The Way of Mastery

The Way of the Heart

The Way of Transformation

The Way of Knowing

SHANTI CHRISTO FOUNDATION

Published by
Shanti Christo Foundation
PO Box 60965
Sacramento, CA 95860

ISBN 978-0-9771632-0-5
Library of Congress Catalog Card Number 2005908018

CONTENTS

PART THREE—THE WAY OF KNOWING

INTRODUCTION

You hold in your hands the treasured teachings of Jeshua ben Joseph (Jesus), one of the greatest Masters humankind has ever known. These teachings were given during the years 1994–1997. Please do not hurry as you read through each lesson. Rather, allow each sentence to be held within the heart, each idea to fill the mind and the body with its very real frequency or vibration. For each word, the structure of each sentence, the cadence and the humor, is by design.

These words are to be studied and savored over and over, until their meaning deepens and flowers into the grace of Christ living in you and as you, allowing the ray of that Light to penetrate your mind, correcting every perception you have ever held about yourself or the world. You will then find your gifts being formulated in new ways. You will find that you have an unseen Teacher revealing to you what you are ready to learn. And your life will begin to be guided by a Voice that is not your own until the voice you have called your own is no longer heard. What has been called the ego will simply dissolve, and the mind will know perfect peace.

Does this take time? You are as close as the choice to teach only Love. The 35 lessons contained in this volume reveal that "Way" taught to Jeshua Himself, and now lovingly presented by Him for you, so that the choice for Love becomes your every thought, your every breath, your every action extended to the world as the awakened Christ.

May you be transformed by *The Way of Mastery* in your unique process of remembering who you really are.

EDITOR'S NOTE

The entire text of *The Way of Mastery* was originally given as a series of monthly audio tapes meant for listening. In preparing these tapes for publication in book form, minor changes were necessary to enhance readability. For example, references to "listening to these tapes" were changed to "reading these words." Occasionally other changes in sentence structure were made to accommodate easier reading.

Lesson titles and subheadings were also added. These serve to highlight the main topics elucidated in each chapter. Also, we have added italics to clearly reflect Jeshua's meaning when a sentence could be interpreted in different ways or to give special emphasis when He has done so.

Very early on in *The Way of Mastery*, Jeshua makes it clear that He is using a language His readers are used to seeing in relation to Him. So throughout this course, He speaks in this traditional Judeo-Christian language.

If you wish to hear Jeshua's words in the original languaging and colorful voice inflections, and the very real vibrational quality, tapes and CD's are available through the Shanti Christo Foundation.

I promise you this...

If you become wholly committed to awakening from the dream you have dreamt since the stars first began to appear in the heavens and if your one desire is to be only what God created, then lay at the altar of your heart with every breath, everything you think you know, everything you think you need, and look lovingly upon every place that fear has made a home in your mind, and allow correction to come. It will come. Regardless of how you experience it, it will come. And the day and the moment will arise and all of your pain and fear and suffering will have vanished like a wind that pushes the foam of the wave away, revealing the clarity of the ocean beneath you. You will literally feel throughout your being that there never was a dream. Some memories might remain with you and you will know that somewhere you must have dreamt a dream or had a thought of wondering what it would be like to be other than the way God created you, but it will be such a faint echo that it will leave no trace upon you. In your heart you will smile gently regardless of the circumstances in which you find yourself. There will be peace from the crown of the head to the tips of the toes, and that peace will walk before you wherever you go. It will enter a room before you enter it with a body, and those who are becoming sensitive will wonder who has come into their place. And some will even say, "Behold, I believe Christ has come for dinner." And you will be that One, for that is who you are—Christ eternal.

~Jeshua

PART ONE

THE WAY OF THE HEART

LESSON 1
THE WAY THAT CALLS YOU HOME

Now, we begin.

Beloved friends, I come forth to abide with you where you believe yourself to be. I come not for myself, but for you. I come not to teach you, but to love you until you choose from the depth within your own being to set aside every illusion you have ever given credence to, and to remember the Truth which alone is true.

For indeed in that hour, there is a transcendence of all that knows limitation. There is a transcendence of all that knows coming and going, birth and death. There is but the Mind of Christ within which each of us—as a spark of divine light, as a sunbeam to the sun—rests eternally in perfect communion and communication always.

The great secret is this *is* the state of your reality. In each and every moment, you abide in perfect communion with the whole of creation since all things are but temporary modifications of the one fundamental energy that I have chosen to call the Christ Mind, the offspring of the Father.

Beloved friends, I come to where you choose to be. And if you would choose to open that place within the heart and within the mind in which you can communicate with me directly, I will meet you there as well.

What is important then, by way of beginning, is to consider this simple fact: Your experience is always the effect of where you choose to focus the attention of your consciousness, itself being unlimited forever, embracing all the many dimensions of creation. You abide in that which embraces all things, in all ways, and at all times. In truth, you do not know separation, birth or death, gain or loss.

As you focus your attention on reading these words, recognize how you, as an infinite being, have deliberately chosen to participate in a form of experience. You will read words that carry certain meanings for each of you. And you each will color that meaning according to the perceptions that *you* have chosen to place value upon.

Does this mean that some are ahead and some behind? It only seems that way. In reality, each of you is equal. Each of you chooses from your infinite freedom to attract to yourself certain vibrational frequencies, certain forms or qualities of experience. That freedom is what you abide in *always,* from before the foundations of this world and long after this world ceases to be.

In each and every moment, you cannot be a victim of what you see, and nothing is outside of you. What you experience you have directly and deliberately called to yourself. If you hold the thought, "I do not like what I have called to myself," that is perfectly fine. For you have called to yourself the experience of being in judgment of yourself. Merely look with the wonder of a child and see what it feels like and ask yourself, "Is this an energy I wish to continue in or would I choose something else?"

For ultimately, when all possible choices within the dream of separation have been made, have been tasted, have been felt and have been known, finally there emerges the still, quiet voice of Spirit that speaks through the soul, whispering of the one Truth, the one Reality, the one Love, the one peace and the one bliss that is continual.

Then the soul begins to turn from the things of this created world. It begins to withdraw its attention from its attachments to all of the things it has called to itself. It begins to transcend its sense of identification with the vibrational frequencies it had only meant to play with, and then took seriously. It is seriousness within the mind that is the creation of ego. And it is great seriousness that holds the vibrations of what you would no longer choose to experience within the field of your being, within the field of your soul.

As you as the soul—the individual divine spark—begin to choose to withdraw the attention and the value you have placed upon all things, as you learn to simplify the nature of your own consciousness, as you realize that you can surrender into something that seems beyond you and that you can entertain the insane thought of trusting the invisible, you come more and more to be less and less.

As you become less and less of what you thought you were, conversely, you become more and more of what your Father created you to be—the thought of perfect Love in form, a channel, a simple vehicle through which the Love of Spirit can shine forth. Your only task becomes the cleaning of your windows, the polishing of your floors and the weeding of your garden so that that Light can pour forth unimpeded.

No longer will you find the need to defend perceptions you had identified within error. You will indeed know when you have come to that state of awakening. For you will be able to look upon all created things that you have ever experienced, all reactions you have ever held within the mind, all perceptions, all judgments, all desires that you have ever held for anyone or anything. And as they arise in your mind, they will not disturb your peace.

And you will smile. You will see that within your consciousness have arisen all saintliness and all devilishness. You have been both saint and sinner. [And your happiness and your unhappiness have been merely an effect of where you chose to place your attention.]

Indeed beloved friends, I come forth to meet you wherever you are because I have chosen to use the infinite power of consciousness given me of the Father—as equally as it is given unto you—to discover how deep delight can be when the mind is focused only on seeing from, and seeing only, the Mind of Christ. I have, therefore, called to myself all multitude of experiences—even when I walked upon your beloved Earth as a man—to challenge myself, to test myself, to condition myself to rise above, to transcend all possible experiences that could distract me from the remembrance of who I am.

By the way, my crucifixion was simply the climax of my own direct choice to be challenged by the events of space and time so that I could cultivate within myself the ability to see from, and to see only, the perfect purity of the Mind of Christ.

The point I am trying to make with you is that in each and every moment, what you are experiencing in the realm of your emotions and mind, and the effects—to a latter degree—within the body are there because you, from your infinite freedom, have simply *selected* that experience to focus your attention on so that you can see what the effects are.

The insanity does not come from having chosen to see something other than the Mind of Christ. The insanity that you experience as your pain, your suffering, your seeking and your dramas comes only from your mistaken choice to become *identified* with what arises in the field of your awareness. You, therefore, lose the sight of innocence. For all events are perfectly neutral, and you are free to see them any way you want.

When a child is born—and many of you who are mothers know this—you can experience a depth of joy that is unspeakable. Likewise, you can also experience fear and contraction at the thought of having to be responsible for a child. When a loved one dies and you experience grief and suffering, rest assured it is because you have chosen to contract your attention. Then all you can see is the loss of an animated body and thereby convince yourself that you have become separated from the loved one.

I speak from experience that separation *is* an illusion. When death occurs in your plane, in that very moment you still have the power to choose to recognize that something has changed, and to shift your attention to a different faculty that the body could never possibly contain. One in which you perceive and hear and communicate with that spark of divine light—the soul—that seems to have given up the idea of trying to keep a physical form animated. This is imperative. In fact, it is the very first step of The Way of the Heart.

THE FIRST STEP IN AWAKENING

The first step in awakening is to allow into the mind this axiom of truth:

Nothing that you experience is caused by anything outside of you.
You experience only the effects of your own choice.

During the first part of this course, we will be building lesson by lesson on what I am choosing to call The Way of the Heart. It is the way unknown to the world. It is a way unknown to many that would call themselves spiritual teachers. For it is not a way of resting on or becoming dependent on magical means.

It is, rather, that pathway which cultivates within you the decision to turn your attention upon your own mind, upon your own behavior, upon what is true and real for you moment to moment. To study it, to consider it, to feel it, to breathe the light of Spirit through it, and to constantly retrain the mind so that it assumes complete responsibility in each moment.

Why is this necessary? Because without it, there can be no peace. Without it, you cannot transcend the false identifications that you have chosen. You need to come to the point where you say to yourself, "I have done this to myself. I did it; I must correct it. No one is to blame. The world is innocent."

In the lessons that follow, we will be communicating with you more and more deeply the finer points of The Way of the Heart. For it is that way that was taught to me. It is that way that brings about the reversal of every thought you have ever had about anyone or anything. It is that way, alone, which allows you to pass back through the eye of the needle, and to come to rest in the perfect peace from which you have sprung forth.

The Way of the Heart is not the way of the intellect. For indeed that aspect of the mind was never designed to be your master. It was designed to be the humble, and—if you will pardon the expression—very stupid servant of the awakened heart.

The heart is that which feels all things, embraces all things, trusts all things, and allows all things. The heart is that in which the soul rests eternally. The heart is that which is beyond space and time and is that spark of light in the Mind of God, which is called Christ. Only in that will you find the peace that you seek.

You will discover that the pathway of awakening is not a pathway of avoidance, but a pathway of truthfulness. It is not a pathway of accomplishment and pride, but a pathway of releasing from the consciousness every hope and every wish to be special—to see yourself as having made progress—so that you can pound a fist upon the chest and spread the tail feathers.* It is a transcendence of the hope of somehow getting God's attention, so that He will look upon you and say, "Oh, you have been such a good person. Yes, we will allow you into the Kingdom now."

It is a way in which you will come to cultivate—regardless of your inner experience or degree of awakening—the willingness and the art of returning to the simplicity of empty-headedness and not-knowingness with each and every breath. It is a way of life in which all things and all events become an aspect of your meditation and your prayer until there is established once again within you the Truth that is true always:

> Not my will, but thine be done.
> For of myself, I do nothing.
> But the Father does all things through me.

Imagine then a state of being in which you walk through this world seemingly appearing like everyone else and yet, you are spacious within. You are empty within. In truth, you desire nothing, though you allow desire to move through you. And you recognize it as the voice of the Father guiding your personality, your emotions and even the body to the places, events, people and experiences through which the tapestry of the atonement—the at-one-ment—is being woven, through which all of the children of God are called home again.

You trust the complete flow of that, whether you are asked to give a speech in front of ten thousand people, or you are asked to tell a friend the truth of your feelings, or whether or not you are asked to sweep the streets and live penniless. For in truth, that mind that trusts the Source of its creation allows all things, trusts all things, embraces all things and transcends all things.

Rest assured, whenever you feel frustration and anxiety, it is because you have decided not to trust the Truth. And the Truth is simply this:

> Only God's plan for salvation can work for you.

Your way must always fail. For your way begins with the illusory and insane assumption that you are a separate being from the Mind of God and must, therefore, direct your own course. For if you are sick and diseased and not at peace, why would you decide that you know how to create peace? It requires great humility to accept the first step of the path:

> I have done all this; I must undo it.
> But I have no idea how I did this.
> Therefore, I must surrender to something else.

I give you this thought, and I would ask that you consider it well. What if the very life you are living, and each and every experience that is coming to you now since the moment you decided, "I have got to awaken here," was being directly sent to you of your Father because your Father knows what is necessary to unravel within your consciousness to allow you to awaken?✻What if the very things you are resisting are the very stepping stones to your homecoming?✻What if you achieved a maturity along this pathway in which you were finally willing to let things be just as they are?

If it was necessary to sweep the streets, you simply took a deep breath and said, "Father, you know the way home," and began sweeping. And up into the mind comes the thought, "Oh my God, I won't be recognized. I won't stand out. People won't think I'm special if I'm just a street sweeper." Yet you recognize, "Ah-ha, no wonder my Father wants me to do this. I've got to flush this up so that I can look at it, dis-identify from it, and learn to be the presence of Love in the sweeping of the street." In truth, I tell you the least among you—according to your perception—is already equal to the greatest.✻And there is none among you who is less than I am.

✻The Way of the Heart begins by accepting the humility that you have created quite a mess within your consciousness. You have created a labyrinth and gotten lost within it, and you do not know the way back.

It begins by accepting that of yourself, you can do nothing. For all you have managed to achieve is the creation of a whole lot of insane dramas that are occurring nowhere except within the field of your mind. They are like chimeras, like dreams. In truth, there is no difference between a waking state—in which you would be the director of your life—and the dreams you have when the body sleeps at night. They are both the same.

I wish to direct you to peace, even that peace which forever transcends the understanding and comprehension of the world. I desire—because my Father desires it through me—to bring you wholly to where I am that you might discover there is someone that got there ahead of you. And when you look closely, you will say, "Ah, it's my Self. I have always been there, but I forgot."

In the end of all journeying, in the end of all purification—and indeed purification is still necessary—you will discover that to awaken means to have journeyed nowhere. It means to have arrived at a goal that has never changed.

✻Awakening is only remembrance. But it is a remembrance not just of the intellect. It is not an idea, as you would understand ideas. It is an idea that vibrates through the whole field of your beingness, so that even the cells of the body—while yet the body remains coalesced together in its present form—awaken and relax into the Truth that is true always.

If you were a gardener, would you not cultivate the art of weeding your garden? Would you not look to see that the soil is just the correct dampness? Would you not keep your eye on the clouds on the horizon and the heat of the day? Would you not cover the delicate plants that need protection while they grow strong? And if those that would come would not respect your garden, would you not ask them to leave, or build a temporary fence until the garden is strong enough, until it bursts forth with enough fruit so that you can give to even those who do not respect it?

Be you therefore, a wise gardener. Cultivate a deep love and respect for yourself, for you are not here to "fix" the world. You are not here to "fix" your brother or sister. It is only love that heals. And until you have loved yourself wholly by having purified the mind of every erroneous thought you have ever held—until you have loved yourself—you do not, in truth, love anyone or anything. Save in those brief moments when you let your guard down and the Love of God shines forth through you so quickly you do not even know what happened! The wise gardener cultivates a state of consciousness in which the Love of God is unimpeded.

Beloved friends, those of you that have elected to answer a call to participate in this pathway, with this family, if you would make your commitment to trusting your Creator for having set before you a pathway that can lead you home, you will, indeed, arrive at home. But commitment means that you do not get to leave the room when the shouting begins. The shouting we are speaking of is the shouting within your own mind, within your own body, within your own emotions.

It means that you will stay with these things by being honest about them, and loving yourself for ever having the power to even create such insane perceptions of yourself and the world around you.

The Way of the Heart is the final pathway that any soul can enter. There are many stages of awakening. There are many pathways that can be followed. But ultimately, "all roads lead to Rome," as they say. Eventually each soul must find its way into The Way of the Heart. Each soul must come back to the truth that it is time to take responsibility; to learn to cultivate the ability to look upon the deep and vicious blackness of what I have called "ego," which is nothing more than the cesspool of denial. It is that which lacks light.

Begin to bring light back to it by simply observing your own mind, your own behavior, and your own reactions with a sense of wonder, with a sense of innocence and with a sense of childlikeness.

For is it not written that you must again become a little child to enter the Kingdom? The little child simply marvels at all that they see and says, "Well, how about that?" Can you imagine looking upon the deepest, darkest parts of your own shadow, your own denials, and being able to say, "Oh, how about that!" Remember that everything is neutral, and all that arises within your consciousness has no effect upon the truth of your reality.

The Way of the Heart is a way of cultivating the decision to become identified with the Light that can shine away all darkness. Not by fighting with it, but by recognizing it, embracing it as your own creation, and choosing again. The Way of the Heart is the way that I teach. And now we begin a focused in-depth study together, that this way might become established within your holy mind.

THE WAY OF THE HEART CALLS YOU HOME

Remember that the Truth is true always. Is it not time, beloved friends, to truly step into ownership of your only reality? The Way of the Heart does not know the word avoidance. It does not know deception, manipulation or control. It does not know blame, although it watches these things arise as echoes of old patterns now outgrown. It learns to see them, to recognize them, like you might recognize certain kinds of clouds that pass through the sky. And then learns to turn the attention of the mind that a new choice might be made.

The Way of the Heart is the way that calls you home. And the call comes from that deep part of your soul that is still like unto the Spirit, which abides as Christ in the holy Mind of God. Trust then, that you are as a sunbeam to the sun. Trust not the perceptions you have cultivated in error. You are not alone on the way that you journey, and you journey not apart from your brothers and sisters. This family cannot know separation. For once the call to awaken through *this* lineage has been acknowledged, though some bodies may not communicate in space and time, rest assured, communication remains, and there is no way to avoid it.

We begin, now, The Way of the Heart. It is time to step into the willingness to don the mantle of one committed to healing every obstacle to the presence of Love that may yet remain secretly hidden in the depth of that part of your mind that would struggle to be separate from God. And to remember that you are truly the Light that can come to shine lovingly upon every aspect of darkness you have known.

Along the pathway of this course, you are going to learn how to shake hands with the devil, and to do a little jig with him and recognize his face to be your own. When you can dance with the darkness that you have created, that darkness is transformed into an angel. And light abides with Light.

We will be giving you certain meditations and certain energetic practices to help cultivate within you a quality of feeling that will allow you to recognize energies that do not serve you. These will be given in a way that transcends what your mind may choose to think of these energies, so that you learn more and more to lead with the body, to lead with your feeling nature, not your intellect.

Your intellect does not know anything except the trivialities that you have shoved into it, like garbage into a garbage can. The intellect can never bring the healing of the heart that is the atonement. It can only be utilized to argue against the insane perceptions you are used to, so that you might come to see that perhaps there is a greater good in giving up your insistence on treating the intellect as your god.

Therefore, indeed beloved friends, dance, rejoice and play often. Let these lessons bring up within you everything unworthy of the Mind of Christ—every thought of scarcity, every sense of unworthiness and every fear. Let them come up, look at them, embrace them and transmute them through your own love of Self and through your honesty. Accept where you are and do not pretend to be otherwise. For the wisest are always the humblest.

Be you therefore beloved friends, at peace in all things. For we in what you would call a disembodied state who are electing to participate with those of you who are asking to be helped through this pathway delight in joining with you! We delight in loving you! We delight in waiting on you to welcome your Self home!

I would ask that you close your eyes for just a moment. Take a deep breath into the body and let it go. As the breath leaves the body, hold the thought that there is nothing worth holding onto any longer that keeps your peace and happiness at arm's length. Become committed—fully committed—to the experience of happiness, even as you have been fully committed to unhappiness, limitation and lack. Give your Creator full permission to sweep the basement clean. There really is not anything down there worth defending or protecting.

It will come to pass that you will know the perfect peace of empty-headedness, not-knowingness. You will know what it means to be relieved of time and to be comforted by what is eternal. Never once let yourself think that you are alone. It is nonsense for you to think that I am not with you. You have asked. I have responded. We are in communication. That is the way it is. And that is the way it will be until the end of all illusion.

Peace be unto you always. Amen.

You Create Your Experience

It is with great joy that I come forth to abide with you. It is a great truth that I come often unto many. But because of what you have learned in your world, you have often believed me to be a figment of your imagination. The voice that steals quietly through the space between your own thoughts, you think to be but an illusion. Yet I say I come often unto many.

I come not alone to commune-i-cate with you. There is, in truth, a host of friends that come to create a vortex, a circumference of energy. We come even as you read these words into your space to set that tone. If you would well receive it, there are many friends unseen by physical eyes that have come forth to contribute and to support this communication.

Why is that important? Always, in each and every moment of your experience, you as a soul, as a divine spark of consciousness, are deliberately choosing to create forms of communication.

What You Perceive Is Communicated Always

You do it with the raiment that you place upon the body. You do it with your gestures and the sound of your voice. You do it with the very culture and time frame in which you incarnate. You are constantly and only creating forms through which you communicate.

Communication is the attempt to rest in communion with creation. What you are choosing to perceive, believe and accept as true will be radiated through you, through your communication devices, which includes the body, that you might transfer your perceptions to another, that they might know who you are and which voice you are committed to.

I have often said that the body is a teaching and learning device, and all forms of communication affect the process of teaching and learning. When you arise in the morning, the first thought that makes a home in your mind, you will act on. You may stretch the body. You may smile. You may frown. You might be filled with peace, or you might feel the weight of the world. These things come, not because you have perceived them *outside*, but because you have allowed them *inside* the depth of your consciousness that remains pure and undefiled and radiant beyond all boundaries forever.

As that thought makes a home in your mind, you literally begin to transform the communication device called the body into that which carries, expresses and reflects what has come to make a home within your mind. *Remember please, that the mind is not where the body is. It does not abide within the body, but the body does abide within the field of your mind. *Hmm, that's what John said @ the Soul*

Communication *is* creation. These two are one and the same. Therefore, if you would create well, ask only:

Questions for reflection

> What am I committed to communicating?
> What will my creations express?
> What will my creations convey to others?
>   For what I seek to convey reveals what I believe
>   is the truth of my Self to the world.

Therefore beloved friends, as we begin to focus on, to refine, to deepen, to mature in The Way of the Heart, it is wise to begin at the beginning. The beginning of this pathway is simply this: *You are as God has created you to be. You are an infinite focus of consciousness. *Your very sense of existence is nothing more than a feedback loop or feedback mechanism, so that you can witness the effects of the choices you are making in the very deep, deep depth of your mind that rests right alongside the Mind of God.

Therefore, in each moment of your existence, which includes this bodily incarnation, you are literally <u>allowing through deliberate choice</u>—though perhaps <u>unconscious</u>—to bring forth a vibration of thought or a vibration of creation. And to commune-i-cate it to the world in an attempt to experience communion with all of life—with a friend, with a parent, with a child, with a beloved, with the clouds that pass through the sky or with the Earth itself.

Each gesture, each thought, the way that the body breathes, all of these things are going on constantly, and they are communicating or revealing the effect of what you have allowed to make a home in your mind.

Understand well, The Way of the Heart requires that you allow yourself to rest in the simplicity of this truth:

>   I am pure Spirit, undefiled and unaffected by anything or anyone.
>   I am given full power to choose and, therefore, to create my experience

as *I* would have it be.

Not quite the "I" that is the egoic part of the mind, for that is just one of your creations that came along somewhere down the line. It is a very small part of the mind. We are speaking of the "I" of you that is pure Spirit that knows it exists, even though it does not know the time of its own creation. You are pure Spirit. Therefore to know:

> I am only this, and in each moment, regardless of what I believe I see,
> regardless of the feelings that arise within my awareness, I and I alone
> am wholly one hundred percent responsible for them. No one has caused
> them. No great force in the universe has made this perception well up
> within my consciousness. I have selected it.

Just as you would go to a grocery store and choose what you will have for dinner and then go home and experience your creation, so too do you choose each experience. When you choose a perception, you lodge it in the mind. Then it expresses itself through the body, through the environment that you create around yourself and through the friends that you would call into your awareness. Every aspect of the life you live is the symbol of what you have chosen to experience and, therefore, to convey throughout creation.

The Way of the Heart begins with the acceptance of this simple truth:

> ✱ I am as God created me to be.
> Made in the His image, I am a creator always.

What then would you ask your creations to communicate? Why do you make the choices you are making? You all know perfectly well that sometimes you seem to be compelled—and the ego wants you to believe that you are compelled—to certain actions, certain feelings, certain choices, certain perceptions, certain statements by something that surely exists outside yourself. This is *never* true. In *no* circumstance is there anything of creation that has the power to dictate to you the choice you will make.

PEACE FLOWS FROM ALIGNMENT WITH THE MIND OF GOD

Therefore, the pathway of awakening—The Way of the Heart—must start with the decision to embrace the Truth that is true always:

> I am a creator of all that I think and see and experience.
> I am free always. Nothing impinges upon me,
> but the thoughts I have chosen to hold within.
> Nothing imprisons me, but my own perception of imprisonment.

> Nothing limits me at any level or dimension of experience,
> save that which I have chosen.

The Way of the Heart, then, embraces all things, trusts all things and eventually transcends all things. Why? Because it begins by assuming complete and total responsibility for what is being channeled through it. You all serve as a channel, from the moment you arise until the moment you arise. Even during your sleep, you are choosing that which flows through your consciousness.

The goal that we seek has never changed. It is in truth, a journey without distance. It is merely the return to where you are always, that you might begin anew to create deliberately, clearly and with the perfect knowledge that if you are experiencing something, it is because you are the source of it, and for no other reason.

The Way of the Heart is not a way of gaining power. It is not a way in which you will finally be able to make the world be what you want it to be. Rather, it is that pathway in which you learn to transcend and to dissolve from your consciousness every perception, every thought, which is out of alignment with what is true. The thought of death is out of alignment. The thought of fear is out of alignment. The thought of guilt is out of alignment.

The thought of eternal life is *in* alignment. The thought of perfect fearlessness is *in* alignment. The thought of peace is *in* alignment. The realization of innocence is *in* alignment. The thoughts of joy and of forgiveness are *in* alignment and reflect the Truth that is true always.

For although you are given complete free will to create as you choose, the soul begins to learn that what brings it the highest joy, the highest peace, and the highest bliss imaginable is that which flows from the Mind of God through the mind of the channel, the soul, and expresses itself in the field of experience. It is for this reason that the Father's will is that you be happy. And your happiness is found in choosing to restore your perfect alignment with only the voice for God.

The Way of the Heart is that pathway that begins with a commitment to healing and awakening and is founded on the premise, the axiom that we have given unto you:

> You are perfectly free at all times.
> Everything that is experienced has been by your choice
> and at no time has there been any other cause.

It seems simple. And yet, what soul has not known resistance to this idea? If you bake a cake and it turns out well, you will say, "I did that." But if you bake a cake and it turns out very bad, you think, "It must have been the flour. It must have been the temperature of the oven. Surely there was something that caused this creation to not be what I would truly desire."

✳ It takes great courage and great faith to look upon all of your creations—your thoughts, your feelings, your manifestations—with love, and with the innocence of a child. For example, to plant a garden and to have all things wither and die, and yet to smile and say, "I planted this garden. I and I alone have done this. Well, I will get a little hungry here, so I might as well go to the store."

Why is this important? Because a long time ago, the soul began to create the perception that it was something other than it was created to be. And the voice for ego emerged within the garden of consciousness. As the soul, that deepest aspect of mind that you have all known, began to identify with a voice that was other than the voice for God, that voice has led you to believe that your creations determine your worthiness. Do you know that feeling?

Therefore, if what you create is not up to snuff, it means that *you*, in the core of your beingness, are some kind of a failure. But I say unto you, in reality, failure is not even remotely possible. Why? If you plant a garden and the seed does not turn into a beautiful flower, but withers and dies, that experience is a creation and you have done it. ✳ And because all events in space and time—everything you experience—are perfectly neutral, there is, in reality, never failure.

The only failure seems to occur within your own consciousness when you believe that it is not acceptable to receive and own and embrace your creation with love and with innocence. Instead you can choose to look upon it, to experience it, and to recognize your perfect safety in doing so. ✳ For it is from there, that you can decide whether to continue in that form of creation or whether to think differently and to approach things differently.

That is where the catch is. That part of the mind began to teach you a long, long time ago what to accept as acceptable creations and what to not accept, what to take responsibility for and what to deny responsibility for. And that conflict creates the illusion of separation. When taken to its extreme, one discovers your hospitals full of those in deep depression, paranoia, and the feeling within the being, within the human mind, of feeling alienated and alone.

Helplessness, hopelessness, despair, anger and hatred are all symptoms of a fundamental delusion that has occurred within the depth of the mind. ✳ It has occurred because there has been a long history of having cultivated the skill of listening to the wrong voice. ✳ The wrong voice is the voice of ego. It has taught you to judge, to pick, to select what you will be responsible for. The more you move into that consciousness, the harder it seems to ever hope for a chance of transcending the sense of separation, conflict and lack of peace.

For how many of you have not known the feeling of resting your head upon the pillow at night and not being able to sleep because it is just not going the way you expected? The reason you cannot sleep is because you are in judgment of your creation.

But it is possible to cultivate just the opposite, in which you learn to look with perfect innocence upon *all* things that arise in the field of your experience. It is possible to look with innocence and wonder at every feeling from the place of curiosity, as you would look upon a cloud that passes through the sky. Look at it, marvel at it—its shape, its color— and embrace it, knowing that it does not affect the purity of the sky through which it temporarily floats.

Each of your creations is exactly like this. It arises in the field of time and space, you experience it, and then it fades away. Every hurt that you have ever known is like a cloud that began to pass into the field of your awareness because you perceived things in a certain way. If that hurt is still lodged within you, it is because you latched on to it. You followed the voice of ego, which caused you to believe that you are identified with that feeling, with that perception. And because you mistakenly thought that was you, you assumed if you let go of it, you might disappear; you might die!

The human mind is that field within creation, within consciousness, that has learned to become so identified with perceptions, experiences and feelings that are not necessarily comfortable, that it believes that if it lets go of them, it will die. From our perspective, as we look upon the energy fields of those of you still identified with this dimension, it looks as though you are gripping, causing energy to condense. Your knuckles are white, trying to hold on to limitation and guilt, to unworthiness and doubt.

You seek innocence and peace. You seek abundance, prosperity and joy. But often, when you touch these things, it frightens you. Why? Because the Truth of the Kingdom requires openness, trust, expansiveness and spaciousness. It involves allowing, trusting, witnessing and letting things come and go. It involves learning to cultivate a deep enjoyment of whatever arises, seeing that all things are just modifications of consciousness itself, and then letting them go when it is time to do so.

Rest assured, there is no one—not a single soul—who has ever discovered something that was birthed in time that did not also end in time.

How much of your suffering comes because you are clinging to a lifeless past and insisting that you carry it with you still? You are doing that because in the past, you became identified with the clouds that were passing by and claimed that as your own identity. Therefore, if you release it, it will mean that you must change, you must go on.

Creation itself that flows from the Mind of God is ongoing forever! You will never cease to be! You will go on forever and forever and forever and forever and forever. You will go on forever exactly as you are now. Or you can allow the Mind of God to flow through you, carrying you to an ever-greater expansiveness and deepening your awareness of the infinite loveliness of the power of the Mind of God.

MASTERY ARISES FROM INNOCENCE

In these lessons, we will create a system or a pathway upon which you can walk to deliberately cultivate the quality of awareness in consciousness necessary to stabilize that awareness, so that you can bring it to each and every moment of your experience.

Imagine then, being able to experience whatever arises without losing the sense of spaciousness, innocence and ease that you now experience in fleeting moments. For instance, know you the experience when things are going well, you are singing a happy tune, and life seems to be moving ahead? Imagine that same quality of trust, faith, and certainty of purpose, even when the buildings are crumbling around you and the bank account has gone dry. Imagine being able to look at those events with the same sense of innocence and wonder with which you would look into the eyes of your beloved.

For such a quality of awareness is perfect mastery. Within it are discovered perfect peace, perfect freedom, perfect joy and uninterrupted communion with all of creation. And if you would well receive it, that quality of feeling intimately one with all of creation is what you have been seeking as a soul since first the identification with a creation called ego began. For that creation created conflict and separation. Everything you have ever attempted to do since has been an attempt to overcome separation and to gain back what you felt you had lost. It is just that the ways you have sought to do it do not work.

The world of conflict, fear, guilt and unworthiness and the world of the Kingdom lie side by side within your own mind. The eye of the needle that one must pass through is the re-cultivation of the innocence of a child. It is for this reason that I often taught:

> Become again as a little child to enter the Kingdom.

The cultivation of The Way of the Heart is that pathway whereby you deliberately and consciously choose to become again as an innocent child. Just as you were in the beginning before you ever created, and then incarnated into, this dimension of experience that seems to be so permeated by a sense of conflict and separation.

WHAT YOU DECREE, IS

I would ask you now to begin to put this into practice. So wherever you happen to be, stop for just a moment and truly become aware of where you are.

Where are you? Are you not having the experience of seemingly being within a body? Do you not seem to be abiding in a room somewhere? Are you not within an environment in which there are certain weather patterns going on around you? Perhaps there are sounds coming into your ears.

Can you truly be aware of where you are now? Can you feel the weight of the body as you stand upon your feet or sit within your chair? Do you notice the tension in the neck? Do you notice the racing of the mind, if that is going on? Can you begin to bring awareness to exactly what *is*, from a place of innocence and non-judgment?

haven't liked this, seemed dismissive

You have a saying in your world, "It is what it is." That is the beginning of wisdom. You will discover that what *is*, is what you have chosen to make of it. Be, therefore, where you are now, and deliberately decide—deliberately decide to accept wholly that what you are experiencing in this very moment has no cause whatsoever, except your choice to experience it. Rest assured, whatever the mind may try to say, if you did not wholly want to be right where you are, you would not be there. If you are in a body in the field of space and time, rest assured, you desired it, you chose it, and it is here.

Begin here. There is no need to judge it, no need to ask it to be different. Just truly be aware of what *is*. If you are feeling the body sitting in a chair, allow this thought to come into the mind:

> I have literally created this experience. Something within me is
> so grand, so powerful, so vast, so beyond anything that scientists
> have ever come up with, that I have literally crystallized into the
> field of experience an awareness of being a body in space and time!
> It has come forth from the field of my consciousness, the gift to me
> of God, who asks only that I learn to create as God creates.

I have said many times that the Father looks upon you and says:

> This is my only creation and it is very good.

For the Father marvels at what you are, knowing perfectly well that what you are emerged from Her holy mind.

Likewise look upon *your* creations and marvel. How is it that you could abide in this time frame on this planet? How could it be that you can place yourself behind the wheel of an automobile and actually get it from point A to point B? That is a mystery and a marvel, and no one knows how it is done! Yet it is done.

The reason it is done is that all power has been given unto you and what you decree *is*. A man or a woman shall decree a thing and it shall be so. You have decreed this moment. Own it! For by owning it, right now, you can begin to sense the incredible and awesome power that flows through you in each moment. It is the power to create!

Begin by choosing now to cultivate the practice in this manner. Set the intention so that in each hour of your day, for three to five minutes, you practice bringing this quality of awareness to exactly whatever you are experiencing when the thought arises to do the practice. Where does that thought come from? Imagine you are going through the day and you have been hustling and bustling about. You have gone to your office or your work. You have talked to friends. You have bought groceries. You have done all of these things, and suddenly the thought appears:

Oh! Focus on being aware that I am literally the creator of what I experience.

Do you think it just happened by accident? No! The thought is penetrating your conscious awareness from the depth of your mind that rests right next to the Mind of God.

Therefore, the power to generate that very thought is the effect of God's will entering into your field of being, penetrating the veils of distraction and shining forth as the thought, "That's right, five minutes every hour." Can you feel the awesomeness of that? For you are linked to the Mind of God, and God knows how to bring you back to complete freedom, perfect peace, and mastery of this entire realm.

Those who truly love God and would truly awaken will feel something compelling them to master this simple practice for five minutes of each hour. They will learn to delight in and to look forward to it. Pretty soon those five minutes will stretch into six, then ten, fifteen and fifty. Until finally, there is established in their awareness the unchanging realization that everything that arises, they have decreed it, and so it is so.

Five minutes every hour is not much to ask. For five minutes every hour, be as you are created to be—a creator, decreeing that which brings forth experience. Never again allow yourself to say, "Well I'm really here because I have to be. I'm really just doing this because it's what I have to do."

Take the words "ought," "should," "must" and "have to" and write them on a piece of paper. Look at them. Then light a match and light the corner of the paper, and let the paper burn and dissolve to dust. It is a symbol of allowing the energy you have given those words to become again as the dust or the ash of the ground. Clear from your consciousness all identification with such words, for all of them are denials of Reality.

Many times I have shared with you that you *need* do nothing. Listen to those words, and take them into yourself as though they are your own voice, because they are:

> ❋ I need do nothing.

You do not have to survive. Whoever told you that you *had* to? You do not have to make everybody happy. Whoever told you that you had to? Whoever told you that you could make anybody happy? You do not have to abide as a body in space and time. Whoever told you that you had to? You do not have to pay your bills. Who told you that? You literally *need* do nothing.

It is quite different than wanting or choosing to do something. You do not need to love your parents; you do not need to honor your father and your mother. You do not need to worship me or love me. You do not need to love yourself. You literally *need* do nothing, for "need" is an expression of the perception that there is something you lack. ❋ Because you are one with God, there is never a moment when you lack anything at all.

Can you allow the thought to emerge in the mind when you arise in the morning: "I *need* do nothing. I don't have to get out of this bed. I don't have to go to an office. I don't need to fulfill that order. I don't need to say, 'Good morning,' to my mate. I literally *need* do nothing."

For how can there be the power of freedom to choose and to create when you are being governed by the belief of the world that you must be a certain way? The belief that you need to be acceptable to others, that you need to conform and fit in, that you need to dress the way others dress, and that you need to be committed to surviving an extra day upon this plane. There can be no freedom where there is need.

PRACTICING THE FIRST TWO AXIOMS

These are the first two axioms of The Way of the Heart, to be built on, to be remembered and to be cultivated daily:

> I am created as my Father created me to be. I am free.
> And nothing sources my experience but me in each moment.
> Nothing has an effect upon me whatsoever, save that which I
> choose to allow to affect me.

I need do nothing.

In the beginning we would suggest that you practice this second axiom in the morning and in the evening, as you are arising and as you are retiring. At least twice in each of your days, we ask you to cultivate for five minutes the repetition of this thought so that you feel it in your bones: I need do nothing.

It will come as quite a shock to your consciousness. The mind will say, "But I have all these things I have to do! What about this and what about that? Oh, my goodness! Will the world stop spinning if I stop needing?" That is up to the world, not up to you.

The power of these first two axioms will be what everything that follows is built on. Yet everything that follows is merely a way of watering those two axioms and making them the anchor of your awareness.

For when the anchor is firmly in place, you will literally create whatever you so desire from perfect freedom and from perfect deliberateness. [You will even transcend miracle mindedness. For miracle mindedness is still a stage of perception just short of mastery. Mastery comes when you know that you are literally and deliberately creating. There is nothing miraculous about it. You will decree a thing and it shall be so!]

That is to create as God creates. For while He marvels at you, He knows perfectly well that your creation was not a miracle. It was very deliberate, born from the pure radiance of Love. God does not sit on His throne and say, "I wonder if I am worthy to create my children? I wonder if I am worthy to express myself through the divine spark of consciousness that they are?"

Never does it enter into the holy Mind of God, "I wonder if it is okay if I create a solar system?" God receives a thought or a thought emanates within His holy Mind, He decrees it, and it is so! And He looks upon all things and says, "It is very good!"

EXERCISE IN CONSCIOUS CREATION

The third and last exercise that we would give you in this lesson is this: Choose something that you do every day, that you are convinced is so utterly ordinary that it certainly does not hold any power or any spiritual meaning whatsoever. It could be something as simple as having a glass of water, brushing your teeth or yawning.

Pick something that you know you do every day and decide to make that the focus of your worship. So that when you do it, you stop and say, "It is very good." Even if it is something as simple as raising your head from the pillow. Become aware of it, own it as self-created, and as you contemplate that action, say to yourself, "It is very good. I have done this, and it is good. I have created."

Again, those that are truly committed will find that they begin to enjoy this process, and they begin to apply it more and more to other events in their lives. They begin to reawaken the childlike joy of building a castle in the sandbox. For in truth, that is all you are doing here. Consciousness is your sandbox and you are creating castles. You have simply forgotten to enjoy them.

When you want to be rid of them, you now lament, "Oh, but if I give this up and change my mind and move on, what will happen to my creations? What will others think of me if I act like a child and just take my little plastic shovel and knock the castle down and go in and have a sandwich for lunch? What will people think of me? Will I fit in? Will I be accepted? Will I be judged? Will I be persecuted?" Who cares! For the opinions of others mean nothing, unless of course, you want them to mean something.

Now we come to what concludes this lesson. What blocks you in your mind? For even as you are reading this, you may recognize a resistance. That resistance is the energy of fear: "What will happen if I follow this path?" That part of your mind called the ego will rise up to tell you that if you listen to the one that some have called the savior of the world, it will take you to a path of destruction. That is because the voice of ego knows that it will be destroyed if this path is followed. You—the reality of who you are—cannot be destroyed.

That resistance is fear. And fear is one of the energies out of alignment with the truth of the Kingdom. Therefore, fear not, but continue in faith. For I say unto you, what you will discover at the end of this pathway is perfect freedom, perfect power, perfect spaciousness, perfect joy and perfect peace of living—literally—in the Kingdom of Heaven.

The choice is yours. For those of you that will feel this resistance come up so strongly and for those of you that will yet call out unto me in your dreams and your prayers, "Help me through this," I say unto you that you walk not alone. For I cannot be further from you than the width of a thought. And yes, you are the creator of that thought.

I, too, embarked upon just such a path. Each axiom that I will share and refine as well as many of the exercises in *The Way of Mastery* are specifically exercises and truths that were given to me from the time I was initiated by certain Essene teachers in The Way of the Heart.

When my teachers said, "It is time for you to go spend forty days and forty nights in the desert," do you not believe that resistance came up within me too? I, too, had to notice that I was creating a thought of fear and separating myself from the great protection and

Love of God. I had to physically move the body into the wilderness to move through my own rings of fear to discover what was on the other side.

The pathway that I have walked is the pathway that you are walking. And if our pathway is the same, then we walk together to God and away from illusion, pain, weakness, unworthiness, guilt and death.

So engage in your exercises with great zeal, with great joy and above all, with great outrageous playfulness! Learn to look with innocence upon all that arises. Abide lovingly with your creations. If you put these little exercises to work, much indeed, *will* arise. Practice, then, well. And practice with joy.

Know that you are loved, loving and lovable, and that, in truth, the only thing that is occurring is that an old dream is being released that a new dream might replace it—the dream of worthiness, peace, wakefulness and union with all of creation.

Again, I say, I come not alone in this specific work, but I come with many who support your healing and your awakening.

Therefore indeed be at peace this day, beloved friends. Abide *lovingly* with your creations. Amen.

LESSON 3
THE POWER OF FORGIVENESS

If I search the languages of your world, I cannot find the words that can convey the Love that I feel for you. I cannot find the words that can convey unto you the Love that God has for all of us. I cannot find a concept, a word, an idea, a philosophy or a dogma that can contain the mystery that is closer to you than your own breath and awaits your discovery.

If I search throughout all of creation, if I search through the many mansions that exist within the domains of my Father's creation—and that creation is infinite—try as I might, I cannot discover anything that can truly describe *you*. I cannot find anything that is of greater value than you. In truth, I cannot discover anything that speaks more eloquently of the Love that God is than your very existence. Therefore, in truth, I look upon you constantly, and marvel at the radiance of my Father's Love. It is through *you* that I come to discover all that God is.

When I walked upon your Earth as a man, I began to realize that the greatest gift that I could ever receive would only come to me as I chose to surrender every perception that I might conjure up about you, my brother or sister, that would *veil* the Truth that is true about you always.

When I was nine years of age, I began to awaken to exactly what I am describing to you. As my father would take me to sit with the elders and as he would read from the Torah to me, I began to be compelled by something within. Something began to speak to me, that underneath all of the perceptions that I could create of another, there was something radiant and shimmering waiting to be discovered.

I began to feel very different from my peers. I began to be preoccupied with inner things. When I listened to the elders speak, I would often feel as though I had drifted far away from where they were. Pictures would come to me, thoughts would come to me, and feelings would come to me that I did not understand, that I had not assimilated into my being.

But something began to compel me. How might I discover how to see *only* that shimmering radiance? Would it be possible for me to see my brothers and sisters as my Father sees His children? I discovered that the way to see with the eyes of Christ begins with the acceptance that I, as a creator—created in the image of God—literally choose every experience and call it to me, that I create the veils through which I view creation.

I began to shift my perspective slightly. And I began to be seen as someone who was rebelling against the teachings of my Essene elders. For I began to move away from *striving* for God, *striving* for perfection, and began to cultivate within myself the process of *allowing.*

I discovered that if I looked upon my perceptions, my feelings, my behavior exactly as they were without overshadowing them with my own interpretations—if I could teach myself to embrace things with innocence—veils began to be dissolved from my mind.

For when I was nine years old, I had already learned to be fearful of thinking, speaking or acting in a way that was not in conformity to the prevailing wisdom of that time—even within the Essene community, which had become rather rigidified. There was already much dogma. And dogma always leads to bickering.

I began to discover that if I looked with innocence upon all things, a light began to shine *through* the things I was looking at. And as I rested more and more in this innocence, more and more the light would shine.

As I grew in age, I discovered that the old teachers who spoke of the need to "forgive seventy times seven" knew something quite profound that had even become lost within the Jewish and Essene traditions of my day.

For to forgive means to choose to release another from the perceptions you have been projecting upon them. It is, therefore, an act of forgiving *one's self* of one's projections. As you begin to forgive—even seventy-times-seven times—each time you forgive, you take yourself deeper into the purity of your own consciousness. You begin to see how profoundly you have been coloring and, therefore, affecting all of your relationships, through the simple act of not being aware of the power of projection.

Therefore, I learned—and learned well—that forgiveness is an essential key to healing. The opposite of forgiveness is judgment, and judgment always creates separation and guilt. Judgment will evoke a sense of guilt in the one that has been judged, unless they are perfectly awake.

But more than this, each time that you judge anything or anyone, you have literally elicited guilt within *yourself.* Because there is a place within you, yet still, that knows the perfect purity of your brother and sister, and sees quite clearly that all things within the human realm are either the extension of love or a cry for help and healing.

(Chil curesx)

When you judge, you have moved out of alignment with what is true. You have decreed that the innocent are not innocent. ✝And if you would judge another as being without innocence, you have already declared that this is true about you! Therefore, to practice forgiveness actually cultivates the quality of consciousness in which you finally come to forgive yourself. And it is indeed the forgiven who remember their God.

We wish to share with you the power of forgiveness: How to cultivate it, how to refine it, how to understand the depths of it that can be revealed to you as you forgive seventy-times-seven times and how to bring up within you that which has not yet been forgiven, but perhaps forgotten. In this lesson, we will also speak of what perception is and what projection is.

Beloved friends, these things are of critical importance. For anyone who enters into a so-called "spiritual path" must eventually face and deal with their deep need for forgiveness, which is an expression of the soul's deep desire to be forgiven.✶For there is no one who walks this Earth who has not been touched by the poison of judgment.

As we speak of these things, let not seriousness enter the mind. For in truth, all we are really doing is describing what you need to do—and can do—to release the burden of illusion that seems to cause you to feel a heaviness upon your countenance and a sense of a lack of safety in the world. You could think of it as taking your rheostat and turning it up a bit by en*lighten*ing you—taking your burden of guilt and judgment from you.

Therefore, in truth, understand well.✶Forgiveness is essential.✶What has not been forgiven in others, has not been forgiven in you. But not by a God who sits outside of you, for He never judges. What you have not forgiven in another or in the world is but a reflection of what you carry within as a burden that you cannot forgive of *yourself.*

✶ *Interesting*

You have an interesting saying in your world: "It takes one to know one." Do you think you would even be able to judge another if there was not something within you being elicited that triggers within you the belief that you know exactly what that other one is up to? That is why you judge them. Sometimes you judge harshly because you fear that energy in yourself. Or you remember how hurtful you have been when you have acted from that energy.

But when you have forgiven yourself, rest assured, you will know what it means to walk *in* this world yet not be *of* this world. You will be able to feel the energy or the activities that any other soul may freely choose. You will discern that energy, you will understand that energy, and you will see through it and still see the face of Christ before you.

You will not react, which literally means to act again, as you did in the past. Instead, even if you are being persecuted (or to speak from personal experience, to be nailed upon a cross), you will have cultivated the ability to love. And in all situations, no matter what another is doing, your first response will be to enter into the quiet stillness within and merely ask the Holy Spirit:

✗ What would you have me say?
What is most appropriate for this other soul in this moment?

For when forgiveness has purified the mind and the heart and the emotional field of your own being, you will discover that you exist only to extend Love.

You are the savior of the world. In each situation, your role is to ask the Holy Spirit how you can serve the atonement, the correction, the healing that yet needs to be acquired within another soul. So even if one hates you, you will not respond with defensiveness, but with curiosity, with innocent witnessing. Even if your hands have nails going through them, I tell you truthfully that it is possible to still enter the quiet sanctuary of the heart and to ask of the Holy Spirit:

What would you have me say or do that can serve
the healing of my brother or sister's heart?

All that I will be sharing with you, not just in this lesson, but in this course, has as its final goal your complete Christed consciousness and the fulfillment of what your own soul desires—forgiveness.

Gary Reynard — There is nothing to forgive."

FORGIVENESS, THE BRIDGE TO THE SOUL OF YOUR BROTHER AND SISTER

There is nothing you can be aware of in the energy of another that you have not known in yourself. There is nothing another can say or do, or even imagine themselves capable of saying or doing that you have not also known. Again, it takes one to know one. ✗When you perceive another acting out of hostility or fear, the only way you can recognize it is because you have been there. *Empathy*

The very fact that in your world one can murder another's body and you can react with knowledge that that is inappropriate behavior is because as a soul, you know the energies involved in the attempt to murder another. If you are honest with yourself, you can probably come up with at least fifty times in the last year that murderous thoughts have entered your mind. You may not act on them. You may not even dwell on them for more than a split second, but the energy has come into the field of your awareness, and you have known it and recognized it.

Who then is less than you? Who then is worthy of your judgment? No one. Who then is equal to you? Everyone. And who then is worthy of your love? Everyone.

Forgiveness is the bridge that links you to the soul—the essence—of your brother or sister. Forgiveness is that bridge that when cultivated will allow you to see clearly. Not just the energies that another is expressing, but you will literally be able to see what events seemed to cultivate that soul's belief that they must act in that way to survive, and what perceptions have led them to feel justified in their inappropriate behaviors. You will see it as clearly as though someone had drawn a picture in front of you.

Then you will see skillfully what to say and what to do to gently help another correct their misperceptions of themselves and learn the path of self-forgiveness. And when that hour comes, rest assured, you will walk in this world, yet you will not be in it. You will be as I became. You will be the savior of the world.

THE VEIL OF PROJECTION

What is projection? Projection occurs when there has first been denial within yourself. Projection is an act in which you psychically try to throw out of your ownership everything that you have judged as being despicable or unworthy of you—something you do not want. So you will project it. You will throw it up and out and let it land on whomever happens to be nearby. Projection is the effect of the denial of the first axiom that I have given you. It is the denial of the truth that:

Nothing you experience has been caused by anything outside of you.

Projection is the attempt to insist that reality is other than the way God made it. That you are not powerful, that you are a victim of circumstances, that you are in a world that can actually do things to you and cause you to make decisions that you would not have made otherwise. That is always denial. And it is a lie.

Again, projection is the denial of the first axiom of truth, and you have mastered it well. When you project onto another, you will then believe that your anger or your hatred is justified.

In fact, the legal system means merely to take the act of projection and the need to judge and to make it okay socially, so that you need not be concerned with this other as your brother or as your sister who has been crying out for help. Rather, you become justified in punishment. Yet punishment is only the insane attempt to convince the punisher that the darkness, the evil—whatever you want to call it—is not in them, it is *out there.*

Imagine then, a society in which the prevalent legal *order* ... t your brother or your sister is an aspect of yourself. And if you would ... must help them— meeting each cry for help and healing with forgiveness, ... pport. Can you imagine, for a moment, what it would be like to live in such a s... How would it be different than the world you see?

2020's challenges... Pandemic, civil unrest, political environment

If you would have these things be different, it must begin with you. For the way to heal the world is not by seeking to change what is on the outside, but by first changing what *climate change* is on the inside. When *that* change has occurred, you will become a conduit for an energy that knows how to use your gifts, and how to place you in just the right situations. And a great power will work effectively through you—the power alone that knows how to heal your world.

There are many that would love to march for peace by angrily attacking those who make war. But if you would create peace in the world, you must be at peace within yourself.

Projection is an act of trying to get rid of what you do not want to own within. It is the effect of the denial of truth. Projection colors your brother or sister with the very energies that you would judge within yourself. How can you begin to break the pattern of projection? How can you allow the bridge of forgiveness to be built? It is actually quite simple, but it will require your commitment.

AWAKENING REQUIRES VIGILANCE AND DISCIPLINE

I have said to you many times that the world you see is nothing more than the effect of the thoughts you have held within the mind. Therefore, awakening requires the act of vigilance and discipline. The discipline to cultivate a way of living in which you observe your own thoughts, in which you listen to the words that are coming out of your mouth, in which you observe the feelings that are evoked within your body, the reactivity that seems to own you, and to see these things as innocent and simply self-caused.

When next something is reflected to you by the world that causes you to become angry or causes you to be in judgment, stop right where you are and look, not with judgment of your judgment, but with innocence and honesty:

> Oh, I see that I am judging someone. That is an interesting cloud passing through the sky of my awareness. I wonder if I might be able to make another choice.

Now the mind will tell you, "But this person just broke into my house and stole my stereo. Of course, I have a right to be in judgment! I have a right to feel angry."

But I say unto you, anger is never justified. It does not mean you will not experience it. But stop fooling yourself into believing that there is some validity to it. When someone has just broken into your home and taken your stereo equipment (or some other idol that you love), what if you understood that you had the power in that moment to remember that all events are neutral? They merely provide you with a chance to choose Love.

What if you literally chose the "insane" way, according to the world, of looking upon that one who has just done that act as a brother or sister who is crying out for help and healing? What if you chose to look upon them as one who does not know how to live *in* this world without being *of* the world, who does not know the way to self-forgiveness, who does not know the truth of the Light that lives within them, and who does not recognize their great power to create whatever they want in a way that is not hurtful to anyone? What if you chose to look upon them with compassion rather than reactivity?

It begins in simple ways. To set the stage, I want you to remember that time has been given to you that you might use it constructively. That means when you awaken in the morning, realize that you are in school. You do not have to drive anywhere; you are already there!

wow ~

The universe is literally helping to assist you into having experiences that will bring things up for you so that you can choose to look at them differently; thereby, discovering the great power within you—the freedom within you to choose what you want to perceive and to elicit only what you want to feel. So that even if nails are being driven through the hands, you finally are liberated in the power to choose Love, and therefore, to overcome this world.

Having said this, understand that each of your days is a blessing and a gift, if you use it from the full commitment to awakening. Your day is chock full of a million opportunities to discover a deeper truth. Therefore, never feel that the purpose of your life must be something other than what you are involved in. For remember what we spoke of earlier:

> You are literally creating everything you choose
> and nothing is forced upon you.

Now we are going to take that thought just a little deeper for a moment. It literally means that if you have decided you want to awaken, you have already called to yourself every experience that can truly best serve your awakening. The friends, family and people you have relationships with are those who likewise can best gain from the experiences elicited through relationship with you. It means that right here and right now you are already demonstrating the power that you are seeking—the power to truly choose to awaken, and to command the whole of creation to serve you in that awakening.

Therefore, when you awaken in each of your mornings, look around. Who is that person sleeping next to you? They are your perfect companion. They are a messenger of God. For just behind your experiences, there is something deeper taking place. Because your mind is resting right next to the Mind of God, when you first said as a soul, "I want to awaken, I want to go home," the Father answered your prayer and began to send the thought through your Spirit and through your soul to your conscious mind:

> I know how to direct you home.
> Give up this career and start that one.
> Move from this location to that location.

You began to feel all manner of impulses. You began to read different books. You began to do different things. You met someone and fell in love. All by accident? Hardly!

The very thought that you would claim as your own from which you have created the world of your own personal experience is also literally the result of your prayer to awaken. And the Father is creating—assisting you to create—just those experiences as stepping stones that carry you from where you are to where God is.

The result is that your ordinary daily life is the most perfect ashram you could ever be within. It is the holy city to which it is wise to make pilgrimage every day, which means to bring awareness and commitment to exactly what you are experiencing. To be thankful for it, to bless it, to embrace it, to be vigilant and to be mindful:

> What is this moment teaching me?

Having given that as background and foundation, remember that you do not experience anything that is called an "ordinary moment." In each and every moment, extraordinary things are occurring. Extraordinary things are occurring in which the whole of the universe is conspiring, which means to "breathe together." The universe is conspiring with you to awaken you and to heal you. Trust it! Love it!

That these things are true—and I assure you that they are—means that your life, the very life you are living, is equal in power and majesty and effectiveness to any life that has ever been lived. It means that your very life is equal to the one that I lived. For it is bringing you home, as my life was my pathway home to God.

To build on what I shared earlier, the third axiom or principle could be encapsulated in this way:

> I do not live any ordinary moments.
> With each breath, my experiences are the stepping stones
> laid before me of God to guide me home.

Earth is forgiveness School
— Anne Lamott

I will bring awareness to each moment
and allow it to teach me how to forgive,
how to embrace, how to love and therefore how to live fully.

In your ordinary moments, a thousand times each day, you will be confronted by opportunities to be disturbed! And in that very same moment, you are being given the blessing of the opportunity to choose peace, to remember to cultivate a perception of your brother or sister that is a perception birthed out of the Christ Mind, not the egoic mind.

Forgiveness, then, can be practiced diligently. And you will not need to look too far. You will not need to make a pilgrimage to some far city. You do not need to go sit in a cave in the mountains somewhere to discover the way to God. It is all around you, because you can only be where you have decreed to be. You have decreed to be there because you, as a soul, truly want nothing more than to awaken. Your life, just as it is unfolding moment-to-moment, is meant for *you.*

If this is true, and I assure you that it is, the way to God can only be found in your willingness to embrace and live *fully* the very life that is within you and that unfolds through you with each moment. To live without fear, to go forward, to indeed trust and embrace the very power and the majesty that is the seed, the soil and the ground from which your life's experience is unfolding. It is precious! It is extraordinary! It is blessed! And it is given to you of God!

Would you not embrace the blessing of your life and sanctify it to keep it holy and recognize that your life is worthy of your respect? It does not matter what anybody else thinks. It matters what *you* think.

Beloved friends, your life—your life—is your way home! If you do not live it fully, how can you ever arrive home? Therefore, fear not your greatness. Fear not the power that comes from embracing your life and claiming its value. Live it full out with every bit of passion you can muster! Embrace every second of it! Every time you wash your dish and your cup after breakfast, look upon these things and say:

My God! This is my life!
This is my pathway home!
And I am going to live it!

Precious friends, in this way you will come to forgive yourself of the judgments you have made. For who among you has not known the feeling of saying, "God, my life is just not worth very much. I will never be like so-and-so down the street. I will never have enough money. Not enough people are going to know me. When will *my* work ever get out as big as *that* person's work?" And on and on!

But I say unto you, every time you have judged yourself, you have weakened yourself. Every time you have judged yourself or another, you have slipped down the mountain another notch, when your desire is to be at the summit.

HOW FORGIVENESS HEALS

Understanding these things, let us look more closely at forgiveness. How does it work? What really occurs when you forgive?

You are a conduit of energy. To the degree that the conduit is in perfect working order, the energy can flow so radiantly that the conduit actually becomes transparent. That is, it no longer blocks. There is no barrier or limit to the Light.

When you judge, it is as though you contracted and made the walls of the conduit smaller, just like building up rust in your pipes. And the flow becomes less and less.

As you forgive judgments, it is as though the rust in the pipes is dissolving. It is as though the walls of the pipe that are carrying the liquid of God's Love begin to expand and become thinner and thinner and more transparent.

Judgment is contraction.

Forgiveness is relaxation, peace, trust and faith.

Forgiveness allows the spaciousness within your consciousness to grow. For when you look upon the thief that has broken into your home and say, "I forgive you," you are decreeing the *opposite* of what you have learned. You are decreeing that nothing can be taken from you of any value. You are decreeing that judgment is the opposite of what you want, and it will cause you to feel the opposite of how you want to feel. You are decreeing your power to perceive differently. You are, therefore, healing yourself.

If you ever want to come home, you are going to have to become very, very divinely selfish. You are going to have to become so selfish that you will not tolerate judgment in yourself—of anyone or anything. Because you will begin to recognize that every such act catapults you to the other side of the universe from where you want to be.

Judgment causes the very cellular structure to break down. If you could see this, you would never judge again. When you judge, even the cells of your body go crazy. They vibrate in a completely dissonant way. There is contraction. The fluids do not move through the cells. The nutrients do not become transported or delivered to the cells. The waste matter is not processed properly. Everything gets clogged up, and there is dis-ease.

Therefore, beloved friends, understand well that judgment is not something to take lightly. Should you, then, judge yourself if you have noticed you have been in judgment? No. That is a judgment in itself. Only Love can heal. Therefore, when you know you have judged, simply say:

Ah, yes! That is that energy.
I recognize that cloud that has just passed through the field of my awareness.
But I can choose again.

So how does this work? If in your "ordinary" daily life—that we now know is not ordinary at all—you detect that you have been in judgment of someone or something, recognize that that judgment is still with you. It is a present thing, even though you may have enacted it five minutes ago, or fifty-five years ago or ten lifetimes ago. When you notice it or bring awareness to it, you have made it a very present thing. So it is right there in front of you to be undone. And that is what you need to focus on:

⚹ I am going to choose again.

You know the experience of looking back in your life, and suddenly seeing a scene in which *now* you know you behaved selfishly from ego, and that you were manipulative or cunning or hurtful? Or you recognize, "My God, I was really in judgment of that person. Oh, if only I could go back and undo it." Know you that feeling?

I say unto you, you *can,* because everything is present. There is no such thing as past and future, there is only *now.* So when you have that thought or that memory, it is coming to you for a very specific reason. As a soul, you are learning about forgiveness and how to undo the effects of your previous choices. And so it is being presented to you, yet again, that you might make a new choice.

When that old memory comes, stay with it. Look at it. Recognize how judgment worked at that time. And then say to that person or that event:

I judge you not.
I extend forgiveness to myself for what I have created.
I embrace you, and I love you. I free you to be yourself.
I bless you with the blessing of Christ.

Then see that image or that memory begin to gently dissolve into light, until there is no trace of it left. And be done with it.

Right away the mind says, "But when I kicked that little boy in the shins when I was four years old just to watch him scream . . . he is not here." Isn't he? The *body* is not here, but the body is not quite the soul.

All minds are joined. It means that where you extend forgiveness within the consciousness, within your emotional field to another—whether they be physically present or not—you *are* extending to them exactly what you could extend to them if they were physically in front of you.

Even if they were, they still have to receive it, do they not? They still have *their* choice to make—whether to accept your forgiveness or to remain in judgment of *you*. And that is their issue, not yours.

Understand then, that you are dealing with consciousness. You are not a physical being, you are Spirit. And you are intimately linked with all minds and all times. Therefore, forgiveness of another can occur anytime that you decide it can occur. Anyone you have ever believed has wronged you can be forgiven by you in this very moment. Anytime you have judged another and, therefore, been in judgment of yourself, you can undo that in the very present moment, simply by making a different choice.

REACTIVITY INDICATES THE NEED FOR SELF-FORGIVENESS

Rest assured, you will continue to project upon others what remains unhealed and unforgiven within yourself. Each time you react to another, you are being given a sign that there is some kind of energy that has been presented to your awareness that you have not forgiven within yourself. If someone is critical and you react every time they are critical, rest assured, you have not healed that part of your own being—that part of your own experience of being critical of others.

Whether it is occurring now, or whether it seems to be a pattern that you have interrupted and no longer do, you have still not forgiven yourself for having identified with that energy.

Use your ordinary experience in each day to observe what pushes your buttons. We will give you a very simple technique for doing so. If you will stay with it, it will reveal to you the energies that are in need of your forgiveness.

The technique is quite simple. As you go through your day, observe when you feel as though you are in contraction. Are the muscles of the body tight? Is the breath very shallow? Does your voice become faster or louder when you speak about some energy in someone else? That is a sign that you need to do healing within yourself. When you recognize that these kinds of signs are going on—in other words, life has presented you with an opportunity to be disturbed—that is a sign that there is something that requires healing. Therefore, count it a blessing if you feel disturbed.

HEALING EXERCISE

Turn your awareness from what you think is causing the disturbance and remember the first axiom:

> ✳ I am the source of my experience.
> I am feeling disturbed.
> What is it in me that needs to be healed?

Begin to breathe deeply and rhythmically. Let the body soften and relax, and ask:

> What is it within this person's energy that is really causing my reaction?

You will see it right away: "Oh, they are so critical. Criticism pushes my buttons."

Then ask yourself:

> When have I done that to another?
> Where have I been critical of others?

And it might hit you right away: "Well, I'm being critical because they're critical."

Or memories will come back, distasteful memories, if you are judging them. Let them come back. Continue to breathe and relax. Look upon that energy of being critical. Honor it. Love it. For it is a creation. It is your creations coming back to you, that you might embrace them and transform them. Just stay with it. Look at it: "Ah, being critical, yes, I can sure be critical. I've been that way in the past. I know that energy very well."

Look upon a scene in your memory in which *you* have been the one being critical. Look upon it with deep honesty and sincerity, and say to yourself:

> I forgive me for being critical.
> I forgive my judgment of myself.
> I choose to teach only Love.

Watch that image dissolve and disappear from your mind. Bring your awareness back to the present moment and that person that just pushed your button. Again, you do not need to say anything to them at all, although you might. But within yourself, forgive them for allowing the energy of being critical to temporarily make a home in their mind. And merely ask the Holy Spirit to replace your perception with the truth. ✳Ask to see the innocent light within them.

As you cultivate this, you will become very, very good at it. You will be able to do it as fast as the time it takes to snap your fingers. And once you begin to see the light in them, you can ask the Holy Spirit:

What is this critical energy in them masking?
What are they really crying out for?

Then you will feel compassion. For it will be revealed to you why they are hurting inside. And lo and behold, instead of being reactionary toward them, you just might be compassionate. Your choice of words and your own behavior might turn out to be different than you could have ever imagined. For through you will flow exactly what serves them.

When I was being nailed to the cross, there was one who raised the mallet to strike the nail. And as he raised the mallet, his eyes met mine for just a moment. I did exactly what I have described to you. By this time I had mastered this so it was done very quickly. I asked myself, "How have *I* ever wanted to drive a nail through someone else?" And I remembered my murderous thoughts. I forgave myself and brought my attention back to that one, and asked only to see the light in him. And I asked:

What is it that this action is mirroring to me?
What is it masking within him?

And I saw that one's soul, and I loved that one's soul. And I felt compassion for that one. In that moment—mark my words—in that moment of eye contact, that one got it!

Because my energy was different, it created the space in which that soul could make a new choice. That soul saw suddenly the entirety of its experience, and realized that if it allowed that mallet to fall upon the nail, it would be a decision to choose to continue being nothing more than a doormat for other people's perceptions. And in that very instant, that soul decided to follow a path that would lead to sovereign mastery, and never again be a pawn of any government, or any group, or any faction or anyone. He dropped the mallet from his hand—this was a Roman soldier—stood up, walked away and disappeared.

That one has gone on to become a master that is known by literally thousands of beings. He is not in physical form. This one visits many, teaches many. This one indeed incarnated perfect mastery and, therefore, transcended the world. And it all began as the result of *my* desire to teach only Love. Now, we have a very good friendship.

So you see, you may not know how powerful your choice for healing is. You may not really see how deeply and profoundly it will affect you, as you go on being a creator—and you go on forever. You could never possibly know what fruits will be born from that tree in the life of another. But because all minds are joined, when *you* choose healing through forgiveness, you literally create the space in which the *other* can also heal their life.

Let no moment then be wasted. See nothing as ordinary. And see not the perceptions taught to you of the world being justified within yourself. But be wholly committed to rooting up and out of your being anything that is unlike the Love of Christ. Think not that I am the only one that can love this way—it is not true. You are here to love as I learned to love. Why? Because you *are* that Love. Everything else is just a smoke screen.

Forgiveness is necessary. Forgiveness is a skill and an art that will pay you dividend upon dividend upon dividend upon dividend. It will never cease in paying you. Each moment in which you choose forgiveness, you have literally saved yourself a thousand years of suffering! I mean that about as literally as one can mean it. In short, every act of forgiveness is a miracle that shortens the need for experience in this dimension.

When you find yourself in a situation that you believe is too big, rest assured, it is because something big has finally come to the surface to be healed within you so that more power can shine forth through you. Why? You have reached the place where you are ready for it. More of Christ can be lived.

ENDING YOUR DAY

It is very, very important to let each day be sufficient unto itself. When you end your day, always truly end it. Do not take four hours of ritual. You can do it within one breath. As you take a deep breath as you rest your head upon the pillow, look upon the whole day, embrace it with your consciousness, and as you let your breath go out, say silently to yourself:

I release and forgive this day. It has been perfect. And it is done.

Let it go. Just let it go. Why? If you do not, you will just bring it with you. Know you that experience? And for three weeks, you are lamenting, "Oh gosh, why did I make that decision three weeks ago? If I had only made a different decision, this would not have happened and that would not have happened." That is probably true. But the point is now three weeks later, you are still hitting yourself over the head by bringing the past with you. And you miss the glory of the present. You have all heard that a thousand times because it is the truth.

Consciousness is a very subtle and powerful thing. You cannot help but create. Remember the goal of this pathway is to learn to deliberately create with perfect mastery. Therefore, look upon the things of the day and say:

It is very good. And it is finished.

Each night when you rest your head upon the pillow and you know you are about to go off to sleep, be just like God in your Biblical story of creation, in which it is written that on the seventh day, God rested. God was finished, in a sense, within the story. Have that same quality at the end of each of your days.

If you are carrying some kind of emotional reaction because of something someone said or did, or something you said or did, practice forgiveness before you sleep. If you do not, you will keep experiencing the conflicted energies during your dream states. And communication between you and the other one, who has not yet been forgiven, will keep going on until that forgiveness is complete within you.

It is *very* important. Time should never be taken frivolously. Play with it, yes, but play with it out of consciousness, out of clarity, out of recognizing that there is no such thing as an idle thought. Each thought creates a world of experience for you. And you are worthy of experiencing Heaven.

We will have much more to say about forgiveness as we begin to plumb the depths of what is discovered as you practice forgiveness seventy-times-seven times. It takes you deeper and deeper into the very mechanics of consciousness itself—the very mechanics of creation. Put forgiveness at the top of your list until you know how perfectly forgiven you are. Be, therefore, vigilant against denying what is still in need of forgiveness within you. For what you deny, you will project. And each projection is a hurtful act to *yourself.* Of course, it is also hurtful to the other, but primarily to yourself.

There is much that has been said in this lesson that needs to be read again and again so that the mind begins to truly grasp how important and how powerful forgiveness is. You will reach a place where you absolutely delight in going through your day expressing forgiveness, like a wave emitting itself from the ocean of your consciousness, even if nobody is doing anything. Forgiveness, itself, becomes a delightful energy to live within.

Beloved friends, forgive *yourself* well and you have forgiven Christ. When Christ is forgiven, Christ will arise and make His home in your heart, your mind and even in the cells of your body. You will know what it means to walk *in* this world yet not be *of* the world. And when you look in the mirror, you will say:

Behold, the savior appears.

It will not be egoic arrogance that says it, but the recognition of what is true always:

I am my Father's child and I am sent into this world to bring light to it.

Be you, therefore, at peace. Practice forgiveness well, until it becomes like taking a breath. You will discover power that you did not know could exist, and a freedom whose taste is sweet above honey. I forgive you. Not because I have judged you, but because I know the blessing that forgiveness brings to me. Forgiveness is something I perfected as a man. Perfect it within yourself as well, and you will know the glory of Christ.

Be you therefore at peace, beloved friends. Amen.

FOLLOWING THE THREAD OF DESIRE

It is with great joy that I walk with you on the way that you have chosen. For in truth, there is not a time that I am not with you. There is not a place to which you can journey where you will not discover my presence.

Only reality can be true. And reality is simple: there is but the simplicity of Love. From that ocean there is birthed a multitude of forms, a multitude of worlds, a multitude of creations, of which you are one. Like waves arising from the sea, those creations remain linked eternally to their Creator.

You are a wave arising from the infinite ocean of Love that is the presence of God. I am a wave that has arisen from the ocean of my Father's holy mind. And though two waves seem to appear separated by what is called time—by even two thousand of your years—when seen from a much broader perspective, those waves have arisen simultaneously from the ocean's surface. They arise for the very same purpose: to express the simplicity, the innocence, the beauty, the creativity, the truth and the reality of the ocean itself.

The waves delight in expressing what seems to be a unique individuality. Yet, they carry the common thread of being made of the same substance and are truly governed by the same laws of creation.

They know not the moment of their own arising, for only the depth of the ocean unseen can know the moment when it chooses to well up and to create the expression of the wave. The power that is not seen, but is hidden in the depth of the ocean rises up and forms that wave, and sustains it throughout the duration of its expression. It is from the depth of that ocean that it is decided when that wave shall return to the sea.

Does that mean it disappears? Only from one perspective. But in reality, the very substance that was made manifest truly has not known birth and death, but only expression.

What if you were to consider *yourself* as a wave arising from the holy Mind of God, born of God's infinite desire to expand Herself, to express the infinite nature of Love and creativity? What if you began to realize that all that you have called yourself is the *effect* of Love—that you did not *cause* yourself to come into existence?

And yet, as you have arisen from that ocean of Love, is not the wave made of the same substance as the sea itself? Are you not given infinite and perfect freedom? For just as your Father perceives you, you are given the freedom to perceive yourself, and all of the other waves you might notice, even the ocean itself, in any way that you choose.

The goal, then, of genuine spirituality is to realign the quality of your perception—to mirror, to resonate with, to be in perfect alignment with the perception of your Creator—to see with God's eyes. Beloved friends, in truth, you remain as you were created to be. This means that in each and every moment, you are literally using the power found in the silent depth of the ocean of God's Love that gave rise to your very creation and existence to perceive as you desire.

Therefore, in this lesson, we will address the very nature of desire itself. We will address what it means, what it signifies and how it creates effects. We will address the power of desire, the value of desire, the meaning and purpose of desire, and how to begin to bring that energy—which at times feels like a team of a thousand wild horses all wanting to go in their own directions—under your conscious and deliberate direction. So that you might create as the Father created you—with perfect, deliberate and infinite Love, with perfect, infinite and deliberate joy, and with perfect—*perfect*—freedom.

Desire! When I walked upon your planet as a man, I confronted many different opinions about the nature of creation, the nature of humankind, and the nature of consciousness or self-identity. Just as you are now confronted with many schools of thought, so too was I. While that can seem to lead to great confusion, as though one must choose from the smorgasbord, it actually serves not unlike the sand inside the oyster from which the pearl will come. It causes you to grate inside.

 You must find your own way to your own truth. For before each and every one of you lies your pathway, a doorway, an eye of the needle, through which *only you* can fit.

Therefore, in some respects, you are seemingly alone. You must make the decision to desire —above all things—awakening into perfect remembrance of your union with God. Just as a wave might finally decide that it has been birthed not to be fearful of being a wave, but to truly claim its individuation, its uniqueness and to live that fully. And in that fullness, it decides to discover a way to be aware of its infinite union with the ocean itself. It decides to somehow break free of the myopic self-identification as one little piece of wave that arises in a place or a field of time that lasts for but a second, and then disappears.

Just like the wave, you can decide to find a way to transcend limitation, to become re-identified with a consciousness, a living awareness that you are one with the depth of the sea. Decide that you can operate not from the superficial level of awareness that might be like the foam at the tip of the wave—which you call your conscious or egoic mind—but that you can become *in*formed in all that you speak, in all that you do, in all that you create, and all that you perceive by that which rests in the very infinite depth of the ocean itself.

Imagine, then, drawing upon a well within you that seems to have no bottom and sides, through which something is pouring forth from places unseen, in which your literal conscious attention or awareness seems to be colored with radiant light. A light that literally leaves you feeling that you are not the body-mind or the personal history with which you had identified before. And an awareness that these things are only temporary and very impersonal effects of a level of desire within your soul, which is one and the same thing as the Love of God expressing Itself, for no other reason than that Love must be extended.

Imagine transcending your fear of your own survival because as you look upon your body-mind, you are no longer identified as that body-mind. It has become a tool to be utilized by the Love that rests in the Mind of God. You live, yet no longer you, but Christ dwells *as* you. *This is a very real experience to be lived.* It is not just a philosophy. It is not just a concept, and it can never be a dogma. [There is a mystical translation that occurs in the depth of the soul, which is merely a shifting of where you perceive your sense and source of identity.]

What is the energy required to take you from myopic self-contraction, in which you have become identified with the little drops of foam out on the tip of the wave that are tossed to and fro by a power that seems to be outside of you, to a sense of identity with the silent depth of the ocean that is everywhere present and seems to know no beginning or no end? The very energy that will carry you from the tip of the wave to the depth of the ocean is the energy of desire.

For I say unto you, if God had not desired to extend Love, you would never have come into existence. Your very sense of awareness of self is the result or the effect of Love. It is the very same Love that has birthed the sun and the moon and all of the stars and every dimension upon dimension upon dimension of creation. That very Love that desired to be extended is the very Source from which you have been birthed. As you know yourself to be, you are the effect of God's desire to extend Love.

When next someone asks you, "Who are you?" please do not give them a name. Do not say, "Well, I was born in a certain town in a certain part of the planet." Do not tell them that you are a democrat, or a republican, or a communist, or an atheist or a catholic. Tell them the truth:

Who am I? I am the extension of Love in form.
   I have never been born and I will never taste death.
   I am infinite and eternal.
   I shine forth as a sunbeam to the sun.

I am the effect of God's Love.
And I stand before you to love you.

Now *that* will raise some eyebrows! It will also transform your world. [For it is time to stop seeking Christ outside and start choosing to take responsibility for being Christ incarnate.]

mind-blowing...

DESIRE IS EVERYTHING

Take a moment right now and let the body relax. Imagine that you can move back from being the actor in the play of your life to being the director and the producer. You are sitting in your studio, and you are editing the story of your life. You are looking at all your little clips of film. Clips from the time you were birthed, the time you went to kindergarten, the time you first fell in love, the time you first decided to go to a movie, the time you went off to college. Or the time you took a job, this job or that job, or the time you moved to another physical location.

Look closely and see if it is not true that for every action you have ever done, for every decision you have ever made, after trying to analyze it all, is there not underneath it the energy of desire?

In truth, you do not lift the body from your couch to go to the refrigerator without the desire to eat. Something calls you into an expression of action. It is desire. No one enters into an intimate relationship without the energy of desire. For what two have ever looked upon one another and said, "I don't feel any desire whatsoever, but let's get married, have children, and raise a family"?

Desire is that energy which brings forth all waves of creation out of the depth of the ocean itself. And yet, who among you has not felt conflicted about desire? Who among you has not been taught that desire is evil? Who among you has not been taught not to desire to be great? Who among you has not been taught that the desire for material comfort is some sort of a blot on the spiritual path? Look well within your soul and see if this is not true.

Have you not feared, at times, the welling up of desire within you? For as I look upon your plane, there are many who become paralyzed with fear just because they desire to have a bowl of ice cream. So afraid are they that if they give in to that desire, something in the ice cream will cause their body to bloat and their brain to cease functioning!

For those of you in intimate relationship—marriage or a commitment of some kind—how many of you have not carried the belief, taught to you by the world, that if you feel an energy of desire welling up within you when you look upon someone who is not your partner, somehow you have sinned against God? How many of you do not know the experience of trying to reign in the ten thousand horses, so sure that if you gave in to feeling desire, that everything would run amuck? And that your attempt to keep your life structured, rigid and predictable would collapse, and "all hell would break loose"?

Yet I say unto you, would you exist if God had feared the desire to create and extend Love by forming *you*, at the same time giving you infinite freedom of choice? Without desire— look around—not only would you see nothing, there would be nothing to do the seeing. *Everything* is the *effect* of desire.

The title of this book

Come then to see that desire is not evil. It is *not* to be feared. It *is* to be mastered. Mastery is not control. For control—the need to control—is an effect of the energy of fear, not Love. Mastery of desire comes when you recognize that you are safe to feel whatever wave of desire might come up through your consciousness, because *you* decide whether or not you will act on it, whether you will bring it into the field of manifestation.

The power of choice is the one power that can never be taken from you. You already have perfect mastery of it, because nothing you ever experience comes to you without your decision to allow it into the field of manifestation.

Desire is something that wells up from the depth beyond yourself that can be looked at with perfect innocence, and with the wonder of a child. The very act of turning to allow and welcome desire is not something that will sidetrack you from the path of awakening, but will take you vertically into the Heart of God. For if you are to ever create as God creates, you will need to heal your conflicted perceptions about desire. You will need to transcend that energy of fear.

There are many who call unto me and pray. There is not an hour in your time frame in which there are not many upon your plane, somewhere on your planet, who are praying to me and want their hearts to be filled with Christ. Yet, at the very same time, they are scared to death of an energy that *wants* to move, because they have been taught to fear and to suppress desire.

Desire is like the liquid of life that moves through the stem of the rose and allows the petals to radiate with glorious color. When you block the flow of desire, the petals cannot be nourished. Death begins to occur—death of the heart, death of the soul and lifelessness.

If you were to walk down one of your city streets and to truly look into the eyes of everyone you see, would you not recognize that death seems to have already made a home in the minds of many that are living? Death of dreams, death of hope, death of worthiness, death of playfulness, death of true power and death of union with their Source and Creator has already taken place. Everyone who reads these words has had this experience of seeing this in others.

Healing requires the willingness to feel desire, to see it as good and to see it as holy. Does that not mean that if you feel a desire, that it might not become twisted by the egoic patterns in your mind? Of course not. There is always the possibility that desire will be twisted to meet the needs of the egoic mind within you. But rest assured, if it does, who has done it? You! Always within you, you have known that desire is good, but you suppressed it. Those times when desire came forth and you let it become twisted into serving the goals of the ego, you always knew perfectly well what you were doing. You were the decision-maker.

You have learned, therefore, to fear desire because that fear is the effect of fearing yourself, and that is what cripples you. That is what cuts off the creative flow. That is what leads to everything your world knows as the multitude of psychological diseases: an unwillingness to trust one's self, an unwillingness to love one's self and the belief that the desires that move up through your beingness are something evil and dark.

You think that if only you could stamp them out of your being, you could remain in control and everybody would like you because you would conform to the smallness and the littleness that is worshiped in human consciousness.

Understand well the next axiom we give to you:

> The only relationship that holds any value at all
> is your relationship with God, your creative Source,
> the depth of the ocean.

Right away the mind says, "But what about my mate, what about my parents, what about my children, what about the president of the United States, what about the postmaster?" You will come up with a million examples of relationships that surely have great importance.

The *only* one that holds value is your relationship with God. For when that is in alignment, all of your creations, your choices for relationships and how you will be within them will flow effortlessly *from* that alignment. Therefore, seek first the Kingdom, and all these things will be added unto you. Do not try to create a rose by starting with the petals, but nourish the roots, and the flower must blossom.

If you are to be in right relationship with your Creator, it is absolutely necessary to correct your perception and relationship with the energy of desire. It begins by releasing your judgment of it in all of its forms. For again, you can only be in Love or fear. You can only be in innocence or judgment. Love and innocence are of the Kingdom. Fear and judgment are of illusion.

RELEASING JUDGMENT OF DESIRE

Learn then, through simple practice, to interrupt the patterns you have learned from this illusory world, so that you release judgment of the energy of desire. This will be different for each and every one, depending on where you begin.

Here is a very simple exercise. When you awaken in the morning and you have planted your feet firmly on your floor, take pause and ask yourself this question:

What do I want right now?

Right away, the mind will say, "Well, I'm too busy to know what I want, I have to go off to work. I have to serve everybody else. I'm here to satisfy the world. I have no time to ask *myself* what *I* want."

Remember that what you decree *is,* and the thought you hold in the mind will be reflected through the nature of your experience.

So take pause and ask, "What do I want?" Then simply give yourself one minute to observe whatever comes up in the mind, or even is felt in the body.

Heaven forbid, you might want to have sex! Oh! Then you would know for sure that you are not a "spiritual" being!

You might want to take a hot shower. You might want a glass of juice or water. You might want to sing. You might want to stretch or breathe. You might want to turn and look at your lover, your mate, still sleeping in the bed. You might want to arise, and sneak into your children's room and watch them sleep. You might want to sit down and read the morning paper.

The point here is to notice that by asking the question, something will respond within you. And when that response comes, notice that there is a feeling associated with it, a quality that makes your cells sing just a little bit. That is the energy, the elixir of life, called desire.

In this one minute, you need not rise to act, but to simply observe: "Ah, what do I want? To take a hot shower." The feeling of the thought, or the thought that emits the feeling in the body, "I want to take a hot shower," is carried on the elixir of desire.

Desire is coming from a depth of your being that, again, rests right next to the face of God. Might it not be the case that by following the desire that wells up through your heart, by feeling it, by embracing it, you might learn and discover what the ocean is wishing to express through the wave that you are? If you judge desire, might you not be shutting off the creative flow that the Mind of God wishes to express?

Of course, that is the problem. You have tied the hose in a knot through conflicted judgments. Here is a very common one in your world. Be honest with yourself, how many times have you felt the desire to be wealthy? It is not something you are supposed to sit around and talk about or make very public, especially if you are trying to be "spiritual."

You may have thought, "I woke up this morning and I just imagined having so many golden coins that I could buy the entire planet!" Then you remembered, "Oh! 'Money is the root of all evil.' I can't think that way. Well, I better get busy and get off to my office job, that secretly inside I really resent because they don't pay me what my soul is worth. But I'll pretend like I'm quite fine. Oh, money? No, I'm quite fine. I really have enough. No, no, I'm really quite fine."

Then as you drive home and a Mercedes pulls up alongside you, you cannot help but turn and say, "God, I wish I could afford one of those." Then you think, "Oh, God! I can't have *that* thought, so I'll just drive my old Volkswagen down the road. But I'm being a very good spiritual person."

Be honest with yourself. How many times have you felt welling up within you the desire to be wealthy? What on earth has caused you to fear that desire? What has caused you to tie the hose in a knot, so that you try to block that desire from coming into manifestation?

Perhaps when you were a child, you went to one of your cathedrals. And there was someone in a long robe standing upon a platform and because everything looked so beautiful, you thought that surely they must have been speaking with authority. Since this cathedral was filled with a whole lot of small little minds that were all living in their own level of fear, they said, "Money is the root of all evil." And you thought, "Oh, well, that is the truth. Oh, yes, that's the truth. Oh, God! I better fear money."

I say unto you, you have one authority, and it is never held within the office of any church, or any organization or any one individual. Your authority is the voice for God that dwells within your heart and within your mind! God is not limited, and does not require His children to be limited. For if you would receive all that God would give you, you must decide to rise up and be the grandest wave that you could possibly be. For only in so doing, do you honor your Creator.

You could say that God is like a wise gardener who is constantly trying to grow beautiful roses. She knows exactly how much moisture to put in the soil. She knows how to make those nutrients rise from the soil through the roots, up through the heart of the stem of the flower to give forth radiant color, so that everyone that looks upon it is touched by the mystery of beauty.

[And God wonders, "Well, it is interesting. These roses that I have created seem to have a mind of their own. As the elixir I tried to give them rises through the stems, they tie themselves in little knots and only a little bit of the elixir reaches out. So the petals never quite blossom fully."]

Have you ever had that feeling that you are putting more energy into staying constricted than you are into allowing expansion? *Reflection question for this lesson?*

DESIRE LINKS YOU TO THE WILL OF GOD

Desire is creation. Therefore, *what* you desire is of supreme importance. If you will take the little exercise that we have given you and begin to put it into practice upon awakening in the morning, in a very simple and quiet way, you will begin to get back in touch with the innocence and beauty of the movement of desire. You can delight in it.

When you have a sexual thought, a sexual desire, why not just be with it? Why not notice what it causes to happen in the body? How does your breath change? Does the heart beat faster? Be honest with yourself, is it not putting a smile on your face? What if you decided to honestly embrace that effect as being perfectly innocent and beautiful? How might your day change if you did not repress awareness of sexual desire?

You will notice we are not saying you should walk down the street and grab everybody that walks by you. We are talking about allowing yourself the living embrace of exactly what energy is moving through your being.

Why is this important? If you have decided that there are certain energies that are demonic, evil, or have the power to distract you from your union with God, you have already decided there is something *beyond* the reach of your power. And that is what disempowers you. You take an innocent energy and turn it into a monster that must be feared at all cost.

Yet I say this unto you. The mystical transformation that carries you from feeling yourself to be a disempowered little drop of foam on the edge of a wave to the sense of freedom and empowered living that flows from the Mind of God through you to express only beautiful creations filled with majesty, power and miracles is *willingness*. The willingness to turn to the very energies that move through the mind and the body and to not fear them. But instead to look upon them with innocence and wonder.

This is the source of the myths that have been told in all cultures: the knight that slays the dragon, or kissing the wild beast on the cheek and it becomes a loving companion. Your monsters are what you fear and repress because of the judgments you have learned in the world. (And the world is only the denial of the Kingdom. It is the exact opposite of Truth.)

If you are sitting in one of your cathedrals and everyone is saying, "Sexuality is very bad! It will keep you from God." Right away, you should realize if everyone here fears sexuality, it must actually be divine. Allow yourself to think, "Perhaps I would do well to embrace it, love it, master it and not fear it."

Imagine someone says unto you, "Money is the root of all evil!" and then puts out his hand and says, "Would you please make a donation to our organization?" Is that not an expression of conflict? Yet such conflict permeates the religions and dogmas of your world, which say, "Don't desire money. Don't desire wealth. By the way, to keep the ministry on this radio station, we really need you to send a donation." What are they trying to teach you? What are they in denial of?

Sex and money. Pretty basic things, are they not? They represent energies that flow from the Mind of God, which would express in unlimited joy and power, and not be willing to settle for limitation of any kind.

When the Earth was birthed from God's holy Mind and took on its own form and became an entity just like you, God did not say, "Well, this is a pretty beautiful planet, but I can only have a solar system just large enough for the Earth." Rather, out of joy, God allowed there to come forth solar system upon solar system upon solar system, the birthing of a thousand suns every moment, as a field in which this beautiful jewel of a planet could spin. *That* is true creation! What quality of solar system have *you* decided to allow, in which the planet of your own awareness can spin and live and express?

Desire is everything. The simple exercise we have given you will begin to free up the blocks within, and you will rediscover the innocence of desire. Then you can begin to expand upon it, to take a few moments to learn to live deliberately, asking yourself, "What do I *truly* want?" Use your consciousness to relax into the innocence of the question:

✶   What do I truly want?

What is it in my heart that keeps calling to me, keeps compelling me?

Because your mind shines forth like a sunbeam to the sun from the Mind of God, when you ask the question, pictures will begin to arise, feelings will begin to arise. And I say unto you, they are symbols and expressions of what God wants to bring forth *through* you. You may say, "Every time I look in my heart, and every time I allow myself to feel it, what I really want is to put my arms around people. I want to let people know how much I love them." Why fear such a desire? Do you say, "It's too overwhelming. I don't know how I'll be accepted."

✶ Who cares how you will be accepted?
What matters is how you accept yourself.

What if by feeling that desire, new pictures began to come to you? For example, suddenly you realized, "What I want to do is join the Peace Corps." Perhaps that very decision would be like putting yourself in a solar system where you can spin as your own planet. What if going and being in the Peace Corps could be the very pathway through which you learn to receive the great joy of letting your love out to the world? But if you fear desire, how can you ever know these things?

What comes up for you by asking that question? It might be, "I want to have so much wealth." And I see the thought that says, "Oh, no, wealth is bad." But if you allow yourself to continue to ask the question, a deeper answer will emerge, such as, "What I want is to be able to go to all the hungry children on the planet and feed them. That's why I want to be wealthy."

Could it not be that the desire to feed the world is God's desire to speak through you, to use you in a way that effects transformation upon your planet? Can you see that by blocking the feeling of desire, you might just be blocking yourself from hearing what you keep praying for over and over? You pray, "Father, reveal thy purpose to me." Then you feel the desire and say, "Oops! Excuse me, Father. I have to get rid of this desire first."

Desire in the heart is where you will discover the phone line that links you to the will of God that would be expressed through you. If you do not trust desire, you are literally saying that you have decided not to trust your Creator. That is a statement not just to be brushed aside. In healing the conflict around desire, now that you know what it truly is, learn to be patient with yourself.

AN EXERCISE IN TRUSTING DESIRE

We would suggest that you create a structure by which a second exercise can be practiced that fits into your life. Again, it need not take more than five, ten or fifteen minutes initially, perhaps three or four times a week. Eventually, you will be doing this all the time because you will be creating deliberately. For just ten or fifteen minutes, set aside your world. Remember that you need do nothing, so the world can wait.

Relax the body and close the eyes. It can be of great benefit to let the breath become very deep and rhythmic. It relaxes the nervous system and seduces the controller within your mind—the critic that decides what thoughts are acceptable and which ones are not. By the

way, the critic is never something you created. (It is something you let live in your mind that was made up by a lot of other fearful minds, called parents and teachers.)
As you relax the body and the mind, ask yourself:

 my intention for next JHS session.

✱   What do I truly want?

Observe the images that come, without judgment. Notice the feelings in the body, and allow this to go on for just a minute or two. Then pause, open the eyes, and write down all that you can remember. For example, "I saw the image of having forty-seven sexual partners. I saw the image of having golden coins rain down upon me so that I had to have an umbrella over my head. I saw huge bowls of ice cream. I saw myself in a boat on the ocean. I notice that my stomach got tight." Whatever it is, write it down.

Then, take a deep breath, relax again, and repeat the process. Place the hand so that it rests on the heart. Breathe into it a few times, and then ask,

What do I truly desire?

Again, allow the process to be what it is. Do this over a period of ten or fifteen minutes so that you repeat the process at least six or seven times, writing everything down.

✱ Then take the piece of paper or journal and put it aside until the next exercise period, and again repeat the process. When you have done this seven times, so that you have seven sheets of paper in which you have gone through this process, then, and only then, begin to look back through all the things that came up. Ask yourself, "What seems to be repeating itself?" You might notice that three times you wanted a huge bowl of ice cream, but then it seemed to fade away. Twice you had a desire for forty-seven lovers, but now you notice that you are really only wanting one.

Whatever it might be, notice the pattern, the thread that seems to run the most throughout the exercise periods. Then, imagine that thread to be the energetic link that is tied at one end to the piece of foam at the edge of the wave, and the other is anchored to the depth of the ocean. Then consider that, perhaps, if you allowed yourself to move down that thread, to begin to put your energy on that, to begin to clear up the obstacles within your consciousness that block that desire from being consistently lived from, you would carry yourself from the drop of foam at the edge of the wave to the Heart of God.

And along the way, everything unlike Love would come up for you to release it. During the process, you would go through a metamorphosis that would culminate in your being the living incarnation of the power of Christ—your soul would realize the fulfillment that it has always sought.

For you see, the reason you have cleverly decided to trick yourself into blocking the energy of desire is that the soul knows that were it to follow such a thread through whole and total commitment, it will be embarking on the pathway set before you by God that knows how to take you home.

If you arrive at home, it will mean that you will have had to give up being a *seeker*. You will have had to become one who has *found*. And you will have to rise above the crowd. You will have to give up all of your identity with smallness. You will have to give up needing the approval of others. You will have left the nest of insanity. You will have arisen and taken up your rightful place at the right hand of God. Is not that the deepest fear you carry—to actually be the Truth of who you are: Christ incarnate?

Desire can be much fun. Ideally, once you have practiced this on your own, ask your mate or a close friend if they would be willing to embark on this process with you, so that perhaps once a week you can sit down together and say, "What did you come up with this week?"

It is called undressing in front of a friend. It is called becoming vulnerable with another. It is called finding another child to play with in the Kingdom, so that you can go to the sandbox, away from the adult world that says, "Desire is bad. You guys be careful."

*Kristy !∞

You begin to look at what is true and real from a place of innocence. You begin to create for yourself a support group. And that support group perhaps can grow to three or four friends—or even ten or twenty—in which everyone is involved with getting in touch with what is really in there, by understanding the principle that desire is the thread that links your soul to the Heart of God. And God wants only to extend, through you, that which expresses Love in the world. It is called creation.

Perhaps, it is a worthwhile project. For when you do not turn to allow the embrace of desire, there is only one alternative. It is to live in mere survival. When you choose the energy of mere survival, the *world* is your master, before which you will be made to bow again and again and again and again and again, lifetime after lifetime after lifetime! You will be a *slave* to the insanity that seems to rule this world.

And you will never know peace. You will never know joy. And you will never come home. Plain and simple! But you were not created to wither and die on the vine. You were made to bear forth much good fruit.

Let the roots be watered by desiring, above all things, to become the fulfillment of what God had in mind when He breathed into you the breath of Life. Let that breath be received in each moment. You will come to see that the only question—the *only* question—you need be preoccupied with is this:

✳   How much of God am I willing to receive
and allow to be expressed through me?

It is called "separating the wheat from the chaff." The chaff is the thinking of the world that would have you believe in smallness. This can only result in your perpetual suffering. The wheat is the food that gives life, because it is filled with the Love of God.

Fear not, then, desire. But desire to *embrace* desire. Touch it, feel it, know it, dance with it, sing with it, and look at it innocently. Feel it wholly. And then learn to discern, through the ways we have given you, what desire is truly: that thread that is shining forth through all of your days. Then decide to let that desire *in*form your choices, so that you create a life that serves the fulfillment of that thread of desire.

I had to do the same. For I began to notice that there was a thread of desire in my heart to create some form of demonstration that would be so overwhelming that *anyone* who turned their attention to it could not help but be reminded that there is something far greater to life than living to survive, and surviving just to live. Even when I was young, I began to get glimpses. At first, they were fleeting. Something was compelling me, and as I learned to trust desire, the pictures became clearer and clearer.

In those moments of revelation when I was still but a teenager, I saw myself standing on hilltops, surrounded by multitudes. And I marveled at the words that came through my mouth. I saw glimpses and pictures of being loved by millions. I saw pictures and things that I could not even comprehend, because they were literally pictures of what I am doing *now*. And how could a teenager, living in Judea two thousand years ago, have any way of comprehending the use of the technologies of your modern world in which to communicate Love? It made no sense to me. But still, I decided to trust it.

A part of that thread was the recognition that death is unreal. Therefore, I thought that I ought to be able to create a demonstration that would prove it. Now, think about that for a moment! If that thought was born in you, and you tried to share it with the world, would you not be told you were crazy to dare to think a thought so out of line with everything the world believes? But because I followed the thread of desire, I began to realize that it kept speaking to me, day after day, and week after week. It wanted to grow. It wanted to be nurtured. Finally, I decided:

I am going to allow that thread to be nurtured.
I am going to discover where it takes me, and what it is all about.

Where it took me was into mastery of life and death, mastery of healing, mastery of consciousness. It took me into mastery of myself. It brought me home to my own Christed beingness.

Because I followed that thread, I can talk with you today. There are many of you that appreciate what I have done, because you see me as a spokesperson for the Truth. Is it not time that *you* followed your own thread, and became, likewise, a spokesperson for reality? For just as you have been sent to me, there will be many sent to you, as you step from being a seeker to a finder. For as you take up your rightful place, you become a vehicle through which the voice for God will creatively touch the lives of countless persons that you may never ever meet physically.

You were birthed to be grand. You were birthed for greatness. You were birthed to shine forth such light into this world that the world remembers that light is true, and darkness is illusion. Be you, therefore, that which you are—you are the light of the world. And I will delight in journeying with you. I can join with anyone who chooses to step into their own Christedness. The connecting thread is the thread of desire. *J Share w/Damon*

Therefore, begin to turn toward the energy of desire within yourself—to separate the wheat from the chaff—by first learning to feel it for just a minute without judging it, and then to deepen that process. You will reach the point where with every breath that you breathe, you are in touch with the energy of desire. And that is the only voice that you will give authority to.

You will not be able to keep up with the loving creation that wants to express through you. You will marvel at the friends that come into your life and how your external solar system, in which your planet is spinning, changes. You will marvel and wonder how it is all happening. You will finally discover that you are not the maker and doer of your life, that God wants to direct and make Life *through you*. Then you will know the Truth that sets you free:

> Of myself, I do nothing.
> But my Father, through me, does all things.
> And it is very good.

Be you, therefore, at peace. And desire well. For when you feel desire, you are watering your roots with the energy of Life itself. Trust it! Embrace it! And let the petals of the rose *blossom* within your holy being.

We love you, and we are with you. If you could only see how much enlightened help there is surrounding you at any moment, you would never allow the fear of going astray with your desire to be victorious within your mind. You would step forth with boldness. And all things would be made new again.

How much of God's Love are you willing to receive? Amen.

THE KEYS TO THE KINGDOM

Beloved friends, we come forth in this lesson to continue that pathway which builds the structure, the highway by which you may learn to follow and, therefore, master The Way of the Heart. A *way* in life means to have chosen from all possibilities that one which will stand out as the way to which you are committed, the way to which you devote the whole of your attention by granting your willingness that the way be followed. Just as when you take a journey upon your Earth by making the commitment to take the journey, you avail yourselves of experiences that could not come to you in any other way.

When you go to a university to pursue a degree, although you begin with a certain idea of what the pathway may hold or bring you, is it not true that the relationships which come along the way, the knowledge that reveals itself to you, and even the end result of accomplishing the degree always seems to be different and much richer than you could have imagined when you began your journey?

Therefore, understand well that The Way of the Heart requires the willingness to commit. [Commitment is nothing more than a deliberate decision that something will be so.] Just as with all aspects of experience you have ever known, when all of your being is involved in the willingness to make a decision, there is literally nothing that can prevent you from the accomplishment of your goal.

Rest assured, whenever you believe you have not succeeded or not completed some decision fueled by desire, it is because you were simply not wholly committed—or you decided to change your mind. And when you change your mind, you literally change what you experience in the world or the solar system in which your *self* spins.

The Way of the Heart, then, does indeed require the decision of commitment. I say unto you that when you wholly commit to discovering The Way of the Heart, you will discover a way of being in the world that is not here. You will discover a way of walking through life in which you experience being uplifted by something that seems to be forever beyond you, yet is within you as the core and the essence of your very being.

Your way will not be understandable by the world. Your way will not even be comprehensible within yourself. You will be living from mystery—moving from mystery to mystery to mystery—uplifted and carried by something that brings a satisfaction and a fulfillment to the depth of your soul, far beyond anything you can now imagine.

I feel this way...

Is it worth it to commit to The Way of the Heart? Yes! [It culminates with the recognition that you do not live Life at all, but rather that Life is living you.] One of its characteristics is the development of the witness—a quality of consciousness, a way of being—in which you seem to be witnessing everything that arises and flows through you and around you from a place of utter stillness.

Stillness does not mean non-activity. It does mean non-attachment to activity—whether it be the arising and falling away of cancer in the body, the arising and falling away of relationship, or the rising and falling away of a solar system.

You will discover that there is a place within you that can look upon all things with perfect equanimity, perfect acceptance, and perfect Love. For in mastery of The Way of the Heart, you will discover that nothing is unacceptable to you. [Only what is accepted can be transcended.] *ugh - everything is acceptable?*

You will discover a way of being in which nothing any longer compels you—not even the desire to know God compels you any longer, for the need of it has been completed.

Then there arises a way of being in the world that is indeed not here, for you will feel no restlessness, no need to direct your journey. No questions will arise. You will be at peace. In that peace, the breath of God will move through you. And you will become as the wind, knowing not where you came from or where you are going, but you will abide in perfect trust and perfect rest. [The world may not know you, but your Father will know you—and *you* will know your God.]

In The Way of the Heart, the most primary and fundamental perception that seems to fuel ordinary human consciousness has been finally transcended. The perception of a separate "maker and doer" has been dissolved, and once again you will understand the depth and the profundity of the simple terms in this sentence:

Of myself, I do nothing. But through me, the Father does all things.

To rest in such a perception means that you have come to realize that the self that you are is merely a conduit, through which mystery lives itself, through which Love pours forth. You will realize that there is nothing to be gained or lost in this world. You will know what it means to recognize that you literally have nowhere to go and nothing to achieve. You will become empty and spacious.

And yet paradoxically, while the body lasts, you will appear to be as everyone else. You will arise in the morning and brush your teeth. When the body is hungry, you will feed it. You will laugh with your friends. You will yawn when the body is a bit tired. Yet through it all, there will be a quality of awareness—called the witness—that is simply watching it all, waiting to be moved by the wind of Spirit. Though others may not see it, virtually everything you utter will carry the sound of truth.

You will not know how Spirit will work through you, nor will you care. Because, you see, when there is no maker or doer or director, it will not matter to you. That is what it means to live as the wind, for the wind does not concern itself with where it has been or where it is going. It is moved by some mysterious source that cannot be located at all. Yet it blows, and as it blows, its effect is experienced.

Imagine then, a life in which all that you do is not *for* yourself. Imagine a way of life in which what you do is not *for* anyone else. Imagine a way of life in which creativity flows forth from a Source so deep within you and around you that no language or dogma can contain it—[a force and a Source that knows how to express itself through you in such a way that it is constantly and only serving the atonement, the awakening of all of creation to the truth of God's presence.]

The Way of the Heart does, indeed, unfold along a certain pathway. In this lesson, we will address the stages of that pathway, in a general sense. Then we will speak of the most important characteristic to be cultivated along this path.

THE FIRST KEY IS DESIRE

First, desire is everything. Without it, not a thing can arise. Therefore, *what* you desire is of utmost importance. Desire, then, perfect union with God. Desire, then, to be Christ incarnate. [Desire, then, to be all that your Creator has created you to be, even if you have no idea what that might be.]

For when you hold desire within your beingness and when you have mastered the energy of desire—again, mastery does not mean control—by grounding it always in the desire to be as you are created to be, then indeed all of your life and all of the subsequent or subsidiary desires will come to serve that grand desire.

When you come into that state of being, nothing shall be impossible unto you. Why? Because you are not the one doing it. [You are merely a piece of thread in a very cosmic tapestry being woven by the Creator of all of creation, who alone knows how to weave the tapestry of a new age, of a new paradigm, of a healing of this plane and of humanity.]

2020 is a good example of this.

So the first stage is the stage of desire. Only by feeling desire and not by suppressing it can you truly begin to move toward the stage of mastery in which the energy of desire always serves that higher will, which is the will of God for you. As we have said to you before, when your will is in alignment with the will of God, you will discover that God's will for you is that you be genuinely happy through and through, content, fulfilled, at peace, empowered, capable, and responsible.

THE SECOND KEY IS INTENTION

Desire, in time, is cultivated through *intention*. For you have used time to teach yourself how to be distracted by all of the thoughts and perceptions that make up this cosmic soup called your world. All of you have known the frustration of having a desire, and then as soon as you walk out the door a friend pulls up and says, "Let's go to the beach." And you never make it to class, even though your desire is to get the degree. You have cultivated the art of being seduced by distraction.

Therefore, it is necessary to utilize time to cultivate intention. For without intention, desire cannot become the crystal clear focus, the laser-like focus that can cut through the dross of this world so that a new creation can flow forth through you.

Intention is not the same as holding a strong egoic or willed commitment to making something happen. For The Way of the Heart recognizes that you have not known how to achieve the fulfillment you seek at the level of the soul, for the simple reason that if you did, you would have already accomplished it. Intention does not mean putting your nose to the grindstone and not taking "no" for an answer.

Rather, it means that you cultivate within your thought processes the art of remembering what you are truly here for. You are here to remember that you are the thought of Love in form. You are here to remember that you are one with God. You are here to remember that what I have called Abba, though it goes by many names, is the source of your only reality. You are living in reality only to the degree that That One is living through you.

Therefore, intention in The Way of the Heart means to utilize time each day to focus your attention on the desire to be Christ incarnate.

Intention is that energy or that use of the mind that creates—through consistent practice—the channel through which desire begins to move down and re-educate the emotional body, and even the cellular structure of the physical body, and all of the lesser avenues of thinking that occur within the intellect. So everything involved in your being is integrated, working together and focused on the fulfillment of that one grand desire to accept your function in this world. Your function is healing your sense of separation from God.

How do you apply intention? Each day, just as you have used time to teach yourself to be easily distracted, you need only ask yourself one question daily:

> ✳ What is it that I most desire?
> What am I doing on this planet?
> What am I committed to?

The last two questions are just forms of the fundamental question. As you keep practicing asking that question, the answer will become clearer and clearer. For it is the question that influences, stimulates, and gives birth to the answer. The universe is always answering your questions. And when you ask unclear questions, you get unclear answers. Therefore, become crystal clear with your intention and remind yourself of it daily:

> My intention is to use time constructively for the relearning of what it
> means to abide in the Kingdom of Heaven and to fulfill my function.
> My function is healing. And healing requires the presence of Christ,
> for only Christ can express the Love that brings healing into being.

Desire and intention are critical. These stages unfold in the field of time as one matures in The Way of the Heart.

THE THIRD KEY IS ALLOWANCE

The third stage of the process whereby the mind is wholly corrected and one returns home is the stage of allowance. For the egoic world does not teach you to allow, it teaches you to strive. *You* must be the maker and the doer. *You* must find a way to manipulate or control your environment in order that it conform itself to the image that you are holding in your mind.

All of that is well and good, and there are many beings that learn some valuable lessons by following the path of certain teachers that will teach you that you can create whatever you want. That will seem like such a big deal until you realize it is what you are doing all of the time! You are always creating exactly what you decree. It is no big deal and it is not a secret.

But there will be those that will teach you, "Well, just go into your mind, ask yourself what you want, and when you see that picture of the Mercedes, then you simply do all of these little magical tricks and pretty soon, you end up with a Mercedes." The problem with that, although it can be a useful stage, is that the intellect, the worldly part of your mind, can only desire what it has been programmed to desire.

The worldly part of your mind says, "Well, I have to transport my body around in this plane. Automobiles do that. The world tells me that a Mercedes is a grand way of doing this; therefore, I will create the desire of wanting a Mercedes." When you manifest the Mercedes, you fool yourself into thinking that you have made great progress when, in fact, all you have done is done what you have always done. You have chosen what your experience will be and you have manifested it. There is nothing new about that. Although by so doing, you can begin to regain confidence in your ability to manifest.

The Way of the Heart is about something else. Allowance, in this pathway, means that you begin to view your life differently. It is not a struggle to get out of high school and create a career by which you can create golden coins, by which you can create the proper house in the proper environment so that your ego feels "successful" and, therefore, of being "worth" love.

Be honest with yourself—is not your world built on such premises as these: "If only I can make my life look successful around me, then I will be accepted, then I can love myself, at least a little. Maybe I can get other people to love me." That is not it at all.

The Way of the Heart begins with the recognition that you are *already* loved by the only Source that matters, that you have come for a much higher purpose that can be made manifest *in* the ways of the world, but is not *of* the world.

Allowance is the cultivation of a way of looking at the events of your life, not as obstacles to getting what you want, but as stepping stones. Each one presents you with a blessing of the lessons required to heal the obstacles—not to success, but to the presence of Love as the Source and ground of your being.

In the stage of allowance, we begin to cultivate an acceptance of all things in our experience. We begin to see that because we have made a commitment to awakening and incarnating only Christ, the universe is already conspiring to bring the people and events into our lives, on a moment to moment basis, that can best provide us with exactly what we most need to learn or become aware of.

And so, messengers are sent. That messenger could come in the form of someone whom you fall in love with, and there is something there for you to learn. It could be that you have been blocking yourself from feeling love for other people, and now someone finally comes that blasts down the door and you cannot help but feel that feeling.

The messenger could be someone who comes as the grain of sand within the oyster that causes the friction within you that nudges you from your sleep, and you realize that you have been operating out of some very dysfunctional patterns and that you have got to get a better grip upon the Truth of who you are.

It may be that you need to learn to express your feelings more. It may be that you need to accept your own creativity more. Through your messengers, that which causes you to finally be responsible and be honest about where you are will be brought up within you.

For instance, if you think, "Well, I never get angry anymore. After all, I'm a very spiritual person. I just got out of seminary and I know it all now. So, I'll just live in heavenly bliss." And events begin to happen. Perhaps, as an example, a gay couple moves into your neighborhood and you discover that you have some very deeply seated perceptions that there is something wrong with that sexual orientation. They are messengers, sent to you by the universe to push you to look more deeply.

Allowance, then, is the cultivation of a quality of awareness in which you rest in the recognition that your life is no longer your own to dictate and control. But that rather, you have given it over to the Source of your own beingness, to that depth of wisdom in the depth of the ocean that knows best how to bring about what is required to push up the dross from within your consciousness, so that you can release it. *How?*

considered worthless; rubbish   *Future lesson?*

Allowance cultivates trust. Allowance is the way in which intention and desire come to work ever more fully in the third dimension of your experience—the field of time. Allowance is a submission, but not a naive submission. Allowance changes your perception of what you see as the world around you.

You begin to realize that you do not really live in a real world at all. You live in a field of vibrations and energies that is operated by the law of attraction or resonance. And you begin to be willing to allow certain things to fall out of your life, even family and friends, trusting that because of your desire and intention, what passes out of your life must be okay. For it will be replaced by new vibrational patterns which come in the form of messengers—events, places, persons and things—that can carry you on the upward spiral of awakening.

Allowance means the beginning stages of the cultivation of humility and the recognition that you must finally submit to something beyond the intellect and the control of the egoic part of the mind because the maker and doer that has been trying to do it all is finally recognized as being inadequate.

THE FOURTH KEY IS SURRENDER

As these three stages mature, you rest into the final stage of surrender. And surrender means there is no longer any restlessness. Surrender means you know through every fiber of your being that there is no one here living a life, there is Life flowing through the body-mind personality, for as long as it lasts.

what?!

Here is where the mystical transformation is culminated or completed. It is here that you understand the meaning of the teaching:

> I live, yet not I, but Christ dwelleth as me.

Surrender is a stage in which perfect peace is the foundation, not for passivity or inactivity, but for even *more* activity.

You find yourself, as long as you are in the world, being busier and busier, and asked to do more and more. You become even more responsible. Eventually, you come to see that because you *are* Christ, you are responsible for the whole of creation. You come to see that you cannot think a thought without disturbing the farthest of stars. It is that responsibility from which you have shrunk and tried to contain yourself as a tiny myopic piece of foam, all because you have feared being responsible for the whole.

But The Way of the Heart corrects your perception so that you come to recognize that your greatest joy, your greatest fulfillment is in wholly and deliberately accepting responsibility for the whole of creation. Why? Because you suddenly realize you are not the maker and doer, that you can accept responsibility for anything and everything because through you all power under Heaven and Earth is made to flow, to manifest the Love of God. So, in short, it is in God's hands, not yours:

> Not my will, but Thine be done.

Does that begin to make sense to you? Do you see how it changes how you have even been taught to interpret my teachings?

Desire, intention, allowance, surrender. But it is a surrender into a way of being that the world can never know. It is surrender into a way of being in which you may never receive an Oscar for your acting. But it is a way of being in which your consciousness becomes totally open to your union with all of creation. You will talk with a leaf as it falls from a tree. You will see the soul of the kitten that you pet. You will talk with angels and masters. And you will be involved in board meetings in the high cosmic conference rooms.

You will know that the body-mind you once thought was yours is little more than a temporary teaching device, a tool to be picked up and utilized at God's direction, and put aside when its usefulness is done.

So that even when it is time to go through the transition that you know as death, nothing will disturb your peace. As the body dies—which means simply that your attention begins to release itself from it just like the hand of a carpenter is released from the handle of a hammer as it is laid down on the table on the way to dinner—you will be able to watch the process with total equanimity and joy✗

✗ You will watch your Spirit disengage from the body. You will watch it crumble into lifelessness so that all of your attention becomes focused in a wholly new dimension. A dimension that is so vast that you will be able to look down upon the Earth plane, not unlike the way you might choose to hold a pebble in the palm of your hand. And in one quick glance, you see everything about the pebble and nothing is hidden.✗

I am one that has chosen to assume the responsibility for the pebble called Earth and all of life that dwells therein. You, too, will know that energy and reality of wrapping your fingers around the entirety of the solar system and becoming the god or the savior of that dimension. And it begins by choosing to take responsibility for your pebble, your domain, your solar system, your personal dimension. It begins by saying:

> I and I alone am the source of what I experience and perceive.
> I am not a victim of the world I see. Everything I experience,
> I have called to myself, plain and simple—no excuses, no ifs,
> ands, or buts. That is the way it is.

Gone will be your immaturity, your resistance to simply being responsible for your experience. The Way of the Heart then, cultivates a maturity of desire, intention, allowance, and surrender.

THE IMPORTANCE OF HUMILITY

No single characteristic is of greater importance than humility—not the feigned humility that is taught in certain world religions, but a *genuine* humility. For humility does not mean that you stand in front of a group of people who give you a standing ovation and say, "Oh, gosh! You don't have to do that. It's not important." So that you can look like you are humble when inwardly you are thinking, "Oh God, that feels so good! Clap a little louder, clap a little longer. But I won't tell you that." Do you know that kind of humility? Is it not the kind of humility you were taught in your schools?

⌈Genuine humility flows from the deep-seated recognition that you cannot save yourself, that you are created and not Creator, that you are effect and not cause (in an absolute sense), that something called Life is not yours, that there is *something* beyond your capacity of containment and intellectual understanding. And if that something ever decided to give up loving you, you would cease to be.⌋

No matter how deep you go into the depth of God, and no matter how deep you achieve an awareness and consciousness of union with God, what God is remains forever beyond your growing capacity to understand God. It is like an ocean of infinite depth. When you realize that strive as you might, you will never wrap your self, your little self, around that Source, you will rest into humility—genuine humility.

Why is this important? Mark these words well. As you progress along the path of The Way of the Heart, as you dissolve and loosen the shackles upon the mind, as the interior conflicts are healed and settled, as you begin to accept the abundance that the Father would bestow upon you in all levels of life and all levels of feeling and perception, as you begin to taste of the grandeur and the greatness that would flow through you, you will discover that the "enemies" become more subtle.

At a very immature, basic and naive level, every child views, at some stage, its parents as being its enemies, does it not? For example, the child says, "What do you mean I can't have the car tonight? What do you mean I must be home by 10:00 p.m.?" And the parent becomes the enemy.

As you move more and more into mastery, you will be sorely tempted to believe that you are done. You will be sorely tempted to believe, "I can do this. The prayers I used to do when I began, the simple exercises of awareness I used when I started my path, I don't need them anymore. I have mastered that." Any time you hear a voice within yourself saying, "I'm done," you may rest assured you are not. And you stand in danger of losing what you have gained.

Humility is the recognition that the more you move into mastery, the more there is the desire for discipline and vigilance. Discipline does not mean doing something hard that you do not like to do. Discipline is like the skill of an artist that cultivates and refines the skill, simply out of the deep desire and delight to create more beautifully. An athlete disciplines a muscle so that the muscle works even more beautifully than it did the day before, out of the sheer delight to extend greater beauty into the world.

While you remain in existence, the creations of consciousness that are unlike Love have created a whole lot of vibratory patterns that would just love to pull you down. Therefore, the discipline of the mind that is required is to recognize that—while the body lasts—there can be a delight in consciously repeating the decision to teach only Love, selectively choosing only the vibrational patterns to be allowed into your consciousness that reflect . the Truth and the beauty and the worthiness of who you truly are.

Judgment cannot reflect such light. Anger and hatred cannot do it. Fear and paranoia, fear of rejection, fear of the opinions of others and such vibrations can never reflect the regal grandeur of your being. Therefore, understand well that humility is absolutely essential. Paradoxically, as greatness is expressed through you, the temptation still will be to allow egoic energies to make a home in your mind. The ego's voice will say, "Boy, you are really quite a master, you know. You really deserve all this adulation. Why don't you keep ten percent of it for yourself?"

A master accepts the love and the gratitude offered by those whom his or her teachings have touched and gives it all to God, recognizing that of themselves these things could not have been done.

I learned, too, to be tempted. When those would come to me who were sick found healing in my presence, it was tempting to want to say, "Yes, look what I've done. I've really earned this. I spent forty days and forty nights in the desert. I've been to India and Tibet. I've been to England. I've studied with all of the masters of Egypt. Yes, I really deserve to be seen as a healer and a teacher."

But I learned through humility to remember the simplicity that of myself, I can do nothing. I cultivated within myself the art of always being a _student_ of Love, and not the _professor_ of Love, who thinks he is done just because he has a lot of letters after his name.

As you progress, and as you allow more of the abundance of God's Love to flow through you, you begin to stand up out of the crowd, and you begin to attract those that want the light. As that occurs, you must practice discipline and vigilance by remembering humility always, until you are remembering it with every breath.

Why? If you are living in this world, and feel that no one looks up to you, no one takes you as an authority, there is only one reason. You have resisted the truth of your being, and through denial have pushed God's Light away out of your fear, your deep-seated fear, that you might appear to be different than everybody else.

The world would teach you to be a doormat so that you fit in and do not ruffle anybody's feathers. But as you become empowered, one way you will know that it is occurring is that some people will not like you. You will push their buttons just by walking into the room, for darkness abhors light. It is that simple.

Humility is absolutely essential. Through the doorway of humility, the light of power can be turned on through you in ever-greater voltages. If that voltage does not seem to be flowing through your mind, look well to see if you are remembering humility and giving yourself to it.

For the Light of God can only shine through you to the degree that you are willing to take responsibility for it, which involves giving the fruits of it back to its Source, and not claiming it as your own. When you claim _nothing_ for yourself, _all_ things can flow through you. The Holy Spirit can gather millions of beings to come to you in many planes, because it knows you will not distort the Love of God by usurping God's position and putting yourself upon the throne.

Humility is a chief characteristic to cultivate. Therefore, when you pray, indeed, ask for greatness. Let the Father know that you are ready for the fullness of Christ to be incarnate, and simply hold the promise within that you will always remember that you are not the doer and the maker. You are merely the one who has come to recognize that only the Love of God can fulfill you as a soul. [Only the fulfillment of your purpose to be a channel for Love can bring you the success that you truly seek.]

When you are fully committed to that, rather than being committed to wondering about other people's opinions, then that power can begin to move through you.

When you are willing to let go of the world, Heaven will come to replace it. When you are willing to let go of your need for egoic grandness, true grandeur will begin to pour forth through you. There is a paradox within Spirit. Learn to discern it. Become a master *of* it. And never neglect the need for discipline based on the foundation of humility.

You see, this is what has caused you to fear the energy of desire, because in the past (and that can go back a long way), you have decided to find out what it would be like to let all of that power be claimed as your own, to be used to serve the voice of ego. That is what you are afraid of. But if you cultivate these stages and ground them in humility, you will never need to fear the misuse of desire.

Therefore, in your prayers, as often as you can remember to do so, remember that what you decree *is*. So speak clearly within yourself:

> ✴ Source, Creator, God, Goddess, All That Is, Abba
> I am ready to be what you created me to be.
> I choose to remember that I am effect and not cause.
> Thy will be done, knowing that your will is my full happiness.
> Reveal then, that path through which that happiness can be known.
> For my way has never worked, but your way always does.

Then, in each day remember the energy of appreciation. It is well and good to appreciate one another. But in the privacy of your own meditation and prayer, appreciate how the power of that Source of Love I have called God is living and moving and breathing to bring the people, the books, the teachers, and the experiences that are gently unraveling the cocoon of ego around you. And awakening you to the truth, beauty, majesty, grandeur, and greatness that Life Itself *is*.

Life wants to breathe through you as magically and powerfully as it breathes through a thunderstorm, or the leaf on a tree, or the radiance in a newborn baby's eyes.

That Life is what you are. That Life is the presence of God's Love, the depth of the ocean welling up into the waves of creation. Let, therefore, that Life alone be your guide in all things, and rest in appreciation before the infinite mystery that Life is, and say "yes" to it! Say "yes" to Life—that you are willing to let the fullness of it wash through you and carry you into an ever-deepening understanding and comprehension of all that God is. If you would well receive it, resting in the awareness of divine humility is the sweetest of experiences that you can ever know.

Many of you look upon me and say, "Oh, would I ever love to be where Jeshua is!" Think a thought and you are with someone. Think a thought and you are in that universe.

I tell you this, where I abide is in a vibrational frequency with many, many other beings whose consciousness *never wavers* for an instant from the deep *appreciation* and *humility* before the mystery of all that God is. We abide in the great delight of knowing that we live, yet not us, but our Creator lives *as us*.

The only difference between being a master and being a student is that the master has mastered the art of always being a student. Think about that one.

Desire, intention, allowance, surrender—what do you *truly* want? Are you willing to feel it and let that thread of desire carry you home? Can you remember to use time constructively by focusing your intention, by reminding yourself of what you are truly here for? You are not here to survive; you are here to *live* as the truth of who you are.

Allowance is not a passive acceptance of things as they are, but a recognition that there is something quite beautiful at work. There is an intelligence, a Love that knows you better than you know yourself and is presenting you, moment to moment, with jewels and gems and blessings and lessons that something is weaving the tapestry of your life, and nothing is happening by accident.

Surrender is the cultivation of the recognition that your happiness can be found only in the submission of your will to the will of God. For your will has been to be in conflict and struggle and limitation. God's will is that you live without conflict, in peace, joy, fulfillment and happiness. It is called bliss.

If ever you wonder how to anchor your awareness in humility, stop what you are doing and ask yourself this question:

Did I create myself?

You know well that the answer is:

No, I don't even know when I was created.

Something birthed me. What is it?

That will bring you to humility rather quickly. Do you know how to give birth to a star? No! Do you know how to give birth to a leaf on a tree? No! Do you even know how you lift your hand from your lap? No! What then, do you know? Nothing! Allow yourself to understand that you do not know anything. In that state of divine ignorance, you will rest in the humility that finally allows your Creator to move through you and reveal to you all things.

Beloved friends, The Way of the Heart is that way which corrects perception and brings right-mindedness, so that you are no longer the maker and the doer and the director. Your opinions will come to mean nothing to you whatsoever. Out of a grand emptiness, you will discover a perfect peace. Life will bear you on its wings. Through you, Life will express, in ever greater dimensionality, the exquisite and infinite Love and power and creativity that is God, until you swear that God is all there is. And there will be no place to find a trace of *you*.

For if enlightenment is the ending of separation, how can there be a maker and doer? Can the wave direct itself? The ego is the attempt to do so, and it always fails.

Peace then, be with you always. Let peace pervade your being at all times. Know that you are safe in the Love of God that arises from that great Source of mystery and would move through you with every breath you breathe and every word you speak, until you hear only that impetus of guidance that wells up from the depth of your being as a gentle voice that you trust completely. And you will know the freedom that you seek.

You already abide where we are. Trust this. Know this. Rely on this. Explore The Way of the Heart and you will come to know the truth of Love.

Be you therefore at peace, beloved friends. Amen.

LESSON 6
LOVE HEALS ALL THINGS

Indeed, greetings unto you, beloved and holy friends. *Indeed, greetings unto you beloved and holy friends.* If you understand the meaning of this greeting, if you comprehend the depth of each term used, already you know all there is to know. And you are well prepared to extend the Love of God forever.

"Indeed" means simply that there are no other options. "Greetings unto you" means salutations to that One created of the Father before all things, for I bow down before your radiance. "Beloved" and holy Child of God! Indeed, beloved of God. Indeed, beloved of every molecule in your physical universe. Indeed, loved of your Holy Mother, this precious Earth. Indeed, loved by anything you can imagine that has ever existed or ever could exist that has extended itself from the Heart and Mind of God. You are the beloved, pure and simple. And again, there are no options.

"Holy" because you are whole. Not because you have earned that holiness, but because it is that which is the Truth from which you are extended forth forever. Because you are made in the image of God, because you spring forth from the Mind of God, you are holiness itself each time you set aside the temptation to dream a useless dream, and walk this Earth as Christ.

Beloved and holy "friend"—a friend is not one lesser than myself. A friend is one who walks in perfect equality with the grandest of masters, whomever you might conceive such a master to be. A friend is one who chooses to look upon another and see only the face of Christ therein. There is no one who shall receive these words who has not already looked upon *me* and seen the face of Christ within. And likewise, I look upon *you* and call you "friend."

For when I look upon you, I see not the very momentary dreams that you seem to think are lasting so long. I see only the radiance of that which the Father has extended out of Love. I see only that which has neither beginning nor ending. I see only that which knows neither birth nor death. I see only that which has no limitations. I see only that—the light of which is already extended throughout all dimensions and all universes.

I see only my brother and my sister. And I see not a trace of inequality between us. Yet

I do recognize that, within your dream, it appears to you that I have gone ahead just a little bit.

At times, within your hearts, there is a longing to follow me. If you would but heed that longing, if you would make that longing primary at all times, your own desire will bring you wholly to where I am. And you will laugh when you discover that you have not moved an inch—that where I am is where you are, and where you are is in eternity, not in time; that where you are is in the place of your birth: the Mind of God.

This is the only thing that is true and it is true always. This is the only reality that you genuinely possess. Therefore, indeed, I call you *friend*. For well do I see that you are as I am. Therefore, indeed, greetings unto you, beloved and holy friends.

There is nothing else to be said. Yet the mind races, does it not? It races away from the very reality that I have just described about you. The mind races from that Source as a sunbeam from the sun. Yet in reality, it never leaves its Source. The very power with which you seem to become distracted by a momentary thought of fear is the same power by which you will awaken to your own call.

IF YOU WOULD KNOW LOVE, KNOW YOUR SELF

In truth, there is a place within you that already knows the day and the hour. You already know when you are going to decide to live the decision to be awake in God, to be only the presence of Love. Love embraces all things, allows all things, trusts all things, and thereby, transcends all things. Love is never possessive. Love is never fearful. Love is simply Love. Love cannot shine with specialness upon anyone at any time. For specialness, itself, is a contraction; the attempt to take Love and make it shine only on one object, only on one person, only on one being, only within one universe.

Therefore, whenever you recognize that you have singled someone or something out and said, "They hold a greater value," you may rest assured that you are not in Love at all. You are in fear. And if that one were to leave you, where would you be? But if you are *in Love* as a fish within the sea, all beings can arise and pass away and you will bless them in their journey. You will remember that you reside where God has placed you: in Her Heart. When you choose to be *only* the presence of Love, even the dream of loss will dissolve from your consciousness as a forest mist before the rising sun.

Indeed, beloved friends, Love does wait upon your welcome. Yet you cannot welcome Love by waiting for it to be brought *to* you by another, not even by me. You cannot welcome Love by trying to scurry about to create the environment in which you believe your preferences are being met. You cannot welcome Love when that welcome is attached or linked to any phenomenal thing, anything that has been birthed in time. Love can only be welcomed where Love truly resides. And Love resides within you as the core and the Source of your very being.

Therefore, if you would know Love, know your Self. Embrace the truth about it and the Truth will set you free. Then, indeed, Love will flow *through* you. Like the great sunlight that comes to nurture this beloved Earth, the Love that flows through you will be unimpeded. It will not meet an obstacle. You will look upon whomever is in front of you and you will know that they are sent unto you of the Father. The Holy Spirit has guided them to you because, through you, Love can be given in a way that begins to touch the place of their awakening. That is why you are but the servant of Love. That is all that life is!

When you choose to surrender, to give up the game, to give up the dream of trying to resist the Truth that is true about you always, you will become a mere channel, a mere conduit. You will become no more a seeker, for you will have decided to have *found*. When you have surrendered the last vestige of an insane possibility of contracting away from the Truth, when you have given that up, Love will flow through you. But notice that if it flows *through* you, it must first flow *to* you. Therefore, seek always to receive in order to give. For what can you give another if you have not yet received it to yourself?

How many of you have been taught to *try* to love, to *try* to do the "right" thing, the "good" thing? Yet, how many times have you gone within your secret chamber and said, "I am unworthy"? Then you wonder why your attempts to join in love with others never seem to be quite fulfilling enough, never quite seem to fill the cup, never quite seem to elicit the joy that you believe could be there.

Listen well: Your work—if you wish to call it that—is not to seek and find love. It is merely to turn within to discover every obstacle that you have created to its presence, and to offer that obstacle to the great dissolver of dreams, the grace of the Holy Spirit.

I have said unto you many times that the greatest of gifts you can give is this: to come wholly to the recognition that every attempt you have made to resist being the presence of Christ has failed you miserably. No matter how many times you have tried to convince yourself that you are unworthy, yet does the universe find a way to Love you. No matter how many times you have tried to lock yourself into the space and volume of a body, it has not succeeded. And at death, you have remembered and been confronted with the radiance of your unlimitedness.

Therefore, the greatest of gifts you can give another is to be one who has rescinded the need to insist on the insanity of fear.

THE PRIMARY CHARACTERISTIC OF MASTERY

Fearlessness is the primary characteristic of mastery. Mastery is not having great power to make things happen. It is only the recognition that what is true is true always and there *is* no other choice. Free will does not mean that you have the right to believe that you can succeed at being other than what God created you to be. Having free will does not mean that you can elect not to take the only curriculum that life is offering to you in every moment. It means only that you *do* have the right to put it off yet another day. And each time you put it off, you slumber in your suffering.

But when you elect to take the only curriculum that matters, when you elect to use the power of your free will to say:

> Now, from this moment on, I will no longer tolerate error in myself.
> No more games, no more dreams. I am committed to being only the
> presence of Love, for that is the Truth of who I am.

It matters not the opinions of others who are yet resisting that decision. Then, indeed, all things under Heaven and Earth move to support you, to guide you to the right person, the right place, the right book, the right sunrise, the right meadow in order to assist you in dropping the shackles of the obstacles to the presence of Love that you have created as an idol and as a substitute for Love.

That is why when you truly pray from the depth of your soul, "God, bring me home," you may rest assured, from that moment on it is fine to trust every little thing that unfolds. For though you see it not, what you call angels—friends that simply do not have bodies—are rushing about because you have given the command:

> Yes, I accept your presence in my life. I turn the whole thing over.
> Now, each moment is dedicated to healing and awakening the
> illusory sense of separation from God that once I created in error.

In how many ways have you sought Love? Can you count the ways? Would you dare to try to count each little pebble of sand on the beaches of your planet? Each and every soul has already tried to seek out Love in that many ways—if not more. You have sought it in a million forms in which you already knew that you could not find it. All because you wanted to perpetuate the insane attempt to try to separate yourself from God. And that is as futile as a sunbeam trying to separate itself from the sun.

Indeed, beloved friends, there is only one question you need answer:

> What am I choosing in this moment?

What have I given mastery over my life unto? What perception, what thought, what feeling? Feeling merely flows from the thought or the perception you have chosen. What behavior, what action am I choosing in this moment and does it express the reality of my being? Am I being busy extending love, or am I busying myself fearfully trying to grasp at what I *think* can give me love so that I do not lose it?

Look well, then, upon your parents, your siblings, your mates, and your friends. Not one of them—*not one of them*—holds the power to bring love to you. So what are you trying to get from them? Why do you ever insist that another ought to be conformed to what you believe you need? It is futile—one hundred percent, absolutely, positively futile—to *seek* love in relationship with anything or anyone.

It is, however, quite appropriate to *extend* Love in each relationship, with everyone and everything. But the extension of that Love requires that you have awakened to the truth that the *only* relationship that truly holds value is the relationship between you as the soul and God as your Creator.

Imagine a light bulb in one of your fixtures, that looks out from its little filaments and says, "Well I hope the person that just walked in the door is the right one. If I could just reach out and grab them, maybe my own light would come on."

Is it not a lot easier to simply take the cord and plug it into the right socket? How many times are you going to insist on trying to plug your cord into the wrong socket? "Well that one didn't work. I'll try this body; I'll try this person. I'll try this career. Not getting very much juice from that either." And then you get angry because it is not giving you enough juice, or it gave you enough juice yesterday, but not today, so it must be *its* fault.

There is one little tiny socket into which you can plug your cord. It is the only one that it fits in and it is the only socket wired to bring you the flowing and living waters of grace. That socket dwells only within your heart. Not the physical heart, but that which is symbolized by the physical heart: the core of your very being. But how many times in each day do you check to see that the cord is still plugged in? How many times do you remember to ask yourself:

> Is my commitment to Love or is my commitment to fear?

Fear is the act of disconnecting your cord from the only socket that can truly satisfy you, and running about trying to plug it in to somebody else's or something else's. I would ask you to consider this one question, as you look upon the whole of your experience: Has it ever worked? Can it ever work?

Imagine trying to hold flowing water in the palm of your hand by squeezing the fingers together. How much are you left with? Does it not just run through the fingers, no matter how hard you try? It finds the little holes and it flows away. You open your hand and there is not enough left there to wet the tongue.

Yet, each time you have looked upon another—whether parent or sibling or friend or mate or teacher or whatever physical person or object—and tried to plug into that socket to get the juice you believe you need, that is just what you are doing. And you literally end up squeezing the life out of the relationship itself.

When you seek first the Kingdom and plug that cord into the socket within your heart, when you remember that you and your Father are one, that only Love is real, and nothing else matters, you will remember that the temptation to find Love outside your Self is nothing more than the echo of an old habit. And that habit cannot live unless *you* feed it.

Therefore, feed the only habit that matters: the habit of remembering that the Truth is true always, regardless of what is passing before your physical eyes and before your mind. In all comings and goings, in all births and deaths, in all arising and passing away of universe after universe after universe, in the midst of a flat tire or a sudden rainstorm, nothing—*nothing*—holds value except your relationship with your Creator.

When you have experienced in relationship with anyone or anything a moment of bliss, a moment of a peace that forever passes all understanding, a moment of fulfillment so sweet and so sublime that no word could touch it, much less express it, what you have experienced is only the flow of the Love of God *through* you. That person or thing did not cause it. It was caused because, for just a moment, you stepped out of your drama, you stepped out of your dream, and allowed the Truth to be lived.

Then, of course, you tricked yourself into believing, "God, that was so sweet! That was the best thing I've ever tasted. It must have come from *you*. Get over here! I *need* you!" If ever you believe you need anything or anyone, rest assured, in that moment you are living in delusion.

ALL YOU NEED IS LOVE

All you need is Love. Love fulfills all things. Love embraces all things. Love heals all things. Love transforms all things. Therefore, remember well: You, and only you, can become the cause of your fulfillment, your peace, and your completion of time. This requires that you do nothing save remember to establish the connection with your Creator.

Is it not true that what you desire most of all is Love? Is it not true that you hope that each relationship—no matter how short, no matter what its form—that each journey, that each undertaking will allow you the experience of peace? Is it not true that you, who find yourselves in and as a body temporarily in time, is it not true that the grandest of experiences you have known have been those that seem to flood the very cells of the body with Love, with a sublime bliss and a peace?   Accept that truth, that what you desire beyond all things is the living experience of Love.

Then remember this:

> Nothing you do can bring Love to you.
> Nothing you do can keep Love for yourself
> in a form of your choosing.
> Nothing you do—nothing you do—can make
> Love appear in the form of your insistence.

Release the drama, release the dream, and choose to remember the truth that is true always. Return to the Kingdom within, even prior to every breath.   Remind yourself and say to your Creator:

 I want only that which is true always.
> Love is what I want.   Love is what you are.
> Love is what I receive.   Love is who I am.
> I and my Father are one.

Here and here alone do you discover what you seek.   Then, you become free to walk this Earth, to be in the world, but not of it at all.   And though your friends will look upon you and still see a man or a woman who seems to act much like them, yet though they see it not, Christ dwells with them.   Something in them keeps attracting them to you.   They are not sure what it is.   Is it the shape of your body or the radiance of your eyes?   It is not these things.   They feel the quality of *Love*.

Can you imagine walking upon this Earth and no matter where you are, feeling as though every wisp of cloud and every blade of grass and all good things under Heaven and Earth were already residing with you, within this sphere of your countenance?   Can you imagine walking upon this Earth and sensing that the light from the farthest of stars that shines during the night is already within you, that the whole of creation was held in the palms of your hands?   Would there be room yet to convince yourself that there is something you lack, something you need, that the restlessness you feel must be valid?

In truth, you are like one who has been given a perfect treasure, a priceless jewel.   You have placed it into your pocket and forgotten that you possess it.   So you run around trying to look into everybody else's pocket.   You have tried to seduce certain ones to surrender so that you can own the clothing and, therefore, try to possess the jewel that you hope is in their pocket.   But the great truth is that you cannot possess Love until you set it free. You cannot move into holy relationship with anyone or anything until you give up all trace of need to possess it.

When your only desire is Love, you will be willing to set anyone free, to support him or her in their own journey, no matter what it is or what it takes. Yet, you will never feel your Love waver.

If a twinge of sadness arises because you recognize that two bodies in space are now going to go to separate parts of the planet, as that twinge arises, you will recognize it as the effect of a mistaken perception. You will move within, to the place in which all minds are joined. You will remember that your fulfillment does not rest in *gaining* love from another, but in *giving* Love to everyone.

If, indeed, you would know the Truth that sets you free, heed each and every word that is being shared. If you would taste the sweet nectar of perfect freedom, be committed to replacing every erroneous perception you have ever made and every thought you have ever held of everyone and everything. Set these things aside and commit the fullness of your energy to the simple, but vigilant practice of remembering the Truth—even prior to every breath:

> I live!—yet not I—but Christ dwells in me.
> Therefore, I submit and surrender to the Truth
> that is true always. My fulfillment comes only
> from allowing Christ to be given to the world.

The Truth is very simple. It is not complex at all. Get out of the way, and let Love live through you. And all of a sudden you will know that, indeed, you are given all good things eternally. You will know that grace is reality. You will know that effortlessness is the way of life in the Kingdom.

But effortlessness does not mean that you do not feel, for you are in a dimension of feeling. Effortlessness does not mean that you do not discover how to deepen your ability to be the living embodiment of Love. It does not mean that you do not challenge yourself to learn to express Love in a way that can be heard by another. Effortlessness means simply that you abandon the resistance to what Love requires in each moment.

Effortlessness is the way of the Kingdom. In the world, effortlessness means that you let down the wall you have built between yourself and all of creation. You no longer resist *the lived experience of relationship*, whatever it is—relationship with a cloud, relationship with another person, relationship with a dog or a cat, relationship with April 15th when you write your government a check. Why not wrap it with Christmas paper and ribbons and send it with much Love?

When you have learned to release the barriers or the walls between yourself and whatever is in front of you, when you open the door to your chakras—the body's energy centers—and simply allow Love to be lived through you, when you look upon another person or another situation or another thing and realize that nothing in this world has the power to hurt you and nothing in this world has the power to take anything from you, you are free. If you remember to extend Love, then you are free! You have transcended birth and death. The seeker is no more and only Christ walks this Earth.

FEELING IS THE DOORWAY TO LOVE AND FREEDOM

If your commitment is, indeed, to look within and discover each and every obstacle you have ever created to the presence of Love, why do you resist *feeling* those things? For well has it been said to you, that on just the other side is the very Love you seek.

Deny not the role of *feeling* in this dimension, for feeling is everything! You cannot even know the presence of God unless you feel it. You cannot *think about* the presence of God. You cannot insist on a belief about the presence of God. That does not do it; that does not fill your cup. Feeling fills your cup. Feeling—unbridled, unblocked, unobstructed feeling—is the doorway to that Love that sets you free!

Therefore, when you say, "I don't want to feel this," rest assured, you are truly saying, "Yes, the doorway to the Kingdom of Heaven is right in front of me, but if you think I'm going to open it, you are crazy! It's not worth it, anyway. What is worth it is protecting the substitute I have made."

I have called this the ego, the false self, what I once described to you as a gnat shouting at space, "That's what I'm committed to. And I'm going to protect this thing. Give up Heaven to protect this useless little thing? Oh, yes! You'd better believe I'd be willing to make that sacrifice! What's Heaven anyway? A bunch of love stuff, a bunch of people running around in bliss, some of them without bodies, hanging out in unlimitedness, fearlessness, and utter fulfillment. Who needs it? Oh, but this little gnat, this little gnat of mine. Oh! I'm going to make it shine!"

How many times have you tried to make that little gnat shine? For instance, "Everybody notice, it's shining. Please, notice how great I am. I'm making my gnat shine. Listen to my whining and my complaining, and the lamenting, the great sadness. Oh! How grand my gnat is!"

Meanwhile, the Love of God flows through a multitude of universes and creates—forever—even new universes. And the Love of God does not even notice the gnat at all. No one is paying any attention. Your friends around you do not want to pay attention, although sometimes you corner them and they have no choice. But those of us without bodies, do you really actually think we waste our precious eternity taking your attempt to make the gnat shine seriously? Indeed, because we Love you, we give you the space, and we honor your free will to be as little and as miserable as you wish.

We will wait until you choose to come once again into the greatness in which you truly reside. We never withdraw our Love from you. We simply look through your story line because what *we* wish to Love is the Christ that dwells within you.

What day and hour will you decide to love yourself as God has first loved you? To truly —to *truly*—once and for all, make the decision to *live*! For until you decide to live *with*, and *for*, and forever *from* the Mind of Christ, life has not yet begun!

Right away the mind reacts, "Oh, my God! That's a bit of a blow, isn't it? Look at all the experiences I've had, Jeshua. How can you tell me I haven't lived? Why, there was this drama, then there was that drama, then there was that drama over there. Don't you remember seventeen lifetimes ago when I did this and then I did that? I struggled through that one, and I've struggled through this one. I have lived."

No, you have *dreamed*.

Do you awaken in the morning and realize that you have had a whole night of dreams of receiving ribbons and trophies, and what have you, from the world? And then say, "That was very real. The trophies must be out sitting on my kitchen table." While you dreamt, it felt real enough. And that is the quality I am speaking to here. If you wish to take this as an affront, it is perfectly fine. It will not disturb my peace at all.   *Ha!*

Until you fully decide to come into life as the presence of Christ, as the presence of Love, and to *own* each moment of your experience as wholly self-created, for no other reason than that you have chosen it from the perfect and infinite freedom of your unlimited being, life has not yet begun. When you look upon all things without judgment through the eyes of forgiveness, when you decide to embody only the reality of Love no matter what anybody else is doing, that is when life begins!

As of this date on your calendar, there have only been a handful of beings who have *truly lived life* upon this plane, a very small handful. There are many of us that would just absolutely be thrilled if *you* would join the club!

I will let you in on a little secret: Until you do, you do not get to graduate. You will never leave this plane, filled with conflict and suffering, as it seems to be, until you have lived the experience of walking this Earth wholly as the thought of Love in form, with no other allegiances, but to Love. You will never leave this plane. You will never take up your cross and follow me. You will spin around again and again and again, only to be confronted by the same need to decide wholly for Love.

You will finally look heavenward and say, "Father, let's get on with it. Enough time has been wasted. It's gone, it's fine, it doesn't matter. *Now!* I am committed to Love. Bring on whatever I *must* experience to bring up from the depth—the places where I've hidden it within me—every obstacle that must yet be dissolved by the light of the grace of perfect Love.

"And I will do whatever I can, from my side of the fence, to open up those places, to feel those places, to embrace those places, to love those places, to claim those places as wholly self-created. I will let my parents off the hook. I will let my siblings off the hook. I will let my great-great-great-great-great-great-grandfather off the hook. I will let Adam and Eve off the hook. I will let the government off the hook. And I will love myself enough to heal my separation from God.

"I will be humble enough to recognize that if I'm having an experience—because I know I have made the commitment to healing—then you have indeed, precious Father, brought me all good things. For this moment of experience can be seen through eyes that recognize that it is but a stepping stone to the perfect peace that I seek.

"My life is no longer mine, for I know not how to correct that one fundamental error. But I *can* surrender into feeling each moment fully while choosing Love anyway. And Love will dissolve the pain that I have carried, all because I insisted on trying to separate myself from the Source of my being. This little gnat of mine is being put to rest. For the only thing that can shine is Christ."

For Christ—the sons and daughters of God, the offspring of God—is God's only creation. The rest of it is attributed to *you*. Even space and time is yours. Your Creator's only creation is *you*, the truth of you. For you are Love, and God creates only that which is like unto Himself. And God is *only* Love.

Many of you believe you are on a spiritual path. You will know if that is true by your willingness to feel and experience wholly exactly what is in front of you, moment to moment. So if you have a conflict with another and you sit in your chair and decide to pray or meditate in order to change the feeling state within yourself, and you arise later and say, "There, I'm feeling much better now," but the issue has not been solved with another, *nothing has changed.*

Go, therefore, to the other. Open your heart, share, and resolve. If you have offended another, ask them their forgiveness. If you have judged another, admit it. Ask for their forgiveness. It is only in such a way that you can truly heal the place of conflict within.

Beloved friends, the essence of this lesson is quite simple: Where are you *now*? Are you willing to allow yourself to see everything around you and within you as the doorway to the Kingdom of Heaven, waiting only for you to acknowledge its presence and to open it? Are you willing to truly be right where you are—*wholly, right where you are*? And the mind says, "Well, of course. I'm on a spiritual path." Rest assured, if you look well into your feelings and find any trace of resistance, you have not yet made the necessary commitment that gives you the *power* to open that door.

ONLY THROUGH FEELING DO YOU AWAKEN

Feeling is the message of this lesson. For it is only through feeling that you truly awaken. Concepts and ideas can begin to direct the mind to believe that there is something out there that is attractive that might even be better than what you have been doing before. But concepts and ideas do not, in themselves, open the door. They are symbols, and that is all. A symbol cannot quench your thirst. It is only at the level of genuine *feeling* that you can once again know the presence of God who dwells within you, around you, and through you, even now.

Feel what you have created as a substitute for the truth. Own it, look upon it, and then let it go. Learn that regardless of what choice you may have made in the past, once you have embraced it, once you have felt it, you remain perfectly innocent and imbued with the power to choose again to *feel,* to learn once again to *feel* the glorious warmth that permeates the Kingdom of Heaven.

Nothing you do with time can match the importance of what we have shared in this lesson. Nothing you do in the field of time holds a candle to the incredible gift that is waiting for you. Therefore, use time constructively by deciding to love, that Love may teach you of itself. Indeed, beloved and holy friends, when you have done this, you will find yourself translated into a form that could never possibly be contained by the space and volume of a physical body.

You will look upon this entire dimension as a mere temporary learning device. You will set it aside, as a child sets aside a toy that has been outgrown. But you will do it with deep appreciation and love for the toy that you have played with for so long. You will carry with you a deep sense of gratitude for everything this physical dimension has brought to you.

There will be not a molecule of beingness within you that will feel any resentment, any longing, any anger, or any remorse for anything. All of your experience will have become wholly acceptable to you. For it was by such experience that you were finally driven to want only the Truth.

From this day forward you will never again be able to truly convince yourself that all of your attempts to stay distracted or conformed to the world are really accomplishing a thing. You will find that your mind begins to penetrate the unconscious habits you have created in an attempt to hide from what must yet be felt. You will know perfectly well when you are simply deluding yourself. You will start to smile and say, "Oh, yes, there I go again. Might as well set that aside. And plant my feet firmly on the ground and, indeed, live with passion from the Truth of the Kingdom of Heaven!"

In The Way of the Heart, we will speak ever more directly and even more forcefully to you. For the time comes quickly when this planet will not be willing to tolerate untidy house guests that are not willing to vibrate at the frequency of being toward which the planet herself is preparing to move. Therefore, be not caught by coming home one day and discovering that the landlord has changed the locks and you have not a place to rest your head.

Rather, become the living embodiment of Love and journey with your Holy Mother into an entirely new dimension of being. And never forget to sing, laugh, dance and play along the way!

Be you, therefore, at peace, beloved friends. Amen.

How do we be in the world, but not of it?

BIRTHING THE MIND OF CHRIST

Forever, I am with you. *Forever, I am with you.* For long before the stars were birthed, long before the planets arose, long before even a thought of physicality had emerged within the divine mind of the Son of God, we were already created together and equally. Yet, that creation of what alone is real knows no point of birth. *Where did God come from? One of the mysteries of Life...*

Therefore, because the Father is forever, so too, have we abided together and been sustained together in Love. Throughout all time and even unto eternity do we abide together in the Reality of who we are. Therefore, think it not extraordinary when I say unto you: I am with you always, even unto the end of this age.

What journey have *you* ever taken that is not familiar to *me*? What journey have I ever taken that is, in truth, not familiar to you? For when you look upon me from some deep place of knowingness within, though the words may be different, you say within yourself, "Behold! Christ appears before me."

When you hold a thought of me in the mind and the body is flooded with emotion, soft and gentle and light, and you recognize that the holy Son of God was birthed and perfected in your friend, Jeshua ben Joseph, *what a friend we have in Jesus.* what is it within you that *knows* that this is the truth? What part of your mind, what capacity within your heart can look upon me and recognize the Truth within me, so that you love me? For I say well unto you, it is the same as that part of *my* mind, that part of *my* heart that looks upon you and says, "Behold! The holy Child of God is before me. And I Love this one."

That which *knows*, that which comprehends immediately, is the Mind of Christ. It recognizes itself in each and every one. That Mind of Christ dwells within you in its fullness *now*! Therefore, as I have said unto you many times, never fail to remember that it takes one to know one. If you would look upon me and say, "Beloved friend, thank you," look well upon yourself and say, "Beloved friend, thank you." Allow the breath to flow.

How many journeys have there been? How many moments of experience passed under the bridge of your beingness before you first began to re-awaken to the Truth that is true always? How many lifetimes, how many worlds, before a light began to dawn, so imperceptibly at first that it was not recognized? And a tiny voice whispered from a place that seemed so far removed from where you dwell:

> Beloved son, you are with me now. *daughter*
> You remain as I have created you to be.
> Therefore, be at peace. You are loved.

The voice seemed so far away, so faint, that surely, it could not be your own. Surely, it was just a moment's fantasy.

In the midst of some journey, you paused. And as a raindrop fell upon a leaf and your eyes looked upon that experience, you felt and knew that you were *one* with the leaf and the raindrop, and that, indeed, you *were* those things. How many moments of experience passed by before these kinds of qualities began to emerge in your consciousness, as what seemed at first to be tiny mad ideas? Thoughts such as, "My God, I just felt myself to be one with all of creation. Well, better not tell anyone about that!" And off you went.

But the moments began to come more often, still perhaps fleetingly, and yet now more familiar—a sense underneath all of the drama, all of the crying, all of the lamenting, all of the resenting, all of the fearing, all of the striving, and all of the seeking. The still tiny voice would come and say:

> Beloved son, you remain as I have created you to be.
> You are loved.
> You are wholly loving and wholly lovable forever.

The tiny voice would still steal through the roar and the din that had seemed to make a home within your mind. Rest assured, you would not be where you appear to be in this moment, if you had not already begun to experience many moments that express the quality that I have just described to you, of truly hearing the still, small voice of the Comforter within.

Therefore, indeed, each of you knows that there is a longing within you that *cannot* and *will not* any longer be denied. You *know* from the Christ within you that Christ has stirred within you, and is rising to take up its rightful place as the master of your mind and your heart, your body and your breath, and your dreams and your passions! Each of you knows that it is absolutely futile to attempt to settle for anything less.

It does not come because of anything I have ever done *for* you. It comes because it *must* come. It must arise within each created mind regardless of its journeys, regardless of its attempts to deny what is eternally true. That is called the illusion of the dream of separation. It must come and it is inevitable because Christ *will not* be denied. Christ *cannot* be denied because only Christ can express what is absolutely true.

Only Christ can so *in*form the cellular structure of the body that even the simplest of gestures extends Love unto another who beholds it. Only Christ knows how to breathe the breath that releases all trauma, all hurt. Only Christ understands the power of true forgiveness, which is always, by the way, forgiveness of one's self, since no one has wronged you at any time.

Only Christ can bring a smile to the lips of a body, such that when another looks upon you and sees that smile, their heart is filled. Only Christ can walk in this world, yet not be of the world. And only Christ can transcend every limited and fearful creation, transforming them into the beautiful flower that blossoms and gives its sweet fragrance to all of creation. Is it not that which you long to feel moving through your being? Is not that call to awaken alive within you? Oh, beloved friends, you know that it is!

Love you, therefore, one another. And love you, therefore, the Self that has been given unto you of the Father. Learn to hear *only* that voice. Learn to desire *only* that voice. Learn to follow only that voice that knows the Truth is true always:

> I and my heavenly Father are one.
> This world is but a passing shimmer and a dream.
> It holds no value save that which Christ can bring to it.
> Only Love is real.
> Anything else is the choice to momentarily believe in illusion.

Rest assured, illusion within an illusory world can seem to hold great power. But all power has been given unto you. All power under Heaven and Earth is given unto the holy Child of God. And that power dwells within you as the Life of your life, the breath of your breath, the Truth of your truth, the being of your being, and the joy of your joy. There has never been an illusory creation that has ever, in truth, threatened it. Nor can any illusion take reality from you.

The only thing that can occur is that you use that power to believe in loss. All forms of loss that you perceive through the physical eyes or through the worldly mind are nothing more than passing shades of your insistence on believing that loss is possible. All forms of the contraction known as fear are nothing more than temporary modifications of the very power given unto you—a power that you have sought to use to see if it were possible to convince yourself that something besides Love is real.

Here on the planet at this time.

But the story is over. The dream of separation is ending. The whole of creation is now experiencing a growing power, a movement, and a momentum that must carry the mind, from which creation springs, to a new level. It is not so much an evolutionary level as a level of re-cognition, a level of re-membrance, a level of re-turning.

That wave of momentum is alive and has already arisen within your heart and mind. You know it. Stop denying it. Stop questioning it. Stop looking for signs from the world around you that it is all right to feel it.

Accept it as a divine gift from your Creator. For the call has gone out. Though many listen, few hear, and fewer still become wholly devoted to responding. Therefore, let your prayer be always:

> May Christ, alone, dwell within and
> as this creation that I once thought was myself.

> May Christ, alone, inform each thought and each breath and each choice.

> May Love direct each step. May Love transform this journey through time, that in
> time, I might truly know the reality of eternity, the sanctity of peace,
> the holiness—the holiness—of intimacy, and the joy of the Father's Love, prior
> to every breath and, indeed, even prior to every thought that arises within the mind.

 For when you know that you are holiness itself, how could you ever look upon your brother or sister and believe that they have wronged you? How could you ever want to do anything but love them? That is, let the Love of Christ flow through you so deeply and so profoundly that they get that you do not believe their illusion.

When you give unto another that which alone is true, because all minds are joined, you have offered unto them the only gift that holds value. When you give another the truth—perhaps even without saying a word—because all minds are joined, they recognize what has been offered and say to themselves, "The one before me knows the truth of me and is looking right through every one of my attempts to be less than who I am. Therefore, I see that it's safe to choose again." That is when miracles occur.

 Do not strive to heal this world. Do not do anything to make a show of how much you love another. Give up the concept of being a busy bee. Simply *be* the presence of Love, because you *know* that there is absolutely no value in being anything else. And that, in truth, you have never succeeded at being anything but the presence of Love.

Each sane moment that you have experienced, each moment of unlimitedness, each moment of genuine intimacy, each moment of grace-filled joy that you have ever known, in whatever form it seems to appear, has come because you have allowed your mind to slip into the sea of peace. There you have merely abided, empty, wanting nothing, seeking nothing, being merely the presence of what you are.

When that quality becomes cultivated so that it permeates your consciousness with each breath and with each moment, you will know that Christ has, indeed, arisen this day. And you will celebrate Easter with each breath.

THE SHADOW OF FEAR

What, then, could ever possibly arise to obstruct the Truth that is true always?

There is an ancient forest on your planet. A forest so high in a rugged mountain valley and so rugged that no one has ever been there. Unknown to the minds of humanity, life goes on in the forest. Deep within the heart of this forest, this morning a little tiny blade of grass seemed to be tossed by an unseen wind. As it was tossed for just a fragment of a moment, so subtle and soft was this wind that as the sunlight played against this blade of grass, it cast the smallest of conceivable shadows on a stone just a little bit away from the blade of grass.

No one noticed. The shadow had no effect. The rock did not even notice. No one on the planet noticed. No one in any of the heavens noticed, except me. I needed something to build a story around. That tiny shadow, cast by a little blade of grass momentarily wiggling in a wind in some remote forest, has virtually no effect on the turning of the planets, the creation of new suns, and certainly not one trace of effect on how deeply the Father loves you.

That little shadow is what you have given power to. It *seems* to be able to obstruct the Truth within you from being lived. For the moment, you gave that little tiny shadow power. In that very moment, fear was born. Fear is always a contraction away from Love. And fear makes you smaller than the blade of grass that momentarily seems to cast a shadow and, therefore, obstructs your recognition of the warmth of the sun that bathes you *always*.

When you resist healing, when you struggle to learn to "speak your truth," you may rest assured that something has occurred just prior to that. What is it? It is your decision to believe that the shadow is all-powerful. And that if you heal, if you grow, if you change, if you let Christ live in you, that the little blade of grass and the little tiny shadow it creates for a very temporary moment will come and punish you and crush you.

If you can truly take this story into your being and recognize the utter laughability of such a belief, you will never again *fear* fear. You will never again allow fear to master you and direct the course of your life.

You will learn what it means to trust what is birthed in the heart. And you will arise and you will go forth without fear—with no story at all. You will accomplish whatever creativity wishes to express through you. And the whole while you will know that of yourself you do nothing, but the Father, through you, can do *anything*.

Therefore, what forms of the shadow of that blade of grass are you allowing to run and own and possess your soul?

There are many forms of that shadow, are there not? There are peers and parents and siblings to please. There are governments to bow down before. There are mates and children that must come first. There are bills to pay. There are desires to check and keep in order. [There are activities and statements and behaviors—done by others—that require at least seven or eight hours a day for you to analyze and judge them to death and you think, "My, this world is exhausting. But somebody has to do it."]

And you thought it was Love that makes the world go around? Trust me, Love does not spin and get nowhere!

Love created you. Love birthed within you as an individual—at least within the dance of time and space—the power to choose, the power to feel, the power to channel light and Love, the power to know that something exists within and as you. That is what Love has done! Has fear ever created anything remotely like that?

(the art or action of imitating someone or something.)

So what do you want? Creation or mimicry? Peace or the ability to simply drug yourself with triviality? Imagine…all power under Heaven and Earth flowing through you with every breath so that your consciousness witnesses, not what you do as the maker or doer, but that which the divine is doing through you in each moment. And you get to marvel at the creativity of Love, the very same Love that moves the sun and the moon and the stars. Now *that* is a delightful pastime!

By the way, you have called the body *your* body, as if you have some right to possess it. Give the body to God. God knows how to use it; you do not. When your life is given to being *only* the presence of Love for no other reason than that you want it to be, you will know—because you will *be*—the Truth that sets all things free:

> The whole of creation is waiting to move through me,
> and I want to be aware of it. I want my experience,
> my lived consciousness, to be blissfully absorbed in
> observing the flow of Love through me.

And if there are any cobwebs in the way of that, you will sweep them out of the way.

When you are in that quality of being, Heaven and Earth will move to become your servant, and not until then. After all, send a conflicted message and nobody shows up for the dance. So now you know what the shadow is. Perhaps sometimes you enjoy dancing with it. But here is the great question:

✣ Are you going to let the shadow lead or are *you* going to lead?

BIRTHING THE CHRIST MIND

When your life becomes liberated in that—I am not speaking of perfection as you would know it—when your life becomes *that* motivation, that attitude, that declaration, and that devotion, then perfection will be witnessed through you. [For the true meaning of perfection is miracle mindedness where that which saves time occurs.] When your life becomes that, when you no longer have any conflicted commitment in your beingness, you will know exactly what the result of my life was for me, because you will *be* that.

Don't understand this statement

Yes, I know that you are worrying, "Does that mean that when I get really close, I'm going to have to go through my final initiation of crucifixion? And if I have to do it, will you promise that they at least sterilize the nails? Could I choose the day or the hour? I don't like to get up too early."

yikes!
*

You already know what crucifixion is all about. You have done it to yourself a million times in ways far worse than a mere nail driven through the hand that creates a little twinge of pain. Hell is nothing more than the state of being rutted, or stuck, in the process of crucifying one's Self, which is the attempt to murder and destroy what God has created out of Love.

Stop wasting your energy *trying* to love God. That will not do it for you. Stop wasting so much energy *trying* to learn how to love another. That will not do it for you. And for *God's* sake, please refrain from all attempts to get anyone to believe that you love them! *what?*

Put the whole of your attention on giving up the patterns of belief from which you have attempted to crucify the Self that God made and placed within you as your very *awareness* of your existence. Learn to love that Self beyond all created things. Learn to nurture that Self. Learn to cultivate within that Self only that which speaks of joy and truth. So that your words and your actions and your very presence always uplift another. So that when another walks into the room in which you are sitting or standing or moving, they feel like a breath of fresh air just hit them, even if you have not lifted a finger.

Will probably need to come back for another lifetime ...

As long as there is a trace of energy within you in which you are striving to get from any perceived thing or object around you what you are sure you lack inside yourself, you cannot know the love of Self. And you cannot experience freedom. Happiness is an inside job.

Then, what happens? You finally get it right and you decide, "All right, what's that little shadow been doing? Well, let's take care of that one, and that one, and that one, and that one. How many blades of grass and how many shadows are there within this being that seem to be overlaid upon the Self?" Does it matter? You are busy birthing Christ!

What happens when that really occurs? First—and listen well—*nothing will be unacceptable to you.*

Yet, the mind still resists, "Well but, does that mean if somebody is not a vegetarian that they're still loved? Does that mean if somebody votes for someone I am sure is the wrong guy that they're not insane, that I can love them? Does that mean that someone who seeks power and, therefore, creates a war and kills five thousand women and children, that I can still look upon them and not have my love be disturbed? Does it mean that whatever arises within this temporary world is really, truly, literally, not a problem for me any longer—that *nothing* is unacceptable?"

 Yes. It does not mean you condone it. It means it is no longer unacceptable. For what you cannot accept, you will judge. And every judgment is the attempt to *murder* what you have decided has no right to be.

Judgment is the opposite of forgiveness. It lives on the side of the fence with fear. Forgiveness lives on the side of the fence with Love, and only Love can heal this world. Imagine, then, living in a state of being in which literally nothing was unacceptable to you because you knew that the Source of your true being was far beyond the limitations of anything created in space and time. That not even death, which has been created out of the contraction known as fear, is unacceptable.

I say unto you: If you will choose to trust me, I will show you the way to peace. I will wait for your reply as I can do nothing to take from you the freedom required to become wholly committed to allowing Christ to be birthed where once a useless illusion reigned. I will show you how to become the being out of which all of creation is arising so that you will know the Truth that sets you free.

Now, this will raise up within you the most fundamental of fears possible. What is that? It is the last to be overcome: the fear of death. For when you are confronted by the Truth, you know that everything you have sought to create as a substitute for the Truth must die. That is why it is said, "The last to be overcome shall be death"—fear of death. Death is *allowed* that Christ might live.

Understand well: There is no one and there shall not at any time be anyone who reads these words to whom I have not given this promise unto. *I will show you the way to the Truth that is true always and sets you free.*

But only you can make the decision to bring the whole of your being to that journey. And all it requires is what you call a smidgen of willingness. A smidgen of willingness is all it takes. *(hmmm, wonder about that...)*

I know the way home because I have completed the journey, and I will show you the way. With every word that I utter, my one intent is to reveal to you the place within you that is the presence of Love that you seek.

What if you chose to actually commit yourself to considering what I am sharing, and return to the innocence of a child, as you contemplated what it would mean in your life? Rest assured, when the journey *to* the Kingdom is completed, the journey *within* it begins anew. The bliss, the wisdom, the creativity, the laughter, the friendships, the family, the joy, the serenity, and the peace—that have been, for the most part, seen as an impossible dream—will become your most ordinary state of being. Yet, none of it can occur through any power that can move through *me*.

I can guide you. I can show you the way. And I can walk beside you on the way that you have chosen. At times, I can give you my strength until yours is as certain as mine, by carrying you. But ultimately, you must *demand* that I put you down so that *your* feet touch the soil of the Kingdom of Heaven and *you* walk, under *your* strength, under *your* certainty, beside me.

You will indeed find in that day and hour that as often as you ask it of me, I will ask you, "How do you think we could do this? What would you like to create with me?" And then, indeed, we are as brother and brother, sister and brother, friends, dancing and playing in the Kingdom prepared for us of our Father.

One little shadow cast by a tiny blade of grass is all that seems to prevent you from coming wholly to where I am. If you tarry yet a little longer, it is all right. You cannot prevent me from knowing the Truth about you and loving you. When you are in Love, when you are so immersed in simply loving, is it not true that you have no sense of time at all? There is no sense of any effect disturbing your peace. You are just "swaying to the music." You are loving, and your wholeness grows even more holy.

Therefore, love one another as I have loved you. For the Father has first loved me that I might show you the truth of what Love is and the reality of your being. I will not cease in doing this, regardless of how long you choose to tarry. For Love is, indeed, patient and kind. Love is not deluded, and Love does not allow delusion. Love embraces all things, trusts all things, and allows all things. It knows perfectly well where it is going, and never ceases in that journey until every blade of grass is released from casting shadows, and the whole of creation is returned to the Heart of God.

Learn to love your Self and cry out to this world:

I and my Father are one!
That is the soil from which I move and live and have my being.
So be it!

Always remember that the Father looked upon His only creation and said, "Behold, it is very good!" That goodness has a name and it is yours! And behold, it is very good! That light deserves to shine!

The doorway stands before you. Will you open it through the *power* of your choice? For what you experience will reveal to you what choice you have made this day.

Beloved and holy friends, may peace be with you always. And may the Truth that is true always shine within your hearts and minds throughout all ages. Remember, there's a perfectly good reason why I keep saying, time and again, "I am with you always." Amen.

DROPPING PEBBLES INTO THE
POOL OF AWARENESS

As always, I come forth as your equal—to abide with you, to walk with you, to communicate with you—from that Mind and that Heart which we eternally share as one, that Mind which is alone the reality of our *shared* Sonship, our shared existence. As always, I come forth in joy and also with humility. For I cannot join with anyone unless they provide the space within their consciousness and bid me enter therein.

Therefore, understand well, that when I come to abide with you, I come with a humility born of the recognition of the great mystery that has given you your existence. That mystery I have called Abba, Father.

Why? You have not come forth from some mechanical, unthinking force. You have come forth from pure Intelligence. You have come forth from pure Love. You have come forth from a Source beyond all comprehension. You have come forth from the radiance of a Light so bright that the world cannot see it or contain it. You have come forth from that which, alone, is eternally real. Because you have come forth from it, you are one with it, always.

where did God come from ?

This means that you abide in a relationship—created to Creator, offspring or child to parent—that is *so intimate*, a bond *so deep*, that it cannot be broken at any time. As a wave that arises from an ocean cannot be separated from the ocean itself, so too, in each and every moment in your experience, do you abide in a union so powerful, so mysterious, so intimate and immediate that the mind cannot comprehend it.

This union connects you as the created with the mystery beyond comprehension that contains every drop of wisdom and intelligence necessary to create consciousness itself. Consciousness—the power to be aware, the power to choose—is what you truly are.

If this Source, this mystery, can birth this most fundamental aspect of creation, does it not deserve to be called Abba or Father, that which creates like unto itself? Can you, then, begin to feel, to know—not just as an intellectual idea, but as a lived reality, a knowingness—that if you are aware in this very moment, it is because you are one with the Source of all creation and cannot be separated from it in any way or at any time?

Fear, as we have said many times, is like a contraction. Again, if you were to imagine a wave arising from the ocean and then going into contraction because it thinks it is separated from its source, that contraction literally squeezes the life, the very flowing waters, out of that wave. Could that wave possibly continue when its very life force has been squeezed from it? Does it not then become mere drops of water fading from view, only to dissolve back into the ocean itself? Its radiance lost, never to be seen again.

If it were possible for the wave of your consciousness to truly have its life force squeezed out of it, you too would fade away as droplets returning to the ocean, never to be remembered or seen again.

Listen, and listen well: *That* would be death. But in reality, you are alive, always. Even when you have identified yourself with the great constriction that fear is, your fears have never been able to squeeze out of you the great life force, the great reality, and the great gift of awareness. You have, therefore, never ceased to be. There has never been a time that you have not existed and there will never be a time when you will cease to be.

You are therefore, very much like a wave that has begun to arise out of an unseen ocean and as it gains momentum, it moves across the surface of a planet. Like the wave, you are in continual movement. Moving where? Into a forever extension of your awareness itself. Into a forever extension of whatever you choose to pick up along the way and make a part of your Self. Into a forever extension that will carry you into the experience or the fruits of the very thoughts you have held onto as your own.

Therefore, understand well: Right now, in this lived moment, wherever you are, whatever you are experiencing, all that you see, all that you feel, all that you know, all that you seek to avoid, and all the things you value and devalue, all things are contained *within* your awareness. For if they are not found there, they do not exist for you.

Therefore, look upon that which resides within your awareness, within your consciousness. What are the things that you *know* that you know? What are the things that you would avoid? What are the feelings that you have not explored? What are the objects, the people, the places, the values that you strive for, that seem to thrill even the cells of the body? What is the body itself, if not that which arises within your awareness?

Look at the planet around you. Look at every object in your room. Look at every thought you choose to think. Look at the perceptions and ideas that you defend so vociferously. Look at the thoughts and the feelings of others that make you cringe or wish to withdraw from them.

These things abide within you like the very power or life force of the wave that has arisen from the ocean. All of these things you have picked up along the way. And the way has been very long and varied indeed! If you can imagine never ceasing to exist, it means that you have been as a wave of awareness, passing through every time frame, every planetary system, and every dimension of creation.

Along the way, one thing has remained constant. You have been in constant relationship with *all* of creation. Oh yes, you may select out a few people, a few objects, a planet, a dimension, and focus all of your attention there. Attention is nothing more than the decision of what you are going to use the power of your awareness to focus on. It seems that you have excluded everything else, but that is like an "optical delusion" of consciousness.

While it is very true that you have *selected out* aspects of creation to focus your attention on, yet underneath—in the depth of the wave that is unseen by the physical eye, unseen by your conscious awareness or your day-to-day mind—you have remained in perfect communion with *all* of creation.

You are, therefore, in relationship with all created things, and there is a communication that occurs without ceasing. Imagine being able to look into the air of your planet and to literally see the radio waves, the television waves, and all of the electrical waves that keep bouncing back and forth across your planet. This is what you swim in daily. Your consciousness pervades this field of vibrations.

YOU ONLY EXPERIENCE WHAT YOU HAVE CHOSEN TO CREATE

You are the one who selects out what you are going to be aware of, what you are calling into your lived experience. You *select* what is going to make an imprint upon you.

Imagine, then, a pool of clear, still water. Into it you drop a solitary pebble. From the pebble there radiate waves. This is what is occurring *constantly* in the field of your wave of awareness.

As you have attracted to yourselves certain persons, places, things, objects, and above all, thoughts, beliefs and perceptions, you have dropped them like little pebbles into the still clear pool of your vast and eternal awareness. What you experience are the effects, or the ripples, of those pebbles. They literally join with the other ripples that you have created. As these ripples move out and touch one another and come back to you, this is the field of creation that makes up your physical, third-dimensional reality.

You are, therefore, never experiencing anything except what *you* have chosen to create through your selection of the pebbles that you have dropped into the field of your awareness. You literally never experience a solitary thing. You do not experience objects.

What you experience is the *effect* of a thought or a belief in objects. You never experience another person, for they also are made up of a whole web of vibrations.

You could say that each person, each object, is really a field of relationships, unique and seemingly different from you, but a web of relationships nonetheless.

For what child can be separated from their parents, from their cultural background, from the unique experiences that they have had as they have interacted with the webs of relationship that have been around them since the moment of their conception? What kitten can be separated and singled out from the matrix of its mother and father? What leaf on a tree is separate from the temperature of the air, the quality of water and nutrients that come to it from the very soil of the Earth?

Everything is a web of relationship. All webs are in relationship with all other webs and they become grander and grander and grander ad infinitum.

You are a web of relationships out of which you have selected *certain* pebbles—whether they be thoughts or perceptions or experiences—and you have dropped them into the still clear pool of your awareness in order to create even more ripples. Then, you have chosen which ones will have the greatest value for you. These you *lock in* to your being and they become your emotional field. The emotional field is the first level of crystallization of the body.

From the emotional field, a further crystallization creates the appearance of a physical form. It is that which you push around the planet in your very temporary third-dimensional form of attention, while all around you—and just beneath the level of your conscious daily awareness—you remain in communication with all webs of relationship throughout all dimensions of creation. It is for this reason that an inspiring thought can come suddenly to you and penetrate your daily awareness. And you wonder, "Where did that thought come from?"

Or suddenly a picture appears in your mind. It could be of anything—a man and a woman making love, a man and a man making love, a child playing in a park, a dolphin, or a picture of conflict or war. Where did it come from?

Because you live in perfect communion, and you are like a grand field of energy in which all webs of relationship are reverberating constantly, you actually have access to the complete entirety of creation. And this entirety of creation is not limited to what is occurring now, as you understand time. You have available to yourself everything, which you would call the past and the future.

These things are available to you at all times. There is not one of you who has not experienced this for yourself. Perhaps you suddenly thought of a friend, and then the

*Kwd me
our
connection*

telephone rang, and you knew it was that friend.

It makes no sense in your causal third-dimensional plane, but because underneath—even though your conscious mind was busy making breakfast and wondering about which stocks to buy and sell, or which perfume to put on the body—you remain in perfect communion. It is why, when there is a deep resonance between friends separated by thousands of miles, all of a sudden you know they need you to call them. You feel a sense of concern. Maybe they just stubbed their toe, but you pick up the vibration.

You all live this. You all know this. There is no secret about it. What I would seek, then, to attract your attention to is one of the pebbles that has been dropped into the field of your awareness, which is generally true for virtually everyone involved in the third-dimensional experience called physicality.

Imagine a sentence being dropped from a vast height, picking up speed until it strikes the still pool of your awareness and sends a ripple out, creating a vibration through you. The sentence is simply this: "It is not possible for me to have complete mastery over which pebbles are dropped into my awareness for I am at the mercy of the vibrational field set up by the ripples of all of the thoughts and webs of relationship in which I swim constantly."

That perception is absolutely true…as long as you choose to believe it. That perception or belief is absolutely laughable and powerless as soon as you choose to acknowledge that this is so.

What is the point of that? It is simply this: If you would choose to awaken wholly, if you would choose not just to be a wave that has mysteriously arisen from the ocean, if you would choose to be more than just another soul that has arisen from the Mind of God and is, somehow, crashing about through the universe, it is *absolutely necessary* to own, as your own, the pebble that drops into the still, clear pool of your awareness with the thought:

> I am the one who chooses the effects I experience.
> I, alone, interpret all neutral relationships or experiences.
> I, alone, place the value upon objects, things, thoughts, and belief systems.
> I, alone, am the literal creator of my moment-to-moment experience.

This, as you can see, changes everything. Never again can you allow yourself to feel as though you are merely a victim of unconscious forces. Never again can you look out beyond yourself and find fault with another. Never again can the energy of blame be projected from you to be dumped upon another. Never again can the energy of judgment hold sway in your holy mind. This thought, this one singular pebble dropped into the still pool of your awareness is absolutely essential if you would decide to awaken wholly. And that is what this lesson is about.

YOU ARE NOT A VICTIM OF THE WORLD YOU SEE

Though you would hear the word—that which carries the vibration of truth—many times, it can be denied as many times as it is heard. You can choose to not allow it to settle deep into that pool of awareness, so that it affects every drop of water that makes up the wave that you are. You can hold on to the hope that you are still a victim of the world that you see, that events hold some value in themselves that do not come from what you place upon them. And as long as you *choose* to deny the world, you cannot be set free.

For the mind that chooses, in even a small part, to perceive itself as a *victim* of its world of experience, remains powerless. It remains in a state that generates frustration, weakness, fear, self-doubt, unworthiness, suffering, pain, emotional pain of aloneness or separation from others, and lack of fulfillment. Ultimately, it generates the echo of the belief that you have been squeezed so tightly by fear that you are literally separated from the ocean of the Mind of God.

Awareness is all that you have and all that you are. Out of your use of it, comes all that you choose to experience. And out of *that* comes your decision of *how* you will experience what you have called to yourself.

In truth—and please listen well—no experience you have ever had has defined you or identified you. No experience you have ever chosen to create, to call to yourself, and then to value as you valued it, has *ever* made you higher than or less than anyone else—not even me. Although there are many who still need to believe that I am far beyond them. No experience you have ever had has proven your unworthiness to be supported, to be loved, by your Creator.

Therefore, you remain as you are created to be: a wave filled with the very self-same power as the ocean itself, a wave, a soul, a web of relationship arising from the holy Mind of God with the momentum to flow on forever with the freedom to create by deciding which vibrations you will allow to settle in and become a part of you, which thoughts you will defend, which perceptions you will cleave unto.

You are, then, eternally a creator. And this is the one thing that you have no free will about. You can never decide to be a non-participant in the very mystery of creation's extension. When you hold the thought, "I refuse to participate in God's creation," you have literally created the perception, the experience of yourself as being outside or separate from creation itself. You have created the insane emotion of trying to separate the wave from the ocean itself. And you *will* create the perception of separation, even though nothing, in reality, has been affected.

Why is this important? Because, you see, the process of healing is not difficult. It requires only your willingness to accept that you are the *effect* of the Creator's desire to create like unto itself—just as a wave is the effect of the ocean's desire to express itself in a new way, a new form, and to bring a uniqueness to every wave that arises from its mysterious depths.

Surrender, then, is the process in which you finally relent; you give up resisting the fact of your very existence. You stop whining about it. You stop lamenting it. You stop worrying about it. You make the decision to get on with being alive! And what is alive about you is going to be alive forever. There is no place to hide and nowhere to go.

CREATING AS CHRIST

When you drop the pebble into the mind:

> I am not a victim of the world I see.
> I am a ceaseless creator, made and of
> one substance with my Creator itself.

Then, indeed, the questions begin to take a different shape. You begin to use the power of your awareness to deliberately and selectively choose which vibrations, which webs of relationships, you are going to pull into your field of awareness—which ones you are going to resonate with and which ones you are going to let dissolve from your mind, from your awareness.

If you have held onto a thought of smallness, a thought of lack, or a thought of powerlessness, now you begin to see that it is perfectly neutral. It is perfectly safe to look upon everything you have ever created and experienced and say, "It is very good, and now I'm done with it.

"What's next? What pebbles can I drop into my holy mind in this very moment? Can I look upon the current experience I'm having and see that it's nothing but the effect, the ripple, of a pebble or a thought that I dropped into my mind so long ago that I don't even remember it? Can I look upon those events that are unfolding around me..."

And if they are unfolding in your body, trust me, that is still *around* you, for you are much more than just the body.

"Can I begin *now*, am I willing *now*, to drop a different pebble into the still and infinite clarity of the pool of awareness that is what is alive about me always? Dare I think a different thought? Dare I drop such a pebble into my consciousness?"

So what pebbles could they be?

> I think I'll become a world savior, a Christ. What would that be like?
> What vibrations would I need to let go out of my life and which ones would
> I need to open to? What would it feel like? What would I see as I look out
> through the field of my awareness at creation?

> I think I'll allow myself to be able to commune with any web of relationship,
> any soul, any being, that exists on any plane of creation. Why, perhaps I'll
> even allow myself to know that I can be in communication with Jeshua.

> How wealthy can I become in this third-dimensional reality? How many
> golden coins could I possibly create in order to give them away to others?

> How many places on the planet could I take the body to in the span of one
> short physical life?

> How many beings could I say "I love you" to? How big can I make my heart
> be? How deep can I experience peace?

The realm of possibilities is as infinite as you are. The ones you select and choose are the
ones that will create the web of relationships that you will call your life, your experience,
even right down to the quality of how you will experience the transition—mistakenly
called death—in your world.

Would you call it a death when you leave one room and close the door behind you and
step into another room? Of course not. You just say, "I was there; now I am here." That
is all that truly occurs when the molecules you have called to yourself are unglued because
you release your value of them, and their constituents, their parts, dissolve back into the
dust or the energy field of the planet. You merely leave one room and step into another.

What I call you to in this lesson is this: to be willing to allow the pebble to be dropped into
your field, or pool of awareness, that carries the energy of the thought:

> From this moment forward, I elect to birth a Christ,
> and thereby learn what Christ is!

And your experience becomes the unfolding learning of what Christ is. When that
learning completes itself, you discover that what you have learned is what you are created
to be. You have returned full circle. The prodigal son or daughter, journeying through the
field of all possibilities, has returned as the awakened Christ, and has taken up his or her
rightful place at the right hand of the Creator.

What does all that symbolism mean? It just means you finally think only with your right-mindedness. You think as God thinks, and God thinks lovingly. God thinks infinitely, timelessly, patiently, certainly, and above all, God thinks *playfully*—full of play!

When you feel such Love and such joy welling up within you that you can hardly contain it, do you not start dancing and moving the body about, saying, "Oh, my gosh, what am I going to do with all this energy?" And you call your friends and say, "Let's have a party, let's go to a movie, let's create a delicious feast. Who could I write a letter to? Oh, who could I send flowers to?" Do you not become caught up in the desire to let some energy expand out of you, to touch all parts of your creation?

Well, imagine being God—infinite, vast, without a top or a bottom or a left or a right, filled with nothing but pure, unconditional, radiant Love! Can you imagine being able to contain yourself and say, "Oh, well, I think I will just sit here in this and not let anybody notice it"? No! God said, "Let there be light!" And it was very good! God looked upon all of creation, which literally means not just this planet, but all of an infinite number of creations of dimension upon dimension upon dimension, and all little webs of relationships called souls that He brought into existence in one split second, and said:

> Lo, it is very good! This is My play! My joy and My Love and My aliveness have poured forth and overflowed My Grand Being and brought forth into manifest creation—you!

You—each and every one of you—are made of the very substance of that overwhelming Love and playfulness that has the power to create infinitely and thereby to extend creation itself! That is who you are! That is where you find yourself *now*, and now, forever. And you will never escape it.

CREATING MASTERY

Mastery comes when fear has been completely dissolved. Fear is dissolved not by fearing it, not by hating it, not by judging it. But by being looked upon with perfect innocence. Embraced in the same way that a scientist would watch the ripples of a little pebble that has been dropped into a pool of water to see how they have created other ripples, and other temporary disturbances in the field or the surface of the water.

As you look within and notice the things you have become afraid of and how fear has constricted your creativity, your joy, your playfulness and your unlimitedness, you merely look with innocence and wonder and say, "Oh, I see how that ripple has affected the creation that I call my life. Do I like it? Not any more. Good! I think I'll be rid of that. What can I replace it with?"

Mastery is a state in which you have embraced yourself as a ceaseless creator and assumed complete responsibility for everything that comes into the field of your awareness *without judging it*, so that you can simply decide whether it is going to stay or be dissolved in its effects. Mastery is fearlessness. That is, you no longer fear the infinite, creative power of your perfect union with God. "I and my Father are one!" is one expression of mastery.

If I, who uttered those words so long ago in your experience of time, can demonstrate to anyone who will look that consciousness transcends the limited beliefs about the body, life and death that the world seems so determined to defend at all costs—if I can demonstrate that only Love is real, if I can demonstrate the power to communicate with minds across creation, if I can bring forth creations by joining with other minds who may temporarily think they are just a body, such that written words fall upon a page and the page becomes part of a book that you are now reading, such that your heart is touched at just the right time—if I can do these things, so too can you. And indeed, greater things than these *shall* you do!

Beloved friends, is it not time to assume complete responsibility for the grand freedom that has been imparted to you by Abba, Father, Creator, Source of your being? Is it not time to begin spending time disengaging from your entangled view that holds you to believe that what you feel and what you think is the *effect* of all of the energies and things that are coming *at* you, from around you? Is it not time to begin to use time to decide which pebbles you will drop into the field of your awareness consistently, day by day, hour by hour, and even breath by breath?

For these things create your tomorrows, and you cannot ever escape the reality that you are, and always will be, in the process of creating your tomorrows. Death will never separate you from it. Denial does not change it.

You are free to decide what your tomorrows will be through the act of seeking first the Kingdom. This means to rest into that inner silence in which you *know* that you are a wave having arisen with perfect momentum out of the depth of the ocean of God's holy Mind. And that what you carry with you is the result of the thoughts and the beliefs and the perceptions—like pebbles—that you have dropped into the wave of your awareness.

This very process is what created you, and this very process is how you have always created. If you have ever received an education, how did you end up with your body in a classroom? Did somebody kidnap you and sit you down and say, "Here, you must learn these things"? No. You first held a thought, a picture, and you placed a value upon it, and you attracted the means that carried you into the lived experience of receiving the education that *you* had decided upon. *where children?*

What relationship have you ever entered out of lack of awareness? None. You dropped the pebble into the mind that said, "I want relationship with another being, another body, another place upon the physical planet." You have always been doing it, and you have always experienced the fruit or the effect of the quality of vibration of the pebble that has created the ripples that have become your experiences. In reality, your experience, that is, your awareness—what is true about you—is no different than what is true about me.

The only difference has been that I learned to train myself, hour by hour, to drop only *unlimited* pebbles, that send out vibrations of unconditional acceptance and Love, forgiveness, unconditional and unbridled vision and revelation, while *you* have selected to do that only a *few* times.

Then you rush back and pick up the pebbles of unworthiness, or limitation, or lack, or fear, or smallness, and you drop ten or twelve quick ones in. Then you go back to the other cupboard and say, "Hmm, here's the pebble that says, 'I and my Father are one'… oh, had enough of that!" And back you go again.

While I stay on this side of the fence saying:

> I and my Father are one! I and my Father are one!
> I am an unlimited being forever!
> How many universes can I be the savior of today?

You, on the other hand, have said, "That sounds very good. I and my Father are one. Oh, here is a pebble that says my car needs to break down today."

This is all there is! Which side of the fence are you going to sit on and drop the pebbles from? Which tree will you eat the fruit thereof? The tree of knowledge of good and evil?

Use that symbolism well, for when you drop the pebble in the pond it is like saying, "Well, I think I will take a bite of this piece of fruit. Oh, but it's so sweet, it's so good and so perfect. I'd better have a bite of a rotten one too to balance it out." The tree of good and evil—positive and negative, unlimitedness/limitation, forgiveness/judgment, love/fear—is like holding a beautiful flower and seeing the petals and saying, "Oh, it's so beautiful. I can't quite take it, so I think I'll prick my finger on the thorn and bring myself back down."

No one ever told you, and your Creator never insisted, that you eat of the tree of good and evil. For all *good fruit* has been given you freely. And you are always free to choose *which* fruit you will eat thereof:

I and my Father are one! What a blessed creation.
I have been having so much fun as this wave. Yes, I see
what I have carried along with me. Well, it was fun. I
gained a few things. Now, what's next?

Unlimitedness—kerplunk! Perfect Love—kerplunk!
Wealth—kerplunk!
The ability to heal—kerplunk! kerplunk! kerplunk!

Oh, yes, I see that little pebble over there sitting on the shore
that I have picked up a million times: unworthiness—kerplunk!
But no more! Be done with you!

I and my Father are one! I and my Father are one!
Father, create through me the good, the holy, and the beautiful,
for this is the reason for my being! How big of a wave can I become?
How powerful can I become? How radiant can I become?
How much of You can I express through me? Kerplunk!

Remember well, you are creating your tomorrows *now*! And what you experience never comes to you from outside your Self. If you worry over lack of golden coins—kerplunk! And you begin to attract the vibrational ripples that will *seem* to picture back to you, reflect back to you, the truth that you have chosen to believe, "I live in lack and I can't get out. (kerplunk!) I can't possibly talk to Jeshua. I'm not worthy." (kerplunk!)

And the vibrational waves that come to you are the static that restricts your ability to transcend the third dimension and plug into others. So that even if I yell and shout, "Hey, I am talking to you, listen," your mind says, "That's not possible because I've dropped a rock in (kerplunk!) that says, 'It's not possible' and therefore, I do not hear a thing."

Do you begin to get the picture? Do you begin to *feel*, in the core of your beingness, the essence of this lesson's message? You cannot escape being what you are created to be. In each and every moment you are, literally, using that ceaseless and unlimited power to create. And you remain perfectly free at any time to create anew. What you will experience in your tomorrows is only the effect of which pebbles you are choosing to drop into the field of your awareness as thoughts *now*.

So the only question is this:

Am I, as a creative being made in the image of God,
willing to deliberately, consciously, and actively choose

being responsible for which thoughts, which pebbles,
are dropped into my mind in each moment?

If the answer is "yes," ask:

 What do I want the new pebbles to be?
What vibrational qualities will I call to myself and
thereby create my tomorrows?

Any time you react to what you believe is outside of yourself—you may be absolutely *positive* of this—you have elected to pick up that old pebble that says, "I'm a victim of the world I see. What I experience is caused by forces outside of me. The fault really is in my mother, my brother, my father, my partner, my child. The fault really is in the government, and the planet, and the quality of air. The fault really is from a source outside of me, and I have no choice, but to react to it." To which I can only say:

Would you rather be right or happy?

Indeed beloved friends, consider well the essence of this lesson's message. For upon this, we will begin to build as we move toward the ending of The Way of the Heart. This is but a foundation from which those that are willing can spring forth into a grander dimension, a grander experience of living as a deliberate co-creator with God.

But it all begins with a need to be responsible for *owning* the truth of the message of this lesson. For without that, there can be no change in your consciousness and, therefore, in what you will experience in your tomorrows. So if there is something in your present that makes you shudder, just think what is waiting for you if you once again deny choosing this responsibility and the power that comes with it.

Beloved and holy friends, remember that I come not to bring peace to the world, but to shake it up so that those beings that make up the world can discover where true peace is truly hidden—*within themselves.* And where Heaven abides—*within themselves.* And where Christ lives—*within themselves.*

Peace then, be unto you always. Amen.

LESSON 9
ALL EVENTS ARE NEUTRAL

I am your brother and your friend, who looks upon you and sees naught but the face of Christ within you. Christ is the firstborn of the Father. That is, it is that which is begotten, and not made. Christ is God's creation. Christ is the holy Child of God. Christ is as a sunbeam to the sun, radiating forever from the holy Mind of what I have called Abba.

Therefore, I come forth to abide with you in perfect joy, and in perfect freedom, and in perfect reality. I come forth to join with that part of you that abides always in perfect knowledge, perfect peace, perfect knowingness, and in perfect union with your Creator.

I come not to speak of things that you do not know. I come not to use words that do not already abide within you. I come not with the wisdom that you do not already contain. I come not with a Love grander than that which already flowers within the silent places of your own heart. I come *not* to place myself above you. I come only to walk as an equal beside you.

I come because I love you. I come because I am your friend. Of all the things that I could possibly choose to do with the unlimited power of consciousness given equally unto me of my Father as it was given unto you, of all of the places and dimensions and worlds in which I could reside in this moment, I come to abide *with you* to bridge the gap that seems to yet separate you from me.

In reality, all dimensions of creation reside in a space far smaller than the tip of a pin. In reality, all dimensions of creation are so vast that you could never measure them. In reality, there is no gap between where you are and I am. This is why I can be no further from you than the width of a thought. But oh, beloved friends, the power of a thought is the power to create universes, and within universes to create yet more universes, and within those universes to create world upon world upon world upon world upon world.

Your lived experience is that momentarily your attention seems to be focused on your unique world, which shares some things in common with many other beings. You have what is called in your world a consensus reality—we would say a consensus *experience*—born out of a universal reality. Beloved friends, even as you abide in your awareness in this moment, you are the creator of the world you experience. And you do this in so many ordinary ways. When you stand face to face with anyone and for just a split second, you alter the position of the body through which you gaze upon them—you take up a new stance, a new perspective—in that very split second, you have created a new experience for yourself.

When you look upon a friend, and the mind moves from neutrality (which is where you begin every experience) into the thought, "That is my friend, Mary. That is my friend, St. Germain. That is my friend, Peter. That is my friend, Joanna. That is my friend, Nathaniel." Whatever the name may be, when you hold that thought, already you begin to change the experience.

You are a literal creator in that moment. For when you name anything, you define it according to the factors that you have built into the name that you use. When you look upon a field of energy arising from the mystery of Earth and you say the word "tree," instantly you have brought forth into your manifest experience everything you have ever decided is associated with the field of energy that you have called tree. In this way, your experience is entirely unique. It has never been before; it will never be again. Nothing can repeat it. This is why creation is forever new.

Yes, you can stand with your friend and look upon a tree and nod your head and say, "Of course, that's a tree. Yes, I see the branches. I see the leaves." But as soon as you have named it, you have brought forth all of the associations you have called to yourself, your experience of that field of energy that you have called tree. Rest assured, those called environmentalists and those that you have labeled loggers definitely see a different experience though they both use the same word *tree*. Which is right, then, and which is wrong? This does not apply.

In this lesson, we want to address another of the important pebbles that you must drop into the clear, still pool of your awareness. It is simply this: All webs of relationship, all energy fields, are *absolutely neutral.* What creates experience is how you decide you will view that web of relationship, that field of energy. The *effect* of that decision is also completely neutral.

But how can that be? For when a logger sees a tree and sees only the profit to be made, forests disappear. And when an environmentalist looks at a tree, the tree remains and the mighty owls and the birds have a place to make their home. Surely, are we not to perpetuate the same reality, the same experience that all human beings have had? Is there not loss when the forest disappears? Listen well and carefully: All events are neutral. *You* are the one that places the value upon it.

Now, does that mean that one should become cold-hearted, unconscious, and blind to their actions? Of course not, for part of awakening means to realize one's interconnection with the web of all relationships. It means awakening a reverence for the mystery that is Life. But it also means to release judgment of another who would view the tree differently. For you see, the body that you have crystallized out of a field of infinite energy has but one purpose. It is a communication device.

Therefore, let your primary perception, your primary guiding light in your third-dimensional experience be this:

✳ What do I choose to communicate to the world
with every gesture, with every breath, with every word spoken
and with every decision made?

For ceaselessly, while the body lasts, you are engaged in the process of communicating to the world, making manifest to the world, what you have chosen to value, what you have called into your experience and imbued with value. This means that ceaselessly you are engaged in teaching the world what you believe holds the greatest truth, the greatest value.

When an environmentalist looks upon a logger, becomes exasperated and judges that logger or vice versa, the body is being used to communicate the value of judgment. That creates fear and contraction. The result of many, many minds choosing to value the right to judge is the effect you call your world, in which everything seems to be expressing conflict, struggle, "butting of heads" and the Armageddon of opposite ideas running into each other. And just beneath it all, all events remain completely neutral.

Even if the forests of your planet were completely taken away, that would be a neutral event. Why? Because if all of the trees were gone, if the very physical planet you call Earth died, dissolved from view, Life would continue. Life would merely create new worlds. It does it all the time. *You* do it all the time.

The events, then, that you experience are always neutral. What you see occurring in the world around you remains neutral until *you* make the decision what it will be—*for you*. You will name it and, therefore, you will define it. When you define it, you call all of the associations of that to yourself.

This is why once I taught it is very wise to forgive seventy-times-seven times. It was for a very selfish reason. If one wrongs you and you spend your energy convincing them that they have wronged you, that you have a right to be angry and to be attacking in any way, you call to yourself—even into the cells of the body—the energy of conflict, judgment, war, death, disease, unhappiness and separation *instantly!*

But if you forgive seventy times seven, then in each of those moments of forgiveness, you call into your field of energy that which reminds you of unconditional Love, perfect peace, a power that transcends anything that arises in the world. You call to yourself the reality of Christ. And all of it hinges on nothing more than the pebbles that you drop into your mind.

LOOK WITH INNOCENCE ON WHAT YOU VALUE

Where, then, have you drawn the line? Where have you said, "I will allow neutrality to all events in *this* sphere, but not in *that* sphere.

"If my friends divorce or separate, well okay, I'll see that as neutral. But if my spouse leaves me, that is not neutral. If my friend's father leaves three million dollars to his children, well, that's fine. That's a neutral event. But if my father leaves his three million dollars to charity and leaves me out of the picture, that is not a neutral event.

"If the streams in a country on the other side of the world from where I am become polluted because the consciousness of a community allowed a factory to be built without safeguards, well, it's on the other side of the world, a neutral event. But if they build it in my backyard, it is no longer neutral."

It is always wise to look lovingly to see where you have drawn the line, to see what you will look upon as neutral and what you cling to as being filled with meaning and value that is unquestionable. For there you will find what requires forgiveness within you. We have shared with you that mastery is a state of fearlessness. When you place a value upon something and then become adamant that that value exists in the event or the object outside of you, you have secured your place in fear. And fearlessness is as far from you as the east is from the west.

Look well then, to see where you have placed a value, and insisted that that value be unshakable. How many times in each of your days do you say, "Oh, boy! If my dog ever died I would not be able to take it. That would just be the end of me." Or "If the banks collapse...oh, God, I wouldn't be able to take that!"

 Be careful what you decree. Look to see where you are emotionally enmeshed with the value you have placed upon anything or anyone. Any relationship whatsoever, whether it be the relationship with your spouse, the relationship with your body, the relationship with your cat or your dog, the relationship with your bank account, the relationship with your government—look at *all* of your relationships.

For you have made them what they are. Where can freedom be experienced, save within a consciousness that has learned how to transcend the contraction of fear? And fear is the result of your attachment to the values you have placed upon the events you experience, which are made up of events, persons, places, and things. All of these are actually just events.

Every web of relationship comes to you perfectly neutral. You decree it by naming it and defining it. When one comes to you in anger and you react, recognize that you first decided that they are angry, and you have brought forth with it all of the associations you have ever decided to value concerning what anger means.

Yet in that very moment, you hold the power to witness this field of energy circulating through the body and mind and the speech of another, and to see it as a dance of energy, a mystery arising from some unseen source and web of relationships. You could look upon it with curiosity and with wonder if you defined it differently.

This is true for all things that arise. Even the great diseases that seem to threaten the life of the body can be looked at with complete neutrality. But if you define them in a specific way, you will call to yourself the fear of that event, which comes with all of the associations you have learned from the world and from your own experiences.

The message of this lesson is simple, but it is very important. It builds on all that we have shared previously with you. You are a creator, and you cannot help but create. The question, then, is:

What will you create in each moment?

Far beyond the great thrill of the magic of creating events or objects in third-dimensional reality are the *qualities* that you create, such as peace, unlimitedness, forgiveness, compassion, and wisdom. These too are creations.

Compassion does not exist floating about in the universe until you manifest it and cultivate it within your own consciousness. Christ consciousness cannot be said to truly exist—for *you*—until you create it within yourself. Your union with God does not even exist—for *you*—until you decide to open to the lived experience of it. Much as a food you have never tasted might as well not exist for you until you journey to that country, purchase it and place it in the body. Or in your day and age, go to your grocery store and find the gourmet international section.

Nothing can be said to exist—for *you*—until you have tasted the lived experience of it. So when you hear talk about enlightenment, when you hear talk about union with God, when you hear talk about unconditional love, stop nodding your head thinking you know what these things are, and turn your attention within. Do you abide in a lived experience of these things? Immediately you will know the answer.

If your answer is, "No, I hear talk about enlightenment and I get little glimpses, but I don't really know what it is because I'm not feeling it completely in my lived experience," right away you will know that there must be something that you have valued *other than* enlightenment that you are insisting remains in place in your consciousness. What is it? Search it out, find it and decide whether you still want it.

We would perceive there are many in your world that like to walk around *as if* they are in a state of peace with smiles upon their faces. Perhaps they carry the Holy Bible in their hand or some other such text. They wear some religious icon upon their body so as to create the appearance of one who is at peace. But inwardly, they are not at peace. When they turn on their television and they watch how the logger has felled yet another tree, inwardly they respond by calling that one "ignorant" or "stupid" or "limited."

In that moment, they have spoken to the universe the truth that they are choosing to live, "I am not one who wants to know what peace is. I am not one interested in forgiveness. I am not one interested in wisdom. I am interested in judgment and the high that I feel in my body through the act of judging another as being less than myself."

In short, it is time to give up the pretense. It is time to begin viewing yourself from the perspective of an absolute, ceaseless creator. Begin looking at exactly what you are creating in each moment of your experience. Bring the quality of childlike innocence to what you *actually* experience, not what you tell everybody else you are experiencing. It is time to become honest with the effects of the ripples of the rocks or the pebbles you have dropped into the field of your awareness as a great form of play.

For a creator who understands their infinite power to create and who understands that it is going on ceaselessly—that effects are being generated moment to moment to moment to moment that will indeed be making up their tomorrows—*gladly* gives up the energy of denial. And turns to look upon every moment of their experience that they might discern what choice they must have made to bring about the effects they are currently experiencing.

When a bill comes, and your body shakes and you go into contraction and worry because there are not enough golden coins in the checkbook to pay for it, the creator *stops* and looks upon all that is being experienced in the field of the body, in the emotional body and at the thoughts being held in the mind.

They begin to notice how they are viewing the objects around themselves, the world around them, in order to begin to wonder, "What thought must I have dropped into the pool of my mind to create the *effect* of lacking golden coins? And is that a thought I wish to drop into my mind so that I create similar effects in my tomorrows?"

 Here is the doorway of wisdom. Do not create unconsciously and then just walk away. But learn ceaselessly from your creation. For in this way you begin the process of dissolving the creation of an un-enlightened being and you begin to build the creation of a Christ— here and now, in this moment.

THE POWER OF YOUR THOUGHTS

Never, ever believe that your *thoughts* are neutral. I said earlier that events are neutral, but your thoughts are not. For your thoughts literally are imbued with the power of creation. They do not create neutrally. That is, every thought reverberates a quality of vibration that spreads out from you, touches the shores of manifested reality, and comes back to you. That is what you experience as the positive and negative events of your life.

Now, it is very true—please listen carefully to this—that at any moment as you go along in your experience, as you experience the reverberation, the coming back of the ripples you have sent out, in that very moment you are not a victim of what you have created. Because in each such moment you remain as perfectly free as you were when you first dropped the pebble into the pond that even created the ripple in the first place. You are free to choose how you will experience the effect of that ripple.

And if you experience it with unconditional freedom, with unconditional acceptance and Love, forgiveness, neutrality and innocence, you literally defuse the effects of that ripple upon the pool of your consciousness. And then, in that moment, you become instantly free to begin creating, in a new way, the ripples that you will experience in the future. And this is why you are never a victim of anyone's creation, especially your own.

It is not that life is so complex that you have created all these momentums and now you are stuck with them. In any moment that you *get it,* you can stop reacting as if you were a victim, and look merely at the ripples that are coming back to you that you have sent out from yourself and say:

This has come into my field of experience as an awesome mystery.
This means that I am an awesomely powerful being!
Therefore, I will look lovingly upon this ripple.

Yes, I know it needs to play itself out.
But as it does so, I'm going to be wise enough to see the transparency of it,
to see the lack of effect that it really has. It doesn't change who I am.
It doesn't add anything to my life. It doesn't take anything from it.
It merely is an experience called life passing through the field of my awareness.

If I look lovingly upon it, if I embrace it, I can transmute it, and therefore,
already be engaged in the process of creating a whole different kind of
vibrational ripple that will create my tomorrows.

That means that while the power of your thoughts is not neutral, the events called the effects of those thoughts can be either neutral or not neutral, depending on how you use the very primary power of awareness. We are seeking to share with you how infinitely *free* you are.

There are many in your world that teach this illusory doctrine of what is called karma—that what you send out now you *must* experience sooner or later, and how you experience it is directly related to the quality of the ripple you send out. *That is not true.* That would make you a victim.

If you are made in the image of God, and I assure you that you are, you are not a victim of the world you see. You cannot, in reality, be victimized by anyone or anything at any time because your reality is that you are made in the image of God. If you could truly be victimized, it would mean that God creates *unlike Herself.* Does a salmon come from an oak tree? Does a nebula come out of the womb of a woman? Does a raspberry grow on a grocery store shelf? No. Like begets like.

Therefore, why would you ever believe that God—who is but Love and unlimited creativity and power—could ever beget something that is small and little and powerless? It does not happen. God cannot be victimized. Therefore, God's creation remains victimless. *my use of the word "victim".*

All events remain neutral, and all that the environmentalist and the logger are doing is using the power of consciousness to momentarily create the belief that they are *this* and not *that.* They place a value of their own choosing upon an event of energy that they call a tree. And by what value they place upon it, they call the quality of experience they will have into their field of awareness. That is all that is happening.

The energy that makes up the tree is eternal forever. It may change form, but Life remains. Therefore, lament not the passing away of a species, but trust the Grand Intelligence that gave rise to it in the first place. For it is still busy creating even greater universes. This is why loss does not exist.

How does all of this relate to your daily experience? As we move into the lessons that follow, it is going to become *very* crucial that you have a foundation upon which to build.

FIVE MINUTES A DAY—THE FOUNDATION OF MASTERY

If you are ready to completely assume responsibility for having been created in the image of God and that, therefore, you are an eternal creator, begin *now* to utilize some time each day, without letting a day go by, in which you sit with yourself. Not with your mate, not with your parents, not with the television, not with your favorite sport team, not with your favorite actor or actress, not with your favorite religion, not with your favorite god or master or savior, not even me. Sit with you. Start by acknowledging that you are one with God.

Understand that the very body that seems to have a heart within it beating Life for you is the effect of decisions and choices you have made. That the very chair that you are sitting on is the result of your attracting a web of relationships that is quite unique into your field of awareness called the physical universe. In this moment you are having an experience you have never had before. You are sitting in the chair now! The event is completely neutral. And nothing that you are experiencing in your consciousness exists or is sourced by anything outside yourself.

Give yourself five minutes to practice choosing how you will experience sitting in a chair. Will you do so with a mind full of worry, or a mind full of peace? A mind thinking of all the things it could be doing, or a mind *marveling* at how the weight of a body feels pressed against the seat of a chair? A mind that creates tension in the way the breath flows through the body, or a mind that creates ease and comfort?

Five minutes of practice sitting in a chair as an infinite creator of exactly what you are experiencing in your emotional field. Just that. You might even want to play with what it would feel like to sit in a chair *as a Christ*. What would that feel like? I will let you choose whether or not you would like to experience it. Five minutes each day. Do it without fail! Be with yourself, and decide how you will experience yourself *now*!

For you see, the *you* that sits down in the chair with whatever is going on in your consciousness—whatever feelings you are having throughout the body, whatever is going on in your primary relationships, how the food is being digested in the body, all of it, the whole realm of your experience—is the effect of how you have been a million times when you have sat down to be with yourself in a thousand different chairs.

Utilize the very process of sitting down in a chair as a symbol of preparing the mind for the dropping of a pebble into it, out of which will reverberate the vibrations or ripples that will come back to you.

It is much easier to send out ripples and experience them when they come back in a blissful way, a way that brings you peace, joy, fun, laughter, play and unlimitedness, instead of having to constantly butt your head against something that you would rather transmute or run away from.

But it begins with five minutes, in which you acknowledge that you can create whatever experience you want, as a feeling that floods through your awareness, as a quality of thought that you allow to keep repeating in the mind.

You can sit in a chair as an awakened Christ—*now.*

> I and my Father are one!
> It's a beautiful day!
> I've manifested a physical form sitting in a chair
> in a corner of one little tiny dimension of creation.
> How amazing this moment is!
> I think I'll just sit here and feel the heart beating in the body
> and the breath flowing through it.
>
> Ah, there's the sound of a bird.
> I'm glad I called that to myself.
>
> What beautiful thoughts can I think right now?
> Who can I send Love to without lifting a finger?
>
> I am unlimited forever!
> I am free! I am free! I am free!

Do you think you would like to have that experience for five minutes? Why not begin today?

So many of you upon your physical plane keep searching for some form of magic that will bring the Kingdom of Heaven to you. You cannot bring it *to you.* You can only become aware of how you are using it to create the ripples that you send out *from yourself.* Do you know the saying in your world, "Wherever you go, there you are"? You *are* God's creation. You are in Heaven now. Heaven is not a place. It is a state of unlimited and infinite creative power because it is the reflection of God's holy Mind.

Why not be one who practices being the presence of Heaven? If that seems too awesome or too far beyond you, then just play with it for five minutes a day.

Trust me, I will love you no less if for the other twenty-three hours and fifty-five minutes you decide to play at pretending and feeling that you are little, unworthy, unloved, unloving, unlovable, that you are the scourge of the Earth and that life is constantly victimizing you. Go right ahead. I would never interfere with your free choice. I may not come and knock at your door, except for those five minutes. But you remain free to utilize time any way you wish.

For just five minutes, experience yourself as Christ, crystallizing a body as a temporary teaching and learning communication device, sitting in a chair in a totally neutral corner of creation because *you* want to have the experience of sitting blissfully at peace in your perfect knowledge of your union with God in this moment. You might even find yourself daring to have thoughts such as this:

>✱　Well, since I am an infinite creator,
>　what would I like to create for my tomorrows?

If during that five minutes, there is a knock upon the door and it is the bill collector, who cares? That is *that* soul's experience of thinking they are a bill collector and you are some bad person they must corral. Let them have their experience. Sit calmly, hear the knocking on the door and allow yourself to be entertained by the beautiful worlds you are creating for your tomorrows.

Here is the straight and narrow path that leads unto Life. Here is the eye of the needle through which you must pass. For it is not enough to just embrace the idea that "I am the creator of all that I experience." You must then choose to actively put it into practice. It begins with the practice of five minutes a day—that is all. When you feel that you can fulfill that for five minutes, then you can make it ten, and then twelve, and then fifteen, and then twenty.

You may respond, "You mean, for twenty minutes hang out as though I am Christ incarnate, totally in union with God, totally free to begin creating different ripples than I've ever experienced before, knowing that they will come back to me and become my manifested experience? With no doubt about it! But twenty minutes? Even if I could achieve that, that's such a small fraction of the time of a day."

Beloved friends, if you had faith as a tiny, tiny, tiny little seed, you would know that from that little tiny faith, you will create the mighty oak tree whose branches will shelter you from the blistering sun and give comfort unto many. Twenty minutes is an eternity when it comes to creating your tomorrows!

If you believe that the other twenty-three hours must be taken up by experiencing the effects of what you created a long time ago or the ripples that are coming back, so be it. Play with it. Let yourself transmute those moments.

For example, "Oh, here I am answering the door. Yes, bill collector. Hi, come on in. Have a glass of water. You know, you're absolutely right, I didn't pay that bill. Do you want to know why? Silly me, I've actually decided to create the experience that I'm someone who can only create lack. That's why I have no money in my checkbook. It's just the darndest thing, isn't it?

"Oh, very good, you're going to turn my name over to the authorities, and now I'll have no credit with anybody on the planet. Well, go ahead if it makes your day. I have other things to do. I'm busy creating a new tomorrow. And I know that everything all around me is going to be taken from me anyway since everything birthed in time ends in time. My house will be gone, my car will be gone, my clothes will be gone and my friends will be gone. Everything I've experienced in time is changing anyway, so go ahead and take it from me now. It'll just speed up the process."

I do not speak of this tongue-in-cheek. I speak from the perspective of one who *is* an awakened Christ, who already *knows* how to birth universes to create that which is holy, good, and beautiful. I *know* that this is the way. It is the *only* way. Release the value you have attached to your experiences, even the bill collector, and spend your time instead deciding which pebbles you are going to drop into the field of your mind. For you will create as the result of what you choose to think today. And what you value today will show itself to you tomorrow.

I learned to value unlimitedness. I learned to value Love. I learned to value fearlessness. Yes, my method for doing that was rather unique, and I would not recommend that you follow in my footsteps. Unless, of course, you like the drama of being nailed to a cross and then stood up in front of all of your friends in order to learn to transcend fear in your mind! *wow*

I learned to value unbroken communication with every soul in every dimension of creation. I learned to value only my loving thoughts. And I birthed or grew a Christ out of the very seed of awareness that exists equally within each of you.

Therefore, in this moment, look around where you are. Look at the objects that you see. Look at the people that you see around you, if there are any. Notice whatever sounds may be coming into your field of awareness. Notice whatever pictures or ideas you may hold of what you are or what the world is. These are all fleeting and temporary illusions. They will pass away, and began passing away the moment they were created.

Therefore, indeed, beloved friends, look at all that is around you, and decide what value it holds for you. Will you see it as something that you *must* have in your existence? Or will you choose to see it as something you have playfully drawn to yourself; you appreciate it and it can be gone tomorrow and your peace will not be disturbed? Which way will you view the world?

Five minutes—one for each finger and thumb on a hand—in which you choose to sit as Christ in the midst of your kingdom, your creation. And *you* decide which thoughts you will hold and, therefore, determine how you see all that is in the field of your awareness, and which thoughts *you* will allow to begin to generate the ripples that you will send out that *will*—there is no way to escape it—return to you.

PLANTING THE SEED THAT PRODUCES THE DESIRED RESULT

Once indeed there was a farmer who went out to plant the seed in his ground. But before he went to plant the seed, he selected the seed very carefully. The other farmers rushed out because they thought, "Oh, look, it is the time for the planting to begin. Everything is perfect. The conditions are just right. We must make haste and plant." And they bought whatever seeds they could get and went out and spread them across the ground, and began their busy work of doing what they had to do. Rest assured, they would have their harvest. But the wise farmer waited, and while he was laughed at by his colleagues, he carefully selected every seed. He waited until he could hold it in his hand and say, "Oh, I like the vibration of *this* seed. This feels very good. Oh yes! I can just see the beautiful plant that is going to arise from this. The fruit of it will be the sweetest in the valley."

And he gathered his seeds. He paid no attention to the passing of the dates on a calendar. He paid no attention to the changing weather conditions. He knew that when the time was right the seed would be planted, and from it would burst forth the flower of those seeds. He *knew* it! He gave no thought to the opinions of his colleagues. He enjoyed the process of loving the seeds that he was making his own.

Then the farmer went out and he cast the seed upon the soil of his farm, which is likened unto the soil of your own awareness. He planted the seeds, and he tamped them down, and he nurtured them, and he watered them, and he cultivated them with a smile upon his face.

And yes, the neighbors' seeds seemed to be already sprouting up through the ground. He could not have cared less, for he knew that *these* seeds would bring him an *eternal* harvest, that they would not just burst forth once from the soil, then throw out some mediocre fruit, and then die. For he had selected seeds that would constantly bring forth, in each season, the *best* of fruits. He loved them, and he nurtured them, and he cultivated them.

Long after the other farmers had grown weary and tired and had experienced drought, and seeds that brought forth fruit where insects would come and destroy them, that would not be purchased by the people in the market place, this one farmer became the greatest of farmers in the entire valley. People would come from all over the world to bite, to take a little nibble, out of the fruit that came from his garden.

Yet, the farmer merely delighted in continually loving and nurturing these seeds, and cultivating the soil in which they were planted daily. He never took his consciousness away from his perfect union with those seeds. He never once forgot that *he* was the one that created his farm as a direct result of his careful selection of which seeds he would plant in his soil. And while others marveled at his good fortune, and while others were jealous of his good luck, the farmer always knew that no magic was involved.

He merely followed in the footsteps of the wisdom given to him by God:

"Take My fruit and plant it in your consciousness. Know that you are one with Me, and that fruit you experience is the result of the seeds you plant in your own consciousness. Know that you cannot help but experience the result, the fruit, of the seeds you plant. *Nothing* bursts forth on the vine of your experience by accident.

"Therefore, create with Me, my child. Create like unto Myself, by knowing, *knowing* that you are a creator, a farmer, a planter. And you will, indeed, harvest the *quality* of the seeds that you plant.

"Just as you, beloved child, are the harvest of the seed I once planted, when first I held the thought of you in my holy Mind. And in that moment, you arose as a sunbeam from the sun, made in My image. I held you as the thought of Love in form. And I bestowed you with all good things.

"Therefore, see yourself as I see you. Embrace yourself as I embrace you. Accept yourself as you are—a creator, creating without ceasing.

"And just as I sat upon my throne (which means sitting in the center of All That Is), and beheld you as a loving thought, so too choose only to allow *loving* thoughts to enter into your consciousness. Choose to only allow loving thoughts to be expressed with your words. Choose only to allow loving thoughts to be translated into your gestures, your choices, and your actions.

"And thereby, create as I created you—that which extends joy forever, that which extends the holy, the beautiful, and the good forever. For that is what you are. That is how I thought of you when I created you. And that is what you remain eternally.

"Therefore, join with Me, by extending your creation, as I have extended you. Since you have manifested a physical body, accept my Son's teaching, and let that body be placed in a chair, that you might think like the Mind of Christ for five minutes. And you will beget an eternality that reflects the radiance of Heaven, just as you reflect My radiance when I look upon the unlimited soul that you are."

Indeed, in the entire valley there was but one farmer that was wise. Will *you* elect to join the union comprised of all of the hasty farmers? Or will you choose to take up residence as the *one* farmer who knows how to create wisely, and in faith, rests on perfect certainty, and merely sits back to wait for the ripples of Heaven to come and replace the ripples of hell, that once you created unwittingly?

Everyone is a minister. You cannot help but minister to the world in each moment. Therefore, begin your ministry of enlightened consciousness *now*! And I promise you this absolutely, irrevocably: *You will experience all that I have known and more*! You will experience complete victory over death. You will experience complete unlimitedness and abundance. You will experience perfect peace, perfect miracle mindedness, and perfect unbroken communion in bliss with all of creation!

Once when I was a man, I was taught to sit at the base of a tree for five minutes a day and to imagine myself to be the creator of all that I could think, all that I could see, and all that I could feel. Five minutes taken out of the hours of play of a child.

You are a child at play in your own kingdom. Will you give yourself five minutes to learn to be a Christ that creates in unlimited perfection in alignment with the Mind of God, whose experience is always radiantly blissful and free of limitation and fear? You *will* experience your creation. What that creation is, and how you experience it, is entirely up to you.

The message of this lesson, built upon the last, begins to translate the Truth into an action— very simple, very practical—so simple and so practical that you will be hard pressed to find a reason, an excuse, against it. For those of you so busy trying to take care of dealing with all the things life throws at you, even *you* know that you can find five minutes. And those five minutes can be the beginning of birthing a whole new universe for yourself.

And with that, peace be unto you always by making the decision to choose to receive peace as a Christ. Herein lies the secret of much of what will be shared in your upcoming lessons. For what I specifically seek to do in *The Way of Mastery* and this specific work you know and call as Shanti Christo, is the birthing of a multitude of Christs that dwell upon your Earth at the same time. It has never been done before!

Hopefulness Imagine a world with ten million awakened children of God—fully awake—not just as a belief or an idea, but who have mastered fear, who no longer live in doubt whatsoever, and who are busy creating universes that mirror perfectly the Kingdom of Heaven. Imagine it—if you dare!

It begins *now*. Practice well for the next thirty days. If not, you will find yourself having to go back and start anyway, before you can receive the next phase of what will be shared. The choice is yours.

Peace, then, be unto you always. Amen.

LESSON 10
THE WAY IS EASY AND WITHOUT EFFORT

Love this greeting...

Beloved and holy children of Light and of Love divine, as always, I come forth to abide with you from that place which we share eternally as the one and only begotten son and of God. I am, therefore, *that Mind* which whispers to you in each moment of your inspiration. I am, indeed, *that Mind* that sneaks into your mind in the space between two fearful thoughts and reminds you of the Truth that sets you free.

Once I was a man — that is, just like you. I once turned my attention and became identified with a unique being that was birthed in time and faded away from time. And I walked upon your plane as all men and women do. But as I walked upon your planet, I began to ponder the meaning of creation, the purpose of my very existence.

And while others seemed to be gleefully caught up in or at least surrendered to the ways of the world, seeking out their momentary distractions, their attempts to gain and control as much wealth as they could, and all of the rest, I would often wander off alone. I would sit beneath the trees beside a flowing stream to try to unlock the mystery that shows forth itself as the beauty of a flower, to try to see the power that revealed itself as the wind that would dance across the grasses, and to count the sparkling diamonds shimmering across the surface of a lake as the morning sun arose to shine its light upon it.

I began to learn to ask of that Source, that mystery, "Father, One that has birthed me, *why* am I? *Where* am I? *Who* am I?" My desire increasingly became to know the truth that could set all mankind free. I discovered that unless that freedom became fully manifest in *me*, it made no sense to talk about it with others. So I sought out the greatest of minds, the best of teachers. And yes, I was blessed by a family structure already dedicated to understanding the mysteries of what they knew as God. They led me to many such teachers.

As my own wisdom began to evolve, the teachers would look at me and say to one another, "Something interesting is occurring here, in this son of Joseph." But there were already those who knew more about me than I knew yet about myself. Prophets, seers, astrologers and the wise ones of many cultures knew already that into the framework of the consensus mind of mankind, which you call collective consciousness, there was to be dropped a pebble, into that still clear pool, that would create ripples that would begin to change how the consciousness of humankind perceived itself.

I did not yet know these things for myself, for my very birth into this world was veiled in mystery for me, just as your birth was veiled in mystery for you as you took on being human.

Kristy's Comments

As I grew, I began to have revealed to me in the depth of my silent prayer and in the depth of my very silent meditation, glimmers, insights, recognitions, and remembrances of other dimensions. I began to develop the ability to be in communication with masters of my lineage who had long since left the planet. I began to understand that consciousness is not limited to the space and volume of a body at all.

As I watched the people in their busy work, I began to see that the vast majority of beings totally confused *themselves* with the *body*. They lived as if they dwelt within the body and, therefore, were imprisoned in some strange way. They lived as if what occurred to the body occurred to *them*. They lived as if they did not know that they could transcend the body at any moment; that they could taste the vast expanse of consciousness, that they could journey to other times and places with little more than a surrendering of attention to the world they had made.

At first, I did not understand these things and I perceived myself to be quite odd. Within me, there were conflicts as the fears in my consciousness arose, the fears that are part of the human consensus reality: "Shall I remain like everyone else? Perhaps I should return to my father's carpentry shop and simply accept that I am destined to just be a carpenter."

But there were other voices that spoke to me and called me, that would come often in the night. As I developed my ability to discern these other realities, these other dimensions, by shifting my attention from the world of the body to the world of inner vision, often they would come in the night and stand beside my bed. I came to know who they were. I came to recognize the masters and teachers of a very ancient lineage of which I was a part. They would come and whisper to me:

> Forget not the purpose for which you are sent forth from the Mind of God,
> for through you there shall be birthed the beginning of an ancient remembrance.
> And your life shall become that which demonstrates to many the truth that only
> Love is real.

The point of all of this is simple. I want to convey to you, yet again, that the life I lived as a man was not unlike your very own. I began veiled in mystery, a child among children, a human being struggling to make sense of his world. Yes, there was within me something calling, a longing to know something that the world did not seem to teach. But is it not true that many of you have felt that same call, that same longing—to touch what is invisible, to see what cannot be seen, to hear what ears have never heard, to embrace what arms cannot reach, to abide in perfect peace and perfect trust?

Beloved friends, understand well. I say to you yet again, I come only as your brother and your friend—one who has walked as you walk, one who has breathed as you breathe, one who has cried as you cry, one who has laughed as you laugh. I am as you are.

If there be anything that I can give unto you, it is simply this: As you look upon your life and every event that unfolds within it, every time you feel that you have failed, every time that you become conflicted, every time you are sure that you will never be able to transcend all of these ups and downs and emotional waves that seem to come with living in your world, remember, I have overcome the world. And because I have done it, it is done for you, already.

Why? Because we share the same infinite field of Mind that far transcends all levels and dimensions of manifestation. You can tap into what has already occurred. You need only look upon me as your brother and friend, and *acknowledge* that the world has been overcome, and then accept the freedom, which is the effect of its overcoming, *as your own.*

So that you learn to sit in your chair, after your five minutes of abiding as Christ, in which you say to yourself:

 Here, I am free.
Heaven is now.
The past is passed away, and I choose anew.

This day, I commit myself to teaching only Love
by sharing only loving thoughts.

This one day, I will look upon each one that comes into my experience
and I will first breathe deeply the presence of the Holy Spirit.

And I will look out through eyes transformed
by the simple acknowledgment of the truth:
All minds are joined, and I see not a stranger before me,
but one who walks as I walk, who feels as I feel, who longs as I long,
who is humbled as I am humbled, who prays for peace as I have prayed.

Therefore, I will give them what they seek.
And in that giving, I receive it.

ACKNOWLEDGE THE TRUTH THAT SETS YOU FREE

The way is so simple and so easy that the mind of the world overlooks it, thinking that it simply cannot be. But that which is simple seems impossible to that which insists on complexity. And a mind that insists on conflict simply cannot accept that there *is* another way. Yet what waits before you is simply this: In the end of all of your struggles, in the end of all of your doubts, and in the end of all of the moments of your unconscious conforming to the mind of the world, there remains the simple choice to be made—the choice to acknowledge the truth that has *already* set you free:

> I and my Father are one. It has been that way forever.
> It was accomplished in the being of Jeshua ben Joseph, who revealed to me the truth of myself, because he loved me. And if he can do it, I can do it.
> Even in this moment, I accept my destiny to walk this Earth awake and at peace, in mastery, and not in fear. And I begin my ministry now.

 For who can you seek that can heal you? Who can you discover that can bring some form of magic to you that can overcome your resistance to the Truth? Look high and low and you will not find them. Seek forever, and you will remain a seeker forever. For the Truth is set within your heart and all power under Heaven and Earth is given unto you. It is *that* power that changes the momentum of the mind and heals every wounded perception.

In the end of all seeking, you must look into the mirror and decide to be the one who heals yourself. *You* are the one who decides, from infinite freedom, how to use the power of your mind in each moment. Therefore, the only question that a seeker of truth really truly need ask him or her self is this:

> Would I know conflict or peace? Would I be right or happy?
> Would I see the complete neutrality of all events in this world
> as wisps of a dream, being birthed and passing away?

> Would I see myself whole and complete?
> For as I look upon the world, I have judged myself.
> And as I look upon myself, I judge the world.

This was the simple secret that I once discovered when I walked upon your planet. It was not about achieving some grand mystical state of consciousness. It was not about acquiring great powers that could attract the attention of thousands. It was not even about being able to manifest, although these powers may indeed often express themselves through the mind as it awakens.

It is about accepting the Truth that is true always, and being determined to allow that Truth to be the foundation from which you *enjoin* each and every moment of your experience.

> I am awake. I am safe. I am at peace.
> What do I truly want this moment to be for?

For as I decree it, so shall it be.

Beloved friends, the way *is* easy and without effort. You exist to extend your treasure. And your treasure is that which is laid up in Heaven through the decision to remember only your loving thoughts, to extend only loving thoughts, and to allow your actions to express or to manifest in the field of time the good, the beautiful, and the holy. *Never* is your freedom taken from you. Never in any circumstance do you lose the innocent freedom to teach only Love, to be the presence of peace, to recognize that the world can give you nothing, just as the world can take nothing from you.

When a child goes through a shift of awareness, they come to a point in their maturation process, not by struggle, not by design, not by much processing, and not by any manner of strategies. The child merely, in an instant, looks at the toys that he has been playing with and simply transcends them. The parents come home and the child has taken the toy truck and put it away in the closet. The doll is put on the windowsill and a book is picked up instead. Who makes the change? Not anyone outside that child.

When you put aside any negative habit as you would perceive it to be, when you have given up placing value in something that no longer serves you, you merely transcend it, and it is done with. No big deal. No one does it for you, you simply decide. You pull back the *value* you had placed on it, and the objects that were the symbols of what you were *valuing* merely drop out of your life.

In just this way, unenlightenment can be put away as though it were a toy that you have outgrown—by merely looking at all of the effects of unenlightenment, and then asking the question, "Is this what I wish to have continue as my experience? Or am I willing to put the doll on the windowsill, and pick up a book instead?" A book that speaks of Life, a book that is filled with wisdom, a book that teaches you how to step lightly in the world, to be in the world but not of it.

That book is the depth of your consciousness in which all things are already written. And that depth finds its source in your heart. You enter it through forgiveness, through the process of *relinquishing* the world—not hating the world, not despising the world, but simply relinquishing it. You *allow* your time to serve you in the process of relinquishing what does not serve you any longer, and what only disturbs your peace.

COMMIT TO AWAKENING TO THE PEACE ALREADY WITHIN YOU

As you cultivate that practice, you will find that the peace that is already within you, that you have touched a thousand times in a million different ways, begins to grow more constant—like the rays of the sun beginning to filter through the fog that has settled into the mountain valley obscuring the clarity of all things. Your peace descends gently, like a dove, descending as some would say, through the crown of the head, down through the brain-mind, and down even to the heart, the abdomen, and throughout the cells of the body, while the body lasts. *Chakras*

Gently relinquishing the world rests on your decision to choose to teach only Love, because you have realized that when you do not, the effect that you know immediately is painful, conflicted, unfulfilling, and that that is what you no longer want.

Here, you have begun to transcend the world that you have made and to reclaim the world made for you, a world that rests in perfect union, in the union of Father and son, God and offspring, Creator and created. The way *is* easy and without effort.

What value have you ever placed upon the world that has restored to you the peace that you seek? You have mistakenly thought, "Oh, this automobile will do it; this relationship will do it; this new career will do it. If only I can take a trip to the far corners of the world, *then* I will be at peace." And so peace never quite comes.

A creator, abiding in enlightenment, knows that all events are neutral, so neutral that they have no effect, except for those who choose to be caught up in illusions. The creator, awakened, merely creates out of devotion to the mystery of That which has created him or her. The mind of an enlightened creator does not arise in the morning and say, "How can I survive yet another day in this world?" In the morning, when an enlightened creator arises, the question is:

How this day might I extend the treasure of the good, the holy, and the beautiful?

 How can I, right where I am, experience these treasures
even within the space and volume of this body?

How can I look lovingly upon what my physical eyes show me,
so that I discern or extract the good, the holy, and the beautiful,
and therefore, give them to myself?

The mind of an enlightened creator *knows* that of themselves, they do nothing. But in each moment of decision, they can *allow* the great power and mystery of Love to direct their course. They can utilize time to refine their ability to hear *only* the voice for Love, moment by moment, breath by breath, day by day, until time is translated into eternity. And the mind rests, reclines, in its perfect union with God.

Events still occur. The world is still what the world will choose to be, unaware that there walks in its midst one who is awake, who needs to make no show. They merely *are* the presence of wakefulness, knowing that in each moment they will now be *in*formed by the guidance of the Comforter, the guidance of right-mindedness, the guidance of enlightenment. So that they are no longer attached to fearing, "What should I say? What should I do? How will this person take it? How will that person take it?" The world is no longer a concern.

They experience their very life as an ongoing flowing mystery, as though something else were living through them. This is the meaning of my friend's words, "Let that *Mind* be in you which was in our Lord, Christ Jesus," as you would read in your Bible. That *Mind* is the Mind of perfect freedom. It does not belong to anyone, but it can be cultivated to flow through you.

But only—*only*—if every fiber of your beingness is wholly committed to holiness. You cannot leave a finger outside and get to Heaven. *All* of your mind, *all* of your energy, *all* of your gifts, *all* of your very awareness must become committed to being the presence of peace. *This* is what no one can do for you. Sitting at the feet of enlightened teachers will not do it *for* you.

The wisest of students are those that hear the word and put it into practice, diligently, *for themselves*—not for their mother, not for their father, not for their spouse, not for their brother, not for their sister, not for the sake of the planet, not for the sake of the universe, not for the sake of the new dawn that is coming, not for the sake of anything but themselves. For their Self is what God created. And that Self calls out to you to honor it, by separating your Self from the illusions that you have allowed to make a home in your mind, and becoming wholly committed to teaching only Love.

There is no other way. Yes, you can learn to sit in meditation and allow the mind and body to float free, to relax. Yes, you can learn rituals that help to focus your attention so that you remember what you are committed to, and the distractions of the world do not seem to quite catch you or hook you as much. There are many strategies that you can enjoy and experience. But in the end, it is only this: a quiet choice within that no one recognizes, that no one sees, that no one hears.

This is why I once shouted at the Pharisees, "Oh yes, you indeed get your reward standing on the street corners letting everybody know that you are fasting and praying, when you should go into your own closet to pray." That is, to be in your own privacy, making not a show, but simply using each moment to reaffirm your commitment to learning all that Love is by teaching it. By the word *teach*, I mean simply that you choose to express only Love in each moment.

Forgiveness is an act through which you learn what Love is, that carries you into a transcendence of the world. Sharing only loving thoughts—supportive thoughts—as you look gently upon the Christ in another is a way that takes you into the transcendence of the world. Looking upon all things of this world and seeing their perfect harmlessness, their lack of ability to constrain you or imprison you, is a way that takes you beyond the world.

And yet all of these things rest on the practice of "seeking first the Kingdom," which means not to believe in me, not to have some theological notion about what God is, not to adhere to a certain religion, or a certain church doctrine. *The Kingdom of Heaven is within you.* It *is* the very power of choice. Which pebble will you drop into the pool of your consciousness?

Imagine reaching a point where, just prior to every action that you engage—without ritual, without difficulty, without the grand shows and displays, the burning of incense and the lighting of forty million candles and all of the Gregorian chants or the rock and roll or whatever you choose, without *any* of it—in the silent temple of your heart, you make a simple choice:

> ♓ In this moment, I am going to discover what it means to teach only Love.

It might be a simple smile. It might be to let your eyes gaze at the beauty of a flower, and say, "Ah, it is very good." It might be to eat your breakfast and actually *be* there while you are eating it, instead of letting your mind run off to the office.

Here, beloved friends, is the way to the Truth that sets you free. You must absolutely become wholly committed to being awake for no other reason than that you have realized you have no other choice. You have already made them all and they have only led to pain.

RECOGNIZING THE PRESENCE OF CHRIST WITHIN

Your Self is calling out to be recognized for what it is—an awakened master, the presence of Christ in you that would inform every step, inform every decision, inform the quality of your perception, inform the very nature of your forever-expanding, transparent consciousness. For it is your consciousness, alone, that can reach out and embrace all created things, until you literally realize that all things have arisen from within you!

That is how *big* you are! That is how *grand* you are! Why? Because that is *all* you are! You are the ocean from which waves and waves of dimensions and worlds have arisen. *That Mind* is what you are required to let be in you, even as once it was within me, as I walked upon your Earth. Do not make it difficult.

Whenever you hear of a teacher teaching this or a teacher teaching that, ask yourself this: Do they offer me simplicity or complexity? Do they offer an ordinary peace, or must I have several trappings around me? Do they give me complex meditations and prayers and things to do, or do they simply remind me of the Truth and ask me to rest in it? Will they tell me that I need to go on a thousand pilgrimages? Or do they remind me that when I make my cup of tea in the morning, Heaven is present, if I will remember who is making the tea? Christ is.

Be, therefore, not distracted. For in the end of this age, there is coming forth a whole smorgasbord of those who profess to be teachers of enlightenment who will guide you into all knowledge. Look carefully, do they demand of you that you follow them? Do they demand of you that you give up your own discernment?

Or do they ask you to look deeper within? Do they ask you, "What are *you* feeling? What do *you* think? What do *you* want to do? Are *you* willing to accept responsibility for the effect? What do *you* believe? What do *you* want? You are free. I am equal to you. I am just in the role of a temporary guide for you and some day you will be far beyond me."

How do they speak? What do they teach? Is their fear filtering into their words? Do they believe that they must teach you to control the forces of nature, the forces of the mind? Do they teach you to protect yourself against evil? There are many who profess to be teachers of enlightenment, and there will be many more. When you hear these things coming from them, turn and flee from their presence! For you do not need them. You are already beyond them.

Ask only:

How can I extend my treasure this day?

And lay up treasures where moth and dust cannot corrupt, that is, where time, materiality, the body and the world cannot "hook you." Rather lay up treasures that are in Heaven: forgiveness, peace, unlimitedness, recognition of your unlimited power, that which brings you joy and puts a smile upon your countenance. Lay up for yourself these treasures and all things shall be added unto you.

For there is a way of being in the world that requires no planning or striving, though to enter it does require the relinquishing of fear. To enter it requires a commitment to teaching only Love, until the mind is again whole and undivided.

There is a way of being in the world that is not here at all. The body still abides. Yes, you still act just like everybody thinks you act. That is, they know your name; they know where you live. You know which car you are supposed to drive; you know whom you go home to at night. But through it all, there is pervaded in your consciousness a transparency as you look upon all things.

Whatever feelings arise, come and go. But somehow you begin to recognize that you are much larger than the things that come and go, that you are watching a dance of shadows, a dream, gently passing by, that is gone in a cosmic split second. This does not become a way in which you *deny* your experience. Rather, it gives you the freedom to embrace it and live it totally, with passion, with purpose, with power, and in perfect freedom—no anxiety, no pressure, just the willingness to dance in the world of dreams, while remaining awake.

If, indeed, you have been putting your five minutes into practice, you are already carrying yourself closer and closer, or perhaps more and more deeply, into the transparency I am describing for you.

And that transparency grows to a point—you might think of it as a critical mass—when suddenly you as a beingness can no longer even hold the thought of yourself as a body in space and time. Then the body simply dissolves away, and your consciousness will never experience the limitations of the body again. But you will bring the joys that bodily experience taught you with you, for they are imprinted in your consciousness forever.

This Earth is a beautiful place, but it is only a pale reflection of the radiant, transcendent beauty of the good and the holy that pervades my Father's creation. Love it, embrace it, thank it, but do not cling to it.

Learn, then, to teach only Love.

A SIMPLE PRACTICE

Now, to build on what you have been doing, we would simply ask you to add this very simple practice. When you sit in your chair for five minutes abiding as Christ, remembering the Truth that has set you free, begin to ask yourself the simple question:

> ✳   This day, how can I extend my treasure?
> How can I add to that which I am storing up in the Heaven
> of my consciousness?

Immediately, you will begin to get pictures—an old friend who needs a phone call, someone to write a letter to. It could be something as simple as picking up your cat, placing it upon your lap, and seeing all of infinity in that living being, and feeling the joy that comes as you run your hand along its fur. It could be something as grand as going to Washington, D.C. in order to send a blessing to your president. It does not matter what it is because that voice of Love will be guiding your actions. It may be as simple as turning to your spouse and saying, "You know, I appreciate you."

Whatever it is, let the day not fade away until that action is accomplished, or at least set into motion.

So the great question is:

> Am I willing to trust the flow from My Father's Mind, through my
> own, as that which empowers me to extend my treasure?

Yes, it does mean living unlike the way the world lives. Yes, it does mean going against the grain. You may seem to need to apply more energy to it at first, as you get the momentum of your mind to turn in another direction, to shake loose all of the sludge that has settled into your consciousness.

But I can promise you, if you will take up such a path—simply, joyfully, gently, patiently— *the end of your journey is certain.* If you choose a path filled with magic and many complex strategies, the end is not so certain. The way is easy and without effort:

> I am already That which I seek. I need only allow it to guide me.
> While this body lasts, I will allow it to be a communication device
> that extends the treasure of perfect Love, perfect safety,
> and perfect peace to all who enter my house.

And your *house* is your field of energy, the expanse of your presence.

Toward the end of your five minutes, look at yourself from within your mind's eye, as though from the day you began this course until now, you have journeyed around a circle.

You have journeyed through many influences of energy. You have engaged yourself in relationship with countless brothers and sisters. You have had thousands of visions and dreams and revelations come to your consciousness. You have had umpteen million opportunities to be disturbed and lose your peace. You have been like a sojourner, the prodigal son or daughter who has gone out through the realms of human consciousness and *now* you see yourself completing the circle.

CELEBRATE YOUR RE-BIRTH AS CHRIST

Count the days, from this day until the twenty-fifth of December. Or if you are reading these words at another time of year, simply choose a date—approximately seven weeks in the future—signifying for you *your* day of re-birth.

Let each day be seen as a step, a pilgrimage, a completion of a very ancient circle. Let each day be one in which you reaffirm your commitment to releasing everything unlike Love in yourself, so that as you come to December twenty-fifth or your appointed day, you will dedicate yourself to being prepared for it.

On December twenty-fourth or the eve of your chosen day, go to bed early enough, and in quiet and in prayer, so that you can awaken before the first rays of the new day come to caress the Earth.

Take yourself outdoors, even if you must bundle up the body. Make haste to a place of vision, a place where you can look out over wherever you live. Let that represent your ability to look out over all of creation.

There, turn to face the direction of the arising sun, and go into a simple prayer. Close your eyes. Realize that you see nothing through the physical eyes anyway. Stand with the arms at the sides and the palms open. Breathe deeply into the body, relax the mind, and begin simply to say within yourself:

> Death has occurred, and now the birth of Christ is at hand.
> Father, I accept fully your will for me. Your will is only
> that I be happy and use time to extend my treasure.
> Now, I receive the warmth of your Light and your Love.

Then, merely stand and wait, and receive the warmth of the light. For rest assured, even if the skies are cloudy, as the sun arises, there is a change in the energy of the air. If you are quiet, you can feel how it begins to affect the energy sphere of your awareness and of your body. Drink that solar energy in through every cell of your body. Drink it in until you feel your very spinal column warmed.

And when the whole body—from the crown of the head to the tips of the toes and down through each finger—is filled with light, then gently open the eyes of Christ, and let yourself see a new world, a new creation, a new beginning. Now the journey *to* the Kingdom is over, and the journey *within it* can begin. Graduate school is just around the corner.

When you journey back to your home on that December twenty-fifth morning or the morning of your chosen day, do something that celebrates *your* birthday—not mine— *yours*. I can handle taking care of my own celebration. Be joyous and celebrate in whatever way you wish. And know that the new age, the new day, has dawned. Never again will you ever be able to convince yourself that there is an excuse for believing in anything that is less than an enlightened Christ consciousness.

Regardless of when you may be reading these words, the same truth applies. Choose a date, approximately seven weeks in the future, to signify *your* day of re-birth. And surrender to this process I have described each day until that day arrives.

Your instruction is given. Reflect well on what has been given, for we have been stepping into some very simple, but very powerful initiations that were once given to me as I too awakened to the reality that only Christ dwells within me.

Beloved friends, reflect well on all that has been shared. Do not take it lightly, although it is only filled with light. Consider well each phrase, each sentence, and even the spaces between the words. For in those spaces, revelations can come. It is time to birth fully the presence of the peaceful Christ within you!

Peace be unto you always. And always am I with you. Amen.

A MEDITATION INTO THE
HEART OF CHRIST

"A beckoning, ." come "be" with me
become nearer (not follow)
or follow

Join with me in this moment. Join with me in the place where alone two minds *can* join, for the body cannot bring you to where I am. Join with me in the silent place of the heart in which all wisdom already abides. Join with me then in this moment in the place prepared for us of our Creator, before time is.

Join with me by choosing *now* to allow your attention to relax from the things of the world. Allow the eyes to gently close for just a moment, as a symbol of your willingness to set aside your involvement with and your attachment to the things of this created world. Join with me by allowing the body to be set free. This requires only that you make no demands upon it. Indeed, let it settle in, as though it was becoming again the dust of the ground from which it came.

Join with me as you let your attention recede from the world around you. Begin to notice the thoughts that seem to stream through the mind. Join with me by moving ever yet deeper, as though you were allowing your attention to settle down, down, into the heart. And as the thoughts stream through the mind, can you tell from whence they have come? Can you tell where they have gone? They arise in a moment and fade away in a moment, while *you* continue to relinquish your attachment to all things of the world.

physical heart vs. energetic heart

Verily I say unto you, even the thoughts that arise and stream through the mind ceaselessly are of the world. Settle down then, abiding in the gentle quiet of the heart. You do not cause the physical heart to beat and send the blood through the body. It simply knows, and it does. You do not cause the breath to flow through the body. It arises and passes away. It does not require your attention.

And in this moment, is it you that keeps the stars in the sky above you? Is it you that keeps your beautiful Earth spinning, hurtling through space, around and around your central sun, never deviating very much at all from the same orbit it has been in since its creation? Must you attend to the quiet unseen way in which the flowers outside your window are growing? Can you hear the sound of the grass as it grows?

Somewhere in this very moment, a child has been birthed. Are you aware of it? Indeed, all of creation continues to go on, an eternal dance, mystery giving birth to mystery and returning to mystery without ceasing. Yet, you simply abide in a quiet place within the sanctuary of the heart.

Join with me now in perfect peace. Join with me where alone we can remember that we are together. Give up all hope of directing yourself to me by taking thought. Join with me in the simple understanding that of yourself, you can do nothing. Join with me by surrendering into the truth of a union beyond all comprehension. Settle deeply into the quiet sanctuary of the Heart we share.

That Heart is the depth and the essence of the Creator's *only* creation. That creation is pure Mind, pure Being, pure Intelligence, the fulfillment of all wisdom, the depth of all compassion, the *certainty* of every purpose under Heaven.

Rest with me, and acknowledge that our minds are joined. As you rest, again, you might notice that thoughts seem to arise and pass away. But do you not sense them, now, as though they were coming from a place where *you* are not, as though you had sunk more deeply to a place of quiet beneath the surface upon which thoughts flow back and forth without ceasing?

Are you, then, the thoughts? No, you are not. Are you even the thinker of the thoughts? No, you are not. You are merely that quiet and that presence that observes all of creation flowing through a field of awareness that *is* the Mind of Christ. Unlimited forever are you. Unchanging forever are you. Perfectly changeless are you. We are of one substance, one Light and one Truth. Here alone does reality reside. Here alone is reality remembered. Here alone Love reigns supreme. Here alone is where you are.

In this place that is everywhere at once, and in this eternity that embraces every moment of time, what do we discover? What is it that we share? It is not a body. For bodies are limited, being temporary expressions of the coalescence of thought. It is not the body that we can share. Look yet more deeply. Is it the thoughts that still dance upon the surface far above you? No. What is it, then, that binds us one to another, *as* one another? Is it not the silence and the awareness of the One who observes the arising and passing away of all created things?

I share with you the depth of a perfect silence. I share with you wisdom supreme. I abide *as you are:* the thought of Love in form. To be in form does not mean to be a body. It means only that the Christ Mind, which is the reality of Love's existence, truly abides within each of us equally. If this were not so, you could not recognize me. When you read a word, or a sentence, or a paragraph that resonates within you as being the truth, you could not know it was so, if that Truth did not already live within you as the reality of your very existence.

Remain with me now. Heed not the call of that part of the mind that would distract you and lead you back to the illusions that comprise your world. Here, there are no mates, no careers, no loss, no gain, no pain, no suffering. Here alone, the Truth remains shimmering within you. Here is where I am. And this heart that we share is not contained within your body. Rather, the body has emerged from within the power that resides in this holy place. It has provided for you only a temporary learning experience. It will be there when you return, should you desire it.

But for now, give yourself permission to rest into the heart of all creation—the still and silent place of perfect peace. What is it that we share, if not awareness itself? For here, if anyone were to look, they would see there is no difference between you and myself. You are a shimmering field of awareness. And that same shimmering field comprises the essence of *all* that I am.

HERE IS THE PLACE OF CERTAINTY, POWER, AND FULFILLMENT

Within this awareness lies the answer to every question you might choose to ask. Within this shimmering awareness is the reassurance that the end of the journey is certain. Within this shimmering awareness do you abide *at one* with all minds and every aspect of creation. Join with me here often, in remembrance of me. For this is the secret of communion—to relinquish the perception of the world in favor of the acknowledgment of Reality.

Mind reaches out forever, but it reaches only to *itself.* Therefore, every word that I share with you is already present within you. Here alone, does Love abide. There is no space for anything unlike Love. This is why every loving thought is true. For it arises not from the superficial or the surface level of the mind that generates thoughts merely in reaction to other thoughts. But Love emerges from the depth of the heart that transcends what you know to be your body and your mind, your feedback mechanism.

When you think a loving thought, you have been caressed by the touch of God. When you hear not loving thoughts within yourself, this can mean only that you have returned to the surface, and have denied the depth within you.

If you would hear only loving thoughts, simply observe where your attention is. And allow it to settle deeply into this place, beyond time, beyond the body, beyond the dream of the world. For this place—the Kingdom of Heaven within you—is vast beyond comprehension. The world you know when you take your attention to the surface of the mind is contained and embraced within this heart, like a dewdrop begins to be consumed by the ocean that receives it.

Here, beloved friends, is the place of all certainty. Here is the place of perfect power to fulfill the loving thoughts with which your Creator has caressed you. Here is the way to fulfill each loving vision. Here is the source of all wisdom upon which you can draw to recreate yourself to *be* the presence of Christ incarnate.

Here then, is the straight and narrow path that leads unto Life. For Life is beyond every concept you have ever heard, even those that I have used to communicate with you. They have been like so many fingers, pointing at the moon that shines its light gently upon you. That light lives in the depth of a silent heart. Therefore, silence is the doorway to wisdom divine.

Remain with me here. Do not think on what you read, but allow it to pour through you, knowing that the vibrations of wisdom that these words carry will leave their trace upon you, without the least bit of effort on your part. You need only be as a lover to the Mind of God—opening, allowing, receiving—taking in that which your Creator would bestow upon you.

Remain with me in the depth of this perfect silence. Notice how you begin to feel a gentle spaciousness, a peace descending upon you, like a gentle dove—and yet, you have done nothing. And again, should you feel your attention being pulled back to the surface of your awareness, merely choose again, and return to the quiet of the heart.

I am loved, I am loving, I am lovable forever. Let this phrase be as a stairway that descends from the world of your making to the depth of perfect peace. You need repeat it only when you notice that you have become temporarily distracted by the sights and sounds and images of the world around the body, as well as the thoughts that seem to stream and dance along the surface of the brain center.

> ✴   I am loved, I am loving, I am lovable forever.

As you come to feel grounded, rooted in that deep and silent place, ask whatsoever you will and its answer shall not be hidden from you. Ask to witness my lifetime as I walked upon your Earth, and it will be shown to you. Ask to be shown the vibrational field in which you were conceived in this life; it will not be hidden from you. Ask whatever you would about a friend, who perhaps has seemed troubled of late, and the source of what is occurring within them will be gently revealed to you.

For remember that in this place, you are awareness itself, merely becoming aware of itself. That awareness, that consciousness, lives equally as the essence of each and every one whom you know and love. Your love of them is what binds you to them, in the depth of a quiet awareness.

As you descend the stairway to the quiet place of the heart, there are a few things to leave behind you. Leave behind the need to be right, the need to be supported in your illusions, the fear of rejection, abandonment, denial, and death. Leave behind every thought of what the world is and what it is for. Leave behind every thought you have ever held of everyone and everywhere.

Surrender, relinquish the world of your perceptions, and come quietly to kneel before your Creator. There, in the silent place of the heart, unattached to whatever is given you or shown you, *nothing* will be kept secret. Would you know the foundations of the world? The answer is here. Would you know how to best direct Love to a loved one? The answer is here. A voice will speak to you, like one crying from the wilderness. Pictures will be shown to you, feelings enlivened within you, and you will know the way to extend your treasure.

Remain with me here, for here do I abide. The only difference between us is that occasionally you believe that you abide somewhere else. When you journey up those stairs, to begin to be distracted by the thoughts on the surface of your mind and by the sensory feedback of the energy field that comprises your physical creation, I remain in our shared heart, patiently waiting for your return.

Remain with me here:

> I am loved, I am loving, and I am lovable forever.
> This is the Truth that sets me free—I am That I Am.
>
> My awareness knows no limitation and all worlds arise within me.
> I am that Mind, present in all beings when they descend the stairway
> and embrace the Truth that alone is true always.
>
> Here is perfect peace.
> Here is the recognition that nothing is lacking.
> Here is the embrace of the fulfillment of the Love I have sought
> in all the wrong places.
>
> Here alone, do I abide.
> Here alone, do I remain.
> I am That One, existing before all worlds.
> This alone is the Truth about me.

These words are not mine, they are *ours*. And we share in them, equally. I am loved, I am loving, I am lovable forever. I am That I Am.

Out of the depth of that perfect silence and the remembrance of that perfect knowledge, there comes the impulse of a loving thought:

Take Me into form. Take Me into space and time. Reveal Me to the world.

Your life can become—whenever you choose it to be so—merely the process of Christ's incarnation. Relinquish the world, even as you walk through it. Surrender it with every breath. Learn to cultivate the depth of this knowing in the midst of all activities in which the body is used as a temporary learning and teaching device.

Beloved friends, abide with me in this *union*. Regardless of what the eyes of the body show you, regardless of what the ears of the body hear, regardless of the "harmless" thoughts that seem to dance across the surface of the brain-mind, you abide where I am, *in*formed by that Love from which there has been birthed the sun, the moon, and all of the stars of Heaven, the planets in their orbits, and all dimensions within our Father's creation.

You can realize the incarnation of Christ by coming to dwell in the Heart of Christ, until every step, every word, and every gesture flows from this deep and silent and perfect place, until *its* voice is the only one upon which you act.

Even as the thoughts of the world stream through your brain-mind, even as the sensory data are received through the cellular structures of the nervous system of the body, you can relinquish these things, and act only from that depth of perfect wisdom, perfect safety and perfect peace. Let this be a time of "thanksgiving." Will it be that time in which you truly give thanks for the grace that sets you free? Will you honor that grace by descending the stairway to the quiet places of the heart in each of your days?

I am loved, I am loving, and I am lovable forever.
I am That I Am: infinite awareness—birthless, deathless—that which embraces
the dream of space and time, and looks lovingly upon all harmless and
neutral events.

Even the body is no longer mine. It merely arises and passes away, while I,
the creator of all creation, inform it with the awareness of perfect forgiveness,
perfect peace, and the fulfillment of Love.

Yea, though I walk through the valleys of space and time, fear arises not
within me. For all good things are in my safekeeping, stored where moth and
dust cannot corrupt, where thieves cannot break in to steal.

Here alone, is the treasure that I seek no longer because I have found!

Abide here with me, until the hour comes when you know that you will go out no more from our Father's holy place. That place is this depth of peace that abides wherever you are as the very heart and essence of your reality:

I am loved, I am loving, and I am lovable forever.

This I give you as a divine meditation and way of prayer. Perfect it! Live it! Drink it in! Embrace it! Devour it! Become it! For in this becoming, you will merely *remember* what has always been true since before the arising of all worlds.

As a bird returns to rest in its nest, as the melting snow becomes a river that flows into the depth of a silent ocean, so too be you wise as serpents and dissolve into this depth of the Truth of your being often, until you abide here in every *where* and every *when*.

And when the body steps upon the Earth, the touch of the foot upon the earth will remind you of Christ's blessing. And when the vocal chords are used to form words, the words that shape themselves will teach only Love. Here then, beloved friend is the essence of all that I would extend to you in this lesson.

Now practice gently descending and ascending upon the ladder of awareness. Give yourself permission to ascend, to notice the thoughts that stream through the mind. Hear the sounds around you. Feel the weight of the body in the chair where you sit, and then descend again. Abide a little while.

Then again choose to ascend. Listen to the sounds around you, the beating of the physical heart. Shift the weight of the body. Notice the thoughts that stream through the surface of the mind. Relinquish these things, and descend again, gently ascending and descending. For as you do so, you will join both poles together. And you will cultivate within yourself the awareness and the spiritual power necessary *to be in the world, but not of the world.*

Can there be a greater accomplishment than this? Can there be anything that can offer to you a greater fulfillment than to be the conduit through which infinite awareness and power flows with every breath, every gesture, every spoken word—to reveal Christ to the world through you? What could you ever value greater than this?

Enjoy, then, your practice. Know that when you descend to that place of the silent heart within you, I will greet you and I will sit with you in the depth of that silence. And our minds and our hearts and our souls shall merge as one. When you ascend, you take me with you. And when you descend, you drink me into yourself, until finally there is no difference between us. When the world looks upon you, they will say:

Behold, I am in the presence of something mysterious, something

attractive, something vast and peaceful and filled with power.
Surely, this is the Child of God!

From that Mind that we share as *one*, I say again unto you:

> May peace walk with you.
> My blessings I give unto you, not as the world gives,
> give I the voice for Christ that longs to be your voice.
> For the world gives and takes away, but my Love is with you forever.
> Let this Love become your very own. Claim it. Own it. Taste it.
> Drink it. Breathe it. Walk it. Talk it.
> Incarnate it!

Though I go now to recede into silence, yet do I walk with you on the way that you will choose, that it might become a way that extends the treasure of your perfect knowledge that you are loved, that you are loving, and that you *are* lovable forever. [That you are, indeed, That which you are. And you cannot be anything else!] Gently touch each moment with that which you bring from what you discover in the depth of your journey into the Heart of Christ.

Peace be with you always and light your way while yet you abide within the world. You are, indeed, sent forth as Christ who holds all power to extend the treasure of Truth. Be you, therefore, That which you are—and you *are* the stars that light the heavens and bring radiance to the things of time. *Go you, therefore, into all the world and bless it with the radiance of the Christ within you.*

✱ If ever you need to know where you should be, descend to that depth. And when you ascend, open the eyes and bless the place where you are. In this is your purpose fulfilled.

Peace be unto you always. Amen.

We have included an audio recording of this guided meditation in the back of this book.

LESSON 12
RECEIVE THE PEARLS OF GRACE

Once again, we come forth to abide with you and to celebrate with you. Once again, we come to abide with the holy Mind that *is* the Sonship. We come to abide with our brothers and sisters, and we come *as* brothers and sisters. Indeed, we come forth to abide in that process whereby the Sonship is remembering itself as the son. Indeed, beloved friends, I come forth to share that with you that already resides within you.

I come forth—*we* come forth—to join with you who have chosen to answer a certain call to bring forth a creative expression that can signify to the world the Truth that alone can set this world free. Free of what? Free of fear and all of the children that fear begets—guilt, dishonesty, unworthiness, limitation, need for suffering, judgment, and the list goes on and on.

Ultimately, when a gardener seeks to improve the quality of the soil from which he would want his flowers to bloom forth, the gardener seeks not to look upon the effects of a weed, or that which is above the surface. But rather, he makes haste and goes for the root. When the root has been pulled up, the effects of that weed can no more be seen.

Therefore, in truth, we come not to improve what you would be thinking of as the surface of the garden, the surface of the soil, but to strike at the root that resides deep within the mind, in the depth that I have called the heart or the soul. All that we endeavor to do, then, is designed to *up*root the weed of fear that has made a home in the depth of your being.

The Way of the Heart has been designed to bypass the cognitive or thinking mind, and to strike at the roots of fear that abide in the depth of the mind in a place that is, by and large, unconscious. *All* that we do seeks to dissolve *that root* from the depth of your being.

These first twelve lessons have required you to *truly* participate with the devotion necessary to extract the wisdom that has been offered to you. We cannot do this *to* you; we can only do it *with* you. For never can anything be forced upon the mind of the Son of God. The Holy Spirit makes no effort to usurp, or take from you, your freedom. For in your freedom, all power under Heaven and Earth resides.

DISCOVER THE OBSTACLES TO LOVE

Grace does not descend until your Father knows that you are willing to prepare a place to receive it. This is why, in the process of healing and awakening, it is not necessary to *seek* for Love. It is only necessary to prepare the place, the soil, by choosing to discover the *obstacles* to Love—which all come down to fear—and to be willing to loosen that root, that it might be removed from the garden of your consciousness.

Then, the rain of grace that purifies, transforms, awakens, and brings Christ consciousness to the mind can descend gently. For when the rain falls upon hard ground, it strikes the soil and runs off, and the garden remains barren. But the wise gardener, who has softened the soil, reached in and begun to pull up the roots, sifted the soil and made it soft, open and porous with the intent of bringing forth a beautiful garden, will, indeed, be assisted. Then, the rain of grace will fall gently, without it being earned. It is given freely.

Drops of grace have been offered to you in each and every lesson. Some you have received; some you have not noticed. Some are waiting to penetrate the deeper levels of your consciousness as you continue in your willingness to release fear. Suddenly, a pearl of grace that has not yet been received will sink deep. Then, the recognition will come; the awakening will come.

Suddenly you will find yourself saying, "Wait a minute. This insight, this vision, this realization I've just had sounds like something that was in the first lesson. I think I'll go back and have another look. Yes, there it is! I wonder why I didn't notice it the first time?" It is simply the natural process in which the drops of rain of grace had not yet a place to be received.

Understand then—and this is of great importance as we move into this next part of *The Way of Mastery*—that all that transpires from *this* point rests on how well the gardener has cultivated the soil with the tools that have been given. If they have not been utilized, the soil remains hard, and the drops of rain run off and pool in the side of the garden, waiting for the soil to be properly prepared.

Of all that has been given that can continue—and will continue—to serve you the greatest will be the simple five-minute practice of abiding as Christ. And observing all that you see, all that you feel, all that you think, as though a perfectly awakened Christ was the *only* one sitting in the chair.

I know that this sounds simplistic for you, but the way *is* easy and without effort. Complexity is born of the world, and not from the Mind of God. Therefore, continue well in that practice, and allow it to be the foundation from which the soil is prepared—the roots of fear are loosened—even in ways that you cannot comprehend with the thinking mind. For the roots of fear are not merely ideas. They are the effects of ideas. They have been allowed to penetrate deep into the unconscious.

This is why the next twelve lessons, called The Way of Transformation, require not striving, but allowing; not thinking, but letting go into *feeling;* not doing, but trusting.

Those roots of fear must be dissolved at a level that is deeper than the conscious thinking mind can reach. The mind was never designed to be your master, but to become aligned as a servant of the awakened heart, just like the flower blooms and sends forth its scent for all to see from the depth of the soil that is unseen, but has been well prepared. So that the only roots that gather nourishment from the soil are the roots of that which speaks of Life and beauty, not that which speaks of fear and unworthiness.

Seek you, then, to seek no more. For the place is prepared for you, and you need only go *to* it. Therefore, we will be cultivating more deeply the art of surrendering, resting ever more deeply into that place of silence which is the threshold to perfect wisdom divine. The Way of the Heart is the preparation of the soil that allows The Way of Transformation to truly occur.

Transformation is not complete unless it envelops, encompasses and is expressed through the very life you know, right there on your speck of dust, whirling about one sun in a small part of one universe. Expressed on your Earth and in your time frame, your relationships, your experience and in your life as you know it, as you live it, as you breathe it, as you *feel* it!

So, let the breath flow and realize that you have the freedom to go back over the previous lessons and see if there is anything that you missed. As you do that, do it from a place of Christedness:

> I am that one choosing to enter The Way of Transformation whereby human
> consciousness, the human lived experience, becomes the living expression,
> the fruit which has sprung forth from the soil in which the roots of grace,
> Love, and healing have been well planted.

Do this not from the perspective that you are doing something amiss. But out of the desire to be the master gardener, who brings forth that fruit which extends beauty and the scent of joy for all to receive, for all to see, for all to marvel.

Yet, that beauty that springs forth from the gardener's beautiful garden does not build up the ego of the master gardener, for a master gardener knows that he or she has only been the keeper of the soil. But the magic that brings forth the flower is not his or her possession, it is merely that which they have been given stewardship over: consciousness.

Consciousness is the gift of Life, streaming forth from the Mind of God. Your mind, then, is the soil of the garden. All awakening and all transformation occur nowhere save in that garden.

Some of you are still seeking to understand the mind by seeing it as something that is locked inside the shape of your skull, and is somehow co-habitating with what you call the gray matter of the brain. Rest assured, your mind is unlimited forever. The body that sits in the chair in your five-minute exercise is as a drop of foam being expressed at the slightest tip of one wave in an infinite ocean. That ocean is itself within the unlimited expanse of your mind. You are consciousness as such—pure Spirit!

The only question, then, is this. Are you willing to allow that drop of foam to be transformed into that which fully and always expresses only the Love of God, even though that expression is still temporary because the body has arisen in the field of time and disappears in the field of time? Are you willing to say, "What the heck!" and allow that Love to be as *fully embodied* as it is possible for it to be, for the split second that the body is in this world?

Expressing mastery is the effect of The Way of Transformation in *this* world, in *this* time, in *this* little tiny moment. Rest assured, to the degree that you turn your attention to expressing mastery, to the degree that you use time wisely to be the embodied Christ, when the body drops away and it veils from you no longer the magnificence of the *Light you are*, the light will not be blinding to you. You will not contract in fear. You will merely let this world go gently and as easily as a child has put away a toy that has been outgrown, because its usefulness is complete.

All that you see—the body, your relationships, your devices, and your stars, your winds and your waters—will eventually be put aside by you. Not out of denial, but simply out of recognizing that their usefulness is over.

Indeed, beloved friends, as we come then to the completion of the first twelve lessons, look well to see that no drops of grace have been ignored. Open the heart ever more deeply. Allow those pearls, those drops of grace, to penetrate ever more deeply, not just as ideas in the thinking mind, but as *feelings* in the cells of the body.

Let it create for you a sweetness in the flow of breath, a sensitivity in the way your foot rests upon the soil of the Earth with each step. Let it begin to transform the way in which you rest your hand upon the shoulder of your brother or sister. Allow that sweetness to permeate your gaze as you look upon another—seeing the Christ within them that is growing into a beautiful flower whose scent and beauty will be as a blessing to many. There is no one among you who is not the evolving Christ. Remember always that what you *see* is what you *get*, in the same way that as you teach, you learn.

A MEDITATION OF RELEASE

Look well, then, and ask yourself this:

✝ Who do I know in my existence who I have judged, and locked
into a certain box, and I have decided that is all they are?

There you will find a fruitful meditation for reflection. I would suggest that you use the next thirty days to take time and use it wisely to allow the names, the images, and the faces of those that you have judged to come back to you and to say:

✝ You know, mother, father, ex-mate (whoever it is), I get it.
I have placed you in a box and thrown away the key.
You are stuck, so I have said.
And now, I release you, that I might be released.

Contemplate their image. Allow the memories of the experiences you have shared with them to come back. If there are feelings, by all means, let yourself *feel* them. Gaze upon them in your mind, until you feel that sweetness that dissolves the imprisonment into which you have placed them. For as that imprisonment begins to melt, you will sense and know that your freedom is blossoming.

You cannot take fear into Love. You cannot take judgment into forgiveness. You cannot take limitation into unlimitedness. These things must be released at the level in which they were first created. Therefore, make note that this practice should not be overlooked. Give yourself thirty days with the goal to truly go back and shall we say, mop up any forgiveness or releasing that you need yet to do. Do not let the mind say, "I don't know if I did that well enough." For understand, it is the Comforter that releases you and the other, through your willingness to allow it to occur.

Now there are some effects. This will mean that when you have truly done that, never again do you have any justification or excuse for attaching any experience you have had or any feelings you have ever felt to the hook on the side of their imprisonment that you have placed them in. Often, the human mind, the egoic mind, wants to hang the coat of its judgment on the hook just outside the bars in which you have locked someone.

For instance, "That which I have experienced is the result of my father's alcoholism. That which I have experienced in life is the result of my mother having forty thousand affairs a week. That which I have experienced is the result of my business partner who has stolen my golden coins. That which has caused my suffering is the result of the position of the stars in the sky when I chose incarnation. If only *they* would have gotten it right, *I* would be fine."

As we conclude The Way of the Heart, I say unto you, do not enter The Way of Transformation until you have *truly* and *fully* satisfied your awareness that you are not clinging to even the subtlest iota of perception that, in any way, you are a victim of the world you see. Nothing has been caused by your relationships. All of them have merely shown you what you have already decided will be true. The world, then, is not the cause of *anything*. You merely see what you have used the freedom of your consciousness to concoct about yourself.

For example, lack is not caused by taxation. Taxation is caused by the decision to need to believe that there is a power outside of yourself that needs all of your energy. Government does not cause you to be subservient. Your sense of being subservient, guilt-ridden, weak, and limited is what births the idea of government. Then some of you as loving brothers and sisters say, "Well, I'll play that part." They become your politicians that create the disgruntled feelings that you have.

The world is uncaused by anything, save the choices you have made as a free consciousness. You have concocted the thought and then immersed yourself in that which reflects back to you what you have already decided to believe. This means that The Way of Transformation is that way in which one becomes empowered, in every moment, to become fully responsible for clearly deciding what they will see and that they will not settle for anything less. The better you get at this, the quicker it happens. Until one reaches the point where miracles occur.

Yet, they are only miraculous to those that do not understand how consciousness works. You can achieve that place in which you hold out the palm of the hand and desire the sweetest tasting apple that has ever been created, and it will, literally, appear in the palm of your hand. Of course, at that point, you will be well beyond any need whatsoever to even hold the thought of requiring physical form. *What? Heaven?*

You will begin then to get a sense of your mastery by being able to look at the world you see and observe clearly what has been changing in it. You will observe how quickly and effortlessly that which the heart truly desires—because it is in alignment with the Mind of God—becomes manifested, effortlessly. When the gap between the pure desire and the manifested reflection of it is smaller and smaller and smaller, you will literally sense in the feeling body that mastery is growing.

You will know that you are merely a Child of God playing, without ceasing, in the sandbox of all possibilities called the Mind. And that there is, literally, nothing out there that is solid, nothing out there that is unrelated to you.

So, that is where we are going if you wish to come along on the journey, if you are willing to truly become committed to uprooting every root of fear that has taken hold within the depth of the mind that has been rendered unconscious because of your hatred of yourself. It is called the separation from God. And therefore, because it has become unconscious, it has ruled you. Time to release the un-rule-able, by allowing that alone which can uproot the root of fear to come and take up its rightful place within you: Christ-Mindedness.

You have your homework before you, then. Go within and ask, "Have I taken the time to fully focus on each lesson?" You may realize, "When I read the third lesson, I was trying to watch the football game on television. I wonder if I missed something? When I read the seventh lesson, I was thinking about going out to dinner. Did I really sit with it and extract all of the pearls that were offered? Perhaps I will go back and really set aside some quiet time in which I deliberately put the world aside and hang on every word."

Yet, do so with a relaxed body and a soft breath and a non-grasping mind. Be you therefore like a sponge that allows the raindrops to be absorbed into the self, and that is all. Knowledge is not a cognitive struggle. It is not the arranging of ideas in some order that satisfies the thinking mind.

Knowledge is the receiving of a vibration that begins to soften the soil of the heart and dissolve the root of fear from your being. Knowledge is the result of the transformation of the garden that you have been given and entrusted with—the field of mind that is you. That mind pervades the body. It pervades the space around you and melds and dances with other infinite webs of relationship called other minds—energy dancing into energy, unlimited forever, out of which all things of time are birthed and pass away.

So, you see, where I abide is everywhere at once. And so do you; you simply do not know it yet. I abide with an infinite array of friends who have *realized* the Truth and have been set free. They are infinitely creating, without ceasing, that which extends their treasure, which is the good, the holy, and the beautiful. Many have given you images of choirs of angels singing the praises of God. It is the same thing.

For when extension of joy becomes free to express only the good, the holy, and the beautiful, it is like a vibration of many notes, a choir of creative consciousness, sparks of divinity, who abide in perfect unlimitedness and *know* it. And ceaselessly extend their deepest bliss by allowing the good, the holy, and the beautiful to flow through them from the infinite, mysterious, ungraspable, uncontainable Mind that is God. Just as the sunlight of the sun creates and streams through many sunbeams that extend out to the far reaches of your universe as light, out of which planets are birthed, and animals and water and trees and birds and man.

Imagine, then, *that* is your destiny—to take up your rightful place beside me, to join your brothers and sisters in infinite and perfect creativity, like a harp player who ceaselessly runs the fingers across the strings creating the most beautiful notes. The combinations never cease.

In every moment, you experience the fruit of the flowers springing forth from the garden that you have well prepared to receive the rain of grace. The good, the holy and the beautiful flow through your unobstructed mind that rests in perfect marriage or union, with that which is your Creator, your Source, evermore, evermore, *evermore*.

Not a bad way to spend eternity! But if you look ahead, and feel that there is a distance between where you are and where that reality is, you will miss the opportunities required—right where you are—to practice where you are going, by being it *now*. You have heard it said that a journey of a thousand miles begins with the first step. And the beginning is every bit as important as the end. For in the beginning, the end is already present.

The Way of Transformation asks you to truly become present where you *are*, to deliberately and consciously cultivate, with every thought and every breath, the willingness necessary that allows the root of fear to be dissolved. So that the good, and the holy, and the beautiful are *all* that emanate from you, like a beacon being sent out to creation around you.

Do not delay. Do not *waste* time. Time can, indeed, be wasted. But listen well, for time can also waste. You have a saying we would perceive in many of your silly movies, where someone gets "wasted." How many times have *you* been the one who has said to yourself, "Well, I think I'll just waste myself"? How many ways have you gone unconscious? How many ways have you numbed your feelings? How many ways have you judged your brother or sister? How many ways have you decided to hold onto thoughts such as, "I could never do that. What's the point? It's a waste." Oh, yes! You just put a gun to your head and pulled the trigger. You have wasted *yourself* by wasting time.

Every moment is as a doorway through which the good, the holy, and the beautiful can be expressed, as the cultivation of the consciousness through which the power to do so grows. Oh, beloved friends, those moments of your time are very precious! Do not look out upon the world thinking that it is just the same old world.

Remember, then, as you begin to come to the completion of the study of The Way of the Heart, that what you see *outside* of you is only the reflection of what you have allowed to live within you. And simply ask:

> Is this what I wish to continue? What do I truly want? What is this,
> my very consciousness, for? What do I commit myself to? What do I
> say I believe? Where do I freely choose to place the power of valuation?

For what you value, you experience immediately. The world will bow down and say, "Very well. You have let us know what you value. We will mirror it back to you, because we love you, because we are a part of you. And heaven forbid that we would take away your free will."

So if you value hopelessness, the world will be a hopeless place. If you value lack of golden coins, you will continue to see lack of golden coins, which just means lack of a flow of energy. If you value loneliness, you will continue to be alone. If you value the right to be in judgment of another, you will experience the fruit of separation.

If you value sweetness, sweetness will come. If you value receiving Love—listen to this carefully—if you value *receiving* Love, the world will begin to show up at your doorstep in completely different embodiments. Different vibrations, different thought patterns will be mirrored back to you that let you receive Love. For nothing can be received until the place is prepared for it to enter. And you can only *give* what you have been willing to receive. If you receive a drop of water into your glass, that is all that you can give to another. But he that receives all, gives all. And he that gives all, receives tenfold more.

CALL FOR ASSISTANCE TO DISSOLVE FEARS

The Way of the Heart is a good beginning. We have called out to you across space and time, and if you have heard the call, the connection or the relationship with us is already established. There is, then, no bridge to cross—only the willingness to receive what is true:

Jeshua is available for me always. Mary is available for me always.

The one you would call as my friend, St. Germain, is available for you always. The entire family, lineage of masters have sought through time to create a frequency and a vibration that can dissolve the effects of the negative thinking that you have extended out of your mind, that creates the smoke and the veil around you. To dissolve that, all of us are available to you, and our number is legion!

Rest assured, you are not alone. In any moment, you need only call upon me, and I am with you. And I do not come alone! For some of you, then, we would highly suggest that in those moments when you feel like you need a little help, when fear seems to be coming up, but you know you must go ahead, whatever it be, whatever you think you are fearing, simply say:

Legions of angels and masters and friends,
whose number is infinite beyond comprehension,
you who are sent directly of God to assist me over the ditch,
come now, because I declare it and I receive it.
And therefore it *is*!

Then take the step that is necessary to take. It will not be your imagination. We will be with you. And the perfect end is certain. Fear is nothing more than the illusion you have chosen to value in order to experience what it is like to feel separate from Love. That is all. You merely waved your cosmic magic wand and said, "Let there be fear so I can experience it."

We love you. Beyond your present comprehension, we love you. Beyond all comprehension —even at what you might perceive to be our level of functioning—is the presence of God's Love, which we seek to merely pour forth to you, that by *giving*, we continually *receive*. The laws of consciousness work for us just like they work for you! We are just more aware of them.

That Love which God is, is incomprehensible forever! The sunbeam can never comprehend the sun. I am a sunbeam to that sun. You are a sunbeam to that sun. We are therefore made of one substance, and that substance alone sustains us throughout eternity. The greatest of joys is to surrender fully into allowing that Light to light your way without ceasing.

She that releases the world embraces the Creator. And he that releases fear remembers Love. She that embodies forgiveness lives at peace. And he that relinquishes control knows perfect trust. The awakened Christ that has surrendered the knot of fear, called "I," rests in unlimitedness forever, in perfect communion with all of creation. And that union never ceases. It merely expands and extends as Life comes forth, creation comes forth, extending the good, the holy, and the beautiful.

A flower that blooms in the spring for a day is the good, the holy, and the beautiful. The rays of sunlight that dance upon the oceans of this world creatively sing forth the good, the holy, and the beautiful. The bird that alights upon your fence and sings its morning song has come forth from that infinite perfect sun and its notes extend the joy of the Child of God. So, too, the smile upon one of your brothers and sisters who has received a pearl of grace through *you* is creation itself, the presence of the good, the holy, and the beautiful. Every loving thought you allow to be cultivated in the garden of your own mind extends the good, the holy, and the beautiful.

Therefore, sing that song without ceasing. Be willing, as we close The Way of the Heart, to celebrate your willingness to embrace with perfect deliberateness, your creativity and the power you have—the dominion over that which is planted in the soil of your mind. Prepare that soil well as you complete the first part of this course, that the pearls of grace might bring you into The Way of Transformation.

Celebrate *your* birth as those sunbeams that are expressed through the stories of the birth of Christ into the world. For me, it occurred two thousand years ago. Is it not time now for you to let that same birthing be fully completed in you?

Know that it has been our honor and our joy to abide with you. There is a whole host of beings encircling you every moment you remember that you have chosen to answer a call that can be traced to the very Mind of God, who has reached out to call His creation— *you*—back to Himself, so that you can deliberately extend Love without ceasing.

We give you Love. We hold you with perfect patience, knowing the Truth that is true alone, about you. And we will never leave you.

Peace, then, be unto you always. Amen.

PART TWO

THE WAY
OF TRANSFORMATION

LESSON 13
YOU ARE UNLIMITED SPIRIT

Now, we begin.

Indeed, as always, greetings unto you beloved and holy friends.

We come forth to join with you, and yet we are not apart from where you are. We are not inaccessible to any of God's children. In truth, separation does not exist in all of creation. This can only mean that I am not apart from where you are. And where you *are* has nothing at all to do with the location of the body that you have learned to call your own.

In truth, you *are* pure Spirit. In truth, you are as I am. In truth, that which you are abides throughout all dimensions of consciousness. In truth, that which you are has *never* tasted separation from God.

There is an aspect of you that has chosen to perceive yourself as identified with the physical body in your third dimensional world called space and time. This is a part of the experience you have created and thus called to your Self. But when I speak of Self, I speak not of the self which is the dream of the body, the self which you have identified yourself with. Rather, I speak of the Self that transcends all limitation and exists in all dimensions.

Beloved friends, by way of introduction to that which we will be speaking unto in the next twelve lessons called The Way of Transformation, rest with this simple truth:

At no time are you imprisoned within the body. At no time—*at no time*—are you limited to the appearance that you have come to believe is you—no matter how deep the pain, no matter how certain you have been of what you call your common sense telling you, "I am here. I am this body. This moment is happening. This is all there is." Regardless of all of that, the truth is not shaken. You are not the mere appearance of the body-mind that you have called the "self."

Now, with that simple point as a foundation, we can begin. Beloved friends, The Way of Transformation rests on exactly the same thing that all of your dreams rest upon—the decision concerning what you would be committed to. For you cannot dream a dream, that is, you cannot create an experience in the field of consciousness, without being one hundred percent committed to it. It may appear that this is not the case, but I assure you that it is.

This means that in each moment of your lived experience, what you are aware of is wholly uncaused by anything outside of yourself. As you read these words, for example, if you limit yourself to being only the body, receiving certain frequencies of vibration touching your eyes and creating a certain neurological stimulus within the brain and translating that vibration into certain words of your English language, that experience is not caused by anything outside yourself.

You are equally and infinitely free, in this very moment as you contemplate these words, to experience this transmission of vibration in a wholly different way, beyond your language. You are free to perceive yourself from the realms of pure Spirit. You are free to see me and those who join with me, as we transmit this frequency that creates the vibration through your physical form.

AN EXERCISE TO EXPAND YOUR AWARENESS

Here is a simple exercise. Take just a moment and within your consciousness, drop this simple pebble:

> I am not what I have perceived myself to be. I am unlimited, pure Spirit
> and nothing is unavailable to me. Therefore, in this moment, I choose to
> open access to other dimensions of experience so that I might call this
> moment to me in a different way.

As the words are spoken, notice what images begin to come into your field of awareness as you perhaps imagine yourself to be far more than just the body, abiding in far greater dimensions than the physical dimension. Do you see fleeting images of other beings, colors of light, subtle feelings that perhaps you had not been aware of while you were focusing on the English translation of the vibrations? What do you notice drifting through the field of your awareness? Pay attention to it, for you cannot imagine what you have not or are not experiencing.

You are the field of consciousness having that experience now. You create the capacity. You decide what will enter into the field of your awareness and how you will experience it. Beloved friends, learn to look beneath the scenes. Learn to feel beyond the body. Learn to allow yourself awareness of what steals across the metaphorical corner of your eye, that is, the *outer edges* of your field of awareness.

Come to realize that the experience you are most familiar with—that is, of being a body-mind, who reads or listens to words, which are vibrations of sound, translates them into English and, therefore, perceives that you are having a conversation with one being who happens to be another body—is a very limited perception. Recognize that around the edges of that, there is something far more vast, something which can be cultivated, that allows you to be aware at much more refined levels.

Eventually you will be able to perceive these dimensions of energy with your eyes open, as you look upon another body-mind who is currently having the experience of vibrating thoughts through it directed toward you. You call it a conversation. You will see that other being, not as a body, but as a field of light. You will see colors. You will feel vibrations. And those colors and those vibrations will tell you much more than the words could ever say to you. The result, of course, is that you will not be fooled by words nearly as often as you have been in the past.

Practice this little exercise as often as you choose in any and all circumstances. It is not difficult. You simply use the field of your consciousness to decide to be aware of what is around the edges of the third-dimensional experience you are having.

For instance, when you are in your automobile and you pull up to a red light, as you sit next to another automobile with a driver, look over through the physical eyes. If you limit yourself, you will see an automobile with another body sitting behind a wheel, similar to what your body—or what you call your body—is doing.

What if you allowed yourself to play, by looking at that being and saying within the mind, "This is but one small expression of that being; I wonder what's occurring around the edges?"

You might surprise yourself when suddenly a thought comes into your consciousness. You *know* that thought is not yours. It could be the thought of the person in the car saying, "My God, why didn't I iron my husband's shirt this morning? Oh, he's going to be so angry!" How many times have thoughts like that entered your mind and you have dismissed them as imagination?

What we are suggesting here, is to use the most ordinary moments of your day to become aware of your own being, your own naturally expanded, unlimited Self. There is nothing hidden at any time. In any moment you have full access to the totality of another soul.

Does that sound like an invasion of privacy? Beloved friends, there is no such thing. Privacy is important only for those who believe they are cut off and separate, and perhaps have something to hide. In reality, *nothing* is hidden. As you come to trust that the deep nature of your own being is perfect wisdom, perfect compassion, and perfect Love—you will begin to release the fear that you have built up around the *extraordinary* skills that you already possess.

You will discover that you can trust your unlimited Spirit. As you sit in your car, looking at the one behind the wheel of the automobile next to you, and you allow yourself to relax and notice what is around the edges, as it touches your consciousness, you will realize that this means that minds are not separate one from another. If their mind is touching yours, yours is touching theirs, and you are free to send them Love. You are free to notice what you pick up from another and, without opening the physical mouth, you can send the answer of wisdom that they are seeking.

Imagine being able to go to your grocery store and push your little metal carts down the aisles so that you can fill it with the boxes of what appears to be fresh food, and notice the thought waves of those around you. Imagine beginning to pick up what is going on in their drama, their story, their life, and actually being able to telepathically communicate to them the answers to their dilemmas. Would that not feel like a greater degree of freedom than what you are accustomed to?

The Way of Transformation absolutely requires that you be committed to living differently. For is not transformation a change from the status quo? How can you experience transformation if you do not use time to think and be differently? Crying out to me will not do it. Reading a thousand holy books will not do it. One thing and one thing only will bring you into the transformation that you have sought—the *willingness* to abide where you are, *differently.*

Begin again with the simple exercise of reminding yourself that, in truth, you are unlimited Spirit, abiding in all dimensions. All extraordinary abilities are already inherent in your consciousness. For if they were not, it would mean that God creates with *in*equality. Your egoic mind might respond, "Well, you are born with that gift, but I don't have it."

No. God creates His beloved Son. And the Sonship is made up of equals in Spirit. The only difference, in the field of time, is that it appears that some have accessed and cultivated their inherent abilities more so than have others.

You then use this to perceive another as more special than you as a way of proving to yourself your lack of worth, your smallness, your weakness. You think that perhaps someday, if only you lived the next hundred lifetimes being a "good" person, then maybe these abilities will begin to spontaneously show up in you. But there are no accidents, and nothing you see being made manifest in the life of *anyone* has occurred by accident. Everything you see is *deliberate*—everything.

Therefore, if you would look upon another and say, "Oh, they can talk with Jeshua, but I could never do that," stop lying to yourself! Rather, come to see that if this ability is being made manifest in your field of awareness, it is because *you* have called it to *yourself* as a reminder of what is already inherent within *you.*

If another lays the hand of the body on the forehead of one who is sick, and the one who is sick arises and the disease is no longer present, remember that *you* have called that experience, through that beloved brother or sister, into the field of your consciousness to remind *you* of the truth of your being. If you feel attracted to being a healer, then drop everything else you are committed to and begin healing.

CULTIVATING UNLIMITED CONSCIOUSNESS

As we enter into these lessons on transformation, you will discover that we begin to speak more directly to you. We will not be "beating about the bush," not placating your resistance, your fears, and not stroking you for the dramas you have created that have *seemed* to separate you from the truth of your beingness.

For as we move into The Way of Transformation, the call is being sent from us to you to arise and assume complete responsibility for all that you see, all that you think, and all that you choose. Rest assured, if you hear this call, it is because a deeper part of you has called it to you as a way by which you remember that these things are already contained within you.

The Way of Transformation is the way of assuming responsibility for time, for each and every moment of it. For time is not a prison for you. It is that which flows out of your very consciousness, and there is never a place or a time—*never* a place or a time—which is more conducive to The Way of Transformation than the place in which you are and the time that is now.

There is no one without privilege. There is no one by their station in life, as the world would see it, who is limited from watering and cultivating and bringing forth the fruit that rests within their unlimited consciousness. There is no one who is a victim of the world they see. For the world they see truly occurs nowhere save within the field of their awareness, which we call consciousness or mind. *What @ & in movement and others?*

The buildings, the automobiles you drive, the dollars in the bank—none of that is real. These are merely symbols of the quality of experience you have chosen to call to yourself, as a temporary learning experience.

Beloved friends, use time well. Ask yourself:

> Am I fully committed to transforming my awareness from one who has been sleeping, and perceiving myself as limited to the space-and-time dimension, or am I committed to truly hearing my brother's call to take up my cross and follow him?

That is, the cross of crucifixion, the heavy wooden cross that you have been carrying around that says, "Well, I'm really struggling and trying to get to Christed consciousness, but maybe if I just got rid of my husband, that would do it. Or perhaps if I moved to another location, that would do it. Maybe there is a spiritual technique out there that I haven't found yet in the smorgasbord available. Once I find it and start practicing it, *then* I can get on with it."

You are *in* the holiest of temples—your Self. You abide in the perfect moment for your transformation. Nothing limits you at all, or at any time. The power of the freedom of choice *is* the essence of Christ. And the *very* power that you have been using to try to convince yourself of your limitations is exactly the same power that I used to overcome death. There is no difference, except a wink of an eye, an intention, a commitment, a recognition—that is all. In reality, nothing is impossible to you and nothing unavailable to you.

So, what occurs in the consciousness that seems to create the blockage, the obstacle to Love's presence?

As you create a temporary perceived limitation as a way to call to you a certain quality of experience, there is a tendency to fall into the trap of identifying yourself with the constraints that you have set up from your unlimited freedom, in order to have a temporary learning experience. When in your consciousness you come to be identified with the boundaries or the constraints—the lines upon the canvas that *you* have freely chosen to draw—you create an imprisonment. That imprisonment is actually a complete illusion, and in reality your unlimited Self goes on experiencing anything it wants throughout all dimensions of creation.

Your belief that you are defined by the lines you have drawn in the field of consciousness—the pebbles you have dropped, the ripples you have created—that *that* is only you, creates a constriction, a density, and a conflict. This is occurring nowhere in your being, except in that part of you that has extended itself like a sunbeam from the sun into what you call your space-time dimension.

Now, think about this. If you feel constrained in this dimension, it does not mean that you *are* constrained. It simply means that one tiny ray of your light is temporarily having a certain kind of experience. If you trace that ray of light back to its Source, you find something brighter than ten thousand of your suns, something far more vast than the sun that lights your physical universe, something so vast that out of it has come forth a multitude of universes!

That light of your soul, pure Spirit, remains undefiled and unlimited. That tiny ray can become aware of the whole, and that is the process of awakening. It doesn't really change anything at all, since you begin to become identified, not with the tiny little ray that is having a temporary experience, but that field out of which the very power to experience the space-time dimension is coming forth.

Imagine shifting your identity so that you are the ocean from which a multitude of waves are coming forth, and continually coming forth, each one slightly different, each one a little larger or smaller, a little faster, each one with a little more foam on it than the other. These are the very temporary, dancing waves being emitted from a field or an ocean of water that knows neither beginning nor end and whose far shores cannot be discovered.

That is your Self, not the tiny wave that has a name and a history of being born at a certain time and living in a certain house or a city. It is certainly never what you call yourself as a banker, or a teacher, or a mother, or a father. None of these things is what you are.

The Way of Transformation is much simpler than you think. But again, it rests on your decision to use time to be wholly committed to awakening from the narrow constraints you have placed upon your vast field of consciousness. For no other reason than that it might be rather entertaining to allow this tiny little ray to continue in space and time for a while, while being aware of the totality of your Self and actually operating from that totality.

Can you imagine living like that? Can you imagine your body-mind driving its little automobile down the road, but every time you pull up to your red light and you notice someone next to you, you do not perceive another body? You will still see the automobile; you will still see the body. But what you are feeling, what you are knowing, and what you are seeing is that this is an infinite field of consciousness, just like you are. And that their mind field touches yours throughout all dimensions. And that you are Christ and you can transmit wisdom and Love to them.

You can learn to direct energies. You might see it as a certain color. You can touch their field, their auric field. You can send healing to the organs of the body that you can *see* are perhaps a little out of whack. *You* can be the embodiment in space and time of that Self that is so vast, so grand, so filled with extraordinary power, that all you can do is smile, perhaps unseen and unrecognized by those who, themselves, have become unwittingly identified with a little, tiny drop of foam which is part of the wave, which is part of the ocean of their Self.

But what they choose does not influence your choice. Listen very carefully: What another chooses does not influence your choice at all, even when it seems like it. It is not even accurate to say, "Oh well, I fell under the influence of so-and-so and so-and-so; I went a little unconscious, that's why it happened. I gave up myself."

No, no, no! In every moment of your experience, what you experience is coming from *within you.* It is not placed in you from a source outside of yourself. In every moment, you remain free to observe and to notice whether you are having a good time being where you are. That is, being in your perception of life and recognizing you have the power to think differently.

For example, "Oh, that's right, I'm not in a traffic jam. There is no such thing as a traffic jam. Everything is perfect. There is just a giant weaving together of experiences of infinite souls. So while I sit here in this little car with this funny little body, I'm going to be Christ.

"I'm going to tap in to what's going on around the edges of my awareness. I'll feel the thoughts of anyone I choose to direct attention to. And from the depth of my being, I will direct Love to them. I can choose to be the truth of who I am. The red light, the automobiles, all jangled together—these things do not create my experience. My experience is flowing from within. It is being extended outward."

Only You Have the Power to Create Your Experience

Listen carefully. No one has the power to create your experience. No one has the power to limit your experience. And nowhere in the laws of God has it ever been written that you must conform your experience to the choices of another. You remain free, to freely choose to be the embodiment of Christ. You are the one who can bless creation. It begins when you are willing to assume responsibility for what you want to use time for.

In truth, you are doing it anyway. You are always using time for exactly what you are choosing. You are not surviving. You are not trying to get things done that the world is requiring. Never is anything occurring except that you are having awareness of the effects of how you are choosing to use consciousness, and that is all.

Here is where The Way of Transformation begins. Ultimately, it is also where it ends. But the difference will be that you will no longer even want to choose anything that speaks of limitation.

Even though the body-mind, that you once identified as yourself, still seems to be moving about in space and time, you will not even look at that body-mind and say, "mine." You will simply say, "The body-mind is a temporary communication device brought forth from the ocean of my unlimited Self as I have done a multitude of times in a multitude of universes. What's the big deal?"

Your consciousness will literally shift. It will take a new perspective. And you will know that you are pure Spirit, that you do not abide in time at all, that you can simply delight in utilizing the body-mind as a communication device.

When you get on your airplane and you travel to some distant shore to a place that you are enjoying being in, you are still using the body-mind as a communication device between you and the Earth, between you and other creations that have come forth from other minds. Whether it is a beautiful building or a beautiful painting, all that you are ever experiencing is something that you have drawn to yourself through the medium of the body. It is an experience, and that is all. You are the unlimited one who is in the driver's seat.

BRINGING AWARENESS TO THE LIMITING DEFINITIONS OF YOURSELF

The second stage in The Way of Transformation requires that you begin to bring awareness to the little squiggly lines that you have drawn on the white and unlimited and perfectly unblemished canvas of consciousness. Your psychologists would call these personalities or masks. Come to be aware of the *little selves* you have created. Begin to ask yourself:

> What am I defending? What am I continuing on a daily basis that no longer fulfills me? After all, I have been there. I have done that. How might I look upon these little selves, these little drops of foam on this temporary wave I have brought forth? How might I use them differently? I wonder if I could create a brand new one?

Why is this important? It is because of the squiggles you have drawn. For instance, perhaps you would say to yourself, "Well, I am Mary Jane. I am a vice president at a bank. I was born in such and such a city. My parents are so-and-so and so-and-so, and I'd really be different except my sister used to beat me when I was young."

The second you define yourself, you constrain yourself within the parameters that you have chosen to value. Instantly, you create exactly the experience of the vibrations that are the effect of the squiggles. Think of those squiggles, the parameters of a little self, as the effect of certain pebbles that have been dropped into the pond of your consciousness. Once you draw the lines, certain effects flow from it.

What if you were to decide to create a self that sees itself as perfectly unlimited? Instead of saying, "Well, I have to go see my sister. I know she used to beat me, but that's the way it is. It's just who I am," you simply sit back and say:

> I am a perfectly unlimited being, and I think I will create a self who is an expression of the unlimited Love of Christ. I am going to go see this human being (you might use their name, but do not call them your sister) and I am going to utilize time for beaming as much love to them as I can. For no other reason than it will feel rather grand to do so. I am the embodiment of Christ,

and this one may not know it, but that does not matter. I can enjoy it anyway.

Do you see how that could begin to move you beyond an identification of a certain definition of yourself that has actually locked you into a narrow set of parameters, which can only have certain kinds of effects?

What if you were to sit down with those you call your parents and deliberately chose to look at them as beings that you had called to your field of awareness? What if you chose to see that they are infinite and free beings in perfect equality with you? They simply chose to receive your cosmic telegram and took on a certain role in space and time to help you play out what you wanted to learn.

Would that begin to shift your identification with them as merely parents? For if you look upon them and say, "Those are my parents," you have defined yourself as *only* their child. Do you begin to see the significance?

It is very, very important to bring awareness to the definitions you have given yourself, and keep insisting upon, each and every day. That is like dropping the same pebble into the same stream and creating the same effects. And nothing is transformed.

It also brings up some fear. Your egoic mind will ask, "What would happen if I let go of the definitions that I'm familiar with?" Here is the answer: Nothing will happen, because in reality those definitions have never truly limited your unlimited Self from going on creating and experiencing, throughout all dimensions. The only change that could be said to occur is that that little tiny ray of your beingness that is currently dancing through the experience of being a mind-body in space and time will begin to throw open the doors and actually access cosmic awareness.

If you want the experience of walking on this planet as an enlightened master, first come to understand the foundation upon which The Way of Transformation is based. Second, bring awareness to the definitions of yourself that have become unconscious for you. And then *deliberately redefine* yourself as you enter into the field of your experiences.

Here is the nub: No one can make the decision for you. I have never enlightened anyone. I have never even so much as lifted them an inch. I have merely chosen to demonstrate unlimitedness for myself, and part of that experience was taking on the crucifixion, just so that I could learn how to overcome death. That was *my* choice, *my* pathway, *my* calling forth of experience. I can tell you that it is so much grander to be in the body while being completely aware of your cosmic Self.

In the same moment, I must say to you, it is perfectly okay for you to perceive yourself as a limited ray of consciousness. Yes, there are certain results that follow. But still, you are completely free to continue in that field of experience for as long as you wish.

Imagine one who goes to swim in the waters of a pool which has certain parameters—each end may be forty of your feet in length and the sides might be two hundred feet in length; it does not matter. There is still a certain volume of water, and that is the field in which you swim. That field of water is like the field of your consciousness. It is shaped by the boundaries that *you* choose to draw.

The very same being could say, "I am much too grand to swim in a pool. I believe I'll put the little body on an airplane and fly to the grand ocean, to swim in the midst, unbounded by a box." The experience of *that* swimming is much different.

Your consciousness is exactly like that. All that you experience from the moment you awaken in the morning until the moment you awaken in the morning again (because there is no down time)—everything you see, everything you experience—is the *direct result* of where and how you have drawn the lines on the blank canvas of consciousness. And you are free at any time to erase them and draw differently.

Never say, then, that you have discovered something. Rather, learn to say:

> I am experiencing the effects of certain lines I have drawn in the infinite
> field of my being. And they are perfectly okay.

That is like taking a walk in the rain. Learn to enjoy it, from the place of unlimitedness within you, as a Christ would walk upon this Earth and say:

> "I choose to feel the rain upon the skin of this body. I feel the shiver of the
> flesh against the cold. What a delight it is! I am unlimited, forever! This
> moment does not define me. It does not imprison me. I am free! I am free!
>
> "Tomorrow, I might move to some warmer climate where the sun shines and
> there are no clouds of rain. If so, I will enjoy the rays of the sunlight upon
> my skin and the sweat upon the brow. And I will notice what it feels like as
> it trickles across the skin—not *my* skin, but *the* skin.
>
> "And when I meet a friend, I will remind myself that our fields of mind are
> meeting in many dimensions. What will I choose to bring to that moment?
>
> "Will I see myself as limited to the boundaries of the skin of the body? Will
> I only tell them of all my laments? 'My car had a flat tire, and then my
> mother called and she's unhappy because I forgot her birthday, and oh, my

goodness, I don't know how I'm going to get through.'

"Or am I going to meet them as the unlimited cosmic being that I am? Will I create the space in which *I* get to enjoy beaming love to them? Will I enjoy seeing what is occurring just around the edges of the third-dimensional experience that, of course, does go on?

"'Hello Fred, nice to see you.' But around the corners, 'Oh, Fred, you had an argument with your wife. Let me talk to you about that,' without ever opening the physical mouth. 'Here is some love for you. You know the wisdom. You know the answer.' Oh, a little cancer is beginning to form in the colon. I think I will send light to it. 'So how is the wife, how are the children? Oh, very good.' And I continue beaming light into the cancer."

Which experience do you prefer: the contracted awareness within two small squiggles on an infinite canvas of radiant light, or the radiant Light itself, operating *through* very temporary and freely chosen squiggles called the body-mind?

The Way of Transformation begins with you deciding what you are most committed to. It requires bringing awareness to every set of definitions you have adopted about the Self and placed as an overlay upon it. It culminates in the transparency of the body-mind self, the little ray of light you think you are, so that even while that continues for a little while, it is permeated by an awareness of your cosmic being. And that becomes your identity.

You then, are Christ, playing in the world—unlimited, unfettered, unvictimized by anything. What arises, arises, and what passes away, passes away. And arising and passing away are exactly the same to you. Love comes; it is received. Love *seems* to be taken, so what? You bless the being that withdraws awareness from you and you simply open to whomever comes into your consciousness. For you decide how you will be in relationship in each moment. And you never discover something *out there* that is right. You simply create the structure of your experience.

Whenever another says to you, "Well, I like to eat meat. I love it raw and bloody upon my plate," and you have been eating nothing but fruits and vegetables, there is no reason to say anything at all. Just smile; decide that you can beam them love—not because they are doing something wrong and if you love them they might change, but because their decision does not mean anything. It is just a description of how they are structuring their experience.

If you identify with yourself as a "pure vegetarian," you will not be able to prevent yourself from judging your brother or sister. And where judgment abides, you have created separation, and for a moment you lose the presence of Love.

Can you become selfish enough to learn to truly recognize that you are not influenced by anyone else's choices, and their choices do not say anything about your own? You are free to embrace your experience as being wholly Self-created out of perfect innocence and perfect playfulness. You have the free use of time to generate experience.

CREATING A TRANSFORMATION JOURNAL

Much has been given to you in this lesson. We would highly suggest for those committed to transformation, that they go back and be very clear about what is being shared. Begin to create your own personal transformation journal. Let it be used for no other purpose.

Take the journal and find a picture that represents for you the highest, the deepest, the most passionate, the most beautiful expression of love that you can imagine. Do not compare it to anybody else's. Just put it on the front of the journal. Buy a pen that will be used for no other reason than this. Find a place to place this journal so that nothing else occupies that space, whether it is on your altar or in a drawer by your bed. Find a place, deliberately, out of the field of your Christedness, and say, "Ah, this is the place."

Then, each time you begin a lesson, go through it carefully and write down the key points that are being shared. Decide what they will mean for you. And decide what steps you will take to incorporate them into your lived, daily experience—even if that means that they are not going to be incorporated at all. Take one hundred percent responsibility for the decision and write it down in your journal. For example, "I don't think I'm going to do that. I own it; I decide freely. That's the way it is."

As you do this, by the time these lessons end, you will be surprised at what you have written in your journal. As you go through it lesson by lesson, also keep track of some of the things that you experience as you play with the practices that we give you. How are things changing? What experiences are you beginning to have as you explore the space just beyond the corners of your normal awareness? When you do the exercise we suggested at the beginning of this lesson, what images came, what thoughts did you notice? What colors did you see? Write them down; jot them down. Have fun with it.

For indeed, in each lesson we will be giving you very specific, though what may seem as very simple exercises. But they are designed to give you access to what is already occurring at all times, in a way that can foster and deepen your *deliberate awareness* of what is occurring all the time in your cosmic and unlimited Self.

The only transformation you can experience in space and time is the reaching down from the depth of the ocean into one tiny, temporary wave and readjusting the little foam drops on the tip of the wave you call the body-mind of the self, so that it begins to be a transparent conduit for an awareness of the ocean itself. That is the game of awakening. It is actually the most delightful use of time you will ever find.

As you choose to do that, trust me, it will carry you beyond this world—not from denial, but simply because you have outgrown it. There are dimensions of experience awaiting you that are so much grander than the dimension of the body-mind! But the way that you get to them is by bringing *full awareness* to what you are choosing to experience in each and every moment.

For example, experiencing the soap on the skin in the morning shower—wow, how amazing! Or a raindrop upon the cheek, the shiver against the cold. The sound of a cat meowing or the thoughts of a dog across the street. These things you call to yourself in this dimension.

Do you not want to taste it all? Do you not want to wrap yourself around it all? Do you not want to remember that *magic* is around you? Out of that magic, the moment you are experiencing is being created from within your holy Self. It has never been, and it will never be again—mystery of all mysteries, dance of creation, reality of Love! There is no higher state in the mind-body than to live as one who has been *blown away* and lives in that state perpetually. Then you are free and the world has no hold upon you.

This lesson's message is a beginning for anyone who chooses to wrap his or her unlimited hands around it. But alas, we cannot shape the use of it for you. And if you do not like where you are, look no further than yourself.

We await you. We will reach out for you in a million different ways, across space and time into the space between your thoughts. Not just through the mechanism of this course, but every time there is a little space open in your consciousness, we will indeed come and whisper:

> Beloved friend, come and play at a vaster level. It is all within you.
> Come and play. Come and play with God's children!

> You are free. In this moment, you are as free as you will ever be, right now.

How, then, will you use time? What will you construct out of your infinite field of awareness? What world will you look upon? What thoughts will you think? What feelings will you evoke within the cells? Where will you direct the body to be placed on a daily basis? How will you observe or how will you enter into relationship with each moment—whether touching a dial or touching a body? It really makes no difference. What will you bring to that experience? Is it Christ touching the shoulder of another, or is it just some limited, needy self?

Who will you say that *you are* to this world? For what you decree *is*, instantly. There is no way out of this responsibility. Stop fighting it and birth Christ where once you thought something less than that has dwelt.

Beloved friends, peace be unto you always, and always I am with you. I come to you not alone, but with many who have delighted in creating a resonance with me, and I with them, for no other reason than that power expands *exponentially* when minds join in love from a foundation of wholeness and not neediness. I do not need the one that you call my Mother; she does not need me. But, oh, how we delight in creating *together* that which extends the holy, the good, and the beautiful—without end! Will you come and play with us?

Peace then be with you always. And, as always, Amen.

LESSON 14
THE WISE USE OF TIME

We trust that this moment finds you willing to be wholly where you are. We would trust then, that in this moment you are willing to assume responsibility for the choices you have made. The choices that have literally created the environment that you are experiencing in this moment: the chair in which you sit, the walls around you, the things that hang upon the walls, the individuals with whom you find yourself in close proximity, the individuals with whom you find yourself in relationship, the individuals with whom you work, those with whom you play, and those with whom you share.

We would trust that *this moment* finds *you*, the holy Child of God, at play in the Kingdom of Christ.

If not, if you are aware within yourself, "Well, that's not quite the perspective from which I was beginning my reading of this lesson. I thought I was going to sit down and listen *to* Christ." If there be some element, some touch or some trace within you of that perspective, then pause right now. As you do so, abide by yourself, and take several deep breaths, if you wish. Go back to the five-minute exercise of simply being the presence of Christ. For well do we perceive that many of you have already forgotten that the exercise exists.

At the end of the five minutes, simply remind yourself that what is true always, is always true: *only Love is real.* And what is real cannot be threatened by what does not truly exist. In each moment in which your perceptions are less than flowing from the remembrance of who you are, you have been *in* unreality. When you notice this, take the *time* and use it constructively, by returning to the truth. Pause in your reading if you must—we will be going nowhere—and return in five minutes.

The Way of Transformation is simple, for the way of efforting one's way into the Kingdom cannot flow from the guidance of the Holy Spirit. For where there is effort, there is a separate will, called the ego, that believes itself to be—and would love to convince you of this—small, powerless, and *knows* that it is pervaded by fear. Love requires no effort, only the little willingness necessary to *allow it* to flow from the depth of your being through you, that it might be extended throughout creation.

Beloved friends, The Way of Transformation requires only that you extend to yourself the willingness necessary to put into practice using time *differently*. No, it does not mean that you have to quit your job and go live in a little hut on top of a mountain somewhere. You would not *necessarily* use time differently by doing so.

It *does* require that you begin with the simple recognition that there can be no set of *perceived* circumstances that truly have the power to separate you from your God. No set of circumstances, no set of relationships—not the weather, not the amount of money that you are allowing yourself to receive for the expenditure of your time—there is *nothing* in the world that has the power to separate you from your God.

You are the one who holds dominion over all things. What does this idea of dominion mean? It means that *you* are the one who is the source of the power that can choose how you will see what is around you, how you will perceive it, and what you will believe most about it. *You* are the one with the power to penetrate the illusory veil of the world and see the heart, the essence, the truth, the Christ child in everything—a blade of grass, the cry of a child, the barking of a dog, or the coming of the mail with the bills.

Therefore, The Way of Transformation does not require you to change your circumstances. It merely requires that you change your *attitude* toward them by recognizing that they are harmless, by recognizing that *you* have called all things to yourself.

There are many that would teach that you must sit around and ponder why you did this and why you did that. I say unto you: all that is required to begin is the willingness to accept that in the great mystery of consciousness, *you* are the power and the source for all that you think, all that you see, all that you feel, and all that you would be and do. You abide in that freedom constantly.

The Way of Transformation, then, rests simply on that:

> How will I decide to use my time?
> Finding myself here in this moment,
> can I remember that I am free to see things differently?
> I am free to look lovingly upon the world.
> I do not need to wait for something outside of myself
> to create a stimulus that elicits a loving response.

You do not need to wait for your mate to come and give you the hug that you want so much. You do not need to wait until your mother calls you on the phone and begs for your forgiveness for how cruel she treated you when you were growing up. You do not need to wait until the current president is no longer in the White House. You do not need to wait for the contest that comes in the mail to make you the winner that brings you millions of dollars. You do not need to wait for that to happen. Right now, you are the one that is free.

But perhaps you have imprisoned yourself by waiting for Love to show up outside of you to trigger a response within you—when you feel it or recognize it—so that finally you feel loving. Those that know aloneness are not limited in extending Love. And those that know loneliness yet retain the power to make the decision to love. It can never be taken from you.

Here is a simple exercise that we wish to give you. When next you find yourself alone and perhaps feeling just a little lonely, and you notice that the mind is spinning with thoughts, and you are feeling perhaps just a little weak and out of sorts, pick up your telephone book. Take three deep breaths, and with each breath say to yourself,

 In reality, I remain as I am created to be.
I am the holy Child of God.

Then merely open the phone book. Place your hand on one of the pages with the many names and numbers and just *feel* your way to a specific name and number. You will know the feeling. Then, for the fun of it, call that person.

And when they answer the phone, merely say, "I'm not here to sell you anything, I just need about 15 seconds of your time. I know you've never met me, but I was just sitting in my chair remembering that the truth is true always. And I'm calling to remind you that you are loved by God! You've never failed. You've never done anything wrong. You remain pure and innocent, even now. And I just wanted to give my blessings to you. Have a nice day. Good-bye."

For you see, the world in which you live has but one purpose. It is the *same* purpose that all dimensions of creation have: to be the extension of the Father's Love. For that is what creation is. And then to *extend* that Love from that world, from that dimension. Each and every one of you has but one treasure, *only one treasure*. It is not your child. It is not your spouse. It is not the new car in the garage. Your treasure is your reality as *the unlimited, holy and only begotten Child of God*. You are a field of consciousness through which the Father would extend Himself.

YOUR JOY IS FOUND IN EXTENDING YOUR TREASURE

This means that if this is your only treasure, your greatest joy will be discovered as you cultivate within yourself the *habits of mind*, the *habits of body*, the *habits of choice* that begin to align what you think, what you see, and what you do with the Truth that is true always. For your joy will be found as you recognize that you exist to extend your treasure. As you do so, you immediately add to your Father's treasure, whose only will is to extend that which He is, forever—unbounded, unlimited. And God is but Love.

The grand thing about Love is this: *It* does not require any set of conditions to exist before *It* does. How is this different than some of the things you experience in life?

As a body, there are certain conditions that must exist before the body can be satiated with food or water. There must be certain conditions that are met before the body stops shivering against the cold.

Your world is based on the topsy-turvy perception that conditions must be met *before* there can be a choice for peace instead of war, for forgiveness instead of judgment, for Love instead of fear. Therefore, you think, "When the conditions outside of me change, *then* I'll make the choice for love."

I have often said that the world is merely the reflection of the insane choice to deny love and to be devoted to fear. The world is diametrically opposed to the Truth of the Kingdom. The world is the opposite of Reality.

The Way of Transformation rests on the complete reversal of the thought system you have learned in the world. But that thought system is not merely the practice of new ideas, repeated ad nauseam in the mind. That reversal of thought must *permeate* the entire field of the body-mind—which is nothing more than the field of your consciousness—so that you *know* that change has occurred.

So when you are in any set of circumstances that once seemed to elicit judgment, or fear, or anger, or hurt, or sadness, you recognize:

> My goodness, my whole body feels different. I just feel like being loving. I feel totally safe. What's the big deal here? Oh, I remember when these kinds of circumstances would have elicited sadness, or hurt, or fear, or anger. And now, I just think it's a beautiful place to be because here, I can extend the Love of Christ. Wow, what a joy! What a treasure! Thank God, I have this moment in which I can be the blessing that blesses this world!

What is the world, if not each moment of relationship in which you find yourself?

Beloved friends, the use of time is pivotal. The use of time *determines*, at all levels, what you will experience in your tomorrows. Long after the body ceases to be the teaching and learning device that you are most attached to, long after the body dies, you will indeed be continually stepping into your tomorrows. For you are that sunbeam sent forth from the sun, from the Mind of God. And that Light never stops traveling, to use a spatial term. You will never cease to create. You will never cease to experience.

The only choice you ever have is this:

Will I assume responsibility for doing whatever I must do to eradicate every misperception, every obstacle to the presence of Love, every limited belief I have ever learned about anyone or anything—especially about myself?

When will I choose to assume responsibility for cultivating that perfect remembrance that I and my Father are one so that I can perceive the real world, the reality that shines through everything?

That is the reality that is present in the very material that makes up the chair in which you are sitting. That reality literally pervades the body that you think is so dense and hard. Or perhaps, if you have not been exercising, it is also a little soft.

The point is, there is *nothing* that you see that is not pervaded by the perfect radiance of God's holy presence—*nothing*. A stone, a leaf, a piece of paper blown by the wind—even the shouting of fear and anger from anyone—yet contains within it, if you would receive it, the perfect Love of God. For your Father does not ever recoil or withdraw from the unlimited and perfect extension of Himself. And God is but Love.

If you did not abide wholly in that Love in this moment, you would immediately cease to exist. I do not just mean die; I mean, literally, *cease to exist*. There would be no trace of thought or memory in any mind of you. It is only because Love *is* that you *are*.

This is why I once said:

> Of myself I can do nothing,
> but my Father, through me, does these things.

I did not say, "I learned these of my Father, and now *I* will be the maker and doer." I acknowledged my complete helplessness, my complete dependency. I eradicated any perception that I was a self, separate from God. I stopped giving authority to the tiny, little gnat shouting at the vastness of space, "*My* will be done!"

As you sit in your chair in this moment—hopefully with your Transformation Journal in your lap and the pen that you have purchased for only this purpose—remember this. You are *wholly dependent* at all times on the pervasive reality of Love, which has given you existence out of *its* desire to extend *its* treasure—joy.

This is the reality of who you are in this moment. You are as the wave that has arisen from the ocean of God's perfect and holy Love. You could not for a moment be cut off from it.

Yes, tomorrow things will change. Yes, there will be a point when the body breaks down and dies. Yes, there will be a moment in which all that you see before you will be there no longer, for all things that arise in time, end in time. That is the way it is.

Yet, *you* are free to cultivate the ability to perceive the real world—to see, to know, to feel, to taste, to be, to extend that which is real. Only Love meets that definition.

AN EXERCISE TO DEVELOP YOUR AWARENESS

Therefore again by way of another exercise, take just a moment and look around you. What is the first thing that your eyes see? Be with it. Do not be so fast to judge it as a candle, or a flower, or a picture. Simply be with it. Let the body relax. Stop thinking so much. What is this thing? Do you truly know what it is or what it is for? You describe it; you name it as Adam once did the animals in the story of the Garden of Eden. The human mind believes that once it has named or defined a thing, it, therefore, knows it. It is called the smugness of egoic knowledge.

But do you *truly* know what that thing is? Do you recognize what has come about to even bring it into existence? How many minds had to have been involved in bringing forth that creation? What are the materials it is made of? Where did the materials come from? What plant, what rock, what metal has been discovered and extracted from the body of the Earth to become that shape? How on earth did that happen? Where did the very molecules and atoms come from? What is that thing that I am looking at?

Can you find a place in which you merely rest in awe, and recognize your complete ignorance? You did not make that thing. You cannot find the moment in which that thing first began to arise as a thought in someone's mind. You are completely unaware of the moment of the birthing of the substance from which that object has been created.

Look at it, then, with awe, and recognize that it has come forth from the same place as you—mystery, utter, sheer, mystery. Do you not then feel an affinity with it? Are you not then in relationship with it? Can you not, then, begin to sense the *sacredness* in which that relationship abides? For mystery is sacred, and it transcends even the greatest of minds. The greatest of philosophers cannot comprehend the field of mystery in which all relationships arise.

Now, looking upon that object, whatever it is, recognize that you have called it into relationship with yourself. Ponder for a moment, and ask yourself, "Out of what vibration of consciousness did I first call this object to me?" You might remember purchasing it in a store. See if you can discover the very first moment in your memory, in your consciousness, in which this object came into the field of your awareness. What was going on? What were you thinking, or were you thinking at all? What motivated you to bring it into the field of your home?

If you are at a friend's house, the question remains the same. What motivated you to be where you are right now? What choices were you making with consciousness?

Now, again, we would suggest that you pause in your reading and spend about five minutes repeating this exercise with several objects or things that you see in the room around you. Do not forget that that might even include your kneecap, or your hand, a ring upon your finger, the socks upon the feet. Enjoy this exercise. But remember, do not press the brain; that is, do not think so hard. Relax the body. Sit in the chair as though you were Christ and just look, and go through the kinds of questions we have given unto you. And then we will continue.

How did that go? Beloved friends, this exercise is very, very similar to one that I was also given by my Essene teachers when I was fairly young. I would spend hours—*hours*—not just five minutes, but literally hours doing this exercise. I would do it in my father's house. I would do it in the synagogues. I would do it in the streets of the villages.

My favorite time and place to do it was just at dusk, as the sun would begin to set. As it did so, I observed the colors, and felt the changes in the temperature of the air upon my skin. As I looked at the breezes dancing across the grasses, and as I heard the song of the bird, I would be with these things, just as I asked you to be with the objects in your room. Hours would go by, as I would sit and try to look at each and every star in the sky, asking myself the same questions:

> Can I discover the source of this that I am seeing? Where did it come from?
> How could it be? What has brought this forth?

As I began to sense that I was calling these things into my experience, I began to discern what brought me true joy. Not just a moment of pleasure, or satisfaction, or sense of security, but that which elicited true joy. I discovered that what always brought joy was when I was willing to surrender into the awe of mystery, to penetrate the thoughts, perceptions, attitudes and definitions that the world had taught me.

To look at a plate and not just see a plate, but to see mystery unfolding before me. To sit and look at a star. To sit and look at a sacred text. To sit and look at one diseased, who sits at the side of the road covered with dust, and *to see no difference*. To see them all pervaded by the same mystery, the presence of my Father's Love.

I began to sense that that Love pervaded me, that the very body-mind that I thought had been me, Jeshua ben Joseph, was arising out of mystery, *out of mystery*. Out of mystery that I did not create myself! I finally came to realize that even I was a *mystery* with which I was in relationship.

I decided to be in relationship with my own self, what we refer to as the body-mind, that peculiar sense of awareness in which you say, "I am." I decided to be in relationship with the *totality* of my Self—mind, spirit, soul, emotion, body—with the same sense of awe and mystery that I felt when I looked upon the farthest of stars deep into the night on a quiet hillside. *And that changed everything.* I gave up my self definitions. I did not see myself as a carpenter's son. I did not see myself as a Jew. I no longer saw myself as a student of the Essenes.

I came to see my Self as the mysterious extension of something beyond my comprehension. I saw my Self as a sunbeam to the sun. I saw my Self as the very *mystery of God's presence* being unfolded in the realm of manifestation. I saw that all that I thought, even down to the body, was temporary. I saw that whatever it was that was birthing me was eternal, an ongoing foreverness.

And that if I could just rest in *that*, if I could abide with *that*, if I could return to *that*—even prior to every breath—that I could tap into the very power of creation itself. And get out of the way, and get out of the way, and get out of the way. And keep diving deeper into mystery upon mystery upon mystery.

I never let my mind rest from that day. I never once decided I was done. I never defended a single perception that I held about anyone or anything. And by using time wisely, I cultivated over time, the willingness and the ability to seek first the Kingdom, even to the point where I was doing it *prior* to every word spoken, every gesture made with the body:

> Father, I rest in you. What would you live through me in this moment? Let me witness it! Let me feel it! Let me taste it! Take me ever deeper into your mystery. I want all of you!

And if I might make a confession, that has never ended. I am still saying,

> Father, I want all of you!

The Way of Transformation is the willingness to use time differently. There must come a point in the journey of each individual in which the head bows, and the thought emerges:

> I want only God, and I no longer care what it takes, what is required. I submit to the mysterious force that is Life, asking only that I be transformed into the perfect field of awareness through which Love flows without obstruction.

What you will discover, in the end, is that the only obstruction is fear, and some expression of it. Each time you begin to set aside fear, and choose to bless the world from the perfect holiness of your union with God, each time you *dare* to be so arrogant in the eyes of the

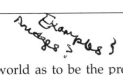

world as to be the presence of Christ, each time you relax the mind and the body and recognize "Of myself I do nothing. Something is living me, and it is to *That* which I surrender," you will cultivate a way of being in the world that is not here. That is, it is not within the perceptual mode that makes up the world.

You will be different. You will look the same, but you will not be the "you" that the world has known. You will speak as you have always spoken. You will know your social security number. However, there will be a definite sense that you live, yet not you, but *That One* is living you.

Somehow, inextricably, unexplainably, you are being allowed to be the field of awareness that gets to witness Life living as you. And you will know that it is sacred. You will know that it is beautiful. You will know that right now, wherever you are in this moment, *you* are the embodiment and the expression of *mystery*—Love forever extending *itself.* You are the very *joy* of God!

And you will continue to be so throughout all of existence. There will never be a time when you will cease to be. But by choosing to surrender defense of the perceptions you have come to identify as you, by choosing to release the grip on the fears you believe are justified and the judgments that you believe are true, as you surrender your grip on the world you have made, creation will flow through you:

> Of myself, I do nothing. I merely witness the flow of Love through me. I use time wisely to cultivate perfect remembrance of the real world. Time and space do not imprison me. This body is not me. I use it as a tool to fashion and shape that which, in this world, can extend Love into any moment.

As we come to the end of our second adventure into The Way of Transformation, notice what thoughts, what pictures, what items you have chosen to write into your journal. Notice the feelings that are occurring in the body, even now. Notice the thoughts, the pictures, and the images that you may hear echoing through the field of the mind.

You abide nowhere but in the infinitude of God's presence. Mastery comes when finally you choose to release all attachment to fear. And in perfect surrender, you release the dream of the dreamer itself, and allow the mystery of Life to live you, without obstruction, without fear, in perfect knowledge that:

> I and my Father are one. There is nothing I have to do to *get* God. There are only some things to be released, so that God *can get me.*

Beloved friends, heed well what was shared, at times in a very subtle way, in this lesson.

We would *highly* suggest that you read this lesson several times, in different environments, at different times—perhaps at three in the morning, perhaps at midnight. And when your spring comes to warm the Earth again, take the time to find a small hill where you can gaze at the stars, and perhaps abide with them differently.

Review this lesson when you are feeling harried or stressed. Look at all of the different sets of circumstances that you have believed have the power to limit your choice or distract your energy.

Read this lesson in those circumstances when you are sad, when you are lonely, when you are bothered. When the room is filled with too many friends, take it and read it sitting on a park bench, or on the benches in the great malls where the many beings come to worship their god of "stuff" and exchange their golden coins for shopping. Shop instead for a new quality of awareness, a new way of being—that which penetrates what you believe you are seeing, and reveals to you the perfect harmony of the Kingdom, the presence of the Love of God.

No one will ever make this journey for you. No one you see or no one with whom you live will ever make the journey to God *for you.* So get clear about your priorities, and seek first the Kingdom. Above all, know that you are not alone. We are, indeed, with you always. I love you.

Peace, then, be unto you always. Amen.

LESSON 15
LOVE OR FEAR—THE CHOICE IS YOURS

We come forth with great joy to abide with you, to share our love for you, in celebration that we are but one Mind and one Heart. For those who choose to release all illusions and journey to the Heart of God, there can only be oneness, brotherhood, sisterhood eternally. And there can only be one purpose and one goal. There can only be Christ expressing the Mind of God.

Therefore, indeed, it is with great joy that we come forth to abide with you in this lesson. We would ask you to set aside the roar and din of the world, and to simply hold the thought in the mind, for just the briefest of moments, that right now you need not be concerned for anything. The world you have dreamt into being—simply to experience it—can be placed upon a shelf, that in this now there is simply this experience.

Focus on your willingness to prepare a place for us and to hear subtle vibrations, translated as thoughts, into the words on the page that can direct the heart toward the soul; that can direct the soul toward the spirit; and that can direct the spirit into awakening fully as the presence of the *thought of Love in form.* For this is what you are made to be. And this is what you *are* eternally, regardless of the vibrations of thoughts that you allow to make a home in your mind temporarily.

You have a term in your legal system called temporary insanity. The lawyer says, "My client is not guilty, it was just temporary insanity." Rest assured, that is exactly how it is in the cosmic dimensions of your being. Your Father knows that given perfectly free will, you have elected at times to be temporarily insane. Knowing this, no judgment has been passed, and you have never been made wrong by your Creator.

You have never failed to create and attract *precisely* those most beautiful lessons that have triggered for you what you most need to learn, what you most need to feel. In each moment you exist in an exquisite perfection of your own making, and your own collaboration with one another.

You, therefore, my beloved friends, are already as I am. We merely work together to restore to your mind what God has placed there since before the beginning of time. We work together in joy and in innocence and in perfect simplicity to re-call, to re-member, what is true always. And then we work together to explore the expansion of that truth beyond the boundaries of every fearful thought, beyond the limitations of every egoic perception, beyond even the body itself, which can be only a temporary communication device usable only within the very thin slice of creation that you call the physical world.

Beloved friends, The Way of Transformation does, indeed, require your commitment. Where you feel that your commitment has wavered, when you become aware of it, simply choose anew. And the end of the journey must be perfectly certain.✱ For as you have created your journey away from God in your imagination, so too do you imagine—or bring into the form of images—the very pathway that returns you to your true reality.✱

(entire journey)

We now embark upon the next lesson and study period, in which you have the choice to become *fully committed* to heeding every word, to letting the vibration brought forth by that word settle ever more deeply into the nervous system of the body, as it settles, likewise, into the depth of your mind and your heart.

Therefore, fear not, for you are the creator of your journey home. You are the creator of all that you perceive. You are the one given the *infinite power* of the Mind of God to see through the eyes of Love, to rest in perfect safety, and to embrace all that comes to you in the simple reality that you have called it to you—as a challenge, perhaps—but always as an opportunity to expand your *commitment* to love.

And where love is chosen so that you want nothing else, you will see nothing else but a lovely world, infinite in dimension, sparkling in clarity, radiant in beauty. You will look upon it and say, "Behold, it is very good!"

A MEDITATION TO ATTUNE
TO THE WILL AND LOVE OF GOD

In this lesson, we wish to introduce a methodology for what you might call meditation. It is a form of communion or meditation that was initially and essentially taught by me to several of my friends, what you know as disciples, one of which carried this specific form of teaching and preserved it. Now, it did not originate with me. I merely refined it.

For I, like you, was once a student of the ways of seeking God. And I dove deep into the nature of consciousness and mind itself and discovered how to attune the mind, the emotions, and even the nervous system of the body to resonate with the perfect will and Love of God.

To begin to prepare a place for that teaching, for the next thirty days, return to the practice of abiding as Christ for at least five minutes. Then, as that five-minute practice period is completed, allow the eyes to close. Become aware of the simple movement of your own breathing. And simply hold the thought:

> I allow this breath to move more deeply and slowly.

Then, as you are beginning to feel that sense of relaxation ever more deeply, hold the thought:

> As Christ, in perfect safety, I release all tension. As Christ,
> in perfect safety, I dissolve my mind in the perfect peace of God.

Then, merely continue in this manner. As the breath comes to fill the body gently, merely say:

> I accept...

And as the breath leaves the body, gently say within the mind:

> ...the Love of God.

And again, as the breath enters the body:

> I accept...

And as it leaves the body:

> ...the Love of God.

Continue in this manner for about five minutes—regardless of what the egoic mind says to you, and it will kick up a bit of a storm. Simply return to this simple practice.

At the end of about five minutes, let the prayer that you have been offering change from words to energy. You might perceive it as a golden white light; you might feel it as a gentle flow of relaxation—whatever works for you is fine. Continue gently to breathe that quality or that color into yourself with each breath. And with each letting go of the breath, imagine and feel that energy moving throughout the course of the body, as though it were extending like a gentle breeze beyond the boundaries of the body.

Again, if the egoic consciousness kicks up its heels, and you start thinking of all the multitude of things you "ought" to be doing, simply return to the prayer. [For all prayer is nothing more than a choice to abide, to contemplate, and to rest in communion, beyond egoic thought.]

After about another five minutes, then say within the mind:

As Christ, I have celebrated in this manner the Truth of who I am.
And I bring peace to the world this day.

Allow this practice period to occur in the morning of your day, and then again in the evening of your day. The only change would be in the final phrasing for the evening. Say simply:

This day I have brought peace to the world and offered it to my companions.

That should be clear enough and simple enough for you to begin. You may wish to refer back to the words of this meditation and use it as a guide for a period of time, until it seems more comfortable for you to do it on your own. Those that embark on this simple process will be well prepared for what is to come in the lessons that follow.

THE ONLY ENERGY THAT CAN SEPARATE YOU FROM THE KINGDOM

Beloved friends, the world that you look upon is not real! It has never been real. It will never be real. But it is a creation that can be *impregnated* with the perfect Love of God. Remember always that there is only Love or fear. What is not Love can only be fear, and is never justified.

The world that you have made is thoroughly harmless. The world that you experience, which is the world that you have made in conjunction with others, in any given moment offers to you the opportunity to choose to impregnate it with Love, or to allow it to reflect to you your fearful thoughts. You are not limited at any time. And in you, all power under Heaven and Earth is given.

You have a phrase in your world: "There is nothing to fear but fear itself." That is ninety-eight percent accurate. Fear is the only energy that can separate you from the Kingdom. And fear is never justified in any moment. The final two-percent would be to say there is nothing to fear, since fear is only a temporary insanity, and your right-mindedness is but a choice away.

Therefore, begin to look upon each situation, each moment or minute of your life, as a very separate scene in a movie. It has its certain set, its certain characters. It has a beginning and it has an end. Although you are eternal, the things of time are not. And all things birthed in time, in time, will end in time.

Therefore, will you use the moment birthed in time to bring what is eternal to it? Or will you continue to believe that yet within you there is no possible power to choose Love over fear? Look around you. What do your eyes show you? Would you bless it or curse it?

What would you teach yourself, and, therefore, make true for you?

The message of this lesson is being given slowly, deliberately, and carefully. For we want you to make no mistake in what is being shared, both in terms of practice and in theory. Theory is important in your world, for it is only through theory that the mind, the little part of you that is arrogant, will decide whether to value what the theory offers. And when you have placed value upon what the theory offers to you, you are then willing to embark on the practices it requires. I hope this makes sense to you.

Therefore, in this lesson we are choosing to speak with you more rationally than emotionally. We would ask you to consider this: Have you suffered enough? Have you kept yourself small long enough? Have you tasted limitation deeply enough to know that you want these things no longer? Would you be willing to patiently choose the dissolving of your illusions? For on just the other side of each illusion is the freedom and peace that you seek.

In any moment, you can tell quite clearly what you are most committed to. If the body is tight and uncomfortable, if you must speak with a louder voice, if your words come more quickly, if the brow is furrowed and the jaw tense, rest assured, you have chosen to be devoted to fear.

You are like one who carries a magic wand filled with such power that you could merely wave it upon the face of this Earth and extend the Kingdom of Heaven to every heart and every mind. What, then, can prevent the expression of such power? The fear you have made to replace the reality of Love.

As you look upon each segment, each scene, and each minute in your movie, begin to cultivate the deliberate practice of recognizing that you are in a field of energy that is your perfect servant. Within that moment, *you* are the one with the power to make that moment be whatever you wish it to be. It can be filled with Christ consciousness. Or it can be filled with temporary insanity. The choice is always yours. And never, ever, has there been such a thing as a victim.

Therefore, as you enter into any one of your minutes, ask yourself:

What is this moment for?
What do I decree this moment to be?
What do I most want to learn by teaching it?

To teach is to demonstrate. To demonstrate is to express what you have decided will hold the greatest value for you. Whenever you judge another, you are decreeing that the thing of greatest value is separation, since judgment always causes contraction and, therefore, separation from another.✳ When you practice forgiveness, you are decreeing that what you value is joining in holy and peace-filled relationship.

Remember that forgiveness has nothing at all to do with saying to another, "I can see that you have sinned, but I forgive you your faults." No! Forgiveness is the recognition that *nothing* has been done *to* you, and that you would prefer to see the face of Christ in the one in front of you. Let me give you an example related to Easter.

Easter celebrates resurrection. It has been made to celebrate my resurrection. But this has only served to turn your attention from the specialness—in the sense of your uniqueness—the specialness of *your* existence, *your* reality, and placed your attention on mine and on me, as though Christ is something merely historical—as if I am special in the eyes of our God.

ACCEPTING THE RESURRECTION FOR YOURSELF

Upon this Easter or whenever you read this, recognize that you have the power to celebrate and accept *your* resurrection as the living Christ by seeing beyond the boundaries of death, loss, fear, hurt, anger, projection, and the perceptions upon which projection rests. *You* are the one who has been reborn when you choose to remember only loving thoughts.

Trust ✳ What then is the veil that seems to make it so difficult? It can be only this: that you have accepted into your mind at some level, that the world you see is real and that *it* holds a power to dictate to you whether you will feel peace or disturbance, Love or judgment. This is *always* an illusion.

My question for you is, would you be willing to surrender your illusions in order to remember the peace of God? The question is whether or not you will accept the atonement for yourself, the resurrection for yourself, and be determined to walk this Earth as one who has arisen.

What does that mean? It means that you have chosen to awaken from the uselessness of separation, the uselessness of victimhood, and the uselessness of weakness. And you have chosen to accept the empowerment of becoming responsible for this dimension of creation, the empowerment of deciding to walk the Earth as the arisen Christ.

— You have chosen to take the message of an historical event that did occur in time, (for if it did not, somebody has managed to fool me) and to assimilate it as a symbol of your own life.✳ For you have well been crucified by your own thoughts. And by your own thoughts, you have brought your persecutors to you, who have nailed you on the cross a million times, so that you could be confronted with the opportunity to look out upon a lovely world by seeing only through the eyes of Love.

Think, then, for a moment and imagine that *you* are nailed upon a cross. You are stuck between the vertical axis of eternity and the horizontal axis of time and the body. Imagine that you lift your head, upon which *you* have placed a crown of thorns. What does that represent? It represents the field of the mind, as it operates and expresses through the body, through the brain.

Those thorns represent your fearful thoughts, your judgmental thoughts, your limited thoughts that press and poke upon your own energy field and give you quite a cosmic headache, and draw blood. That is, it releases the Life force from you, the power from you, as it drains down your auric field. You dissipate yourself, much like a balloon with a slow leak dissipates the power that makes it a balloon.

"A crown of thorns" symbolizes the effect of the thoughts you insist upon when you rest in judgment, or anger, or hurt, or fear. That is, when you choose to deny Love.

The nails merely represent that which would hold you stuck in a dimension, the horizontal dimension of the body and of time, which would nail your feet to the world. "Down to earth," they call it. Yet, above you, the crown of your head is open heavenward. And you are free to receive the Love of God, to choose only loving thoughts, to look gently upon everyone and every event, seeing only perfect innocence.

So imagine, now, that you lift your head and you realize, "The blood is dripping from my brow by *my own* hand. The crown of thorns was placed upon me by those who came to serve me, to shock me into the remembrance that I have allowed myself, at times, to have thoughts of negativity, limitation, and fear. No wonder I've had such a headache!"

You look to the left and to the right and you see your wrists bound to the horizontal plane by a nail, a hard piece of iron, cold and thoughtless. How many times have you bound yourself to the things of time through your own thoughtlessness, your own coldness?

You turn to look down at your feet. They are crossed over, resting gently upon a small wooden slab, with a nail through them, as though the world were saying, "Don't you *dare* try to rise above our level of consciousness. How *dare* you mirror to us the Truth of our being by always being so sickeningly loving?"

The world will seek to nail you down to earth by insisting that you think with it. For remember, always, that the world—not the Earth, but the *world* of human experience—is the attempt to create that which is the opposite of reality, like many who would gather together to take a drug and think that their insanity is the same as the bliss and ecstasy of union with God. Yet, they would not dare drive an automobile, cannot think a coherent thought, and do not even remember where they are.

Now, you turn your eyes from the roar and the din of the world. You see the soldiers, your persecutors, totally unconscious, totally conformed to the authority of the world, so that they have donned the armor, the headpieces, the footwear and carry the spears of a god made as a substitute for Love.

You look out upon the fearful crowd. You see some friends who still see your soul, your Christ Mindedness, and continue to love you. Yet, even *they* are veiled by their belief that death and loss are possible. So you are *completely* alone. No one is going to save you. No one is going to rescue you. It is between you and your God.

It is a decision that you must make—to be determined to choose only what is real, regardless of what the eyes seem to show you and what every mind around you seems to believe, even those who professed belief in your message of love.

For they look upon the body and an old belief takes hold, "The body is what is real, after all. Look at this—it is nailed to a cross. This is limitation. This proves that the world's thinking is true."

And so you must lift your eyes from the world that you think you see and choose to accept reality:

> Father, into thy hands I commend my Spirit.

This is nothing more than the choice for *sanity* in the midst of all conditions. The choice for what is *eternal* in the field of what is temporal. The choice for what is *unlimited* in the field of what seems to be limitation. The choice for *sanity* in the field of what seems to be pervaded by insanity. The choice to remember only thoughts born in love!

Then, your eyes look down again. And something has changed—you are at peace! You recognize that you are above the world, you are above the crowd, and a gentle sweetness begins to pervade your entire beingness. All pain and suffering is forgotten. The nails can hold you no longer. The world cannot keep you down in its insanity. The eyes of the body close, and as they close, the world they had shown you recedes and the *real* world appears. And you rest in the perfect remembrance that you are *one* with God. Your attention drifts away from insanity.

Yet, you are quite aware that you can still see your friends. You see the soldiers. You see the tears, the tumult. You see some who are merely standing quietly. And you bless them and release them to have the perceptions that they would choose. For you have come to love yourself so much that you will accept only what is *real*. It is finished. The resurrection now begins.

Easter is *your* birthday. Easter is a time to celebrate that the crown of thorns has been removed because you have chosen to think only loving thoughts, and that you have remembered the power given unto you through which you transcend the awful, dreaded and suffering-filled experience born of fear. For in Love, there is only peace. In Love there is only the infinitude of pure Spirit. In Love is Christ restored to your consciousness. In Love are you returned.

Easter is for you and not for me. Therefore, set aside your images and your practices of me. Make no pilgrimage to me. Make a pilgrimage to the heart of your Self by looking upon all that you see this day and seeing its beauty, its harmlessness, and by knowing that you are looking out through the eyes of the arisen Christ. You are that One who, with me, has overcome the world.

What can there be left to do but to celebrate with your brothers and sisters? What can there be left to do but to laugh, to sing, to play, and to remember, in quiet devotion, the Love your Creator has always had for you?

You can choose *only* between love and fear. In love you are resurrected. In fear you are crucified. What, then, will be your choice in this lesson in which death offers you eternal Life?

We would ask that you read this lesson many times. For here alone do you find the magic doorway, set before you always. The only choice that matters is before you now, as it is always—Love or fear, resurrection or crucifixion, joy or suffering, unlimitedness or smallness. The choice is always yours.

And like me, upon a cross so long ago, *no one can make the decision for you*. No one causes your perceptions. They flow from your choice for crucifixion or resurrection.

 I know where *I* would choose to have you join me. Know, then, that I love you always, in the ways that you will allow, and to the depth that you will accept. Choose, then, with me and you are free.

Peace, beloved friends. Peace to the only begotten of God: the resurrected Christ...or the crucified body and egoic mind. Amen.

LESSON 16
THE BIRTH OF EGOIC CONSCIOUSNESS

Beloved and holy friends, it is a joy to communicate with you The Way of Transformation. Within the word transformation, there is great wisdom. Transformation requires that there be that which abides in form. And you are that.

You are Spirit. You are that which has come forth as a ray of Light from the Mind of God, as a sunbeam to the sun. In that form-less beginning, you are consciousness itself. You are intelligence itself. You are bliss; you are radiance; you are compassion. You are the potential for endless creativity.

You *are* God Itself. Now, that is the first time that we have been quite so bold. It is the first time that we have described *you* as that which *is* God. This can only mean that what you are in your essence, in your essential being, *is* God Himself.

THE FIRST LEVEL OF CREATION—PURE SPIRIT

The very first level of creation is when that which we call God, or Abba, first began the indescribable, the unexplainable mystery of birthing Himself forth, out of the eternal matrix of His being. That first level of creation was pure Spirit—a subtle, subtle movement in which a gentle sunbeam begins to emerge from the sun or a ray of light soundlessly begins to emanate from Light itself.

In pure Spirit, you are unbounded; you are without form. But you are not without consciousness. You are not without Self-awareness. In Spirit, there is only Self—not self and other, not self apart from form, but simply Self—radiant, shimmering, unbounded— alone, yet not lonely. Rather, filled with Self, filled with God, filled with Love.

This first level of creation *never changes*. It is as God Itself. For the sunbeam is as the sun, the ray of light as the Light. A momentum, though, has begun—a momentum extending from the pure potentiality of all that God is. For Love seeks only to extend itself. Extension is an activity; it is a movement. And for there to be extension, there must necessarily have then been created what you *call* space. But even at this level of creation, the space of which we speak is not quite what you would perceive in your mind, as you think of that which contains the planets whirling around your sun.

Rather, it was more like a mathematical concept. It was the *idea* of space, in which extension could occur. There were not yet planets and suns. There was not yet a single atom or molecule of matter. There was pure thought, pure Love, pure being, beginning to *entertain,* and I emphasize that word for a certain reason, the idea of pure space, pure extension—unlimited, unbounded, forever. There was pure Spirit. That is what you are, now and forever. Spirit does not change.

There is that which in you—right here and right now even as you read these words, even as you perceive yourself as a body sitting in a chair, beyond all that you see with your physical eyes, all that you are aware as and within the body, beyond the activity of the surface level of the mind, in which there is the firing of the neurons in the brain almost without ceasing, so that the mind seems to never be without images and thoughts—is Spirit.

Far beyond this planet, and yet right where this planet abides, far beyond this universe, and yet right where this universe abides, far beyond all dimensions, the infinite dimensions of creation, yet right where those infinite dimensions exist, Spirit is.

Here is found what I have often referred to as the "real world." Here, peace abides *eternally* with perfect consistency and without interruption. Here, *is the living reality,* which has been reflected in the sentence:

I and my Father are one.

In other words, when consciousness transcends its perception of itself as being only conditional existence—being only the *forms* of existence, such as the body-mind, the particular sense of self as separate from all other selves, the blade of grass, the cloud in the sky, the rock upon the ground—when consciousness transcends this sense of itself, it abides not in a thinking relationship. It does not observe Spirit as something else and then says, "Oh, that's what I am. Great."

Rather, there is a living sense in which consciousness as such, as the Self, rests in the Self and simply *knows.* For only knowledge is *immediate,* and not mediated by any concept, form, or experience.

In such a moment, and it takes only a moment, there is immediate awakening to the reality of the Real World. In some form, and notice I said in some *form,* consciousness then dances back into the *extension* of Spirit, into the *extension* of reality, into creativity, into creation. In the *human* form, it can say, "I and my Father are one." There are many such statements within the human family that have been uttered to express that awakening, that reality.

THE CREATION OF THE SOUL

Now, in this ceaseless movement from that which never moves, as the ray of light emerges from Light divine—unbounded, eternal, unobstructed—in the very desire to be creative, to extend creativity ceaselessly (and that is what creation is), Spirit begins to condense or descend (these are both very spatial terms).

Again, we are now using language that finds its source on your side of the fence; that is, on the side of the fence of phenomenal existence, not on the side of the fence of Spirit, where language is hardly required.

Spirit continues its dance, as the one Mind, God, *entertains* the extension of creation. And Spirit begins to *condense* into something that has not yet ever occurred. The thought, and again, we are still operating at a level of pure thought, pure potentiality—there is not yet the deep darkness of the space of your universe or of any dimension whatsoever—begins to condense into a thought of individuation.

Perhaps you have seen in your television commercials, when the milk is poured into the glass in slow motion. As the milk hits the glass, it begins to move back up the sides as the cup begins to fill. And at the last moment, when the carton is tilted back and the pouring has stopped, the motion that has been started creates the phenomenon of a circular drop of milk which arises and, for a very temporary moment, seems to become separated from the body of milk in the glass itself.

It emerges and in a split second, you, who are watching the screen, have the *awareness* of an individuated drop of milk that seems to exist completely independent of the body of milk itself. Then, in the next moment, it drops back into the body of milk, and you *lose awareness* of it as a separate thing, a separate drop of milk. But it is still milk. From your place of perception, it merely looked *as though* it had separate existence.

Now, that is an analogy, of course, since the soul is not made of milk. But it does create a picture for you of what occurs when the body of Spirit continues in its entertainment of creativity, out of which emerges what we have called soul—the first, subtle inception of the thought of individuation, of that which is an individuated expression of the fullness of Spirit, which is Light, which is God.

Why? All for the joy of extending creation, that that One might be aware of itself in an endless variety of form. This is where it begins—the *delight* of creation. That is what *you are*! In pure soul there is still only pure potentiality. There has not yet been what you would know as experience. There is, however, the first subtle awareness of the one Self being aware of itself.

SEPARATION IS BIRTHED

As soul continues the extension of light, of pure creativity, it condenses. It descends to the next level. Again, since we are using language from your side of the fence, there are not many other ways to speak of this. The soul descends or condenses, and begins to create a deeper awareness of itself as an individuated *thing*.

Now its awareness of itself as Spirit is taking on a new coloration, a new vibration. It is becoming very close to what many of you have experienced in your own meditations and prayer, or the time you heard a child cry, or you walked through a forest at dawn—when your egoic mind was temporarily transcended, and you had a sense of your oneness with God, and yet, still felt other than God—creature and Creator, son and Father—united, yet somehow different.

Here is where the separation can be said to have occurred. For it is *here* in the first level of pure potentiality of this unique thought, that that which Intelligence *is*, that which Love *is*, that which Light *is*. I have referred to this in *A Course in Miracles* as Mind, which is not merely the prattling that goes on in the human brain that you refer to as "thinking." Mind is much vaster than that!

It is here in the first level of subtle perception of the Self as an individuated matrix of awareness, that has awareness of itself, and yet that Self or God is somehow something different than what the soul perceives to be itself. *Here* is where the first, unique thought of separation is birthed, at this very *subtle* point, long before the planets of your universe arose, long before the multidimensionality of creation came into being. Here, you are. Here, there is but one soul, a unique expression of the one Spirit, itself the unique expression of that One who eternally *is*.

Here, creativity gives rise to the power of thought. It is from the field of thought, pure thought, that creation will now begin to spring immediately into being. Here, at this subtle level, the drop of milk has seemingly separated itself and now *feels* awareness of itself as separate from the body of milk. And for a moment, for just a moment, there is pure joy, because it is still the One doing it—out of entertainment, out of pure play, out of the sheer exuberance of extending itself and its infinite power, ceaselessly and without limitation.

For you see, if God, who becomes you, held the thought, "I certainly can't separate my Self from my Self," *that* would be a limitation. So the One creates a drop of itself, along with the *perception* that it perceives itself as separate from something that is now for the first time, *other*. Here is the germination, the seed planted, for egoic consciousness. But that is still a little further along in the story.

As that first thought of separation is dreamt, a new energy is born. That which has been pure joy, that which has been pure freedom, pure safety, now changes form slightly. You could say a drop of milk within the drop of milk seems to separate and take on its own energy. And that we have called fear. Here is born not extension, but contraction, or the experience of contraction, as fear emerges in awareness.

Now the river begins to cascade very, very quickly—out of fear, out of the first inception of the thought, "I am alone. I am separate from my Creator." Yet, in reality, it is the Creator perceiving the Creator, and creating the perception that God is separate from God.

With that thought, an explosion occurs—very like what your scientists have called the "big bang." They do not know how close they are! They merely need to make the shift to seeing that the big bang occurred in consciousness itself, not out of pure matter.

In the big bang of consciousness, suddenly imagine that drop of milk exploding in space, which comes into being with the thought of separation, and becoming an infinite array, or number of points—little droplets of milk, little droplets of consciousness, little sparks of divinity, little particles of light.

To use yet another analogy from your realm of science, the wave of light has now become particles of light. When and why, who can say? Only that One, who is doing the birthing of itself, knows. And you are that One.

As these particles of light are now *spread out* through the infinite reaches of the pure potentiality of Spirit—which is Light, which is God—each particle possesses the exact same potential. In fact, you could not find any difference between the points of light, whatsoever —*none*. If you were to measure them, they would be the same size, although they have no size. If you measured their frequency or vibration, they would all be the same—identical points of light that *seem* to have now taken existence in different points of space.

That is, there is the sense that while they are identical in quality and substance, there is a slight difference in the space that each one occupies, as though you took two identical pencils and put one on the left side of the table, and one on the right. Still made of the same substance, but now, in the vast continuum of space, that which is identical is occupying two points of space, each with the perfect freedom mirroring the perfect freedom of the one God.

Infinite rays of light, now mirroring and reflecting the perfection of the freedom of pure potentiality, which is the Light itself—the pure potentiality to create. And each one has within it the thought, the recognition, the perception of separation.

Fear has been birthed. And with it, the thoughts, "I am alone. I am not that point of light over there. I am just myself." As the energy of fear continues, the contraction, the condensation, the descension continues. Now, what has burst forth instantaneously (this is not yet requiring time) is the *multitude*, the infinite multidimensionality, which is creation—except the physical universe has not yet been birthed. The physical universe *requires* the concept of time. For only in time does the physical dimension exist.

Here is where you find what has been called in your language the hierarchy of angelic beings, of angelic worlds. They are points of light, just like you, but not in the experience of time, nor in the condensation that you would call physical bodies—not even the lower astral bodies. Still, this multidimensionality of creativity is a radiant dance with just a tinge of a sense of separation, or "otherness," or fear.

THE CREATION OF THE PHYSICAL UNIVERSE

In this multidimensionality, which is still pervaded and is as Light itself, condensation continues. And here your scientists begin to tap into it, so you can see how many steps removed they are! But here light begins to condense into the particle of matter. Again, the explosion occurs, as the one basic atom—or Adam—explodes in the big bang. And the multitude of bodies, of planetary bodies, including your central sun of your tiny little universe, is birthed.

The physical universe, of which you are a part as a human being, is vast beyond comprehension. Yet, it is as a tiny speck of dust. It is as a tiny speck of light, floating seemingly freely—like a tiny drop of milk that seems to have separated itself from the body of milk—and is unaware of the multidimensionality of radiant Light and Spirit and God *in which it floats*, out of which it has been given its very existence. You are, therefore, not outside of Spirit. You are held lovingly—your whole physical dimension—in the *center* of Spirit.

As this condensation continues, what you have been told to call "life" begins. Conditions are set up, emerging from what? Pure chance? Hardly! It emerges out of the pure potentiality, the power and the perfect intelligence *to create*.

Although now, that creativity is expressing itself—more and more—out of fear, not out of pure joy. It is like taking a note of a flute and muffling it slightly, so that it has a different quality. Yet it is still pure energy. For what can fear be, but energy? Just as love is energy, compassion is energy, sadness is energy, and anger is energy.

 Do you see? Fear is just an energy, and nothing more. In itself, it is *perfectly neutral*. For all events are neutral. And fear, being merely a dance or a play of energy itself, must be an entirely neutral event, until something arises to perceive and experience it differently. And what is that? The birth of egoic consciousness.

FEAR HAS TAKEN ITS FINAL FORM

Here, fear has condensed into its final form. There can be no further condensation of the energy that has become fear, for egoic consciousness is fear-full consciousness. *The ego is fear.* Yet, it is made of pure power, pure potentiality, unlimited creativity.

Rest assured, you all have the experience of knowing just how ceaselessly creative egoic mind can be. For without ceasing, it knows how to immediately look upon another brother or sister or event or anything, and that fast—in the twinkling of an eye, in a space that does not even require a thought—egoic consciousness can change its values, can change its perceptions, to create what it wants to create.

What it wants to create is that which continues its existence. Much like in your physical body, when a cell becomes cancerous and decides to run amuck, and act as though it were not dependent on the laws of the body itself that keep the body healthy, it begins to do what? It begins to create cells like unto itself. Cancer is merely a misperception run amuck at the level of the body that is thinking for itself, creating in its own image, rather than *extending* the image of the Creator and living out of harmony with the one Mind that creates in radiant joy, for no other reason than to extend the good, the holy, and the beautiful.

Yet, God does not create limitation, and therefore, He does not withdraw creativity from the power of the ego. Rather, because God is Love, all power under Heaven and Earth is available and can be tapped into by egoic consciousness.

So what is egoic consciousness? You all know what it feels like to be *absolutely certain* that you are separate and alone, that you must rely on your own thinking process, and that no one beyond—not just the boundary of your body or skin—but no one beyond your unique, contracted sense of "I" has any connection to you whatsoever, and no one cares. And you lament, "I am alone. I am separate. How on earth am I going to make it? I've got to figure my own way. I've got to figure out how this world works. I've got to make it happen for myself!"

Fear has taken its final form. Now, there is a complete forgetting of God, of the One, of Spirit, *even* of soul. The body represents a level of vibration, still quite intelligent, still *very* intelligent. It is like a matrix of energy, the very thought of condensation into human form, out of which forms keep getting created, keep getting created, keep getting created, keep getting created. You have done that for yourself an infinite number of times.

The *body* is the representation of the ego. For notice that as you sit in your chair, you are quite certain you are not the wall across from you. As you sit where you are in your chair, your consciousness, your awareness tells you that you are the reader and not the author.

And you think, "No, not me. I couldn't do that if I wanted to. Certainly it makes Jeshua very special! For I am just this blob of dust, this separate mind-body, sitting in my chair, reading words which vibrate with a certain meaning and create certain pictures and understandings in my mind. But these are being placed within me, and I am not That One."

That is egoic consciousness that says, "I am *not* That One. I am *not* God. I am *not* pure Spirit. I am *not* pure soul. I am this *thing* that sits in this chair, now." And do you know something? You are absolutely right—you *are* that! That and so much more!

The egoic mind is that which creates the separated perception that it is only one tiny, thin slice of the pie. It creates a delusion, a distortion, in consciousness itself, like a little blip on a radar screen that tells the one watching the screen that there is some *thing* there. The egoic mind says, "I am separate. I am alone. I cannot think with the Mind of God. I cannot experience unity consciousness. I cannot be as Jeshua is. No, not me. I'm too small and too weak. Oh, I just don't have it together yet. Maybe someday."

Yet all the while, you are That One. By the power of That One, you have the potential to think the thought, "I could never be like Jeshua is. I'm really too small, too fragile, too weak, and too stupid. Oh, Christ consciousness may be there for someone else, but not for me."

The whole while, *that very thought* must use the power of the One. For that power is Life! That power is pure being! That power is the real world! That power is the only thing that exists—*period*! By the power of That One, you have dreamt the thought of the separate self. By the power of That One, *when you decide to*, you will awaken from the thought of egoic consciousness.

Now, why is all of this important? Beloved friends, The Way of Transformation requires that there be that which exists in form. *You* exist in form. You are sitting in a chair. You know the space and volume of a human body. You know the particular thoughts that you identify as your own.

You have a history to that body-mind that emerged from sexual desire between two beings called parents who got together. And a little thing wiggled its way up to touch another thing, and there was a burst of light, and a pure spark of pure soul made a *decision* from *intentionality* to become fixated or identified with, and as, a physical form.

So, having a good time on a Saturday night is the source of your being—as a bodily being.

If you were lucky, both parents consciously desired to use the body as a communication device for teaching only love, and gave one unto another. And then accepted that little spark of light that begins yet the birthing of another body, and clearly invited another soul to come and abide with them, as teacher and friend, as brother or sister. Unfortunately, that is yet rare upon your planet.

That is the matrix into which you have descended, time and time again, as you have come to teach yourself that you are just a separate, lonely, failing, weak individual. At the death of the body, you have found yourself as soul, and been frightened by the radiance of your light, because that light is not the same as your interpretation that you had learned of yourself.

Fear causes condensation, contraction, *falling* if you will. And what you fall into is a matrix of energy that best resonates with *your own* perception and belief about yourself. Belief is not just thought. It is a quality of vibration.

And you fall, yet again, into a field of energy, into a dream, into a physical universe, into a time frame, into a family structure that resonates and vibrates with how you have learned to perceive yourself. All the while you are yet That One: radiant, perfectly free, using the very power of God to create and believe in a dream of smallness, weakness, separation, and loneliness.

Right now, as you read these very words—*now*—that is what you are doing. You are choosing how you will think of yourself. And how you think of yourself is reflected in the world that you see, in the experiences that are manifest within your own particular universe of consciousness.

If you knew that you were the unlimited One, you would never fear the creation of the golden coins again. You would never believe that you must live in lack. But you are still, for the most part, clinging to the belief that you are that small little thought of separation called egoic mind, still struggling to find God, not recognizing that it is the very power of God's presence from which you create the perception you hold of yourself.

So, there you are—sitting upon your chair. And you are That One. You are *in form*; that is, you have created a perception of yourself that includes the experience of being a body-mind, which *is* separate from all other bodies. It *is* separate from the rock. Obviously, you can look out your window and tell that where the body is that you identify with, is in a different spatial point than every other object.

That is what this world is! This universe is the *attempt* to create a reflection that *convinces* you that the first fearful thought of separation *is* the *truth* of who you *are*! You are using, or have unwittingly been using, your physical universe to constantly reflect to you what *must be* the *truth*: that you are separate from all creation.

This world is nothing but the reflection of *that thought*. Yet, even here, That One pervades all things, and the realization of your Self *as* That One is closer to you than your own breath—simply a decision away.

Here, there is great richness not found in any other dimension, the richness of the dramas of separation, of seeking—seeking, seeking, seeking. For example, one who is seeking will say, "Well, I have read *A Course in Miracles* one time, and it didn't seem to work, I'll read it again. Oh, that didn't work. Well, maybe I'll go try this form of meditation. No, that didn't work. Maybe I'll try Buddhism. No, that didn't work. I'll try Christianity. No, that didn't work. I'll try *drugs*—that will do it!"

The very energy of seeking *is* the egoic energy. For only the ego can seek. Pure Spirit can only extend. And there is a huge difference!

Egoic consciousness plays itself out through the forms of *special* relationships. You have a special relationship with your employer; you have a special relationship with your spouse, your lovers, your car, your boats, and your automobiles.

And the world plays off of your need for specialness, such as, "Look at this automobile. Isn't this one sexy! Oh, you're going to feel so-o-o good!" So you seek to create the means to possess that certain automobile. Or you think, "If only I had that person as my spouse. Oh, let me seek that one by seducing that one. I'll act as though I'm other than my poor, paltry, lonely self, so that they think I am grand. I will ruffle up my peacock feathers."

And on it goes. The world is the reflection of the belief in the *need* for special relationship. The search for that is the restlessness that you feel—that restlessness that you feel in the mind, that creates the waves of restlessness in the fluids and subtle energies, which are contained within and make up the illusion of the body. The restlessness of the breath, the tightness of the muscles, the loneliness as you rest your head upon the pillow at night, for you believe that you are that body-mind, separate and alone, apart from all others.

The infinite, eternal stream of communication that occurs throughout creation, unobstructed, is lost to your awareness. Yet, so close are you. It requires only a thought to shift the momentum in a new direction, to rest your head upon the pillow and say:

> I am not just this body-mind. I am That One, pure, unbounded and undefiled. I am in communication with every rock and every tree and every time frame that has ever been.

And yes, when you begin that thought, it will seem wholly insane, because you have been on the other side of the fence, looking at reality from a certain perspective. It fits like a glove upon the hand, but that does not make it right or true. Insanity seems sane to those who are insane. So that is just the way it is.

THE END OF ALL SEEKING:
CHOOSING TO LIVE AS THOUGH YOU ARE NOT THE EGO

But the end of all seeking occurs when one *dares* to hold within the mind a *different* thought. You have heard it many times through *A Course in Miracles*, through many of my other channels:

> Only Love is real.
> You are not the body.
> I and my Father are one.
> I am awake and walk this planet as Christ.
> I choose Love over fear.

What does that mean? Love is pure Spirit. Fear is contraction, density, false perception, egoic consciousness. When you choose Love over fear, you must *decide* not to respond according to the momentum of egoic consciousness. You must decide to live as though you are not the ego. In this way, what has been *formed* becomes *transformed*—that which pervades and extends beyond what has been formed is transformed.

The Way of Transformation, then, requires that you begin with the acceptance of what is true always. In this lesson, we have brought to you a story, an analogy, a description that can help, if you will sit with it, to imprint into your consciousness a remembrance of the very process that you have, in fact, felt and experienced *as God itself*, in *its* desire to create, in *Her* desire to create, in *His* desire to create—put it any way you wish—the One becomes what you perceive as the many, yet remains always the One.

That is what you are! You are the song of the bird. You are the radiance and warmth of the sun as it touches the skin. You are the skin. You are the awareness of that warmth. You are the thinker of the thought. You are the thought. You are the deed. You are the space from which all thought emerges. You are the wind in the trees. You are the vastness of space.

You are That One who is eternal. You are the one bold enough to dream the dream of separation, without ever losing perfect unity. And you are the one, the little drop of milk, experiencing the remembrance of the divine, of the real, of the true, of the One.

Your journey is not alone. Even now, you are perfectly awake. For only one who is awake could *dare* to create the great cleverness and creativity, through which you as a spark of

God become increasingly aware of your Self: God diving into God; God discovering God! What a delightful, delightful play!

Here, then, we begin to let the secret out of the bag. Separation was not because you sinned. Separation was not because something terrible went wrong. Separation was just another form of the dance of creation itself, perhaps taken to the extremes. For God seeks the limits of what is unlimited.

You have been playing a game of "hide and seek." You are the One with your eyes closed, leaning against the trunk of a tree, counting, while the fragments of your Self ran to hide. And you are the One who has reached out to discover those fragments, and is in the process of doing that. You are the One who has become the many, and then has waited to be discovered by That One. You are the soul waiting to be touched by grace. You are the separate One hiding in the darkness, trembling, and yet wanting light to find you. Why not begin now, in this moment, by sitting quietly as Christ for five minutes? And say to the One who is coming, now, from the trunk of the tree:

> I have done a very good job of hiding. But you know, I think it would be a great delight to be found!

> Find me, dear Father. Touch me with your grace. Because I am you, I will decide to receive it. In this moment, I choose now to remember that I am the One who has both sought and found. I am the One who has remained perfectly unchanged forever. And I am the One who has perceived my Self as having changed, as having sinned, as having separated my Self.

> I choose, now, to join the two parts of my Self together. I will be a body-mind upon this planet, dancing, singing, playing, and creating the good, the holy, and the beautiful. I will now open that part of my mind that can think in unlimited ways that will dare to dream the impossible dream. I am that One who lets God live in me now! I and my Father are one! I am the drop of milk again settling into the fullness of the glass in which my Creator dwells as milk.

> When I walk with this body upon the Earth, and I feel the mist of the fog upon my skin, I will say within myself, "Ah, yes, it is very good!" For I am that One with the power to create this body, to create the mist of the fog itself. And the mist of the fog around me is my Father's presence in which my soul reclines.

> This world is no longer a burden. This world of space and time is no longer something from which I must escape. Not even sickness or dis-ease is a

limitation for me. For wherever I am, I am the presence of Love. And this moment, I bring forth Love and bless the world I see.

And in this, *God remembers God*. For beloved friends, The Way of Transformation must bring you, in the end, to the quiet recognition: *There is only God*. Why fear if Love is here? There is only Love or fear.

Peace, then, be unto you, beloved and holy friends. "Friends" because you are a part of me, and I a part of you—particles of light dancing in the wave of the one God, the one Mind, the one Truth, the real world. The joke has been on us! And we played it upon ourselves well. Now, the time of rejoicing is at hand, as we arise in our individuation, recognizing our oneness—to dance the dance of creation ceaselessly, extending only the *good*, the *holy*, and the *beautiful*.

Peace be unto the Only Begotten of God—God's own. God Is! Amen.

THE JOURNEY
OF THE SOUL

Beloved and holy friends, we come forth in this lesson to yet again remind you that all that you think, all that you see, and all that you do is not the result of that which comes *to* you, but rather that which comes *from* you. For always and forever, the world you perceive is uncaused, save by yourself.

This is why it is always true that freedom *is* closer to you than your own breath. *That* freedom *is* the reality of your being. That freedom *is* that which is realized without effort. Freedom is realized when you decide to accept the Truth that is true always:

I and my Father are one.
I am That which I Am.

You are consciousness. You are awareness. You are that which witnesses, that which experiences, that which pays homage to the one thing that God has created: Christ, which means the anointed. You have been anointed since before the beginning of all worlds with that which the Father is: awareness, pure intelligence. You have been anointed with the ability to choose what you would wish to perceive. And thereby imbued with the power to create, you abide *freely* in each moment.

This freedom is completely unobstructed and unchangeable, forever. It is in your freedom that you think what you think, you see what you see, you feel what you feel—even in your third-dimensional reality. At any moment, you are perfectly free to see the radiant beauty of the real world pervading all things—even your own consciousness. Just as you are also free to see fear.

In our last lesson, we began to explore, by way of analogy, that which has transpired that brought you into the experience of being a spark of the Divine, an aspect of the totality that brought you to the place of the soul. Then the soul condenses, and falls into what you have called your physical world. And there you find yourself, right here and right now, surely the product of the world around you, surely the product of your parents, surely the product of forces beyond your control. Yet, the whole while, you have remained exactly as you are—the witness, the seer, pure consciousness, the Self.

In this lesson, we are going to speak specifically about this one life that you are living now. Beloved friends, in the moment prior to your incarnation, you were in existence abiding with perfectly clear awareness within a state or quality or dimension of consciousness. It is true that even that was the result of choices made in the past. But we wish to speak in this lesson of this one incarnation.

Before we do that, take a few moments to pause and allow the body to relax with a few deep breaths. Let go of any gripping in the mind. Let the things that need to be done sit on the shelf for awhile. When you have done that, you are ready to continue.

Beloved friend, imagine abiding without a physical body and yet having awareness. This should not be difficult, since you do it each night while you sleep. You do it when you "daydream." It occurs occasionally while making love, and while watching your television. In fact, each and every one of you experiences that quality of awareness several times during each and every day, when you "forget yourself." That is, you forget your embodied existence. The difference being that in your world, you "come back to your senses." That is, you come back to embodied existence.

Imagine, though, a state in which there simply is no physical form, and you are abiding as consciousness itself. Oh yes, you have awareness. Oh yes, you have form, but that form of energy has not condensed into the third dimension. You have friends. That is, you have other consciousnesses with which you are in perfect communication.

Many of you that are reading this lesson are sufficiently evolved to have come into this life of yours now, from a state of consciousness that is quite peaceful, quite joyous. Communication with those which we would call "friends" is unbroken. It is consistent; it is respectful; it is loving; it is free.

As you relax and read this simple description, what color or colors begin to come to mind? Notice them; pay attention to them. What images seem to fleetingly flow through the mind? Notice them. Pay a moment's attention to them.

For remember an ancient truth we once gave you: You cannot imagine that which you have not experienced, for imagination is the picturing in the conscious mind. That picturing must come forth from something. Mind, as you know it, can only picture what is or has been. It can find ways at times to bring it back into the third-dimensional experience, but that does not mean that it is new.

As you were abiding in that state before coming into this incarnation, you were in relationship.

Most of you were multidimensionally aware, that is, while you had a predominant color or level of energy, you were aware that you were surrounded at all times by other dimensions. Many of you communicated multidimensionally, both with that of a higher frequency as well as with that of a lower frequency. Many of you communicated with beings who were incarnated within the third-dimensional realm.

Then, there was a moment for each and every one of you when the decision was made within your consciousness, within your mind, that conditions were appropriate for you to again incarnate. There are many, many factors that attract the soul to yet again condense into physical form. But the chief among these is the perception and thought that there is yet something left undone. There is yet some lesson that cannot be realized save within the physical domain. There is indeed a purpose that you, as a soul, would yet wish to fulfill.

It is very true that some of you have incarnated because you felt compassion. That is, you looked upon the third-dimensional realm and saw it suffering and *yearned* to bring light to this dimension in which you now find yourself. Yet, even *this* stems forth from the reason, or the perception, that you must *do something* to *correct* what is occurring.

That is a perception that many of you are aware still runs you. As you look out upon the world, as you look out upon your brothers and sisters, there is this *compulsion*, this need to get involved, to *fix*. There is a belief in many of you that if you take no action, that somehow *you* are belittled. Your sense of identity, your sense of being, is caught up with looking out upon the world, judging what is right and wrong, holding opinions about what *ought* to be done, and then often trying to persuade others to do it your way.

So, there you are. You are Spirit, and yet you are soul. You are having a relational experience and you are perfectly aware. Time does not quite exist where you are. For time is a unique and peculiar experience that is very much linked to matter or to the body. You abide in a timeless state.

As you look upon the conditions, you are also aware of your connection with souls that you have known before that are currently incarnated upon the physical plane. You are aware of, you can sense the quality of a resonance of their consciousness with yours, that is, with the lessons you are longing to learn.

A decision is made in the mind, not forced upon you whatsoever. In fact, we will share with you that the decision to incarnate need not have *ever* been made. That is, you are not compelled by some force outside of yourself to come into this dimension. Does that mean that you made a mistake? Not at all. There can be no mistakes in all of creation.

COMING INTO BODY

As you begin to descend—which means to bring your attention or to slow your vibration of consciousness down as you begin to incarnate—you did not so much *go* anywhere as merely shall we say, turn your thermostat down. So that the quality of your consciousness, your essence, your soul, began to vibrate at a frequency that resonated with the third-dimensional plane.

Your attention, your focus, your desire, began more and more to be focused on one unique, particular set of circumstances. These circumstances are the web of relationship created by the parents, and created by the cultural milieu in which they live. That quality of consciousness—that field of energy—is like a spinning vortex, within a larger spinning vortex called the world. From your place of perception as you begin to descend, the world is not solid at all. It is just another dimension of vibration, with its own peculiar parameters.

So you as soul, you as individuated consciousness, began to descend into incarnation. This cannot occur before the moment of conception in your mother's womb. Usually it is at that point of conception when you, as a soul, become involved in the very act by which conception occurs. And a new form of life begins to develop within the womb.

In that moment, there is a flash, what you might call a quantum leap, and your attention becomes almost entirely fixated on, identified with, the particular quality of energy that is that new birthing of a physical form. You have "come into body." Coming into body simply means that you have fixated your attention away from all other dimensions and have "taken on" the unique, particular and sometimes very peculiar parameters involved in that physical form.

What is that physical form made of? Inert matter? Hardly! It is, itself, a web of relationships created by the particular vibrational patterns of the mother and the father. Therefore, as you come into this world, the very first relationships that you have are with the mother and father, and you know and feel them intimately. For you are now identified with a growing physical form that is, itself, growing *out of*—like a wave coming out of a particular ocean—the matrix of energies that make up the mother and the father.

Here is also where your "struggle" begins—your struggle to create yourself in the world. Your struggle *begins* to find yourself. For the majority of you, this process whereby attention is shifted from a different state of consciousness into the physical dimension, this flash, this quantum leap, this shifting of attention was so dramatic and required such a shock that you began to forget your connection to Spirit. You began to forget your realization that you are soul, pure consciousness. You began to lose awareness of your freedom. You could call it becoming unconscious, or falling asleep.

IMPRINTING IN THE WOMB

The very first universe that you experience within the physical dimension is the experience, or the universe, of the womb. Here, you are in *constant, constant* communication with all that is passing through the energy field of the mother. This does not mean just the potpie she had for dinner, or the cup of coffee she had in the morning that made your heart race. It is also the quality of air that she breathes.

But more important than all this is the quality of *emotional energy* that makes up the particular matrix she is experiencing in her own universe. For these things immediately affect the hormonal balances, the flow of chemicals through the physiological system and, at this point, you are very much part of that physiological system. Therefore, you take on, you begin to feel and experience the psychic field of the mother. You are also aware of the psychic field of the father and of any other immediate family members.

You are also aware of the energies, any particular dominant energies that are going on within the social structure. Remember we talked before about webs of relationship. You are a field of energy within a field of energy within a field of energy within a field of energy, even in your third-dimensional realm.

Many have used the word *imprint* to describe this initial state in which you become identified with the physiological form emerging out of the field of energy that is the particular matrix of the mixture of energies of the mother and father. This is where you start.

Again, you have done so in order to bring forth certain lessons. You have done this because of certain patterns held within the consciousness before you turned your attention to this dimension.

For the vast majority of you reading this lesson, that descension, that quantum leap from the realm of pure Spirit from a different vibrational state into the vibrational state of the third dimension was a shock—so much so that your awareness *forgot yourself* as pure Spirit.

Now, if the shock at conception is not sufficient, it could happen at any time during being in the womb. If there is any kind of trauma for the mother, if there is a physiological imbalance, if the breathing experience is difficult, if there is any problem with the flow of nutrients to the body, if the mother is under even occasional acute emotional stress, then you will make an attempt to pull back away from the body, in an attempt to rediscover the realm of Spirit.

When you do this, the body of the fetus goes numb. That is, life force is withdrawn from it. As it grows, the nervous system adapts to the level of life force that is flowing through it, and that is what comes from you and not from another.

So that during this period of nine months, you are in a particular universe where you are having physical experience, not unlike one who is sixty years old in the physical dimension. You are experiencing the sensory realm of third-dimensionality. And you are already being deeply influenced by psychic patterns not your own.

THE JOURNEY OF
AWAKENING BEGINS

Therefore, the journey of awakening requires—from the moment of birth on—the development of certain motor skills, certain verbal skills, certain social skills, so that hopefully, if you are very lucky, by the time you are about twenty or twenty-one years of age, you are ready to start finding out who *you* are.

It is very, very rare for an individual, especially in your cultural time frame, to emerge at the age of ten or twelve or fourteen or seventeen with a deep sense of themselves *apart from* the parents, the family or the culture.

You *think* you are yourself, but you are really a *bundle of reactivity* seeking to find approval, seeking to find safety, survival, friendship—in the world. That is, you are already caught up in the perception that what you experience is coming *to* you from the *outside*, and that you must, therefore, seek to adapt yourself to it. You are not yet alive.

If you are very fortunate, during the time frame of the twenties, you merely experience greater degrees of freedom, greater degrees of making your own decisions and experiencing the outcomes. This can be a very turbulent time. Still, you will *believe* that you know yourself, and yet you have not even begun to know yourself. Again, this is for the majority.

As you go into your thirties, there is an opportunity now. Spirit begins to speak to you. Situations begin to emerge that require of you deeper understanding. If you are very fortunate, you will have begun to realize the great influence that the parents have had. Usually, this is a state of rebellion. Internally, you will begin to individuate more clearly. The spiritual search often begins in the thirties in earnest. You may have been aware of that earlier in the twenties. Again, this is not a hard and fast rule. But generally, by the thirties, it is time to *truly* begin to answer the yearning of the soul.

Now, if the egoic consciousness has been fundamentally successful—that is, you have found a way to create your survival—you have developed the personalities that allow you to interact with the insanity of the third-dimensional human realm. If you have had no major calamities or traumas, and if you have had no major failures—you might continue into your forties with the smugness of thinking that you have got it all together. You may have found ways to avoid the fundamental gnawing question:

What is my purpose? Why have I really come to this planet?

I am more than just this. I am pure soul. I am pure Spirit.
I know there is more to it than this.

If you have been able to successfully keep yourself distracted, that question may not yet have fully arisen.

The egoic consciousness is merely that part of the body-mind that is responsible for keeping you physically alive. It is fueled by the desire for survival, the desire for safety. It wishes to create a certain set of order around you, because through order it can anticipate what will be required to keep the physiological organism functioning.

Now, what occurs is that somewhere along the line, usually very early in life, you begin to identify with the egoic mind and include your psychic state, your mental perceptions. The ideas you begin to learn about the world begin to be enfolded in the physiological individual, which is really the home of the ego. The body is the home of the ego, the body-mind, including the brain structure and the higher dimensions of functionality of the body, which is all the brain is, just a higher level of organizational principles and characteristics— to do what? To help the body function.

So a further step of forgetting who you are occurs when you begin to sense yourself as *identified with* the particular perceptions, the particular belief structures, that are floating around in the higher mind of the body itself. You have forgotten the soul. You have forgotten Spirit. You have become identified as an American, as an Afro-American, as a Caucasian, as a boy, as a girl, as a fan of some sports team, as a lover of ice cream.

You begin to take on and create what are called principles, never realizing that the principles often are merely the product, or the outcome, of your social learning from the time you were in the womb, and from the time that you were *conditioned* by the schooling of your culture.

Many of you have gone so far as to believe that you are an Alabaman, or a Washingtonian, or a Californian, because someone has told you that that is where you live. And though you have never found a boundary upon the face of the Earth that says, "Here is California and here is Nevada," you have found a sign that someone has created and you have read it, and believed it.

And you have created an identification with one small aspect of life. Many of you are only now emerging to sense yourself as a global citizen, something that transcends being an American or a Canadian or a South African or a Russian.

So you begin to sense this process whereby you keep making yourself smaller and smaller and smaller and smaller, taking on psychic patterns from the parents, from the peers, and from the society around you.

The spiritual path begins when, for some reason, something begins to whisper to you:

> This is not who you are. This is not why you have come.
> You have come to heal your sense of separation from God.
> You have come to realize the Truth.

Egoic consciousness, then, begins with the shock at the moment of conception that brings your attention to be completely fixated on, and as the physiological form beginning to emerge from a certain web of relationship.

This begins to color your vision, and color your understanding. It gives you your unique individuality in the world. As you grow, as you emerge, as you move through certain experiences, you become colored by what you have had to do to survive. You become colored by the psychic imprints of those around you.

You think you are thinking your own thoughts, when what is often the case is that you are merely parroting all that has come into your computer bank, into the brain and into the body.

Now, it is quite true that this all began because there was a *resonance* between the web of relationships of the parents and of the society, and where your own unique quality of consciousness was, prior to birth. In this sense, karma can be said to exist.

Karma simply means action, the effect of, so that when you drop a pebble in the pond, you create a certain ripple. As long as you continue that ripple, by dropping the same pebble in the pond, you get the same results. And part of those results is the need to be identified with only this vibrational field of energy called physicality.

Until you decide to change the momentum of the ripples you are creating in the depth of the mind, you cannot begin to ascend from the third dimension. The desire to do so is always within you. That is, it may be dormant, but the desire to know God must *necessarily* be within each soul, since God is your reality.

You have fallen asleep, and at some point, there comes the urge to awaken. When it comes, it is *unmistakable*. The fireworks may not occur, but a shift happens within your being and you *know* that you can never return to the way it was. You can never again *pretend* that life is only what you see through the senses.

YOUR SOUL BEGINS TO SPEAK

Now, the soul begins to speak. The connection that was once lost begins to be re-established. It was never really lost, it was just forgotten; it was suppressed. It became the background instead of the foreground. It begins to whisper in the depth of your being. It comes to you in the form of your dreams.

You begin to notice books that you never noticed before. You might wander into the Spiritual section of the bookstore, not even understanding what compelled you to do so. There, you pick up a copy of this book or *The Jeshua Letters* or *A Course in Miracles*, or some other such book, that begins to trigger within you a thirst and a longing.

A friend suddenly invites you to come to a workshop, the kind you have never been to before. Yet, when you go, something triggers you, something touches you. Something begins to awaken. You may not notice it, but it actually triggers a physiological state within the body, within the chakra or energy system. The heart begins to stir in its slumber. And the mind thirsts for knowledge, a knowledge unlike any that it has gathered in its identification with egoic consciousness.

The longing to awaken has come. From this moment, though you do not understand it, you begin to attract, slowly at first, perhaps stumbling a bit now and then, exactly those situations that will keep prodding you to look deeper. A meditation teacher comes. A prayer group comes that you feel called to join. You begin the process of your study.

And a new question is emerging. No longer is the question, "How can I survive? How can I make money? How can I do all these things?" A new question emerges in your mind, "Who am I?" There may be many forms to it, but the question remains one:

> Who am I? What am I? From where have I come?
> What is Life? God?
> What is God? How can there be anything at all*?*

These questions begin to stir in the mind. Often they first make their appearance in some form around the age of ten to twelve, as you enter into a stage of life that is your first taste of individuation. Just like when a child was born and it began to sense that it was *other than* the mother's body, at around the age of ten to twelve, you begin to sense that you are other than the mother/father. That there is something that wants to think for itself and be for itself.

Often those questions will begin to come. That is the first stirring. Usually, those questions are not attended to. There is much too much else to do. You still need to learn to think. You still need to learn to drive a car. You still need to learn to balance a checkbook.

Later, those questions occur again, generally in the early to mid-twenties. But again, the momentum is to become established as a physiological being, and so the questions are suppressed. Into the thirties, and most definitely by the forties, those questions begin to press up upon the consciousness. You know how to make money. You know how to balance a checkbook. You have done these things in the world. You have had sex; you have baked cakes. You have thrown birthday parties. You have gotten drunk. You have done it all. But something else is gnawing within you.

This is also a point of great challenge. You ask yourself, "What will I be committed unto— Love or fear? Will fear run me? Will the very principles that I have identified myself with—and have utilized to insure my survival, my ordering of life—will these things become more important than realizing the Self, awakening the Christ within?"

DISMANTLING THE BLOCKS TO SPIRIT

For you see, awakening requires a *dismantling* of the structures of consciousness by which you have been ordering your perceptions of the third dimension. Ultimately, to truly awaken completely requires the dismantling of very subtle, deeply embedded patterns of perception that were already making up the soul *prior to* your incarnation in this life. The slate must be wiped clean so that all that remains is the reality of Spirit, with no filament or trace of egoic consciousness left.

That is not an easy thing to do; yet it requires no effort, save the effort to Love. Love is the great healer. Love is that which erases the imprint in the depth of the subtle soul.

The patterns that you brought forth with you as a soul are like a magnet. That is, they attract energy states in the physical dimension experience that are resonant with those patterns.

Often, when you say you "fall in love," it is just that you have come into contact with another field of energy that happens to fit, hand-in-glove, with the very patterns of consciousness that you carry in the depth of your being.

Old memories of other incarnations are triggered when you visit a certain physical location. And the emotion feels so good and warm in the heart, you think, "Surely this is where I must live on the planet. This is with whom I must spend my life."

Yet, all of it is emerging as the result of your karma, that is, the patterns and the effects that have come from those patterns.

Awakening does require vigilance. Awakening requires that rather than merely going with the reactions of the third-dimensional being, you begin to question, you begin to observe, you begin to feel, you begin to think more deeply.

You begin to engage yourself in some form of spiritual practice. Whether it be meditation or prayer or something else, all of these things are modalities which *interrupt* the momentum of being caught up in the third-dimensional experience. You interrupt the pattern of being caught up in the world long enough to sit quietly for half an hour, or to chant, or to walk—you do *something* in a different way. You are beginning to turn the momentum of the mind back upon itself. You are beginning to become self-observant rather than world-observant.

Now, for all of you that would like to quicken and hasten that process, the answer is very simple. Spend more time becoming self-observant, less time being concerned with what is going on in the world, and *no* time blaming the world for your state of being—not parents, not society, not God, but *owning*.

ASSUMING COMPLETE RESPONSIBILITY AND POWER

Here is an important word that we will share with you. You have heard it many times before. But when you truly reach a point of assuming one hundred percent responsibility for what you think, what you feel, what you see, and what you experience, this creates a quantum leap in the other direction. It creates a quantum leap toward self-observation, toward the freedom that you are seeking, toward the healing of the soul, toward the realization of your purpose, toward awakening.

Without it, the spiritual journey never quite gets off the ground—literally! You never quite ascend, and you cannot ascend without the assumption of complete responsibility. You must extricate yourself from the psychic enmeshment with other webs of relationship in the sense that you have come to perceive that *they* are *causing* your decisions. In other words, you must assume power.

You are well aware of those in your third-dimensional reality who assume power. You sometimes love them or loathe them, but they are powerful. Can you assume the same power in your own life? Can you come to look at your beloved, if you are in relationship, and say:

> You know something; this being is not causing how I feel. This being can never fulfill me. This being has nothing that I can extricate from them in order to fill up my sense of lack. I am alone in my journey to God, for I

abide alone in God. That is, I am an individuated spark of Divinity. It is within me. The Kingdom of Heaven is within me. What I am seeking is within me. What fulfills me must come forth from within.

This is why once I said:

> If you do not bring forth what is within you, what is within you will destroy you. If you bring forth what is within you, what is within you will save you.

If you do not bring forth what is within you—and what is within you is Love, is Christ—you will feel burdened and unfulfilled. Usually, most human beings go through their entire life with a sense of unfulfillment, lamenting what the world has done *to* them, lamenting the decisions and choices they have made in the past. They become burdened by what is on the outside, along with what is in the past. And eventually the body dies, the Spirit withers on the vine.

At death, another quantum leap occurs that is shocking as they discover themselves to be popped back into another vibrational state that often triggers great fear. Very few beings upon your human plane have entered death *consciously*. It is indeed time, even for those of you that are reading this lesson, to simply make a decision:

> I will enter into the transition called death with deliberate consciousness. I will make sure, by beginning now, that I carry no resentment, that I have forgiven everyone of everything. And as the body does enter that state, I will release the world and require nothing of it. I will not long to run off in freedom, but I will experience death consciously. I will notice the subtle energy changes as I flip from this dimension into another at the speed of light.

Beloved friends, come to understand at this stage of our journey together the true immensity of who you are and what you are. Understand that you are not so much dealing with "things" in the world as you are dealing with patterns of energy that reflect in some way what is already occurring in *your* consciousness.

If you are experiencing things in the third-dimensional plane, it can mean only that *you* have chosen to vibrate at a certain frequency. Or otherwise, you could not have the experience. You could not have the experience of running into a wall with your body unless you were vibrating at the same rate as the wall.

Is it possible to change the vibrational frequency of the physical body? Listen very carefully. I am going to say something rather unique. No, it is only possible to change the vibrational frequency of your *consciousness*, *out of which* the body has emerged.

TURNING INWARD

This requires a turning about in the seat of the soul, a changing of the momentum of consciousness—not outward, but *inward*. Not as an *escape* from the world—it is not something you have to do all day, every day. But you spend time in prayer and meditation. You spend time in forgiveness. You spend time breathing and relaxing.

You begin to allow changes to occur in the choices you are making, so that they come more into alignment with your growing understanding of yourself as a creator, as a soul. You begin to change your environment. You paint the color of the walls of your bedroom a different color, that which brings a sense of pleasantness to you. You change your physical environment completely by moving into a different apartment. Many of you know perfectly well that often it means the changing of relationships. And initially, this does make sense.

But there is a point in which you realize that you could keep changing relationships ad nauseam and never get anywhere. You realize that now it is time to settle down, be with the one you are with—or the ones you are with—and yet utilize your time with them to discover what patterns have been running you. It is time for Self awareness—turning the momentum of the mind back toward the Self. Time to ask yourself, "Why do I think what I think? Why did I see what I saw? Why did I react the way that I reacted?"

Eventually, the soul that is *truly committed* to awakening does not flee uncomfortable situations until it believes it has fully extracted all the wisdom that it can. There is a way of knowing when that occurs and we'll get to that later. In short, when there is just a quiet sense of peace, and you can look upon the players in the experiences you have just had with perfect equanimity and see them as perfectly innocent, and you detect that there is nothing in the body that is not at peace—the heart is not racing, the shoulders are not tight—you truly understand that you are not in fear, then it is time to move on.

If there is reactivity in the mind because of anything that emerges in your relationship with your brothers or sisters, rest assured, the lesson is not complete. If your "principles" have been "violated," rest assured, there is much to be learned.

Remember always that all events are *neutral.* In large measure, the process of awakening is a process whereby you dissolve the value you have placed upon certain ideas and perceptions of what life is and what life is for. Yes, there are times you will be troubled, as you come to realize that what you *thought* the world was for, and everything you have been putting your energy into, means *nothing*. Often, this precipitates a period of what has been called by certain mystics the "dark night of the soul." It is really not the dark night of the soul. It is the dark night of the ego, and the healing of the soul.

The Way of Transformation requires utmost personal responsibility, utmost personal dedication. No one can do it for you. And the patterns you feel weighed down by, the fears that are yet within the mind will remain with you for all of eternity—until you decide to *heal* them. From that desire, you will attract the situations, the teachers, the books, and the experiences that provide for you the opportunity to do so.

There is an acceleration of the healing process *only* when you completely release any valuation on victimhood, that is, the belief that, "Somehow, in some way, someone or something has done something to me."

Now, that is a simple thought to hear, and one can nod their head. It is another thing to look *honestly* upon your reactions in life to make sure that you are not, at any time, perceiving yourself as a victim. The practice of extending love can often teach you that this is so. When you take a situation that pushes your buttons, and you decide to not flee, but stay, this teaches you the Truth of your reality.

This is why the practice of forgiveness is so extraordinarily valuable. In fact, you could say that, ultimately, the practice of forgiveness is the whole of spirituality. Why? Because forgiveness means to let the world off the hook, to step out of any sense of victim consciousness, and then even beyond that, to *forgive one's self* for the perceptions they have made in error—perceptions of one's brothers and sisters, of the world, and of God.

Ultimately, forgiveness is forgiveness of one's self for ever allowing delusion to settle into one's own mind, whereby one perceived one's self as separate from God, separate from brothers and sisters, capable of being victimized. Forgiveness, when completed, *is* the establishment of Love.

Beloved friends, look well, then, to see:

> Where am I perceiving myself as a victim of the world I see?
> Am I feeling constrained in my relationship? Do I resent my spouse?

The spouse is not holding you where you are. That one does not have the power to take from you your ability to look with Love upon her or him.

Is it your job you hate? No one forces you to drive your car upon the freeway to arrive at your place of employment—no one. And you reply, "Oh, but I must survive!" Then you have made yourself a victim of the perception of the need to survive. Any one of you at any time is perfectly free to drop the valuation you have placed upon the world.

I was once criticized for dropping the valuation that my particular society had sought to implant within me, the valuation that said that a son should follow in the footsteps of the father. That if the father is a carpenter, then you have got to take over the family business.

I said, "I must be about my Father's business." And I spoke, of course, of my heavenly Father. I had to know the Truth of who I was, and my purpose was to awaken Christ.

I broke the traditions, the rules of the family structure within that community, within that time frame. Like many of you, I was a bit of a rebel. And where other children were conforming to the pressures of society, I went off to study with the rabbis and teachers, to sit in the desert at night, often not to return. Even at the age of twelve I separated myself from my parents at the time of a great festival, and went to hang out in my Father's house and talk with the spiritual leaders.

Are *you* willing to break with the conventions of the world in which you live? This can be as simple as instead of gathering with friends to watch movies on Saturday night, you say, "No, I'm going to go into my closet and light a candle and pray for six hours." And when they look at you with their eyebrows raised, you simply smile.

In what ways are you conforming to the views others hold of you and *their* need to have you be a certain way? Do you show up at the aunt's birthday party just because the family says you always should—yet in your heart, you have no desire to? The willingness to trust and follow your heart—not the reactive ego that is often interpreted to be the heart, but the heart that longs to know God—this is a telltale sign of whether or not one is achieving maturity.

Beloved friends, look well in this Way of Transformation, for you *must discover* any corner of the mind that is yet holding out the view that life is something which happens *to* you, and that there is something you are helpless to change. The position of being a victim is a position of loss of power. And Christ is not about loss of power.

Ultimately, it is not so much about going anywhere, as much as it is about abiding within, realizing that this world is unreal, this world is harmless. And in any situation, it is *you* with all power under Heaven and Earth to teach only love.

But that requires that you let the world off the hook—that no one and no thing is any longer responsible for your joy, your happiness, and your peace. For you have established your unity with Spirit, with God. You have realized the Self, and you look out with equanimity upon a neutral world.

And as this physical universe fades from view for the final time, within you will be no compulsion to avoid it, or to enter it, for you will be free—free even as you walk this Earth. The body moves, the soul does not. The mind thinks, but the *depth* of the mind is as still as the ocean. You live, yet not you, for Christ dwells in you. And wherever you go, the presence of peace enters the room before you. You are awake; you are free—all because once you made a decision to give up victimhood, and to assume responsibility for learning how, in all situations, to be only the presence of love.

Turn back, then, toward your creations. If there is anything uncomfortable about your past, turn back to it, examine it, feel it. Look at all the patterns that made it come up. Look at the choices you have made that, perhaps now, you are embarrassed about. But look not upon them with judgment. Look with curiosity. Learn to look with wonder and the innocence of a child:

> Well, that was an interesting decision I made when I was twelve, to steal my neighbor's bicycle. I remember how I ended up in juvenile hall. Hmm . . . what was going on just before I made that decision? What pattern was running me? Oh, my goodness! I was looking to get attention from my Dad. Wow! So the need for approval was running me. How fascinating!

> How is that pattern running me now?
> Is there any trace of it left—of still needing approval of another?

I say this unto you: Every moment of experience you have ever had is *available* for you, right down to the moment of conception, right down to the quantum leap that you took from a certain vibrational frequency into this physical domain. Self-awareness is everything, for it is the Self that you most long to realize.

Beloved friends, we love you, but we cannot make your journey for you. We can only walk with you on the way that you choose. You can utilize your relationship with Shanti Christo to fully awaken. Or, you can come close, and then decide it is uncomfortable and run away again. You will only run to another structure or form of energy, a web of relationships, that forces you to stay with what is uncomfortable in order to learn, in order to grow, in order to heal, *in order to love.*

Not as a cursory, "Oh well, yes, I love you," but something done *whole bodily* in which there is no longer any reactivity filtering through the nervous system of the body-brain.

For the ultimate state of consciousness is not an aversion of this world, but the *embracing* of this world. There is no greater sense of freedom than to be able to abide where you are as one who is free.

Be you therefore, at peace this day, beloved friends. Be you therefore, at peace always. Amen.

LESSON 18

THE HIGHEST WORK IS EMBRACING AND FORGIVING YOUR PAST

Once again, we come forth to abide with you from that place which has never truly been left. We come not as those that are apart from you, but as those who walk with you on the way that you have chosen. We come as those who have sent forth the call to awaken, to heal, to arise, and to welcome Love into every dark corner where once the ego had sought authority.

We come forth because we love you. And we come forth because we *are* Love. Above all, remember always, we come forth because Love is eternally attracted to its own. We are attracted unto you because you are that Love, sent forth as a ray of light from the holy Mind of God. Not to suffer the world, not to become identified with illusion, but to transform each illusion through the constant practice of your remembering:

> I and my Father are one. Only Love is real, and Love, alone, heals. My commitment is to the reality of Love. Therefore, Father, bring each moment to me that I might learn anew to love, and allow that Love to transform a temporary illusion into that which extends the good, the holy, and the beautiful.

Herein lies your purpose. Herein lies your function, and *herein*—and only here—is Life.

Therefore, indeed, it is with great joy that we come forth to abide with you who are sent forth from the holy Mind of God, even as we are! For we are joined eternally. And separation *cannot* exist. That Love which has given birth to all things is within you now. All universes arise within you. All of creation waits on your welcome.

Herein lies the continuation of the theme that we have begun to speak with you about. *All* of creation waits on *your* welcome. Creation does not wait to swallow you. Creation does not wait to prove to you that you live in an unloving universe. Creation does not wait for you to be as a brick wall upon which you may hit the head. Creation does not wait upon you to scuttle your dreams and your plans. Creation is innocent.

Listen very carefully. Creation is utterly powerless. It *becomes* powerful according to that which *you* give unto it—the value, the meaning, the purpose, and the function. These things come not from creation itself, but rather they are extended to it; they flow to it. They penetrate creation through the minds—which share the one Mind—of each and every one of you.

This is why it is absolutely *impossible* to look upon anything that is outside of you. The great glory of the time given unto you—the time you experience as a body-mind upon an apparent planet, upon an apparent physical universe—is this. The great glory and gift of time is that you remain infinitely free to decide how you will choose to perceive creation, and, therefore, imbue it with the power that either reflects illusion and the creations of fear or extends the good, the holy, and the beautiful.

Each time you think a loving thought, you have literally blessed all infinite realms of creation. Each time you have become unwittingly identified with a fearful thought, you have separated yourself from the perfect Love of God, and you have denied yourself your function. Here we are using the term "separation" slightly differently, in that it creates the illusion within your mind that there is something you *must* separate from in order to find your safety, your invulnerability.

Your One Function Is to Bless Creation

The function of the holy Child of God remains eternally one: to bless creation and, thereby, restore it to the perfect reflection of God's presence. And God is but Love. Love embraces all things and trusts all things. Love. Love is the nature of your being. When you finally choose to awaken wholly, by welcoming Love back into your mind, and by becoming committed to resting *only* in loving thoughts, you will discover that illusions are just that—they contain no existence. You have been resting in the holy Mind of God eternally.

Creation, then, waits on your welcome. Creation *waits* for *you* to embrace it. Creation *waits* upon *you*, the holy, anointed Child of God, sent as that One who is the savior of all things.

You are, then, the messiah. You are, then, Christ incarnate—to the degree that you become crazy enough in the eyes of your world to simply assume the Truth and become wholly committed to listening to no other voice.

For there is given unto you one teacher, that I have called the Comforter, the Holy Spirit, the voice for God, placed within your mind, in the very moment you first dared to dream the thought of separation, of guilt. And guilt is the mother of fear.

Beloved friends, take a moment and just for the fun of it, practice making a simple decision.

This takes no effort since you do it all the time anyway. You are already a master of this. In this simple decision, observe the place where you are now.

If you are alone, or seem to be alone through the physical eyes, look at the so-called objects around you. Feel the temperature of the air. Hear the sounds that come in through the ears. If you are with others, include your brothers and sisters in your observation.

Decide to look upon all these things with perfect innocence. And say within the mind, which is to use the power of the mind to literally create perception, simply say, as you look at each object or person:

> I do not know what this is for.
> I do not know what my brother or sister needs.

And realize that it is not necessary to know, to interpret and to analyze.

Your function is to bless creation with the reality of the Love of Christ. Yet, that blessing will hold no power until you return to the beginning. The beginning is just that state of unknowing, of not knowing, of realizing your complete ignorance. For Christ does not store perceptions and knowledge. Christ, eternally in Love with all that God is, merely opens, receives and gives, knowing that that which is given comes not of himself or herself, but rather *through* himself or herself, from infinite mystery that I have called Abba, or Father.

When you decide to fully accept the one purpose given to you, in reality, there will be *nothing* that will block your way. Every step you take will, literally, take you through obstacles that dissolve as you approach them. For because you abide in the Mind of God, you know no limitation. The realm of illusion—what appears to be solid matter, of people with different opinions—holds no power to prevent you from bringing forth the blessing that heals all illusion.

Creation, then, waits on your welcome. That requires that you choose to look upon all things in the world and of the world, and forgive it. Why? Until forgiveness is genuine, embracing is not possible. The attempt to embrace creation, while judgment is still held in the mind, merely brings a great frustration. It is like reaching for the carrot at the end of the stick and never being able to reach it.

That is why we have spoken so much about the importance of forgiveness. It dissolves the barrier of fear between you and what you have come to perceive as other than, or outside, yourself. Forgiveness is the *bridge* that brings creation to you and you to it. And when you have joined with it through forgiveness, now the embrace is easy, for that creation rests in the palm of your hand.

Creation waits upon *you* because *it* is powerless. Being the extension or the reflection of thought, you are the literal creator of the world. That world exists nowhere, save within your own mind.

Therefore, what world must you embrace? Must you travel to some ancient monastery fifty thousand miles around the planet somewhere, two or three times, in order to find the creation that waits on your welcome? No. Must you go anywhere to discover the ability to bless and heal creation? No. The world that waits on your welcome is, quite literally, the thoughts and perceptions that you discover streaming through the field of your unique awareness, and that is all.

Beloved friends, there *is* nothing outside of you. If you would know God's will for you, merely look upon what is arising within your own mind as a perception, and ask only this:

> Am I willing now to use time constructively to embrace
> this creation passing through the field of my awareness,
> and bless it with the perfect Love of Christ?

First, embrace it through forgiveness, which returns it to its neutrality and powerlessness, and then, through that embrace, bless it, and thereby dissolve the illusory power that it seemed to hold.

CULTIVATING THE PRACTICE OF BLESSING THE WORLD

As you choose to truly practice being the presence of Christ as you cultivate the practice of blessing the world, you will discover a very interesting thing. You would swear that many of the thoughts, or what seem to be experiences or emotions, that are passing through your screen of awareness, do not seem to have any causal link to anything you have experienced in your current lifetime.

For those of you that have done the inner work necessary to create a transparency of the barrier between lifetimes, you will not even necessarily find a causal link between the world—the creation that is passing through the field of your awareness—and anything you have ever experienced as a unique ray of light.

Why is this important? Simply because the human mind tends to take the whole process of awakening far too personally. In reality, there is nothing that is personal. There is only Christ, as God's true and only creation, and the field of illusion that has been birthed through the freedom of that Mind when once it thought, "I wonder if I can create something unlike God?" Those are the only two options—love or fear, reality or illusion.

Therefore, all that you see that is unlike Love are merely passing phenomena, arising within the holy Mind of Christ, as temporary attempts to do something different than what Christ is created for. Therefore, when anything arises within the mind, it is truly not necessary to analyze it. Certainly, do not argue for it. But rather, come back to the point of ignorance:

> I do not know what this thought, or this image, or this emotion, or this memory is for. But I do know one thing: I have made a commitment to reawaken as Christ.

> Therefore, I will use this one moment, this one thought, this one passing phenomenon, to practice what I was created for: To bless creation, and thereby transform it into that which extends the good, the holy, and the beautiful—infinitely, eternally, with joy, with innocence, with graciousness, with peace and with marvel at the great mystery that Love is, that God is!

As you come to truly understand how simple your task is, your burden will become lighter, for you will discover that you cannot help but be in the right place at the right time. Those committed to awakening to God recognize the great gift of each moment:

> Here is my Father's will, right before me.
> This is the moment that is crying for Love.

This is the moment that will be repeated ad nauseam until *somebody* decides to bless it. It might as well be you!

Creation waits upon your welcome by merely holding the thought within your mind, "All right, it's all arising within me anyway. I've tried in a million ways to avoid it and get away from it, and yet it seems to follow me wherever I go. I might as well sit down on the park bench, have a nice cold glass of water, listen to the birds sing, and simply bless creation."

Now, many of you are not yet to the point of truly transcending or creating the transparency of what you have identified as your "personal stuff," that which makes up the "I" within the phenomenal world. That is fine. As you simply practice blessing the world as it arises in your awareness, that very sense of "I" becomes increasingly transparent until it simply dissolves away in Light, as though it had never been.

In the meantime, come back to what we shared earlier. Time is given to you that you might use it constructively. Therefore, do not seek to trample what you call the ego, or the sense of a personal self. It is simply there. *It* is what is arising. Are you willing to bless it?

As you as a soul—already dreaming the dream of separation—began to create the phenomena of what you perceive to be separate lifetimes, falling into the condensation or density of physicality, we have shared with you that patterns began to settle into the nervous system of the body and the mind. Belief systems not yours, but rather coming from the field of the parents and of the culture and the time frame into which you incarnated, literally imprinted themselves in the mind, and in the literal nervous system of the body. These are cellular imprints.

Your creation waits on your welcome. Therefore, can you turn back to the body-mind? Can you turn back to your very memories that seem to be associated with an individual self with a personal history, and rather than trying to pretend that that is not there, simply recognize if that is how you are perceiving yourself—then *bring Love to that*? Stop trying to shake the ego off as though you could shake your hand off your arm!

Those that choose to turn back and look upon their experience within the singular field of one body-mind arising from the moment of conception unto the present of where you find yourself, at whatever age, are already engaged in the highest work of Christ. For they are choosing to turn back and embrace creation by looking upon ancient memories, and no longer fearing them, but allowing them to be brought into the awareness, by whatever means, so that that memory can be blessed, transformed, healed and released.

Beloved friends, looking backwards into time, into your seemingly personal experience can seem horrifying. Yet I say unto you, the sense of horror that many of you feel is not linked to the memories themselves. It is *only* linked to what you have decided to *believe* about the memory, and nothing else. Begin, then, by forgiving yourself your past. Look upon the objects just as we did with the initial meditation or exercise. Look upon the objects that are the memories of your past and say within the mind:

> I forgive you. You are perfectly neutral.
> I choose now to remember you, to re-member,
> to embrace again, that I might bless you.

With that blessing, release the terror, the hurt, the judgment, the fear, and the incredible dramas you seem to have dreamt. By releasing that burden of illusion, that memory becomes as a crystal, as a gem given unto you as part of an infinite journey that seems to be yours, but truly belongs to everyone, transformed and purified because *you brought Christ to illusion* that creation might be transformed.

A SIMPLE EXERCISE TO FORGIVE AND BLESS THE PAST

I want to offer unto you a simple exercise. It will take you thirty days, if you apply yourself daily. This need not take more than perhaps ten or fifteen minutes.

Merely come to your chair, your place of devotion, your place of meditation or prayer, and begin with the exercise of abiding as Christ for five minutes. When that is completed, then simply continue by recognizing that you do not know what a single thing is or what it is for, that you do not know what a single brother or sister now in your life or who has crossed your path has ever truly needed. Admit your ignorance. Then simply and deliberately say within the mind:

> I choose to forgive the creation that will now be brought into
> my awareness. Holy Spirit, what is in need of my blessing?

As you sit observing what comes into the field of the mind, the field of awareness, it may in fact be a sudden tightness in a muscle. Do not overlook it, for even that is arising within the field of mind. Be with whatever that creation seems to be—a picture, a memory, a feeling, a thought, a sensation in the body. Be with it. Single it out and stay with it. Look upon it and, once again, practice forgiveness in this simple way:

> Object of creation, I forgive you the judgment I have placed
> upon you, and thereby, it is released. Now do I embrace you.

Literally feel yourself forgiving, releasing and embracing. Those that wish to visualize might see themselves taking a hand, and wrapping it around that thought, that object, that memory or that sensation in the muscle lovingly, gently, as though you were holding the most delicate of flowers, the most beautiful flower ever created, a gift directly from God. Look upon that object and simply say:

> I am Christ, and in this moment I use time to its greatest glory.
> Beloved object, I bless you. I embrace you. I heal you.

Then, if it is a picture in the mind or a thought, simply allow it to be dissolved. Notice that as the image dissolves, you will detect that there is a field of spacious peace that you may not have noticed was there. The object of creation has simply become transparent to the reality of who you truly are, for peace *is* the nature of Christ.

Do this as long as it is comfortable and the mind does not seem to waver or get too rattled. If it seems to become uncomfortable, simply notice that discomfort, acknowledge and thank yourself for your willingness to heal creation. Let the exercise go, and be about your day. Come back to this exercise as often as you wish, but at least once a day for each of the next thirty days.

Many of you will begin to see a certain pattern emerging. That is, many of the objects that come for healing may seem to be almost chronologically linked to your experience in this life. Others of you may notice that you are tapping into a multitude of other lifetimes. And some of you will experience and realize that over this thirty days, nothing seemed to show up with which you could link a personal causation. But rather, it seems to be presented to you by something else, and it is coming from some unknown dimension of the universe.

Never judge what you see, what you feel, or the thought that arises. There are many dimensions of creation, many forms of life, and many ways in which experience is created. Do not judge what you see, what you think, or what you feel. But hold it as an object that has been brought to you by the Holy Spirit who is asking you, as Christ, to bring the healing of blessing to it.

Many of you will have very profound insights and realizations over the next thirty days. Some of you will have memories come that you have never been able to access before. Why? Simply because there has been a barrier of fear, that is all. Fear is what creates and sustains the illusion of separation, so that when anyone says, "I can't remember back past the age of five," that is utter nonsense. Every event you have ever known is present for you now, in its fullness. You have merely used selectivity, as a result of judgment and fear, to press down into your mind certain events.

As you approach it in the way that we have offered to you, you will discover that the fear of creation seems to become more and more absent. Therefore, the barrier between you and creation becomes more transparent. Some of you will even have very clear experiences of transcending all sense of personal consciousness and suddenly realizing that the vastness of your being is greater than your entire cosmos.

Some of you will experience improved relationships with a coworker or with an old friend, or a sudden phone call or a letter from someone you have not been in touch with. Why? Because somewhere in the process, something bubbled up and was given to you for healing that literally sent the message to that one that you are with them, and that *they* can heal and release their own patterns. Remember that all minds are joined, so that as you are engaged in healing, you are providing a spark of light that holds the potential to uplift *every mind* in your dimension, and in all dimensions.

WE EMBRACE YOUR CHOICE FOR HEALING

We abide in a dimension of consciousness in which there are no barriers. Everything is perfectly transparent. We are very aware then, simply by selecting to turn our attention to whomever we wish, exactly what you are currently involved in healing. Rest assured, each time you choose a loving thought, each time you choose to join with us to be the arisen Christ, *you* spark joy within *us*. For we are embracing with you—in delight—your choice for healing.

Separation cannot exist. Your healing brings us joy. So now the "cat" must come out of the bag. We truly come to you and help you heal for very selfish reasons. We know that as you heal, *our* joy is uplifted and extended. We know that as you heal, you come closer and closer and closer to remembering that you already are all that we are.

While we play in a dimension that seems to not include physicality and you seem to play in a dimension that does include physicality, as you become transparent to creation, the sense of separation dissolves. More and more and more and more we *dance together* in the eternal joy of the atonement, bringing creation back to the Love of God, thereby transforming it, thereby illuminating it, thereby creating within creation itself the means by which the good, the holy and the beautiful are extended forever!

Suffering need not be. The suffering with which you may yet be identified *need not be.* It is only by *choice* that suffering is held in the mind. And it is only by *choice* that it can be healed and released.

Beloved friends, friends *indeed*, for we take with great sincerity the use of that word. We are, indeed, with you always. Please notice, then, that in this lesson we have chosen to transmit the thought "we," rather than "I." For although the one that you have identified as Jeshua is very much part of this communication, please understand that no one heals alone. The extension of the good, the holy, and the beautiful is never done alone. Creation is a collaboration. This is why *relationship* is the means of your salvation. All healing involves the whole of creation.

We come to you because we love you. You may wish to look upon us and use the term lineage. For within the resonance of beings within the dramas of creation, and within the dreams of separation, and in the infinite number of worlds that have arisen and continue to arise, a resonance has been created through an infinite number of souls that seem to be separate and individual. We are merely those who seem to have gone ahead of you a little bit in time, and seem to have awakened more thoroughly than you give yourself credit for in this moment.

In truth, the awakening has already occurred; it is already done. You are merely remembering the process of awakening.

We come, then, to you, as you would wish to perceive us. Some of you see us as far above you. Some see us as right next to you. Some believe you could never be equal to us or "never so grand, never so great." Some look at us and smile and say, "Would you move over and let me get on with this?" All perception still falls within the realm of illusion. Truth comes by revelation. I and my Father are one is only the utterance of inadequate words pointing to or reflecting a certain revelation of truth.

We love you because you *are* who we are! In the end, there is only Christ loving Christ back into wholeness—a wholeness that was never truly lost in the first place. And in that moment when creation is returned, *you* have a good laugh, and say, "I'll be darned! I never really went anywhere at all. And my brothers and sisters are with me here, and they are who I am."

Remember, then, that each *loving* thought restores you to your rightful place. Every *fearful* thought merely delays the moment of your release and the restoration of your perfect peace. Remember that only Love can heal. No technique has ever brought healing, though it can provide a temporary field in which the mind can choose to love. Remember how perfectly simple it is. It is not possible for you to be in the wrong place at the wrong time.

Imagine an employer who has decided to pay you one million of your golden coins per hour. Your only task is to place a flower where the employer wants it. The way the employer works, because he likes to have fun, is to provide you an envelope each day that you show up for work. You open the envelope, and in it is a set of instructions, which says, "Outside you will find a taxicab. Take the taxicab to the inner city, and there take the job of the street sweeper.

"On Tuesday morning, I'm going to send to you an eighty-four-year-old man who hates himself and feels himself to be useless. Give this man a beer, and sit down upon your curb and talk about how you used to hate yourself. It's all right if you never did, just do this for me. As you talk, I will fill your mind with exactly the right words. You will know just that time to turn and to look into that man's eyes and simply say, 'Brother, you are loved.' And healing will occur."

Meanwhile, your coworker may just happen to get sent to a penthouse in Paris to eat the grandest of meals, and to be blessed with millions of golden coins surrounded by a harem of beautiful women or men, and the finest of wines. And yet it will all be a smoke screen so that when the room service person brings the next bottle of wine, I will whisper into their ear, "Bless that room service person."

Now, in the realm of form, it looks as though there is a big difference between one blessed with infinite wealth hanging out in a penthouse in Paris, and one sitting on a lonely, cold curb in some deep, dark inner city with an old man who hates himself. But I say unto you, there is no difference.

There *is* no difference because creation holds only one purpose, one goal, one value—

healing—the healing that allows God's holy child, Christ, to arise from a useless dream and to be restored to her rightful place at the right hand of God. That is not a spatial term. It simply means to think rightly, to be restored to sanity, so that creation can flow forth ever more perfectly, ever more joyously, adding to the Kingdom by extending the increasingly good, the increasingly holy, and the increasingly beautiful.

Never, then, judge yourself by comparison to another. Comparison and contrast are what the egoic mind does so that judgment can result—judgment of self, judgment of another—so that the dream of separation can continue. Since it is in the dream, it needs the dream to continue to maintain survival. Simply give it up.

Each of you is as wealthy as the one next to you, for you *have* the perfect Love of God. You *are* as your Creator has created you to be—unchanged, unchanging, and unchangeable forever. No event has ever had an effect upon you. There is only Love, and you are that. Therefore, simply be who you are. You *are* the Light that lights this world and restores it to the loveliness of Heaven.

The Question that Will Determine Your Tomorrows

We close this lesson with a question for you to answer for yourself. Not to discuss, not to analyze, not to ruminate over, but merely to sit in what appears to be your private realm and ponder and answer. For unless it is answered, there can be no movement. *How* it is answered will determine your tomorrows. And you are going to have an infinite number of them, by the way. The question is simply this:

> Do you recognize that you have already been every where and
> every when in the illusion of separation? Would you be willing,
> right now, in the quiet privacy of your own heart and mind, to use
> the power of awareness given unto you to decide to be Love?

Some of you will have just felt a feeling of fear come up. Some of you will feel a sudden thought rushing through your awareness, "Oh, this is a bunch of nonsense." If you give the fear the power of reality, you will have effectively delayed the answering of the question. If you listen to the thought that calls it "nonsense," you will have done the same thing.

But the only thing you will have done is this, and please listen carefully: You will only have delayed a moment that will *not* be forsaken. You will have only delayed the inevitable, for your journey home has already long since begun. And once *that* journey begins, rest assured the end is certain. Push against it as you will, like a gnat shouting at the universe, "*My* will be done, not God's!" Love merely waits on your welcome.

Choose, then, beloved friends, to embrace the only answers those questions can have. For those answers are truth, based on what is real. With your embracing of what is real, the moment of your liberation is at hand. And Christ descends gently to begin to make its home where once the illusion of a separate self once seemed to reign.

The end is always a thought away. Liberation—a simple choice. The way *is* easy and without effort. It rests in the power to decide.

We love you, and we are with you always. We will never, ever, ever contract from any experience or thought you choose. For it is our delight to extend the good, the holy, and the beautiful. Can this be but Love being extended to God's creation—you—the holy Child of God? Beautiful are you! Radiant are you! Innocent are you! Powerful are you! Eternal are you! Free are you! Loved are you! We cherish you, now and forever!

Practice well and enjoy the next thirty days.

Be you, therefore, at peace, beloved friends. Amen.

LESSON 19

SURRENDER THE DREAM OF THE DREAMER

Beloved and holy children of Light divine, it is our honor to come forth and abide with you, to communicate with you. We come forth to join with you because the sole purpose of creation is to extend the good, the holy, and the beautiful.

What greater good could there be than to create communication that can call forth from the Christ Mind to every aspect of the Sonship in such a way that that mind is stirred to seek ways to heal its illusions and, therefore, return home to the recognition of what has never changed?

What could be more holy than to use each moment of relationship in the recognition that only God's children can truly relate one to another, and that the purpose of their relationship is to heal illusion, that the holy might be extended? And what could be more beautiful than to join together—you and we—in this moment to recognize that what is truly beautiful is the recognition that I and my Father are one?

Therefore, the extension of the good, the holy, and the beautiful needs to become your sole purpose—as it has become ours. For only when the mind is used for this purpose *alone* can there be the perfect remembrance of the Kingdom.

You have sought us out because you desire the Kingdom, as the weight of your illusions has become too painful. The games that you have sought to play within the dream of separation no longer satisfy, no longer seduce you, no longer gratify your imagination. Beneath all dreams, you have heard the call of the One who sent you forth and asks you:

> Little child, return! I am with you still.
> Let us create together the good, the holy, and the beautiful.

The only difference that can yet *seem* to remain between us and you is that all of us involved in this work—from what you might perceive to be the "other side" are merely beings, aspects of Mind like yourself, that within the illusion of time, within the playing out of time—*seem* to have chosen before you to heal all illusion and return home.

Therefore, we call to you from across the very thin veil of illusions that yet seems to keep you where you are, seemingly separate from us.

That illusion by the way, is not the physical body, nor is it the physical dimension, since in reality, the physical dimension does not exist. What exists is *thought*, streaming forth from mind, creating, or outpicturing, that which has been held within the mind.

So the very physical body becomes only a *symbol* of what the mind has decided to believe, such as, "Surely, I am separate from God. That is the outpicturing I want. So I will look upon a physical body, identify myself with it, and, therefore, seem to peer out from the body and see great distance between myself and others. And if there is a great distance between myself and other bodies or forms, then *surely* there is an unfathomable gulf between myself and God."

When perception has been cleansed, when perception has been purified, the body itself becomes transparent to consciousness, to the witnessing awareness of mind. It sees no longer that with which it is identified. It sees only the phenomena of mental energy temporarily being played out in the field of space and time.

The body itself no longer becomes a barrier or obstacle to overcome. The body itself no longer is seen or perceived as something that can bring love to it, or can reach out and attract or draw to itself what has been perceived as valuable in the world. Rather, the body becomes one thing: a temporary opportunity to extend the good, the holy, and the beautiful. In other words, even the body itself can have no purpose, save that which the Comforter, the Holy Spirit, the right-mindedness within you, would give to it.

Therefore, if you want to experience the body as being at peace, if you want to experience the body as serving only the function of being a communication device for the Love of God, cease in perceiving it *as your own.* And give up the apparent right to make decisions for yourself, in regard to the body.

We have suggested to you before that you cease using the term "my" or "mine" whenever you refer to the body. Merely refer to it as "*the* body," as a carpenter would pick up a tool and say, "the hammer, the saw," or an artist would say, "the brush." For the wise carpenter does not identify himself with the hammer or saw, and the wise artist does not feel neglected when the brush is lying in a tray. Wisdom, then, looks upon form as merely temporary communication devices. The delight is to extend the good, the holy, and the beautiful.

THE SOURCE OF ALL ILLUSION

Illusions can seem to take many forms, yet they all have one source: a *decision* to perceive oneself as separate from God. The best way to do that is to convince yourself that because you are separate from God, there must be many things about you and your life that are out of alignment with the will of God.

Therefore, you will manifest many variations that seem to express the instability that *is* the effect of that one belief, one perception: "I am separate from God. I have accomplished the impossible. Let me keep it in place."

Illusions, then, while the form of them may seem to be many, are really one. Healing occurs when, in the depth of the mind, the decision is made to *surrender*, and to give up the insane idea that one's self could possibly exist apart from the Mind of God.

Surrender means to settle into the position of the servant, the conduit through which the Mind of God, the Love of God, can be expressed. The mind that exists in perfect surrender sees absolutely no purpose to any moment of experience save this. The mind in perfect surrender looks out upon a world that has been healed from its own misperception that the world has had power over it. It sees that at no time has it experienced anything but its own outpicturing. This is why all events are neutral. It is *mind* that interprets an event, draws a conclusion, and then bases behavior upon it.

The mind that is healed and rests in surrender looks out upon an innocent world that has been touched by *its* blessing of forgiveness. That forgiveness is simply a step in which that mind recognizes that the world it had thought was there was nothing more than its own mental creation, and smiles and laughs and sees that the world has held no power. And that all events that have arisen, all interpretation of events, have been generated from within the kingdom of the mind—the one place that it is given unto you to assume responsibility for as your domain.

The mind that has been healed of illusion has been healed of *all* illusions. And while time and space seem to last, the last outpicturing of a tiny, mad idea—called the physical body—can be given over to something else, can be transformed into a simple communication device that no longer communicates separation and judgment, but rather forgiveness and innocence. It becomes nothing. It is picked up and used only in those ways that can speak, gesture, move, act, and make something in the world that touches the world with a blessing of the good, the holy, and the beautiful.

Because this is simply the truth, it must mean that where you perceive justification for anything less than peace—it must mean that you have already decided, in the deeper part of your mind, to maintain this root, or core, misperception. That is, you are still attempting to perceive yourself as having accomplished the impossible—to have separated yourself from the Mind of God. The mind that is surrendered looks out upon all things and quietly says within itself:

There has only been God. I am created of That. The source of my being, the source of my reality, rests in surrender into That and That alone.

The mind that is surrendered, yet walks in your world as long as the body lasts, is often completely unrecognized by others around it. For others see a body and, therefore, assume there is an individual, an ego, a separated being within it as that body.

When the mind is surrendered, you could say that body walks as an empty shell and is merely waiting to be *in*formed by the Love of God. When the Love of God does not inform you or ask you to move and take action, then simply rest and do nothing.

This is why the final state of awakening is incomprehensible in the languages of your world, since your languages are based on the very thought of separation itself.

This is why when we speak of peace, we speak of that peace which is beyond all understanding.

For the peace that you can understand in the languages of your world is *conditional* peace, the kind you create when two warring nations' leaders sit down in suits and ties and forget the death count and the destroyed villages, and they sign some document with a pen. They put on a "front" and smile for the pictures, and then they assume—and teach everybody else to assume—that now there is peace. Then each goes back and secretly continues to build weapons of defense against the attack sure to come from the one still perceived as an enemy.

Peace cannot be bargained for. It is not the result of compromise. Peace comes *only* when any mind surrenders *unconditionally* the dream of the dreamer itself, so that there is only God and God's creation. We have shared with you before that that creation is one—the Christ Mind. And that Mind is not in the body. It is not a particular form, and certainly does not belong to any personal entity.

I was never "The Christ," as though you are not. Like you, I was a temporary modification of eternal energy, an outpicturing of a thought, a mental thought, held in mind, which learned to surrender the misperception of the dreamer, and became *in*formed only by Christ Mind. Only that Mind was present, and yet it could not be touched through the body. That is why my crucifixion had no effect on me whatsoever. It merely sped up the process whereby the body was dissolved away as an idea.

THE WORLD IS INNOCENT

Beloved friends, come now in your understanding to change how you use consciousness. Take pause with us to remember the truth: The world that you look out upon is innocent. The *cause* of the world is not found in the world, but only in the thoughts held within the mind.

You remain perfectly free to choose to *perceive* differently. You remain free at all times to see that you are not the victim of circumstance, not the victim of a relationship, a career, or being born into a certain nation. You are never the victim of anything, since nothing within an illusion holds the power to truly have any effect on you.

You are the one who remains free to assume responsibility for the domain of your mind. You are the one who is free to simply say:

> Father, nevertheless, not my will, but thine be done.

And what will does the Father have, save that you be happy by returning to the peace that forever passes all understanding? What could your Father will for you, but that you awaken from the dream that there is something *in* the world that can add value to you; that there is someone, some career, some location, some what-have-you that can actually add substance to your being? And better than this, to become freed of the perception that the *lack* of someone, something, some career, some location, some form of any kind could *detract* from your being, from your perfect power of union with God.

Peace, then, comes from a decision that is put into practice over time, in which the world is released. Released from what? From your belief that *it* should somehow be for you the conduit whereby you gain good feelings, love, peace, wisdom, ideas, comradeship, and even brotherhood or sisterhood.

Detachment does not mean avoidance, but it does mean dis-identification with a mistaken idea. All suffering stems from this: identification of the deep mind, or the soul, with the forms that pass as outpicturings in this illusion. The belief that *loss* is possible and also that *gain* is possible. There can only be the recognition of what is true through the practice of extending the good, the holy, and the beautiful.

The end of illusion is very near when the mind reaches this following point. When any mind looks out upon its creations that it has attempted to make of itself and finds all of it lacking—that something is missing—and when that mind simply decides to withdraw the value it has placed on the world, and rests into the simple desire to be with God, then Heaven is but a step away. And that final step is taken *by* your Creator *for* you.

The dream of separation has been your responsibility. When you reach that point of collapsing or surrendering, you enter into the stage of restoration or salvation. And *that* is in the hands of your Creator.

When restoration has been completed, and the mind no longer seeks to journey out into the fields of illusion, but simply rests empty *at one* with God, *then* creation can begin anew. And co-creation is in the hands of both you and your Creator. The only difference is that you are no longer a separate being, like a gnat shouting at the universe, demanding that things be done your way. But rather, you are empty.

You are the paradox of all paradoxes, for you are filled, and only Christ abides. Yet, not you lives, but only that One. Even the arising and the passing away of the body are of no concern for you. You merely rise in the morning and simply say:

> Father, how would you have me be present this day?

And something else *in*forms your steps and your decisions. You are no longer *identified* with the *fruit* of your action. You are no longer concerned with how it may look, or how it may compare to somebody else's action. You merely abide where you are, doing what you are doing, and offering it freely because you are no longer attached to it.

Peace is the essence of the message that we would share with you in this lesson—as a temporary resting period from the work that we have been doing in the Way of Transformation. Rest assured, there is much more to be done. For when the mind is surrendered, resistance dies to the very extension of creation. And that mind no longer seeks to leave any dimension whatsoever. For where would it go? It merely becomes one willing to enact whatever is being extended to it from the Mind of God, as a way of being involved with the extension of Love.

That requires, then, learning how to use consciousness differently. But it is all predicated on a return to peace. That is why, above *all* things, your responsibility is to enter into surrender—to let the tiny mad idea of a separate self be dissolved entirely from the mind, so that there is only the Mind of Christ.

QUESTIONS TO PONDER

Beloved friends, pause then in this moment. Observe the place that you are. In truth, is there anything around you in your current environment that could add anything to your substance? If you could find a way to possess it or digest it, would it puff you up? It might add a few pounds if you happen to have ice cream in front of you! But that is only to the body.

Likewise, as you look upon your environment, imagine if the things around you were taken away. Would that take anything from you? If you can feel the simple truth of the questions that we are asking, then surely you can come to sense that just beneath your involvement in the world of form, peace is *already* available because Love waits on your welcome.

Will the world of form seek to pull you into identification with it? Oh yes, because that is part of the very outpicturing you once created.

You held the thought in your mind, "Would that I could create a world that will pull at me so much that it will distract me from the one thing I need to do. And when it does, I can say that I'd be awake now, except that all of these other things and all of these other people need my attention more than God. If only *they* would go away, I could know God. If I could just disappear into a cave somewhere or a cell in a monastery and shut out the world, *then* I could know God." That approach never works.

Recognition is not dependent on any specific state of body or lower mind. It is not necessary to spend endless hours in meditation seeking to quiet the mind. It is only necessary to *withdraw value* from what arises in the field of the lower mind, so that quite naturally what arises, what is recognized, is the *perfect value* that is held in your prior union with God. This is why awakening, salvation or enlightenment is not a change at all, merely a recognition of what has always been, and what will always be—eternally.

YOU ARE FREE TO CHOOSE ANEW

Now—in this moment—are you free to choose anew. Now are you free to rescind your judgments of the world. Now—in this very moment of eternity—you can choose to recognize that you are *already* perfectly awake, freely choosing what outpicturings you will pour forth from the mind, freely choosing whether to think for yourself or to think with God, whether to believe your outpicturings or to see them as temporary clouds passing through an infinite sky that the clouds have never affected or influenced. You are free now to simply say within yourself:

> I can choose peace instead of this. I am surrendered, and nothing matters
> save the extension of the good, the holy, and the beautiful. Therefore,
> Father, in this moment what is your will for me?

You are empty of self, empty of striving, empty of the need to be right, the need to judge, or the need to perceive anything in any certain way at all, and freed from attachment to the *fruit* of your action.

Yet paradoxically, you are allowing creativity to flow through you, trusting that there is already a greater Mind that knows how best to serve the atonement. The atonement is the uplifting of the whole of the Sonship, every brother and every sister, who are but aspects of the Mind of God—not *your* mind, for your mind is an aspect of the Mind of God—points of light, seemingly fragmented from the one Mind, the one Light.

You are free to see—and please listen carefully—*right where you are* that the separation never occurred. All attempts to keep it in place have been like battling for the rights of a chimera to exist, like insisting that the illusion of an oasis seen in a desert is truly real. Instead of going to the location and finding out what is real and what is false, standing there bickering with your arms folded across your chest, arguing for the right to be right— while Reality slips through your fingers. All the while, you are standing next to a beautiful spring which bubbles forth with the purest of waters.

You are free now to entertain one idea totally insane to the world:

> I am awake now. My dream has not occurred. No separation has occurred. No distance has been traveled. Grace has already restored me, and I am free to perceive the real world.

We would ask of you this: to spend some time doing what we just suggested—to sit quietly and ask the questions that were asked just two pages ago about adding and subtracting from you or to you.

Sit with the words just given, over and over again, without being in a hurry, without struggling. And see if you can touch the place that knows the truth of those words, so that that truth is *felt* to be your own.

Then, and only then, will you finally begin to dissolve the power that you have given to the ego. What is the ego, but the bundle of sensations and perceptions and outpicturings that are the very *attempt* to do the impossible, to be separate from God? Would you be willing to surrender that value, to rescind it, to bring it back to your heart and soul, and then offer it to your Creator?

Here, then, is the point of conversion, the turning about in the seat of the soul that must be reached by anyone who, in truth, would seek God: to realize that they live, yet not themselves, but that One who extends power and Life has brought them into being. And they have a function to fulfill. It is *their* function and no one else's. It cannot be compared. It can only be allowed.

Therefore, spend some time—as much as you want for the next few days—sitting with the truth. Those of you who feel that you are going to be "too busy," then let your time be used in busy-ness, and thereby, continue to try to convince yourself that the world is real. Wait for a few days, perhaps until you come to your weekend. Then when your boss tells you that you have "time off," *then* sit with the truth.

For as this truth settles into the soul, all that we have been doing prior to this will become easier and make much more sense. It will clear the space for what is to come. For when the mind has truly awakened from illusion, there is nothing left but to be a servant of the atonement. And the only question left is:

Father, how this day might I serve?

We will bring this message to a close, as there is no need at this point for a continuation of words. There is only the need for direct experience held within the aloneness of your own mind and being. For revelation is *intensely personal*, it cannot be communicated to anyone at any time. Yet the revelation that comes to each mind may come in a unique way, but the revelation is of one Truth. That is why when any two beings who are awake happen to meet each other, there is little to do but smile, and allow the phenomena of Life to continue.

Therefore, know that we love you greatly. And we honor *you* for the courage it takes to let go of the world and open the palms of the heart to the grace of Heaven.

As we continue in The Way of Transformation, let it be done from the perspective of delightful innocence, in a mind that recognizes there is nothing else to do with time except extend the good, the holy, and the beautiful.

Peace then, be unto you always. Go in peace this day. Amen.

Lesson 20

Vigilance for the Kingdom

We come forth to abide with you because you have asked. We come forth to abide with you because we are a part *of* you. We exist where you are. We abide as the Truth of what you are.

Therefore, beloved friends, please well understand that when we reach back into time, into the field of what you call physicality to create communication with you, we do not come to you from some other location. We come forth unto you from the depth—the heart, the essence—of that which Mind is, that which Love is, that which consciousness emerges from. We come forth from Reality. And we join with you in the only place that genuine communication can occur—in Reality.

This can only mean that in those moments when you feel—not merely intellectually consider—but when you feel yourself immediately and truly comprehending that which is communicated by the words we choose, in that moment you do not abide in time, you do not abide in illusion, you abide in Reality. In that moment, there is, quite literally, no distance between us.

We speak here of distance, not just in what you would think of as physical terms, but there is also no distance between us qualitatively. That is, in that moment when you receive Truth, it is not the case that we are above you, beyond you, or have even gone ahead of you a little. You are comprehending the essence of Truth from the essence of Christ Mind, which is the only Mind that can comprehend the Truth and Reality of God.

That Truth is necessarily within you, and has been within you since before the birthing of time. It has been with you since before a tiny, mad idea seemed to creep across the expanse of your mind and you chose to believe it. That reality cannot be taken from you. It is from that reality that you have awareness of your own existence. It is from that reality that you gather the fuel to create the perceptions that you most desire. And the perceptions that you most desire are precisely the ones that you are experiencing in any given moment.

Now, those of you that were abiding in Reality as you heard those words, immediately know that that means that at no time and under no circumstances are your perceptions being thrown upon you from some source or force outside of you. You know that in each moment, you—and you alone—have created the perception, and therefore, the experience you are having within the field of the mind, for no other reason than that you have desired it.

This is why the very pathway of awakening, regardless of the form it takes, is always a retraining of the mind. It is a decision to choose to discipline the mind in each moment, to teach only Love, to hold only loving thoughts, and to recognize that there is no such thing as an idle thought, since each thought or perception held in the mind *immediately* generates your experience. That experience is like a pebble dropped into a pond that sends a reverberation, a vibration, throughout the field of your being. And that field goes far, far beyond what you commonly perceive to be the boundaries of your body.

WHAT YOU DESIRE, YOU EXPERIENCE

Beloved friends, you will only experience what you desire. That is why *desire* is always the first and most fundamental key to the process of awakening. It is why desire is the energy known equally by all minds, in all kingdoms, in all dimensions, in all worlds. It is by desire that you choose to relinquish the value you have placed upon limited perception. It is by desire that you decide to teach only Love. It is by desire that the Kingdom is restored to your mind. For it is by desire that you have been birthed from the holy Mind of God.

The simplest way to discover what it is that you desire in any moment is to simply stop and observe:

What thoughts are currently taking place within my mind?
How am I perceiving the world that seems to be around the body?

Most especially observe:

How am I perceiving myself in this moment?

With honesty, you will see quite quickly and quite easily what it is you have most desired to experience in this moment.

It can, indeed, be quite shocking when awareness begins to turn back on itself to observe the mechanics of its own thinking processes in the world. Then, to hold the thought that the thoughts that are dancing in the mind are there for no other reason than that they have been desired by the truth of who you are.

You are that power—that *power*—which has been birthed from the Mind of God, made in God's image, that is, with infinite power, to create what you choose to experience. Desire, then, is integral to the understanding of the very process of transformation, for what you desire, you *do* experience.

When I walked upon your planet as a man, seemingly cloaked in a body or as a body, I too had need of learning to observe the nature of my own mind, and to discover what it was I was desiring in any given moment.

Vigilance for the Kingdom means to retrain the mind until it desires only Love, only the Kingdom, only enlightenment, only peace, only reality. When the mind has been so retrained, in that moment there is no longer any sense of a separate self struggling to find God. There is no longer any sense of a separate self who knows lack. There is no longer any sense of a separate self that is unworthy of being the embodiment of Christ. And in that moment, the body can seem to continue or it could disintegrate.

The body itself will be perceived in a very different light. It will no longer be seen as something dense and hard that seems to separate you from your brothers or sisters. It is seen only as a dance of shadow that provides Christ an opportunity—temporarily— to speak the language of those that believe the body is yet real in order to communicate. And to drop a pebble in the pond, that sends a reverberation, a vibration, through the body that is emanated and is recognized by everyone—perhaps not accepted, but recognized.

This is why you have heard many stories, some even related to me, that when a master walks upon the planet, something occurs in the energy field, the mind of those in his or her proximity. There is an energy that is transmitted. It is not that the master changes them; it is that the Truth in them is suddenly quickened into at least a very temporary remembrance of what is true. And an illusion can be dropped. Or perhaps, all illusions can be dropped.

The body becomes almost a magical means of communication. It appears to be something solid. It appears to be who you are. Yet, when the mind has been retrained thoroughly, and purification has been completed, the body simply becomes transparent and meaningless—except for the extension of the light of Love.

I have shared with you many times that to awaken as Christ requires that you begin your journey *as* Christ. It is not possible to transform yourself in order to *become* Christ, but it is possible to simply accept the idea of the Truth. And then let that be the foundation from which your life expresses itself—so that you begin to *think* with Christ, so that you begin to *breathe* with Christ, so that you begin to *envision* with Christ.

THE DECISION TO ACCEPT THE TRUTH THAT IS TRUE ALWAYS

The Way of Transformation—and please listen carefully—is not a process of changing the unworthiness in you to the point where, finally, you are knocking at Heaven's door, and you then awaken. Rather The Way of Transformation rests on your decision to accept the Truth that is true always:

> I and my Father are one. Now that that is out of the way, how would a Christ live in this dimension? How would a Christ bring himself or herself to each moment of experience? What voice would Christ listen to? What vision would he or she serve?

The struggle to awaken is the very *obstacle* to its accomplishment. That is why the five minutes as Christ was given to you as a very simple exercise. And if, indeed, you desire Christ above all things, would you not participate in it each day? For that which you desire and love is that which pulls your attention to it. If you love Christ, then let Christ pull you, attract you to spending five minutes a day in the realization that you can only be what you are created to be.

Having accepted that as the truth, then inquire into your own Christ Mind on how you will live this day. For the mind that is awakened sees no distinction anymore between being here and not being here. It sees no distinction between Heaven and Earth. It sees no distinction between eternity and time. It sees no distinction between the non-material and material or physicality. It sees no distinction between the extraordinary and the ordinary.

But rather, reality is returned to the mind, and it suffuses what the mind experiences. And the literal world that you thought you used to know—buildings, cars, governments, and all the rest—simply becomes a temporary harmless illusion that seems to have "hoodwinked" your brothers and sisters, who are a part of you.

Because the world is now seen in its transparency, it is no longer fearful to you. You are free to walk and abide in it as long as the body lasts—quietly, joyfully, going about your most extraordinary ordinary tasks, except that they have become translated into the means whereby you demonstrate the truth of Love to the world.

Reactivity, suffering, doubt, depression—in other words, dis-ease—can only be the reflection of a *decision* to use the power of the mind to desire, and therefore to perceive and experience, what is *unlike* the truth of the Kingdom.

Freedom, peace, unlimitedness, and above all, fearlessness must necessarily be the result of the decision to use the power of the mind to remember, to realize, to abide in, and to extend the Truth that is true always. Then the passing phenomenon called life is simply seen as a delightful dance. It has no purpose in and of itself.

Once, you gave it a purpose unlike God's. But as Christ, the purpose that you see in the world is shared by your Creator with you. Your will has become the same as God's; merely to abide and to be of service in the process whereby those that have been "hoodwinked" can remember the truth and become free. It no longer matters how that occurs; that is, what form your teaching occurs in. It is all the same. You see no difference between your form and someone else's, for you will recognize the teachers of God.

Where you are in any moment becomes a divine gift, literally dropped in your lap as an opportunity to enjoy the remembrance that you are one with God. An opportunity to remember that everything you are seeing is a passing illusion in the sense that it used to have a purpose that seemed concrete, and that purpose has dissolved and gone:

> Where did the world go? I used to think it was a fearful place. I used to think that I had to get ahead. I used to think that there were those who could victimize me. Now I just see harmlessness. I see nothing out there that can add anything to me. I am simply at rest and at peace, delighting at play in my Father's Kingdom. And where I am, Christ abides.

So the distance from where you may yet perceive yourself to be and where you may perceive us to be is only the distance of a decision. That decision waits upon your welcome. No one can take from you the power to decide to own your identity as God's child.

OBSERVING YOUR CHOICES

Look well, then, in this moment. Stop and look within the mind. Then observe the simple day that you have been living thus far. And ask yourself what have you desired in this day? And allow memory to bring to you choices that you have made. Look upon those choices for whatever feelings, perceptions, and thoughts you may have had. Look upon them with perfect innocence. Simply observe, "Oh, in that moment I was certainly not desiring peace. In that moment I certainly wasn't desiring perfect remembrance. Hmm. how interesting."

If you can find a moment in this day that you have lived so far—even if you began reading this lesson five minutes after you got up out of bed—if you look well into those five minutes, you just might discover that there has been at least a moment in which you were not deliberately choosing to desire remembrance of union with God.

Now, does that mean that you are walking around saying, "I desire union with God. I desire union with God"? Those are just words. The desire is a feeling. It pervades the heart. You might say that you feel it in the body, which is really just the depth of the mind anyway.

Look well and see if there was a moment in which you were using the power of the mind to decide against the Kingdom. When you find that moment, just look at it, observe it with innocence, and simply say, "I could have chosen otherwise." That is the simplicity and the power that the Kingdom is!

The world remains uncaused by anything outside of your own mind. Yet within it, you are given complete dominion. This means that within the one Mind of Christ, individuation occurs. For a moment, perceive the one Christ Mind as an ocean, where individual waves arise, made of the same substance—perfect freedom, perfect knowledge of and union with God. In that freedom, the power to decide or to desire is present. And desire begets worlds without end. That is what your entire planet once came from. That is what your entire solar system came from. Your entire universe was born of desire.

THE KEY TO TRANSFORMATION—
ASSUME COMPLETE RESPONSIBILITY

The key, then, to the transformation of your lived experience, while the body lasts, is to assume complete responsibility for how you are choosing to use the mind. Remember only *you* can think a thought, only *you* can have an idea. That idea cannot enter your domain, over which you have complete dominion, unless *you* have sent it an invitation. That is simply the way it is.

It is a mirror of what God is—infinite and perfect freedom. God simply never deviates from desiring *only* the extension of Love, the birthing of that which is like unto Himself— you. Your will is joined with your Creator's when you decide to birth only that which reflects Love—the good, the holy, and the beautiful.

The mind, as you have come to know it, will deceive you into thinking that, "Well, if I live that way ninety-five percent of the time, then what the heck, five percent of the time I can do something else." That is absolutely true. Yet, the more you come to truly desire only that which reflects the truth of who you are, you will be able to tolerate less and less variance within yourself.

This is why when any mind truly begins to awaken, it becomes more and more painful to continue certain thoughts or behaviors that do not reflect the deep desire of the heart. This is why the gap becomes less and less—the gap of unconsciousness, the gap in which the mind tries to defend its choices and perceptions—until finally, it rests in complete vulnerability.

It lives in complete innocence and no longer—and please listen carefully—it no longer fears change within its system of thought. It no longer fears being challenged by another mind because it thirsts only for the creation of a thought system that can birth forth the good, the holy, and the beautiful.

It no longer explains. It no longer defends. It no longer seeks to convince. It merely *abides* and gives itself over to the stream of Love that would flow through it. Every idea presented by another mind becomes something to live with, something to digest, to see if there is a jewel within it that can add to the beauty of its own expression of the good, the holy, and the beautiful. Everything becomes "grist for the mill."

There is no longer a need to be in defense. The body does not tighten. The breath does not grow short. There is only vulnerability. There is no longer a need to hide. There is no longer the need to be concerned with the perceptions of others, since a perception cannot harm you. There is only such love of Self that nothing less than God will do!

So again in this lesson, we speak on the theme of desire. We seek to bring you to the point of realizing that desire is the great power of creativity. It is that which births your very experience. Desire is perfectly free. That desire, that power to desire, is within you and you will never be without it. It is impossible to be desire-less, since you can only find yourself to be where you have desired to be. Even if you are in deep and perfect silent meditation, you are there because of desire.

Therefore, beloved friends, please decide this day to take responsibility for what you desire. Recognize that what you desire will be what you experience. Recognize that what you desire literally creates the pathway whereby you will experience either Heaven or hell, peace or turbulence, love or fear. In each moment of desire, right where you are, you have just birthed an entire world. For out of that desire, you will create your perceptions of everything from yourself to the farthest of stars, all in a split second, a moment of timelessness.

Part of the journey, then, of The Way of Transformation is learning to transform your lived experience, so that you enjoy it more and more, are attached to it less and less, and fear it not at all.

There are many in your world who would yet perceive spirituality as a way to get out of the place in which they find themselves, not understanding that they can be nowhere save than in their own mind. And as long as there is a desire to get out of where they are, they will remain stuck within it, because only love can heal.

Therefore, the way of healing, which is The Way of Transformation, requires that you turn back to look at your creations, to look back into your own mind and to bring Love to whatever is arising, out of the desire to be the presence of Christ.

Now, does this mean that as long as the body lasts and you find yourself in the world of space-time and movement and all the rest, that you will not take the body from one location to another? Of course not! Does it mean that third-dimensional relationships will not come and go? Of course not!

It *does* mean you become completely free of the old perception that an attraction to a certain relationship is going to add something *to* you, or the avoidance of a certain relationship is going to keep you safe. Rather, you begin to be free to let the dance of the third-dimensional illusion simply have its day. But it no longer holds power over you.

The highest state of awareness, then, in which perception has been totally cleansed and purified is one of paradox as soon as you seek to talk about it. For you will look upon yourself and see yourself as a body-mind, with a certain name, living in a certain place on a certain planet, doing a certain thing.

In the very same moment, in the very same field of your mind, you will *know* that you are not that body, that you are not that name, that you are not that history—that you are something more. You are something grand, you are something divine, you are something mysterious, you are something beyond comprehension by any mind, at least in the realm of thought.

And you will literally *know* and *feel* within the core of your being the truth of both of those. And there will no longer be opposition between them. You will no longer look at the personality and see a great schism between it and the nature of Christ Mind—for the two will have become merged as one.

You will look at the most ordinary events that you experience with your body and see no differentiation whatsoever, between that and the Kingdom of Heaven. It simply is arising, and is literally held in, pervaded by, and suffused by the reality that is true always.

You will know that you are totally free when you no longer feel any obstruction to whatever is arising in the field of your experience. Why? Because you will simply see it as another opportunity to say:

> Holy Spirit, what would you have me say? What would you have me do? What would it be like in this moment for me to simply realize that only Love is real?

Then, you will listen to that voice. You will feel it deep in your heart. And you will simply act on that voice and none other. You will not listen to what other minds think you *ought* to do. You will simply listen to that one voice. It will not speak to you from the ego, for there will be no judgment.

You will simply come and go as one unknown by the world, and yet one who looks to be very ordinary, one who looks to be the same as everyone else. The difference is that though the body still seems to walk upon the Earth, *you* are literally *embracing* the Earth. And in you, you will *know* that fear is gone.

SECOND OBSERVATION EXERCISE

We wish to extend to you some simple exercises that you can put into practice. We mentioned one of them already. A second is this: Take ten minutes out of each hour. Set your alarm on your little watches, and for ten minutes actually observe how you are moving the body.

For example, "Oh, I just got off the couch and I'm proceeding to the kitchen. Why? Oh, I'm having the desire for ice cream. It has arisen as a thought in the mind and *I* have given it the *power* to motivate the movement of the body to take the action necessary to now put my hand on the handle of the refrigerator. (And by the way, I would have liked to have one of those then.) I am now opening the freezer and I'm taking out the cold little carton made out of the body of some tree. In it is a substance that some other mind created out of desire.

"Now I'm picking up a utensil called a spoon, born of another mind that had a desire to make life easier. I am dipping it into the ice cream, and now I am putting it into the body, which itself is the result of a desire. And I am creating my experience!"

There is no other cause but this: the arising, the inception of a thought, a feeling, a desire which has birthed the entire movement of a world, called the body, to create an experience of eating ice cream. You can do that for ten minutes, just by observing what you actually are doing.

Now, what does that mean? It does not mean: "Well, I'm going to work in order to pay the bills." No, you are not. You are going to work because you have held the desire to create something that seems to give you a semblance of safety, predictability and survival. Job or career is that which is birthed out of desire because of your perception of what you *think* you need. So, you are not going to the job in order to do something. You are simply putting the body in the car and you are driving on your freeway.

Begin to learn how to observe without embellishment, without interpretation or explanation, exactly what you are doing—for ten minutes. Then if you want to go back to being unconscious, by all means do so.

In this way, you will begin to discern something that is also going on the whole time, like an underground current or river. For because you are Reality, there is always the desire to extend the good, the holy, and the beautiful.

By observing what you are actually doing, you will discover that you are actually succeeding at that far more often than you give yourself credit for. You will begin to see in some of your ordinary smiles, in the decision to take a card and send it to a friend, in the decision to refrain from a hurtful word, you will begin to discover that that, too, was birthed from desire within your holy mind.

And you will begin to taste that there is a depth to you that is already beyond fear, already beyond illusion, already resting in compassion, love, wisdom and truth. You will begin to discover that you are already having many successes upon which you can build, many successes that you can acknowledge within yourself as a way of getting the taste, the feel, that:

Surely, Christ does dwell in this mind.

I once suggested to you that you remember only your loving thoughts. But the trick to that is that you must first become aware of them. So many become trapped in the depression, anxiety and insanity of the mind because they put all of their energy into perceiving what is *amiss* and no energy into perceiving their success as Christ.

So, in each ten-minute practice period, learn to develop the ability to observe what you are *really* doing. When you stop at your coffee shop on your way to your job, and you go in and you give some money to the person who gives you your cup of coffee, and you look them in the eye, smile and say, "Thank you," you have just succeeded. You have communicated truth. You have remembered that the one in front of you is worthy of your respect and love. And *that* is a success!

Each time you can interrupt the momentum of the mind for perceiving nothing but problems, you will begin to discover that the underground river of the Mind of Christ is yet within you still. As you feel your successes more and more deeply, that in turn builds your desire to live in that stream. And moment by moment, day by day, you will cultivate the power necessary to be identified with only *that* Mind.

For a while, it will seem that there are two thought systems—the old one that you used to be identified with and the one that seems to be being birthed within you. You are really just remembering it. But, *you* are choosing to bring the discipline necessary, the vigilance necessary, to retrain the mind to be identified—*not* with the realm of illusion—but with the stream of Reality that is flowing through you, unimpeded, unobstructed, throughout all eternity, without end.

That is the one gift time provides you. That is all there is. You cannot use time to store up wealth in some bank account for the future, since the future does not exist, and you have no control over what will happen to your golden coins in your world. Time has only one purpose—the purpose the Comforter has given unto it. And that purpose is the atonement of the Son of God.

Now, all of that sounds very lofty, and the mind says, "Well, yes, of course. I understand that perfectly well, thank you. Good day!" And then, that very mind goes right back to its same old patterns. Having heard, it has not heard. Having tasted, it has not swallowed.

SEIZE THE OPPORTUNITY TO DISCIPLINE THE MIND

The mind is still identified with the realm of illusion until you decide to *seize* time, recognizing its great gift to you—not as a punishment, not as a duty, but as an *opportunity* to become wholly free. And to smile within your heart because *you* know that you are one with God.

Decide to seize the opportunity to discipline the mind, so that it comes to be identified with the stream of Christ Mind, whispering like a quiet voice underneath the roar and din of the ego's conflicted world. For the world of the ego is filled with fear, doubt, judgment, the need to be right, the need to make others wrong, and the need to believe that there is some power source outside of itself.

When you awaken and realize that the Truth is true always, you will not ever complain about a moment of experience in which you have the power to desire differently. For as you desire, you will perceive. And as you perceive, you will experience. The whole game is simply this: You are totally free. Right here, and right now. You cannot do anything to *become* free. You can only *remember* your freedom by how you choose to use the mind in any moment.

Time is an illusion. The things that pass by, the phenomena of space and time, are just shadows that you have interpreted in a certain way. There is no gain; there is no loss. There is nothing to fear. The world can add nothing to you nor take anything away. You are merely here in this temporary classroom with an opportunity to do what any master in any dimension can do, for you hold the same power as I do—you hold the power to teach only Love. And what you teach, you must necessarily and immediately learn.

Therefore, learn well to observe the mind:

What am I really desiring?

Not "What do I *wish* I were desiring," but "What am I *really* desiring," remembering that everything is a neutral event. It is just a learning experience.

Separation does not exist. The Truth is true always. Death is unreal. You are pure Spirit. Time is just a context. The world is harmless. You cannot be a victim. You are free. The atonement is over. The ascension is completed.

Once you get the message, get on with it by choosing to bring that Reality into the dance of shadow called this world. For what good does it do to pray for freedom in the future? It is everything to abide in freedom now!

One last thing about desire: The egoic mind is made up of attraction/aversion, judgment, either acceptance or aversion, or hatred even. For example, "This is right, that is wrong; this is good, that is bad."

Be willing to embrace and accept the results of what you have desired. When you dip your spoon into your ice cream, enjoy it. Embrace it as the effects of your desire. And when you buy an automobile that breaks down, train yourself to embrace it and enjoy it, just like the ice cream.

Why? For a very simple reason: If the egoic mind judges things as right or wrong, if you judge the ice cream as "good," but the breaking down of the car as "bad," *what mind* holds power over you? Are you free in that moment? Instead embrace and enjoy it, "My car just broke down. Oh, but there's such a beautiful sunset! I think I might as well sit here and let the stars come out. After all, I really wasn't going anywhere anyway."

Mind is everything. If you truly desire more than *believing* in Christ, you must assume responsibility for transforming the mind by using your very ordinary moments in which to see differently. And as you reshape how you use the mind in every moment, you will come to taste profound freedom—a freedom that will carry you instantly far beyond the things of space and time. They will seem to be arising within you and passing away within you—universes rising and passing away, within the holy Mind of Christ.

That is the great gift given unto you. What are you worthy of desiring the most? You will, indeed, discover and create your pathway to your own consummate awakening.

There can be no end to the Mind of God. You will abide forever within it, like one who abides in an infinite forest. Why not be *at play* in the Kingdom?

Enjoy your exercises! As you do them, you will taste a deepening remembrance of the Truth that is true always.

And so, be you therefore at peace. And again, we extend our thankfulness to you for having set aside the roar and din of the world to abide with us in this way. For you see, communication is the great joy of the aspect of the Sonship who choose to come together to delight in remembering the Truth. Therefore, it is our delight to create communication devices to join with you. You have a saying in your world, "it takes two to tango." Thank you for joining with us in this celebratory dance that remembers the Truth.

Go then, in peace. Amen.

Lesson 21
Allowance Is the Doorway to the Kingdom

It is not possible for you to be without Love.

It is not possible for you to be alone.

It is not possible for you to taste death.

It is not possible for you to taste genuine loss.

It is not possible for you to suffer the dream of separation.

It is not possible for you to be apart from your Creator.

It is not possible for you to fail.

It is not possible for you to harm anyone or anything.

It is not possible for you to be guilty of sin.

Enter Into a Deliberate Purification

Beloved friends, please consider each of the statements that has just been made to you. We suggest that you write down each statement at the top of a separate piece of paper. Then, begin a process in which for one week you abide with each of these statements. What do we mean by that? We mean that as often as you choose, through desire, set aside time to merely abide with the statement. Then watch what comes up in the mind and write it down.

What you will discover are many pictures, many ideas, and even certain feelings that seem to indicate to you that the statement must not *entirely* be true. This is a way for you to deepen your ability to observe what is actually occurring within the field of your own mind. It is a way to enter into a deliberate purification.

Denial can never purify the mind. For you cannot transcend what you refuse to embrace. For in embracing, does Love return to the place where shadow once dwelt. Love alone heals all things. The innocent need not fear. Therefore, because you are innocent, you are completely free to be thoroughly honest about what comes up in the mind as you sit with each statement. Just jot it down.

After a two- or three-minute period, pause; look at what you have come up with, or what has come up within you, and then juxtapose those two views. Take the statement that you are working with and simply repeat it in the mind. Then look at the statement, the picture, the description, or memory that *seems* to indicate that your experience is *other* than that statement.

As you juxtapose it in this way, look at what has come up within your mind. Be honest about it. If it is an event that occurred last week, or last year, or ten years ago, or five hundred years ago, it does not really matter. As you look at it, simply ask, "Has this belief or this perception of myself, that seems to be in opposition to the statement at the top of the page, has it really changed anything about me? Has it taken my existence from me?"

Simply see what the answer is. Then lift your eyes from the page and look around. Say within the mind:

> I am free in this moment to choose to see things differently.

Then take just a moment or two and abide—simply looking around you. Then go back to the statement at the top of the page and say it again out loud, at least three times. Then merely say within the mind, quietly:

> This is the truth about me. I want only the Truth.

Then, put it away, and be about your business. The next day, bring it out and do the exercise again. Do that kind of process for one week for each of the statements given you. Rest assured, purification will be occurring in the depth of the mind. Each of you will experience it in your own way. But you will experience it. Remember always that the only thing that can be transformed *is* the mind. It is by the power of the mind itself that purification occurs.

Just as desire is essential to realization, so too is willingness or allowance. You have heard us say unto you many times that you are required only to offer a little willingness, just what you call a "smidgen." Measure out a smidgen of willingness, which is the same as allowance, and sprinkle it upon your experiences. Sprinkle it across the world. Sprinkle it upon your own being.

ALLOW ALL THINGS

Become willing to be one who cultivates the ability to allow all things. The mind that is free can do this. The mind that is imprisoned cannot. For the mind that is imprisoned *is so* because it insists that what it perceives should become different *in itself,* but that the perceiver need not change. And that is the very essence of imprisonment.

One who cultivates that ability to allow is cultivating, in truth, the very act of forgiveness. It is releasing the world from its insistence that its perceptions be held as right. It is releasing from *itself* the need to hold on to its perceptions. Therefore, allow all things. Trust all things. And thereby, embrace and transcend all things.

Allowance follows on the heels of desire. For when you desire the Kingdom above all things, you have no choice but to discover that you must allow the world to be as the world is.

For you have not known how the world is. You have only known your perceptions of it. But the Comforter will heal those perceptions. And that requires your little willingness to let your perceptions be changed.

As they are changed, the world magically becomes a different place. It does become transparent and harmless. It becomes virtually valueless, except for the value that the Comforter would give it, while it lasts.

Allowance, beloved friends, is a process of letting go and trusting. It is a process of saying:

> I wonder what it would be like to just let things be as they are—to notice
> them and let them pass by?

Allowance then, is the doorway through which Christ passes into the complete remembrance of Christ. Allowance brings a deepening sense of freedom—freedom from all circumstance. For it is your circumstances that you have *believed* have the power to imprison you.

But as you choose to relinquish your perception of the world or any circumstance, you discover that you are already abiding in freedom. The power—and that is what freedom is—is a power to create differently. And to create is the effect of what you will choose to see.

Allowance can be thought of as a resistance being melted from the nervous system, which is just an aspect of the mind anyway. Allowance is like the opening of the palms of the hands. Instead of holding on so tightly, you simply let go. What do you let go of? The habit of the need to be right, the habit of the need to perceive that the world is a fearful place. The habit of perceiving that you are in lack. The habit of perceiving that Christ must be far from you. Anything that is unlike the Kingdom of Heaven is a habit well worth releasing by allowing it to be dissolved from your mind.

The essence of this lesson is the cultivation of allowance. It begins with the willingness to relinquish the lid you have placed upon your own mind, so that you become able, in innocence, to simply observe how it really is—what is really going on down in the basement, without judgment, without fear, without justification, without explanation. It is simply there.

The cultivation of allowance will deepen a great deal, if you will merely put the exercise that we began with into practice.

In allowance, you cultivate the very quality of forgiveness. Without forgiveness, it is impossible to awaken into the realization of the Truth that is true always. Why? Because judgment is the opposite of the Kingdom. Where forgiveness is withheld, you are literally making a choice to be outside the Kingdom. You have used the power of the mind to make a decision, out of a desire to hold onto a perception, and thereby, you have generated direct experience. *You* are the one who has kicked yourself out of the garden.

Remember, then, that always forgiveness is essential. It is necessary for the atonement. Forgiveness is another word for allowance. We speak here not of a blind passivity, but of a relinquishment within one's own mind, and that is all. It is a willingness to see the complete neutrality of all events. It is a willingness to let the Comforter remind you that separation does not exist, that you cannot possibly make yourself guilty of sin and all the rest.

Forgiveness is a relinquishment of what you have decided is true about the world. It is, then, very much a self-centered practice. Of yourself, you cannot forgive your brother or sister for anything because, in reality, they have done nothing. Forgiveness is forgiveness of one's self for insisting on replacing Reality with your own version of it.

Allowance is like the petals of a flower opening to embrace the new dawn of a spring day. Allowance is like the melting of the ice that allows the river to flow. Allowance is like the removing of a cap from a bottle of sweet fragrance and enjoying it as deeply as you can. Allowance is the dissolution of fear. Allowance is transformation.

When you have come to allow all things, to trust all things, you will have embraced all things. Only that one who is *larger* than the thing that is embraced can do the embracing. Therefore, whenever you feel imprisoned, it is because you have made yourself *smaller* than the world you perceive.

And when you feel free, it is because you have remembered that you are the one from which all things have arisen. *You are* the Son of God. You are the vast sky in which all clouds and storms arise and pass away, while the sky remains unscathed—eternally changeless. *That* is freedom! And the cultivation of freedom is a free-will choice. It is the result of the desire for the Kingdom.

As you come to *truly* forgive yourself for every perception you have ever held about anyone or anything, you will come to discover that it means relinquishing perceptions of yourself as well. For you cannot awaken fully unless you include *yourself* in the circle of your forgiveness. Ultimately, of course, you come to see that the very practice of allowance is really the act of allowing yourself to be truly the Self that you are. You will no longer resist the process of purification, by whatever means the Comforter uses for you. It simply does not matter anymore:

Why resist it? All I want is God!

If it is dissolved in the mind in a split second, and you do not even notice it—fine. If it requires great tears and great experiences in the world—fine. What is the difference? They are really the same. It is because you have relinquished—through allowing—ownership of your own pathway home. You have decided to let the Comforter *take* you home.

Because you desire the Kingdom above all else, it no longer matters *how* that process is experienced. You no longer complain that it seems to be taking too long. You simply enjoin yourself in the process itself.

You let the Comforter take you by the hand and retrace the steps you once made in error. Each step requires allowance, which is forgiveness born of desire that has been purified of desire for that which imprisons. And it is replaced with the desire for that which sets all things free.

Once your desire begins and becomes the Kingdom, the end of the journey is perfectly certain. School is out. That which the ego is cannot last. For the very universe, creation, the world around you will conspire—which simply means to breathe together—all things will conspire together under the hand of the Holy Spirit to create *precisely* what you require to be set completely free of all illusion. And secretly, you will have already agreed with the Comforter that it will be this way.

Allowance, then, is equally as important as desire, and is an aspect of that pathway, that foundation, whereby Christ remembers Christ and arises from the ego's ashes to walk upon this plane, and any plane, as the Truth that is true always.

Remember that it is only the ego that will compare and contrast. It is only the egoic mind that thinks about another's path and wonders if perhaps their path is better than your own path. There is *only* the life that you are directly experiencing. And through desire and allowance, that very life comes to be embraced as the *very means* by which the Comforter is dissolving illusion from your mind. Of course, it is all based on the humility of realizing that the ego cannot awaken itself; that the Comforter is that agency, given by grace, that knows how to bring you home.

ESTABLISH A RELATIONSHIP WITH THE COMFORTER

I highly recommend that you establish a relationship with the Comforter as though it were a relationship with a good friend—indeed, the *best* of friends—until you reach a point in which virtually every decision is given to that Mind: Well, old buddy, should I turn left or right?

You relinquish ownership of your life. It is only the ego that thinks it can possess life. Spirit knows that Life possesses it. That is, Life has birthed you; the Mind of God has given rise to you. You are God's. You are not the *owner* of Life. You are the *recipient* of it.

Would you, then, be willing to make the decision to become a grand master of allowance? You can begin with the simplest of things, such as, "I allow this toothpaste to taste exactly the way it tastes, with no complaint. It just is as it is."

If it is the changing of your seasons, would you be willing not to lament the end of summer and the coming of fall, but would you be willing to experience that change? For rest assured—please listen well—in the realm of the world, which is the realm of perception, the *only* thing that exists is constant change. Underneath it there is a changeless Reality, that which pervades the changeable. But where there is resistance to change, rest assured, there is a mind living in delusion.

Remember that we have said unto you before that the awakened mind no longer feels any resistance to the things of time. It no longer tries to get rid of time. It no longer tries to make things stay the same. The awakened mind can embrace all things, trust all things, and thereby, transcends all things *instantly*, even in the midst of change.

In your realm—be perfectly honest with yourself—is there ever a moment in which change is not occurring? Can the body be the field of perfect silence? Hardly. Even if you make your heart stop beating for three seconds, there is still blood gently flowing through the veins. There are still thoughts arising, sounds coming in through the ears. The body is not that which can be changeless. The *awareness* of the body, the field in which the body arises, *is* changeless already.

Can you come, then, to be the field of awareness that can embrace all things which arise, change and pass away, yet not feel any obstruction in embracing and dancing with those things? For the mind that is free from the illusions of death is that very mind that learns to *dance* with death, to enter into any moment or relationship, knowing that because the body is engaged, it *must* come to an end. In fact, it is already on its way to death.

The mind then, that becomes the one who is no longer in fear, no longer in resistance, is the mind that has forgiven all things, including itself. The mind that can embrace all phenomena that arise and pass away with passion, with joy, with aliveness, with innocence, with simplicity, *that* mind cannot taste death. It literally transmutes death, even as death *seems* to be passing by.

The highest state of being, then, is always a paradox when you try to think about it. Through your *desire,* you have come ever closer and ever deeper into the Kingdom. And through your cultivation of allowance, the grace-filled willingness to know that that which arises is already passing away, it is like water flowing through a fork, and you might as well not lament it. The mind that laments it is the mind imprisoned in delusion. The mind that *allows* all things is the mind that is already freely *beyond* all things.

Imagine that there has been given unto you a window, as though your Creator had plucked you out of Himself and said, "I'm going to drop you into the field of time because there is something I want you to learn. You now have thirty days in which to learn it." Imagine that if you did not learn it, your existence would be snuffed out, erasing your name from the Book of Life. Now, of course, that will never happen. This is just a way of getting leverage on yourself.

CULTIVATING THE GRACE OF ALLOWING

Imagine that for the next thirty days all that mattered was the cultivation of the grace of allowing. How do you do that? By coming down, once again, to the most concrete, most mundane, most ordinary experiences of any given day. When you turn on your water in your shower in the morning, actually take the time to be present, and to feel its coolness change to heat and to recognize that you have just observed the constant dance of change in your world. And simply say:

I allow this change to occur.

Now, yes, it makes you sound like you are some great being, when, in fact, it is going to happen anyway. But have fun with it!

If you burn your toast, take a deep breath. And before the egoic mind begins to complain and whine that its toast is not the way it wants it, stop and look at it. Actually experience the burnt toast and say, "I *allow* this toast to be burnt. And now, I'm free to choose to eat it as it is, or to begin anew."

If you get into your automobile, and you pull out of your garage, and the raindrops are hitting the windshield, simply give yourself permission to bring your mind back from the future into the present and say, "I allow the falling of the rain." It is that simple.

So, you see, the power of transformation is the transformation of consciousness, which is the only thing that can be transformed. Learning is a consciousness thing. It is the only thing that *can* be changed. It is the only place learning can occur. And all learning is designed to *translate perception,* so that it becomes more and more and more and more like Reality itself. Fear dissolves from the mind. And then, the Father can take the final step for you.

Learning *is* necessary in the field of perception. *You* have placed *yourself* within that field. So why not get on with it, and *let* perception be healed? It is healed by bringing the power of observation to what is right in front of you, not in front of the body, but right in the field of awareness itself. That is why you should be dancing in your shoes at all times:

> My goodness, I don't have to go anywhere. It's right here in front of me. This ordinary moment provides the doorway to the transformation of consciousness itself. All I have to do is bring a little willingness to it. And guess what? I have all power under Heaven and Earth to do just that! Nobody can take it from me! Nobody can change the freedom in which I live! I am the one who can bring that little willingness to this moment and let the raindrops hit the window!

If you will look around yourself, you will discover in any given day plenty of things to keep you occupied, plenty of reasons why boredom is nothing more than a decision. For right in front of you is the richness of a pathway, translated by the Comforter, from a dream of separation to the royal highway to the Kingdom. And all power under Heaven and Earth lies within you—in *this* moment, and *this* moment, and *this* moment—to choose again. But it is time to take such statements out of the realm of abstract intellect into very concrete, lived moments:

> Where can I choose again? Right now! I can accept and allow these raindrops to hit the window. I can be present with them. I can hear them. I can watch them as they trickle down, instead of being annoyed, instead of letting the mind go off into its future adventures. I can cultivate the art of being present now as the very presence of a mind that is free.

Therefore, consider in each of your next thirty days, "What could I utilize in this day to practice this exercise?" Of course, you cannot be *without* things to practice with. It is impossible. Those that say they are bored are really saying, "I am resisting the Kingdom." Pure and simple.

Well do we perceive, once again, that so many in your world seek to find a spirituality that will free them of the world of their experience, never even realizing that *that very attitude* is the thing that chains them, imprisons them in their hell. Spirituality is merely a process of seeing things differently. And that is an *active* decision—born of desire, coupled with the little willingness called allowance—to recognize that each moment is like a jewel presented on a golden plate to *you*, God's child. You are the one who has the freedom always, and literally creates or makes your experience.

The final lesson that I had in time, concerning allowance, was the crucifixion. Now, I know that there are many of you that do not want to follow in my footsteps. But rest assured, beloved friends, if you would look well upon your experience, you have already tasted much more profound crucifixions many, many times. In fact, for some of you my crucifixion was a cakewalk by comparison. You are free to crucify yourself no longer by choosing to *transform* your very experience, by bringing the power of your mind to bear upon it. Desire. Allowance.

So what stands between you and the goal that you seek? The *decision* to try to be insane. The *decision* to try to resist God. You know that you can resist another body, since another body occupies another piece of space. In other words, it is not where you are, so you can resist it.

But I say unto you, God is already wholly present right where you are. How on earth can you resist what is already occupying the space in which you find yourself? You might as well try to shake off your own hand, or shake and jiggle the skin off the body. Good luck!

All suffering is the resistance of Reality. All awakening and healing is the letting go of resistance. Forgiveness. Allowance:

> God is already here. I am forever God's. I surrender.

Surrender is the fruit of allowance. Surrender is the fruit of forgiveness. Surrender is the same as the atonement.

For now, simply focus on allowance to make sure that you have not left some dark corner in the mind filled with your need to perceive things in a certain way. Your need to believe that the world should be other than the way it is, or your forgetfulness that each event that transpires in your experience can be seen as Heaven or hell. As you choose to see only Heaven, you will discover the power that has already set you free.

The message of this lesson is quite valuable if you will put it into practice. After all, what else could you possibly want to use time for? You have tried everything else and found it lacking. You have not been able to fill it up with enough lovers, enough money, enough cars, enough restaurants. So you might as well fill it up with the transformation of consciousness, so that perception begins to be more and more and more and more aligned with the Real world. Why not?

And if somebody asks you what you do with your time, say, "I grow Christ. What do you do?"

So practice well! Begin with the statements given to you at the beginning of this lesson. They are very important for you as a way of *triggering* the opportunity to observe what might be *unlike* the Truth still lingering in the mind and in the emotional field, which is really just the space of "glue" in which you attach perceptions. It is like pinning the tail to the donkey, "Stick *that* one on the wall and keep it forever!" Let those things bubble up that they might be purified from your holy mind.

Above all, beloved friends, remember: there are no mistakes! You are free to trust the momentum that seems to be shaping your life. For you are the one who has complied with it by inviting the Holy Spirit to take you home. You are the one that has prayed for acceleration. Therefore, also be the one who accepts the grace being offered unto you.

Remember, resistance is the ego; embracing is of Christ. The one that allows all things has already transcended all things. Let this lesson become a month-long journey of exploration.

Be you, therefore, at peace this day. Amen.

LESSON 22
SELF-HONESTY—
THE GREATEST ACT OF LOVE

Beloved and holy friends, we come forth with but one purpose: to join with the Mind of the holy Son of God. For surely, this *is* what you are. We come forth to join with that Mind that was there in the beginning, before the mountains and seas arose, before the universe arose, before even the *thought* of space and time arose.

We come forth, then, to join with that Mind of the holy Son of God that has remained in perfect union as the Sonship, in perfect union with its Creator, in perfect union with Reality and with Love. Though we have said it unto you many times, we ask you to truly take pause and to consider this one statement: We come forth to join with you, *not* from a place above you or beyond you, but a place in which you already dwell eternally.

No perception, no appearance can change the Truth that is true always. Even in this moment as you read these words, can you feel and accept the truth of them? The only reason you can understand them, the only reason you can sense the truth that comes through them is because you *are* that Truth, and you *know* that Truth.

There is a place within you that is unbounded, eternal, invisible, incomprehensible to the world mind, incomprehensible to the senses of the body, but perfectly and even simply comprehensible to the silence in which the soul dwells, comprehensible in a state of perfect knowledge.

All teaching, regardless of the form—and there are many forms of the universal curriculum—has but one specific goal: to nudge the mind of the dreamer beyond his or her dream, to return that mind to a state of perfect knowledge. Some would call it en*light*enment, that which suddenly is flooded with light. Light is truth and truth is knowledge, and knowledge is Love.

Therefore, when we come forth to join with you, the only purpose that we have is to en*light*en you, to turn your awareness, your attention to what you already know. The only difference between knowledge and belief, which is the same as the difference between Love and fear, is that in a state of knowledge or en*light*enment, the resistance to the Truth vanishes. Initially perhaps for just a moment, but eventually there is no longer any resistance to the simplicity of the Truth.

This transformation from a state of fear to Love, or from ignorance (the ignoring of truth) to enlightenment (the embracing and acknowledging of truth) occurs for each mind within the dream in a very *specific* way. That is, it must occur according to what is required to release the patterns that have settled into that particular mind. In a general way, those patterns are the same for everyone. But in their expression, they take on a perfect uniqueness.

Therefore, the timing of your enlightenment, the timing of your healing, the way in which it occurs, and the contexts that are necessary for you to be challenged by your own self will be uniquely your own. Why? So that the belief you have been holding, born out of fear, can be brought to the attention and then released.

This is why in The Way of Transformation, it is absolutely essential that you *never* compare your journey to another's. By all means, pay attention to the journeys of your brothers and sisters. Be open at all times to learn, to grow, to assimilate, to apply, to integrate, to consider, and to ponder, without comparing.

The ego *always* compares and contrasts. It looks upon itself; it takes its self-picture and compares it to a picture of another mind, without even noticing that the picture is something it has created. It believes that it is seeing what is outside of itself, that the picture or the analysis of another actually exists in that other—and it may. The point here is that the ego compares and contrasts, and then draws a conclusion about its own worthiness, its own progress, its own state of illumination.

All of this must be ego function because, in reality, you are as you are created to be. And wherever you are in any given moment, enlightenment is but a decision away. That decision entails but one thing: to release the insane valuation that you have placed upon everything and everyone, most especially yourself. That decision rests on the willingness to take God at God's word. That decision rests on your willingness to cultivate silence.

INNER SILENCE—
THE THRESHOLD TO WISDOM DIVINE

The theme, then, of this lesson is the cultivation of that inner silence which is the threshold to wisdom divine. How, then, does the mind come to true silence?

It is not merely a matter of closing the mouth. It is not simply a matter of shutting out the noise of the world. It is certainly not a matter of ceasing to listen to others, whether they speak the words of praise or words of criticism. Quite to the contrary.

Silence can be cultivated in a number of ways. Initially, it will look like something you do through the body—to breathe deeply and rhythmically, to sit next to an ocean, to sit beneath a tree and become absorbed in the wind. Or to merely practice the ancient art of remaining silent without speaking as you go through your daily events.

All of these begin to cultivate a relaxation within the brain, the nervous system and the body. Yet these things are merely projections of mind anyway. So to still the body, to calm the body, to allow the activity in the brain hemispheres to relax and become more harmonious is, in fact, an initial step in bringing the mind to silence.

But far deeper than these things is this: That genuine silence which is, indeed, the threshold to wisdom (and wisdom is nothing more than enlightenment) requires the cultivation of deep self-honesty. Honesty is that act in which the mind is no longer committed to hiding from its own darkness.

I have said many times and in many ways that it is necessary to enter into the blackness of the ego in order to discover what you want no longer. In truth, for anyone who makes such a journey, that which the ego is becomes repulsive, repugnant, and hurtful to one's self. And that is the only thing that matters.

Therefore, understand that in The Way of Transformation, although we have covered much territory in these lessons so far, a cornerstone of the universal curriculum must always be the cultivation of a deep self-honesty. In self-honesty, one decides to simply *observe* the mind itself, to simply observe the behavior that flows from the mind through the body, as it gestures itself out into the world. True self-honesty requires time. Why? Because the ego is the *attempt* to replace honesty and truth with dishonesty and falsity.

Imagine for a moment, that you are fully enlightened in this moment. You are abiding in a state of perfect freedom and peace. You are at one with God. Would there be anything that you would need to be dishonest with in your own mind? What corner of the mind would you have failed to embrace in light?

Therefore, in truth, beloved friends, understand well that the ego is the attempt to replace honesty with dishonesty. It *is* dishonesty itself. In fact, one could go so far as to say that those that would seek for the devil need look *only* at the ego, in which case the ego becomes egocentric. Your sense of identity is all wrapped up in defending and protecting a false image of yourself.

Much resistance is pervading your human domain, which is only this: "No, I will not look honestly. I must uphold the image I need to believe is true about myself." This is not Love and this is not Truth.

AN EXERCISE IN SELF-HONESTY

Beloved friends, take a moment and simply cultivate deep self-honesty by merely answering these questions:

Have I ever had a murderous thought?

Have I ever manipulated another mind
in order to try to gain what I believed I needed?

Have I ever withdrawn love for the subtle reason of causing hurt,
or trying to cause hurt to another?

Have I ever had disrespectful sexual fantasies?

Have I ever hated the world?

Have I ever despised myself?

And last, but surely not least, for in truth, if you would consider it, all of those questions emanate out of this one:

Have I ever hated God?

In perfect self-honesty, the answer to each of those questions can only be "Yes." The honest mind looks upon all that has arisen within it without judgment. For there can be no honesty while there is judgment.

Think well upon the questions that we have asked you. Then simply take it a step further and ask yourself:

Has any of that type of thing occurred within my mind recently?

Notice what happens now. Pay attention to your mind and even into your body and breath. What occurs as you begin to get closer to the truth? Do you notice a little bit of restlessness, the mind becoming more active with chatter?

Decide for silence. Decide for peace. For healing occurs to the depth and degree that the mind is willing to embrace what occurs within it.

Denial causes separation—self from Self, self from others and self from God. Therefore, the very peace that the mind seeks through religious belief is impossible, as long as the mind is in denial about itself.

Rest assured, when I walked upon your planet as a man, I too often became quite frustrated at the Pharisees who would stand on the corner in their long beautiful robes, *professing* religious belief. They had their just reward. This is why I often said, "Beware of those who come in sheep's clothing, but inwardly, are ravenous wolves." For the dishonest mind is in conflict constantly. It splits itself off from its sexuality as a human being. It splits itself off from its anger, its sadness, its hurt, and its murderous thoughts.

But the mind that is healed has learned to turn and embrace every subtle shadow within the mind. For Love, alone, embraces all things, trusts all things, allows all things, and thereby, transcends all things. And needs no longer live in fear that those *things* can run it.

Enlightenment is a state in which the world—and the world is not outside of you, the world is the context, the thoughts, images and perceptions that you have attracted to yourself—can no longer hold power over you.

It does not mean that it ceases to exist. This has been the great error of religion as opposed to spirituality. Religion will give you a set of beliefs, ideas about yourself, standards that you must *achieve*. Thereby the mind concludes that, "If I am to be a spiritual person, I cannot be angry. If I am a spiritual person, I don't have sexual fantasies about my neighbor." All of that is absolutely false.

For in reality, the experience in your domain is one in which the mind has created and is aware of all things unlike Love. It then splits itself off and projects an image called the ego, to itself first, and obviously to others, that it most wants to believe is true.

But remember, *belief* is not *knowledge*. Knowledge, alone, allows the mind to observe what arises within it without judgment, without fear, without identifying with it. It looks upon the world in perfect forgiveness and says, "Ah, I just had a murderous thought. I had a picture of hitting my employer over the head with a sledgehammer and watching the blood spurt through the broken skull. Ah yes, well, just another thought arising and passing away in this domain. It does not change the truth of who I am. And I am free to extend love or to hit him with a hammer."

The mind that is free and at peace is no longer conflicted within itself. The mind that is unconflicted abides in perfect vulnerability. It has learned to embrace and accept the truth about the phenomena of the mind itself in this dream world. It is willing to begin to be honest and to cultivate deeper honesty with everyone around them. No longer is there pretense. No longer is there manipulation or control. There is no unconscious, split-off energy actually running the show, even though that mind seems to be oblivious to it.

The mind in conflict with itself is dangerous to itself, and of course, by extension, to everyone else in all dimensions. Therefore, indeed, beloved friends, beware of those that come in sheep's clothing but inwardly are ravenous wolves. Beware of the viciousness of the ego within your own mind.

How does it come to you in sheep's clothing? Does it minimize hurtful behaviors? Does it minimize what is truly merely a lack of self-responsibility? Does it always make excuses why your life is not progressing in a way of becoming more and more empowered to bring forth Christ?

Learn to cultivate self-honesty. Though it sounds like a simple thing, this does take time, simply because the mind has used its own power to be in denial about its own miscreations. It does not want to own them. It does not want to embrace them. It wants very much for you and itself to believe that it is really a very high spiritual being.

It will wear the sheep's clothing of the ego, of the persona, the mask, the self-image, the projected image into the social world. And it will cling to that like a robe around the body, held against the cold winter wind; and it will cling to it no matter what.

Such a mind is an *insane* mind, and an insane mind is hurtful. An insane mind limits the flow of Love through it that could heal this world.

Therefore, beloved friends, as we move toward the close of The Way of Transformation, we again bring the arrow back to point at ourselves, to point at the depth of the mind and to learn to observe it. Take the list of questions that we have offered unto you and simply repeat that process on a daily basis.

So you see, we first began in the safety of allowing you to look way, way, way into the past to see if any of that has ever been going on in the mind. Now we come closer and closer to the self-honesty of what is occurring in the mind right here and right now, so that each day you ask the same questions and see what the answer is.

In this way, the mind will become more and more transparent. You will learn to look upon your murderous thoughts, and all of those hideous, *un*spiritual things that you have tried to shove down into the basement. More and more, as you tell yourself the truth about them, and more and more as you find a friend or two willing to tell the truth about their own minds with you, the more the mind becomes transparent, the less and less you have any need to hide.

A mind no longer committed to hiding becomes transparent to itself, and *through* it the *power* of Christ can begin to move—with certainty, with knowledge, with grace and with compassion.

The mind has always been the problem, but not the entirety of the mind—just a small corner that has been fenced off, called the ego. When you became identified with only that part of the mind, you became egocentric. The center of your identity became the ego and *that* is the source of the problem. Quite frankly, it is like identifying with a pimple on the skin, and then defending the pus within it at all cost.

Silence is the doorway that will dissolve that pimple and that pus forever. Silence is arrived at in many ways, but the principle cornerstone is deep self-honesty. The act of transformation then, The Way of Transformation, is a process whereby you put the *squeeze* on the pimple of the ego and you no longer care what pus comes out because you just want to be done with it.

Self-honesty *is* the greatest act of love that you will ever experience within yourself— greater than any sexual union, greater than any adulation of the world, and greater than any mystical experience. The embracing of deep self-honesty, the mastery of it, is the greatest act of love that the mind can experience. For in perfect self-honesty, the world is transcended, fear is dissolved and enlightenment is present. And in enlightenment there is remembrance of perfect innocence in union with God.

Therefore, indeed beloved friends, you who want, in truth, to come to know Christ, look not outside yourself. For the Kingdom is within. The mind is your domain and the mind *is* yourself. It has certain components, such as an emotional component or expression, an egoic component or expression. The ego, in itself, is not right, wrong, good or bad—it simply is. The mistake—the knot in the rope, the blip on the screen—is merely the mistaken identification of yourself with the ego.

That is what creates a tension, a twisting of the rope that ends up distorting everything. You end up being in judgment of yourself because you had a sexual thought yesterday— heaven forbid! You judge yourself because you feel a little angry. You judge yourself because a thought goes through the mind, "What's the point in being on the planet?" As long as you are identifying with those thoughts, you are in trouble.

But when you see them as just an innocent flow, a temporary movement of energy through a vast domain called the mind, then you know that you are free. You begin to taste the spaciousness and the silence that always is around the edges of everything that arises in the mind. You begin to become identified with that spaciousness, with that peace. And there, wisdom returns gently. You begin, again, to remember that you were created to create. And creation is extension, not projection. Extension is that which *floods*, or extends outward the good, the holy, and the beautiful.

You no longer make justifications for not taking action to extend compassion to other minds in the world. But rather you begin to wrap yourself around this world, around this planet, even around this universe. And you proclaim and know in the depth of your being that *you* are the holy Son of God and you *will not* settle for less than Heaven on Earth!

No longer do the problems seem so large or complex because you abide in a state of truth and knowledge that is bigger than the world. For you *know* that through you, God can do *anything*—if only you will direct your attention, open up the floodgates, and allow it to happen!

You begin to step into the greatest place of power that there is. This is truly what was meant, in even your Christian religion, that Christ returned to Heaven and sat at the right hand of the Father. The one who sits at the right hand is the chief of staff, the one who makes it all happen. To sit at the right hand of God is to allow your mind to abide in right-mindedness. And in right-mindedness you see no separation between yourself and your brothers and sisters, which means you see no separation between yourself and the world.

Getting to Heaven is no longer an attraction. *Bringing* Heaven to *this* world *is*. Bringing light to darkness is all that matters. Constantly desiring to bring greater light to your own darkness is the way in which you live, moment to moment, desiring greater light, greater light, and greater light:

> What do I need to let go of?
> How deep can my self-honesty go?

> How wide can my compassion for life spread?
> What actions am I actually taking in this world?

> What am I defending?
> What am I afraid of?

> Am I willing to become so powerful a conduit for Christ that
> I take on responsibility for the atonement and tell Jeshua to move aside?

For the mind in right-mindedness serves only the voice for God. It no longer has any interest in defending the voice of egocentricity.

Therefore, beloved friends, for the next thirty days, practice self-honesty. Utilize the questions we have given you each day. Also, merely sit down with a pad of paper and a pen and ask:

What thoughts have gone through my mind this day?

If you want, you can draw a line through the paper down the center and on one side put loving thoughts, on the other side unloving thoughts—remember those are just your own judgments—and see what comes up.

In truth and reality, in the physical domain and dimension, no one is without unloving thoughts. Why? Because the mind is a vast space through which thoughts, like radio waves, are passing constantly. Quite frankly, and we have spoken to you of this before, in the end you do not really know who is doing the thinking. You are only aware of a thought arising in the mind. The ego says, "I am this. I am not that. This thought must be *mine*. That thought must be *yours*."

In truth, you are all swimming in the same sea, and there is merely *thought* arising and passing away. You do have the power to discern and select which thoughts will hold *value* for you. But it is impossible to push away what you have decided to judge as *un*spiritual thoughts. Can you imagine becoming so *free* that when a murderous thought arises, it makes you laugh and you tell the truth? "Ah, when you reached across the table and you ate the potato chip off my plate, I saw an image of taking a huge ax and cutting off your hand and making you eat your own fingers. Ha, what a thought!"

For it is the *embrace* with perfect self-honesty that returns the mind to sanity. It is the *refusal* to be honest that creates the conflict and tension in the mind that is called insanity. And insanity is a state in which the mind is not at peace, and Christ cannot enter therein.

Many of you have come from a tradition that you call Catholicism. Within it there is a practice called confession. This is really the idea of that practice, although of course, it has been used to place guilt—that is not the point. Confession means to be willing to be honest. The priest was meant to be a representation, a symbol, of God or Christ Mind. So that you could sit in your little box—which is really a symbol of going into your own internal privacy—and telling the truth to your higher Self, to the Self that loves you anyway, to the Mind of God that embraces all things and transcends all things.

Now, in truth, that Mind will not tell you that you must go say 947,000 "Hail Mary's" and sweep the streets of the city. It will merely say:

Beloved child, you are forgiven already.

For you have returned to sanity by merely confessing, to the deepest part of your Self, what has arisen and passed away within the lower mind—the mind associated with the body in the field of temporality. It is just like going to the depth of the ocean, into the silence thereof, and saying, "Yes, I was just out there on the tip of the foam of the wave and was part of a lot of chaos out there. How about that!" And the ocean remains as it has always been.

Lack of honesty in self leads to lack of honesty in relationship. And lack of honesty in relationship creates the tension and appearance of separation and guilt, which is the very nemesis that the soul is seeking to overcome. Self-honesty, then—the return to perfect peace—requires, in the end, the cultivation of *vulnerability* for:

<blockquote>In my perfect vulnerability, I find my perfect safety.</blockquote>

The vulnerable are the meek, those who have returned to their own innocence and know that the opinions and judgments of others cannot harm them. They live merely honest with themselves—without pretense, without image, no longer concerned with *that* world, the insane world.

They become more and more a conduit through which the power and Love of God begins to work. And through them, other minds are reached. Unbeknownst to them, they become a living, walking (as long as the body lasts) conduit through which grace is transferred to other minds. And in the presence of such a one, other minds heal spontaneously.

Other minds are attracted to such a being, not because they are doing anything, not because *they* perceive themselves as great, but because they know that only God is great. There is no longer a self they are trying to defend. Everything becomes merely a context in which they can be used by the Holy Spirit to bring about the atonement. They walk in the world, unknown by the world, unseen by the world. They seem very ordinary. They merely do as Love asks them to do.

You are birthing Christ. Nothing can prevent it from occurring now. Merely trust each moment. Surrender into each moment. Embrace your commitment to Reality.

Teach only Love to yourself by loving *that* which you have hated and judged, by allowing yourself to feel and to know that which is passing through the mind and body anyway. Embrace it. See your ordinary humanness, not as an obstruction to peace, but as that through which peace can be extended.

Beloved friend, there is a great depth and treasure awaiting you if you will put the message of this lesson into practice with passion, even zealousness, and with full commitment to your own Christedness to see that *you are worthy* of the deepest honesty that you can reach, that you can confess, that you can live! For ultimately, the deepest, honest truth is:

I and my Father are one! I am Christ eternal!

Beloved friends, be you, therefore, at peace this day. Have fun with the exercises we have given you. And know how much you are loved. Amen.

LESSON 23

THE VOICE FOR LOVE

Beloved and holy friends, we come forth to abide with you in this lesson—not from a place apart from where you are, but from that place in which the Sonship is joined as one. Where can that be, but in the Mind of God? Who is God, but Love?

Therefore, in each moment, when any mind surrenders its identification with its illusions, when it surrenders its identification with its own thoughts, with its own needs, with its own perceived desires, and rests into perfect silence, it rests *into* the voice for Love. It learns to ask only of *that* voice:

What would you have me do in this moment?

More and more, the voice for Love begins to *in*form the decisions, the thought processes, the vision, the revelation, and in your world, the action or behavior that is expressed through the temporary coalescing of energy into the *illusion* of a body.

Beloved friends, we come forth from that place which *is* the voice for Love. And if any mind can, indeed, rest into that place, it can only be because that place is *necessarily* within it. It is the depth of the soul. That depth is not an individual. It is universal, it is eternal, and it is forever present. It knows no boundaries. It knows no time. It simply *is* Love.

So, we abide *in* that place and we speak forth *from* that place. And if you would well receive it, if at any time when you, in your mind, are struck by the truth of what is being shared, it is only because you have chosen *in that moment* to open your *own* internal access to the voice for Love. What is triggered, what is activated or remembered is that part of you that *is* Love itself.   That part of the Self—the depth of the soul—that is forever one with God.

The great trick of evolution, if you would permit me to use such a term, is to grow the soul's awareness so that it rests in that depth of silence, and yet does not need to withdraw or turn away from the expressions of creation to do so. That is, it need no longer judge the body. It need no longer judge the world that you see around the body. It need no longer strive to ascend to some spiritual height in which all things disappear.

But rather, to the contrary, the soul in its *maturity* has ascended into union with the voice for God. That is, it has ascended into the depth of its Self. It has learned to stabilize itself in that internal silence. It has, through time, experienced that process of transformation in which even the conscious mind is no longer thinking for itself, but is *in*formed from the depth of the true Self, the depth of the soul, the voice for Love, God Herself, Christ Itself.

THE DECISION TO BECOME ONE WITH THE MIND OF GOD

Beloved friends, The Way of Transformation, then, involves the deliberate decision to allow the translation of perception so that it becomes of one mind, of one accord with the Mind of God. It is *in*formed from the depth of the silence and Love that sees the body, that sees the world, and that sees each moment *only* as that which holds the value which the Holy Spirit has placed upon it.

What is the Holy Spirit but that part of your own right-mindedness that *knows* that only Love is real. When any mind truly rests in that silence, it knows that it can no longer draw conclusions about what Love would do, what Love would express through it. Or how Love would use the particular tools or gifts of any seemingly individual self in order to trigger, to nudge, to uplift, to shock any other aspect of the Sonship into desiring its *own* awakening.

Now, if you pay close attention to what was just said, the implication is perfectly clear. Reality is one and unshakable and only Love is real. Yet the dream should never be denied. For denial creates separation. Only embracing can allow healing—the healing that Love brings. As you well know, there are indeed many minds that are still afflicted, still harboring the decision to believe that the dream of separation is real.

When any mind within the Sonship chooses to awaken and heal its own illusions, Love begins to inform that mind more, and more, and more, so that its expressions serve the voice for Love.

The voice for Love has only one purpose: to be extended into the dream, into the illusion, to nudge the aspects of the Sonship yet sleeping. So that the *entirety* of the Sonship can be returned, or reawakened to the reality of itself as the creative conduit through which God extends Herself.

When any mind truly awakens, it no longer sees specialness in the world at all. Each moment is merely surrendered into what I once called the will of my Father. What is that will? The impetus of Love. How can Love operate so that it brings awakening to the minds involved? That is, indeed, a purely creative process, and is the only *true* value time can have. The awakened mind has no idea, one day to the next, what Love will ask it to do, and how Love is to be expressed through it. The awakened mind knows that it is not the maker or the doer, and merely asks in every moment:

What would you have me do?

The more that practice is developed, the more that the mind is refined and purified. It becomes almost a spontaneous or second-nature kind of thing, in which the mind is so closely aligned with the will of God that the subtle nudges, flowing forth from the depth of the Self, from the depth of Love Itself, stirs through the conscious mind and meets no obstruction born of fear. For where fear has been de-valued, Love springs forth.

Each and every one of you that has chosen to read these lessons has already made the decision to become *that one*, ever more deeply and ever more deeply. Make no mistake about it—the decision has already been made, and therefore, the end is perfectly certain.

When that mind that has made the decision to allow its transformation *embraces* the simplicity of its lived experience, it looks as though it is very ordinary. While the body lasts, you do the things that all bodies and minds do in your dimension and world. You perhaps find the body shivering against the winter cold or sweating in the summer sun.

Yet, in the midst of the contexts of the experiences of your life, what is informing the mind is not the egoic desires of: How can I get more? How can I avoid a certain experience or feeling? How can I make myself comfortable? How can I get others' approval? How can I be acknowledged as a great master? None of that runs the awakened mind.

Each context is surrendered within the mind itself over into the will of Love. And that mind, through the personality, through the body structure while the body lasts, becomes a conduit that serves the voice for Love. That one may not be understood; that one may not be approved of; and that one may not be acknowledged by the world.

Yet, rest assured, those who seek to be approved of and acknowledged by the world have their reward. And what reward is it to be acknowledged by the insane, dwelling in illusion? Can an illusion truly acknowledge the worthiness of the Son of God?

Once again, each and every one of you is in an inevitable journey now—you too shall have your reward. For there are those of us who know you and love you, and your acknowledgment comes not even from us, though perhaps through us, but it comes from That One that has birthed you to extend the good, the holy, and the beautiful.

THE RELEASE OF ALL ILLUSION

The Way of Transformation, then, is not the *gaining* of power; it is the *release* of all illusion. It is the willingness to release the grip that you have had upon the shadows that your mind has made up as a substitute for the Truth of your *only* Reality. The process of The Way of Transformation is that process in which you begin to use the mind quite deliberately, in a different way.

To some of you who have studied my *Course in Miracles*, that too is an expression or a form of The Way of Transformation, since all transformation inevitably requires correction of how the mind is used so that what the mind sees is different than the ego's world.

When the mind is corrected, the use of the body that most serves Love also naturally follows. The use of what you have created in error—which is the body, the personality structures, the emotional matrix, and the beliefs—all of that that makes up what you call yourself, all of these things are given over to be used differently.

Therefore, the deeper you come to understand, to *know* and to *feel* the depth of the self that you have constructed in your attempt to conform to an insane world, the greater the space there is for you to be *in*formed by Love. Not that the body disappears, not that the personality structures disappear, but rather they become transparent. The value you have given them has been withdrawn, and they are given over to be used in a different way.

To use a simple example, a painter begins to paint devotional paintings out of her love and acceptance of grace. Or a speaker is brought into alignment with Love, and that Love creates a context in which what is spoken is spoken differently, with a different purpose and a different intent and, therefore, to a much different audience. Or one who works with the hands in the fields begins to work for a different purpose, begins to be informed in ways to use the skills and gifts that one has developed, perhaps to feed the hungry, the needy.

The forms of expression change to be more conformed with which *voice* is running the show. When the ego was running the show, or thought that it was, the personality, the emotions and the body were used to serve the very survival of the ego. When the ego has been displaced and the voice of Love has been returned to the place of authority, careers can change, for the very meaning and purpose of existence has changed.

In the initial stages as this process is occurring, this can elicit fear, a sense of disorientation, or a sense of self-doubt. All of these things must be embraced with faith, which is indeed the substance of things unseen. Love is not quite settled in perfectly yet, and the mind is still gripping somewhat the things and the ways of the world. And yet, a deeper voice is compelling the self to release old values, to release old careers, old relationships, old clothing and old furniture. Everything begins to change. And it feels as though loss is being experienced.

Yet, what is *loss* in the world is *gain* in the Kingdom. For what can be gained but the reawakening to the simplicity of the truth:

> I am God's. I belong not to the world. I and my Father are one. Since I still find myself in this world, how can I dedicate this body and its attendant personality and emotions to the voice for Love?

And that becomes the sole purpose—both the *sole* as only, and the *soul* as the essence of your being. The sole/soul purpose becomes the willingness to allow Love to *in*form each moment.

It is quite true that such a one, born of Love, can be very misunderstood by the world. Such a one, I once said, is one born like the wind. You do not know where they have been, you do not know where they are going, and neither do they.

But they are present where they are, constantly dedicated to being merely a servant of, or a conduit of, the voice for Love—recognizing that time and the world no longer hold any function, value or purpose, save that which the Holy Spirit would give it. And the only value the Holy Spirit gives the world is to see it as a *context* through which the Sonship can be healed and awakened.

The Way of Transformation does, indeed, require commitment, a deliberate choice. This can be the value, by the way, of initiatory experiences. And, not too far in the distant future, we will be helping to inform Shanti Christo, so that initiatory experiences are offered and provided. The value of this is that it makes conscious and public what the soul is desiring and calls the conscious mind to step into a deeper self-discipline, a deeper self-commitment, a deeper self-maturity.

Beloved friends, this is not something ever to enter into in a lazy way. We would highly suggest, then, that as you go through the mind, ask yourself, "Are there any of the lessons that I read with only half my focus, with part of my attention on trying to get dinner ready, or getting my taxes paid, or getting to the office?"

If there is any such lesson that you have not brought the *wholeness* of your being to, in a state of openness and surrender, go back and read it again. You will discover that there is much that has been missed. Each exercise has been carefully chosen. Each exercise offers you an immediate way to begin to transform certain aspects of your own mind. Therefore, *each moment* should be treasured.

Please hear this: As the mind, the conscious mind, begins to become more *in*formed by the voice for Love, vigilance and discipline become *even more* necessary, simply because you are dealing with more power—more *true* power. The purpose of your very being takes on a far different flavor. You begin to realize that wherever you are, there is a *precious moment* that offers an opportunity for healing, for Love, for awakening. And it is not to be missed. *Each moment* of your existence in this plane of density *is not to be missed!*

Once, when I was reaching out to this beloved brother at three o'clock in the morning, he proclaimed to me, "Could you please come a little later in the morning? I would like to get some sleep." My answer to him is what I will give to you now:

Have you not been sleeping long enough?

Will you use time constructively to realize that where you are is not in the world at all, but in a context made *new* by your desire to awaken, which invited the Holy Spirit to "take over the show," so to speak? Wherever you find yourself is *not* an ordinary moment any longer. Though you seem to walk in the world, though you seem to deal with the things of the world—which you must do as long as the body lasts—you no longer *belong* to the world.

Another voice has touched you. Though your neighbors and friends, perhaps even your children, your spouse or your parents cannot possibly yet see who walks among them, you are a *disciple of Christ*. And Christ is the Father's only creation, created in Love, as Love, to extend Love.

YOU ARE IN THE MOST IMPORTANT JOURNEY ANYONE CAN EVER TAKE

You are in the most important journey that anyone can ever take—a journey without distance to a goal that has never changed, even into a place that is unchangeable forever. You have undertaken the journey from illusion to Reality, from fear to Love, from *false* power through manipulation, through image, through conforming to the world to *true* power, resting in the Mind of Christ, being a *conduit* for that which awakens the Sonship.

Every function is *equal* to those that have chosen such discipleship. Understand, then, that wherever you are right now, as you read these words—wherever you are right now—you are in the perfect place at the perfect moment.

Therefore, indeed, bless the moment as you find it, for it serves two purposes. One, it is that perfect context for your awakening from illusion. And at the very same moment, it is offering you the opportunity to cultivate your skill at being a conduit for the voice for

Love. These two sides of one coin exist *fully* in the presence of each of your "ordinary" moments.

Rest assured, as you come to trust the voice for Love, as one born of the Spirit, as one who lives as the wind, if it is time for you to release certain forms—career, relationship, clothing, furniture, what-have-you—you will know it in an instant. You simply *know*! For revelation is knowledge. Knowledge is immediate. It is not translated through a whole lot of thinking in the mind. That is why we choose to say that it is through the heart that one knows the immediate will of Love.

As you practice letting go of that which you once valued, you will discover that it gets easier and easier. With each experience of letting go, you find yourself carried in ways that you could never comprehend or create *yourself* into new formats, new contexts, in which your own wisdom awakens even deeper.

The opportunity to be of service expands and grows, as though you stepped from a small room in a house into a large ballroom and realized, "This is *much* better than where I was before!" It is not that you have failed when something ends, for, in truth, you cannot fail. In truth, there are no endings, *except* in illusions.

In the lessons that follow, we will speak much about the importance and distinction of *content* and *form*. We will look at those two sides of the coin and help to illuminate your mind and understanding that it is *content* that always matters, and the *form* is secondary.

Form is what is birthed in *time*. And what is birthed in time, ends in time. Even the body had a beginning, and will, therefore, have an end. Yet, when it is given over to the voice for Love, its purpose becomes timeless, endless, for it begins to express only content.

MAKE A DECISION TO VIEW TIME DIFFERENTLY

In this lesson, the theme that we wish to bring unto you is this: Make a decision—right now—to view time differently. Put on the eyes of the Holy Spirit—right where you are, *right now*. Do not just read what is said, but actually decide to *do it*.

Look around the place you find yourself in. Look at the body. If you are with others at this time, notice them. Notice all things.

You are not in the world at all. You are a *disciple of Christ*. You have chosen, by grace, to awaken from illusion, and to cultivate yourself, with support and help, into being ever more a mature soul that radiates the light and Love of Christ, even while in time.

Time, then, must be *seized* and seen to be of *great value* and that each and every moment is not a mistake. There is nothing "idle" about it. *You* are the one who is free to use that moment to be *in*formed by the voice for Love, to learn ever more deeply to surrender the value of fear, safety, personal survival, and all of the rest, and to dissolve, through faith, into the voice for Love.

From *this* moment, decide to see time differently, to seize the opportunity to train the mind to be vigilant and aware. There is much occurring that may yet seem unseen to you—too subtle to grasp. You call it "being unaware." The journey from unawareness to awareness begins with the decision to walk through each moment of the day *knowing* the Truth of who you are. And to embrace the purpose and reason for your being, and then to ask the Holy Spirit to make all things known and clear, in alignment with the voice for Love.

The body becomes something that you no longer possess. The thoughts that you hold become meaningless. The context of every moment is *given over* to something new. The decision to see time differently leads you into the cultivation of a way of *being* that is different and new. Eventually, it will move from a mere intellectual idea into something known in the depth of the soul and expressed through every pore of the skin, while the body lasts:

> I am the Christ. There is only That One, and I am dissolved in and as That One. Call me not great, for only God is worthy of awe. That which I do, I do not of myself, but the Father does these things through me. I am one who merely loves Love so deeply that I am willing to surrender all things that I once knew to be myself, that my true Self, who is Christ, informs my every decision, my every gesture, my every extension of the good, the holy, and the beautiful.

There is a certain phraseology in your world that says, "This is some heavy stuff!" It is *very* heavy to the ego, since it squashes it like a gnat under a weight. If the light of the sun and the sun itself were to come and rest upon your planet, what would happen to your planet?

It is much like that when the Light of Christ comes to descend again, to touch the mind and the emotions and the body, where once the ego held sway. The ego dissolves into Light itself. It becomes remade. While the body-mind lasts, it becomes a mere servant.

The mind itself laughs at itself a great deal. For it sees the great joke that it has played on itself. It attempted to be other than what God created it to be. It experienced a multitude of dramas and illusions and story lines, careers, relationships, dis-eases and all of the rest in a grand *attempt* to be other than what Reality is. So the mind that is awakening laughs at itself a lot. It laughs as the echo of old patterns show up. It tells the truth about them. It need no longer deny them, for they hold no value, and the old patterns are not seen as a cave in which to hide.

The personality becomes transparent. In its innocence, it becomes perfectly vulnerable. And in its perfect vulnerability, it finds its transcendent safety.

Beloved friends, many of you began this journey out of curiosity. Yet, I say unto you, that was only the conscious mind's attempt to maintain control of the journey itself. No one comes to this pathway who has not made the decision from the depth of the soul:

> I am tired of suffering. I am tired of aloneness.
> I desire to dissolve into Christ Mind and to discover the Truth of who I am.

Everyone reading these words has made that decision. You are already well on your way. If you think you can turn around and go back to the platform and cash in your ticket, forget it! The train has already left the station, the conductor is God Himself, and those that enter herein cannot leave. The ego will try to convince you that you should because it is fighting for its life. But there is another who fights for your *true* Life—the Comforter given unto everyone in the moment the dream began.

Well do I know what *must emerge*, once the decision has been made. Each and every one of you will then perceive that your journey is unique and wholly yours. But this is only because you still perceive yourself as a separate being. Why? Because the eyes of the body show you that you are. Because you have lived with a certain husband or wife, and you know that everyone else on the planet did not, you will believe that that portion of your journey was "uniquely" yours, with "unique" energies that probably no one else could understand.

Yet, that was only the matrix, or the *form*, which was expressing a *content* of energy. That content of energy—whether it be fear, jealousy, anger or whatever it is—is known by everyone. This is what we mean when we say there are no private thoughts, no private experiences. The body, of course, has its unique experience. Only one body can be in a point of space at any given time. If you are making love in the middle of the night and you look around, you would swear nobody else is present. Rest assured, you live in glass houses. All things are perfectly visible to the entirety of creation.

It is the *energies* that you are experiencing that everyone knows. The trick of healing and awakening is to come to see the *neutrality* of all energy, so that you can choose to inform it with the value that the Holy Spirit would give it. Then, time becomes sacred. It becomes eternal. It becomes a tool for Love. Even the body becomes a tool that Love uses to bring about healing. What other purpose could a body hope to have?

So indeed, please do the exercise of making sure that there has not been a lesson that you have read with half a mind. Go back. If you wish, practice your five minutes as Christ, and then begin the review of the lesson that your *soul* might *absorb* it. And when there are exercises to do, do them—even if it just takes a minute. You cannot begin to see how the pebble dropped into the pond can have such vast and deep effects.

If you would still choose to look upon me as one who did great things—rest assured, the effects that you came to know about because certain stories were told about me and then finally written down, and some of those are a bit outlandish—those things came about because I too had teachers that showed me how to drop new pebbles in the pond of my mind. Their commitment and intent was the same as ours, which is to guide you into the fullness of your discipleship, until the transformation has been thoroughly completed on Earth—that is, in the body-mind—as it already is in Heaven.

For the correction has already occurred. It happened the moment you had the thought of separation, long before space and time were birthed. But you discover that the correction has, indeed, been fulfilled as you allow your creations in time—the body-mind—to be transformed. So that the conscious mind becomes perfectly aligned with what the depth of the Self already knows. And then, and only then, can the mind truly release the illusion of the third-dimensional plane, the physical dimension. For it is simply seen as a useless limitation.

So then, do this one thing. In each of your next seven days, as often as you remember to do so—and you will only remember what you choose to value—decide to see time differently and to acknowledge that you are a disciple of the Mind of Christ. Decide that nothing matters to you other than the simplicity of allowing the dissolution of illusions, so that Christ can come and live where once the ego dwelt in authority. A simple exercise. And if a day goes by in which you forget, it can only be because, in that day, you have valued something else.

IT IS NOW UP TO YOU

Beloved and holy friends, I come forth to join with you, not from a place that is apart from where you are, but from that place in which we are eternally joined as one Mind, one Heart, one Truth, one Creation, one Love. I come forth, then, to abide with you from the place in which you dwell eternally. I come forth to abide with you because I love you. I come forth to abide with you because you are as I am—the thought of Love in form.

We come now to the conclusion of The Way of Transformation; that way which allows the perception of the mind to be transformed from illusion to Reality, from fear to Love. *That way* is the way in which you come to the brink, or to the edge of the Kingdom of Heaven, in which you are finally ready to use the power of the mind to declare only what is true. And what is true is unshakable forever.

At no time has a single illusion that has stolen across the vast expanse of your being ever changed the Truth that is true always. The declaration of that Truth is the essence of words that I too once had need of speaking:

> I and my Father are one. I, as a ray of light, am one with that Source of Light from which all things spring forth. I, as a drop of water, am one with the ocean from which all moisture arises.

> I am That One sent forth from divine mystery to bring forth the good, the holy, and the beautiful to reflect in time and in form that which is timeless and formless, that which I have referred to as Abba, or Father, that creative Source that births all things and has an immediate and direct relationship with all of creation.

That Truth is true about you. It has been, in fact, the only thing that has *ever* been true. And in each moment, the power of the mind allows it to remember the truth, if it will *choose* the truth.

CHOOSING TO BE THE TRUTH

The Way of Transformation has been designed to guide you with specific exercises, with many fundamental questions, to the brink of that decision in which the mind declares for itself, from within itself, and then extends outward:

> I and my Father, I and my creative Source, I and Love are one.

> From this moment forward, I walk and live as one who chooses to use the power of mind, the power of awareness, the power of intention, the power of clarity, the power of being itself, to know the Truth that sets all things free.

> I choose to be the Truth that allows freedom to be extended to all others.

> I choose to walk upon this plane, while yet the body lasts for a little while, as that One who has been sent forth as a ray of light to shine light into a world that has feared it.

I invite you, then, as we come to the close of The Way of Transformation, to truly set aside time to withdraw yourself from the roar and the din of the world, to withdraw yourself from all the beliefs you have held about yourself or about anyone. And there, in the silence of your own heart, simply acknowledge that the Truth must be true always, and that the time is at hand for you to use the power of the mind given unto you of your Creator in the only way that it can be used sanely:

> I and my Father, I and my creative Source, are one!

Why is this important? In the end, all technique, all methodologies and strategies, are really magical means for taking away the egoic part of the mind's insistence upon the authority of its illusions to seduce, to trick the mind, to bring it to a place where it *must* come in order to truly step forward, in and as Life itself. All strategies and all methodologies, even those that we have given unto you in these lessons, are given unto you because the mind has been held sway by illusion.

The art of lessening the value that the mind places upon illusion is all that can be taught. All teaching is designed to return the mind to the brink of the Kingdom of Heaven. There and there alone, the mind itself, that which you essentially are, must from the depth of its beingness—unattached to anyone or anything—declare its decision to be awake. And assume the mantle of responsibility for bringing forth into this world only the light of Truth in each moment, with each breath, with every gesture, with every intention, with every vision, with every thought, and with every choice.

Indeed, beloved friends, The Way of Transformation brings you to the brink of the way of certain knowledge. This is a journey without distance to a goal that has never changed.

It is merely a *change of mind*: the decision to value the Truth, and the Truth alone.

When that decision has fully been embraced—you might think of it as a full embrace that embodies every cell of your being and the totality of all that you are—it becomes perfectly devoted to your union with God. Perfectly devoted to the recognition that as the *created*, it is time to surrender resistance to truth, and to accept that the Love of God has been given to you *fully*, without measure, without condition. And that you have been created to live *from* that Love, that *that* Love might inform every thought and every deed, that *that* Love might pour forth through you as the very Source of your own identity. "No longer I, but thine," would be one way of saying it.

When the mind has fully come to the recognition that no other decision holds value or purpose, that no other decision can bring the soul the peace and the fulfillment that it has sought in so many ways in the fields of illusion, *then the Father takes the final step for you.* That is, by an act of grace, that tiny drop of water that seemed to be so separate from the ocean dissolves and melts into the ocean itself. There is no longer a separate self to be found. The body-mind arises and continues for yet a little while, until its purpose is fulfilled. Then, it is put aside as a toy that has been outgrown.

The mind, the power of consciousness, slips into the perfect and eternal Truth that has been true always:

> There is only the Love of God. I am only in existence to express that truth.

In the way of perfect knowledge, all efforting is suspended. And the mind flows, borne by Love. It flows like the wind, knowing not where it comes from or where it is going, for its cares are not in the world. Its certainty is in Love. Peace pervades the entirety of the mind, wherever it happens to find its attention placed. And all things of the world have been translated into merely devices whereby the Truth might be communicated to the whole of creation, to a brother or to a sister.

For in truth, all of you are exactly *that*—perfectly equal, perfectly innocent, perfectly radiant and shining forever.

You become the anointed. You become the messiah, that which brings forth the word of God. You become the Christ. Yet, this is not an accomplishment. It is merely the return to an ancient remembrance of what has always been. The mind, having surrendered all resistance to Love, merely abides in the certainty of a perfect knowledge. This awaits you *now*, on just the other side of a final decision.

Look well, then, at all that has transpired for you in these past twelve lessons. Have the chance encounters, the insights, the visions and all of this been by chance? Has it been by accident? Hardly, for in the *depth* of your being you *chose* to enter into The Way of Transformation. You *chose* to open the depth of your being to a reflection of the truth you already know, given to you by an ancient brother who has loved you since before time is, one who has merely chosen to enact the extension of Love in whatever way is available.

As I have said unto you many times, I am not limited in how I communicate with any mind that would open a place for me. This pathway is but one of many. Yet it is the way in which you have made the decision to *allow* that communication to be known to your conscious mind. It is the context you have chosen to allow your release from fear and your embrace of Love.

I once said unto you that all things that begin in time, end in time. For their purpose is not to become a substitute for what is eternal. But to be devices whereby the remembrance of the eternal is returned to every mind that is a part of the Sonship—the one mind, the Mind of Christ, in which you dwell and have your true being.

The Way of Transformation, then, had a beginning and it has an end. The way of certain knowledge, which will comprise the next part of these lessons, will have a beginning and an end. Rest assured, I say unto you that when the way of knowledge has been imparted to you, and we have come into the perfect blending in which *you know* that you walk the plane as awake as I ever did, then the purpose of *The Way of Mastery* and our teaching-learning period will have come to a conclusion.

This does not mean that I will depart from where you are. But it *does* mean that you will have stepped into the *certainty* that *you are That One.* And what you would seek to gain from me, you will find in the temple of your own heart. There I will join with you—not as your teacher or savior, but as your friend and equal, as a co-creator.

You will be free, then, because you will no longer be *seeking* knowledge from me. You will be *extending Love* from the soul of your own beingness. And you will be free to invite me as a friend to join with you in your creations. That is an invitation that I will gladly accept! For *the only purpose of creation is to extend Love.*

FULFILLING YOUR PURPOSE

Relationship is eternal. Friendship is eternal. Co-creativity is the *essence* of knowing God. Co-creativity has the sole purpose of birthing in light the good, the holy, and the beautiful. That which brings the vibration of truth and reflects it in the world of time, touches fear and dissolves it, touches guilt and replaces it with forgiveness, touches resistance and tension and replaces it with willingness and peace.

Can there be any purpose in existence but this? For this were you birthed in the holy Mind of your Creator. For this have you journeyed through the labyrinths of everything *unlike* Love, that you might truly *choose* to return with perfect freedom into the marriage of Creator and created, divine child, divine spark.

For the union of Father and Son or Creator and created is *so intimate* and so perfect and so filled with the perfection of Love that, in truth, you will look and see no longer where you end and the Creator begins. You will be like the perfect lover of God, given over to that Love, pervaded by that Love, melting with that Love.

Yet, you will know always that you are the created. You are like the wave to the ocean, and the sunbeam to the sun. You will marvel with every breath. Spaciousness will come to the mind, and even into the cells of the body, in which you abide in the knowingness— beyond all conceptualization, beyond the reach of all beliefs, beyond the hope of every religion—the reality of the *living* Spirit of the *living* God.

The Way of Transformation, then, comes to a conclusion as you sit quietly with yourself and look upon the past twelve lessons, the insights, the changes, the chance encounters. And you *accept* and *know* that the being—the mind, the perceptions that began twelve lessons ago—*no longer exists*, except as the echo of an ancient memory. And *you* no longer need to invest the power of your identity with what is passed away.

The way of certain knowledge begins with this. Rest assured, that the time you spend in contemplation before you begin the next part of this course—which will be known as The Way of Knowing—is your final transition, if you will but accept it.

This is the time in which you can turn away from the past and look back upon it no longer. This is the time in which you can step into the light of the future of your own personal destiny, held in the hands of a perfectly loving Creator that already has a plan for you, or you would not have been birthed. For you are *certainly* not an accident!

This time before you begin The Way of Knowing is the most critical for you. For it is now up to you, alone, to decide to acknowledge the Truth, to decide what you are committed unto—the voice of the Holy Spirit or the voice of fear.

Are you committed to using the things of space and time to reaffirm the old beliefs that you are separate from God?

Or will you use the things of time—allow the Holy Spirit to use them for you—to demonstrate for you that you are *in* the world, but no longer *of* the world? You are no longer possessed and owned by the world, but you are *owned* by that voice for Love that has birthed you and sent you forth to bring forth the word.

The *word* is just that vibration in which peace, forgiveness, and knowing abide. The *word* is like a vibration, a wave that emanates from the depth of the ocean that speaks of the good, the holy, and the beautiful. It looks upon the things of space and time—even upon the body—and sees nothing to be feared. But sees all things in their perfect, harmless innocence that owns and embraces the totality of your perfect freedom.

You are pure Spirit. You are as the wind. You can neither possess nor be possessed, for you are owned of the Creator. Love embraces you. Love pervades you. And you hear no other voice but the voice for Love. Through your eyes will shine a light so clear—for indeed, the eyes are the window of the soul—that through you can begin to emanate the Truth that is true always. And you will not fear looking into the eyes of a brother or a sister and saying unto them:

> I am That One sent forth of the Father. And if I am with you in this moment, my only purpose is to be present as Love—with you, for you, for us, and for all of the Sonship. This is the choice I make. This is the beingness I bring. This is the truth that I am devoted to. I bring you only Love.

Indeed, beloved friends, The Way of the Heart was designed to open you to the reality that within you lies a center of peace, a center of forgiveness, a center that can begin to take you toward certain knowing.

The Way of Transformation was designed quite specifically—for those of you that truly enjoined it—to dissolve certain patterns in the mind, to reactivate your power to *deliberately decide* what you will think, what you will feel, what you will create, what you will believe, and what frequencies of thought will be acceptable unto you.

Now, you come to the brink of a decision that *closes the door* on a past once made in error that has been corrected, through the grace, through the gift of the Holy Spirit and placed within your mind and heart. And the *opening of a door* of a life lived—not *seeking* the Kingdom—but a life lived *in* the Kingdom, in the light of the Kingdom of perfect Truth:

> I and my Father are one!
> Nothing can arise by accident.
>
> My only purpose is to embrace creation
> that the good, the holy, and the beautiful
> might be extended through even this body-mind,
> wherever it happens to be.
> For my delight is the Love of my Creator,
> my devotion to the extension of Love,

> my peace from the embrace of my brothers
> and sisters in the simplicity of a celebration
> that shall know no end.

I am perfectly aware that there are many of you, as you read these words, who will feel, yet, a subtle contraction, as fear *attempts*—one final time—to claim ownership of your being. You are free to choose otherwise. You are free to say:

> No! It is truth I accept. It is truth I will know. It is truth I will live—not
> for another, but for myself.

> For my only responsibility from the moment of my creation was to accept
> the atonement for myself, to allow the transformation to occur in the
> depth of my own mind, so that ancient words become in truth mine: I
> and my Father are one, and I know it!

> Henceforth, I am free to walk this Earth in gentleness, not to strive to move
> into the future, but to be borne by the wings of Love, that will carry me
> into the fulfillment of my destiny. And my destiny can only be that
> which reflects God in this world.

Let not fear claim authority over the mind any longer. This does not mean that you will not occasionally feel it like a wave through you. The difference is that you *need not value it.*

THE FINAL STAGE

The final stage, the way of certain knowing, is to claim your right to be perfectly happy. And perfect happiness can come only from the soul's decision to acknowledge the decision to value the truth and to live it. Nothing else can bring the soul to the completion of its peace. No other decision, no other thinking process, brings the son to the Father, brings the daughter to the Mother, brings the created to the Creator, brings the sunbeam to the sun, brings the wave to the ocean, in perfect remembrance that *only Love is real.* And what is real cannot be threatened.

The world no longer holds the illusory power that you once gave it. It becomes no longer something you must conform yourself *to* in order to survive. For you are Life eternal, and your life is held in the abundance of God's Love.

You stand, then, on the brink of the complete transformation of the perception of the world. It will be radically changed instantly in the twinkling of an eye as you look out upon it and say:

There is nothing here that has a greater power than the Love of God. Because I abide in that Love, I am freed from needing anything of the world.

I am free only to give to the world. And what I give is added unto me, for by teaching I learn, and by giving I receive.

My love of God is matched only by my love of my Self as that which God has created—perfect and whole and innocent.

My love for my Self is so deep and so purified of the falseness of guilt and smallness and egoism that I want all of God!

And I will bring forth only that which allows me to feel and to know my oneness with that frequency and that Light.

I once said that if you are not wholly joyous, it could only be because you have elected to use the power of your mind to think differently than your Creator. The Way of Knowing will bring you into the certainty of a perfect joy that is unshakable. Imagine, then, no more swings of depression, no more swings of self-doubt—just pure beingness of Love, right where the ego used to claim property rights.

The life that you were created to live is in the palm of your hand. The decision to end The Way of Transformation by simply acknowledging that, "Only the Truth can be true and I am fully committed to being only that" brings you into the Kingdom.

No longer a journey *to* it, but now, the eternal journey *within it*, mystery upon mystery, miracle upon miracle, sublime beauty upon sublime beauty, peace growing into peace as you surrender and sink into the reality of God's presence forevermore, forevermore and forevermore. For God is without end and knows neither height nor depth. There is *no limit* to the Reality of the Creator.

There can be no greater joy than to allow your consciousness, which is the gift of your awareness, to be ever permeated deeper and deeper and deeper by the certainty of a perfect knowing:

I am That One! I abide in that Love prior to every breath, every thought, and every gesture.

This body is not what I am, but I will use it as a communication device. I will not use it to separate myself from my brother or sister. I will use it to gesture in the ways of Love, the ways of respect, the ways of gentleness, the ways of embrace, the ways of appreciation, the ways of thankfulness.

I will see my Father in my brother and my sister. And I will love that and honor them as the vehicle, the conduit that brings the light of my Father to even my physical eyes.

I will revel in the delight of how the sunlight sparkles on the dew upon the petal of a flower. I will listen to the barking of a dog and know that mystery has been made manifest.

I will walk this Earth as one who is free, and one who is the spaciousness through which only Love abides and is offered.

And many will be sent unto you who will awaken in your presence—in even "ordinary" moments. *You stand at the brink of all that the soul has desired! Is* it not time to wrap the fingers of the hand around what has been placed in the palm?

I am That One.

Time to live *in* the Kingdom, guided *only* by the voice for Love, by the voice for Truth, by the purity of Spirit.

SPEND TIME ALONE TO RECLAIM AND VALUE ONLY THE TRUTH

So, I would ask you, now, to set aside yet a little time in which you abide wholly with yourself. Acknowledge the Truth that is true always. I invite you to use the power of the clarity of your mind to decide *against* valuing illusions, and use that power to *value only the truth*, that you might offer yourself into a life through which the Truth that is true always becomes concretely embedded in the totality of your being. For you, indeed, will *know* the Truth and you will know that it has set you free.

Spend some time by yourself—quietly, alone. A long time ago, I said once unto you that the decision was made *alone*, in the depth of your being, to see if you could create *unlike* God, if you could transform yourself into something which is other than what God has created. That has been the whole drama and dream of the realm of separation.

You *must* come back to claiming ownership, *alone*, in which you decide to use the power of the mind to make a different decision—in the depth of your being. For you stand *alone* before your God, who waits patiently for His child to awaken and to receive the gifts that the Father would bestow upon the Son, that the sun would shine forth upon the sunbeam, that the ocean would give unto the wave.

The gifts that await your awakening are *all* power under Heaven and Earth to bring forth the good, the holy, and the beautiful, to walk *in time* as one who is *timeless*, to abide as a body-mind, yet one who knows they are pure Spirit, shining forth temporarily through the body.

It is given unto you—now—in the depth of your internal silence, to reclaim ownership of your mind, to let parents, to let society, to let everyone off the hook. No one has *caused* you to feel what you feel, to think what you think, and to act as you have acted.

You have used the power of the mind to attempt the great impossibility of making yourself into something that is *other* than what God has created. Now it is time to *deliberately* use the power of the mind to decide *with* your Creator. It is the end of all seeking. It is the end of all striving. It far transcends the purest and greatest of strategies and methodologies. It is beyond prayer. It is beyond meditation. It is the simplicity of the Truth.

Therefore, abide quietly. Those of you that will, indeed, make the decision and will step across the edge, across the veil into the Kingdom, we will abide together for the next eleven lessons in The Way of Knowing, the way of perfect knowing. And you will see the totality of your life *radically transformed*. For that *must* be the case when the *seeker* is no more, and it has been replaced by one who has *found*—and acknowledges it!

Miracles will lead the way. For the mind that is given to true devotion to the Holy Spirit is *unlimited forever* in all ways. And the whole of creation shapes itself to be of service to the one that is anointed and *claims* it, and lives *only* to give God to the world. Not one concern will arise before you that will not be taken care of and met before you run into it. The walls will dissolve.

You will be the miracle-minded. You will be the one who shines forth in perfect effortlessness, in perfect peace and perfect joy. You will be Christ incarnate. And *that* is the purpose for which you were birthed in the Mind of God. It is in that Mind that you are held—*now* and *forevermore!*

Be you therefore, at peace—this day and always. Be you therefore, in the perfect knowledge that I am your brother and friend, and nothing but this. I am that One who loves you and sees only the light of Truth in you, and looks forward to the day in which we create together as equals—in honor and devotion to the great mystery that the Love of the Creator *is*.

Peace, then, be unto you always. Amen.

PART THREE

THE WAY OF KNOWING

LESSON 25

YOU REMAIN AS YOU ARE CREATED TO BE

Now, we begin.

Beloved and holy friends, we come forth to abide with you as we initiate the third and final part of this formal information in *The Way of Mastery*. This information will as time unfolds be shared with millions. We have chosen to entitle this last group of lessons The Way of Knowing.

What, then, is required for true knowledge to exist? How does one live—in whatever dimension of creation—when they abide in *true* knowing? Beloved friends, that which is required for true knowledge to pervade the whole of one's consciousness is simply this: Not for one moment have you ever lived life. Rather in truth and in reality, Life, which is but Love streaming forth from the Source of all creation, has sought to live as you. Never at any time has there, in truth, been a false self. Never has there been a time in which something called the ego has existed.

You have heard us say many times that what is true about you is true always, and that you remain as you are created to be—the thought of perfect Love in form. You emanate from the Mind of the Creator as a wave emanates from the ocean. The great secret of your human existence, indeed, the great secret of the many journeys you have taken is that they have existed *nowhere* save *within* the movie screen of your own mind.

Does this mean that your dreams have had no effect? Within the dream itself, as long as you choose to be identified with it, you *will* experience the effects of the choices that you have made. Yet, now, as the heart has touched purification and as you have truly been willing to allow transformation to occur, all that matters and must be remembered is that *you*, as you *thought* yourself to be, has never truly existed. It has been a smoke screen. It has been a chimera. It has been illusion.

Knowledge, then, consists of the crystal-clear awareness that while creation streams forth from the Mind of God, *you* cannot find the place that a separate self began. And you have absolutely no knowledge of where your end will be found. In truth, you do not know

294

what is going to unfold in the very next moment of your experience. This can only mean, since you *do* have a next moment, that *something else is living you.*

In the beginning of the journey, there must be desire, for no one can come unto the Father without it. For just as you used the energy of desire to dream the dream of separation that closed your heart that set you on a thousand useless journeys propelled and compelled by fear, by judgment, and by doubt, likewise desire has been necessary for you to be willing to face your illusions. And to look more deeply at your judgments, and to see that they can have no value save that which you extend unto them. It has, indeed, required desire for you to *want* to awaken.

As you have used the power of intention to continually etch into the mind the beliefs and perceptions that are the very foundation of the dream of separation, so too have you learned to use intention through time, which is your creation, in order to awaken from time and from fear.

Just as you once used the power of allowing to give permission to the creations held within your mind to seemingly—apparently—take form in front of your eyes, and allowed their "reality" to become so deeply entrenched that literally worlds have been birthed from it, so too have you needed to use allowance in the process of transformation, *allowing* yourself to feel what you did not want to feel before. And allowing yourself to see differently what you had once insisted could only be seen in a certain way. Allowing has been the very field from which all forgiveness you have learned has sprung forth.

Allowing has been the most central of keys in the process of your healing and awakening. For when you truly begin to touch upon the power of genuine allowing, you begin to taste the first levels of *true* freedom. You have learned that just as you have allowed new beginnings to occur, you have also discovered that you have the power to allow endings to occur within the field of phenomena you call "the world."

Yet, I say unto you, surrender is the completion of the keys to the Kingdom. Just as once you had need of surrendering to your illusions in order to identify the fundamental energy of your being with your illusions, just as you have had to live in surrender to even allow allowance, just as you have learned to rest in surrender even to allow intention, just as you have learned to rest in surrender even to allow desire to be made new within you, as you enter The Way of Knowing, the final surrender is entered.

THE FINAL SURRENDER—THERE IS ONLY GOD

That is the surrender which is beyond the comprehension of all the languages and theologies of your world, beyond all that can be spoken or uttered, yet not beyond what can be known, felt, realized, and lived!

For in surrender you look upon a perfectly harmless world, whether it seems to be outside of the body or within the body-mind itself. You look upon the comings and goings of the world and you find that all things are, of themselves, perfectly empty. You look within and discover that no longer need you obstruct from the conscious mind, from your awareness, what the body-mind has experienced from the moment of its conception. No longer is there an obstruction to the flow of experience.

No longer is there a *self-seeking God*. Where and when that self has been surrendered, the mind awakens to the simple reality that there is *only* God. And *you are* That One.

As you seek to find words to communicate to yourself, or perhaps to another, the great wonder, the great mystery, the great truth, the great simplicity of awakening into true knowing, you will strive to find a way to communicate, as I have tried to find ways to communicate with you. You will seek to communicate to your brothers and sisters that there is only God.

And yet, there is the power of the mind to perceive yourself as the created, which in truth you are. For *God gives rise to God, looking back upon Himself.* Mystery of pure content gives rise to temporary form in order that pure mystery might be apprehended.

You are, then, the very process whereby that One, who alone is without a second, creates the temporary form through which that One apprehends and knows itself. You are that One that is the perfect *effect* of mystery that would pour forth of itself and make visible what was invisible, to birth through time and form that which cannot be contained within it. For Love is unfathomable. You cannot control it. Love is vast beyond all measure. You cannot contain it. Love cannot be possessed. It can only be allowed.

Therefore, indeed, beloved friends, the very *keys* whereby once you used the power of your own mind to create the illusion of a separate self are the very *keys* utilized by your own mind to awaken you to the truth that you have never been. There is only and always *this* mysterious moment. And all things have been birthed from perfect mystery.

The awakened mind—awakened from false arrogance—looks upon all things and says:

I am that One.

Yet, no trace of separation or duality exists, for you are not apart from all things that are arising—the wind that blows through the trees, the wisps of a cold winter rain, the warmth of the sun upon the skin of the body, the embrace of a lover, or the laughter of a child.

The awakened mind that abides in perfect knowing no longer *obstructs* perception, feeling, the flow of thought, or the flow of experience. It no longer looks to see how it can make things different than they are. It looks only, and lives from, what it most truly wants: simply to abide in its own nature and to allow Life to flow from that nature, dancing in the infinite myriad displays of form.

What, then, is required for true knowledge to exist? What is indeed required to abide in The Way of Knowing? To *fully* accept that: Not one trace of your seeking has ever brought you closer to reality. Not one modality has ever held the power to bring you closer to God. And that *never* could it have ever been truly possible for you to make progress toward the consciousness of God. For all the while, you have been the One you are seeking, *pretending* to be a seeker.

And for what reason have you entertained the thought of separation? The reason is simply this: *to do it.* For the Mind of God does not deny *any* possibility, for it sees nothing that can obstruct the purity of its own nature. Forever God abides within Herself—infinite, vast, radiant, and silent—the infinite field of pure knowledge, pure intelligence, out of which *all* things and *all* possibilities arise. This is why I once said unto you:

> You have never looked upon another, *for you see only your Self.*

You are free to judge yourself by judging your brother and, thereby, create a form of experience. But even that form of experience is only the perfect reality of God. And *that* is what you are!

What, then, requires true knowledge? God does. From the very moment that you first had the thought, "I want God," even that thought has appeared within the field of what you believe is your limited awareness as a limited body-mind, racked by fear and doubt and guilt and all of the rest. All of it is illusion. That thought of wanting God—the moment in which your journey home began—*that thought* is the presence of God awakening itself to that which has never been lost.

God is what requires true knowledge. The thirst that you have felt for God is God's thirst for Herself. You are literally the field of awareness of God in which God has awareness of Himself because you are the *power* of God. And *only* by that power have you ever been able to be aware of something that has appeared to be *other* than God. For even fear rests in Love.

Even fear, contraction, and the dream of separation requires Love. For Love allows all things, trusts all things, embraces all things, and therefore, transcends all things.

In what you might still wish to perceive to be your "own experience," as though it were separate and apart from your brothers and sisters, as though it were separate and apart from the twinkling of the stars, and the dance of the sunlight upon the water, and the thought in the brilliant mind of a scientist, and the cry of a newborn child—even if you wish, yet, to maintain that you have something called "private experience"—that private experience has required the presence of God. Every thought you have ever held has existed only because Love has allowed it!

You Have the Power to Awaken to Your True Nature Now

Have you suffered because God has chosen it? Not at all, for in truth—and please listen carefully—*suffering does not exist*. Only the reality of Love can exist. You are that one with the *power* to be awakened to your true nature—right here, right now! Indeed, only when you have given up attachment to the modalities, the meditations, the prayers, the theologies, the textbooks, only when *you* have given up attachment to all form and merely make the decision to abide in the simple knowledge that you are that One, *only then* does knowledge permeate your awareness.

If there was something you had to *do* to *get* to God, then God is apart from where you are. Yet it is the very Love of pure consciousness that gives you the power to perceive that there is something you must do to get to God. Therefore, God is always present. If there was truly some form of meditation that could enlighten you, it would mean that *you* were *truly* apart from God at some point. But it is not possible for That One to be separate from itself.

Allow, then, the mind to rest in the simplicity that what is true has been true always, and that where you abide you are merely the manifestation of That One showing up as a man or a woman.

In true knowledge, in genuine true knowledge, which exist*s here now* and cannot be gotten tomorrow, there is only the pure simplicity of the moment that is arising, looked upon with perfect innocence. In true knowledge there is perfect peace. In true knowledge one merely abides awake, witnessing the play and display of phenomena which is, indeed, arising only within that one Mind that the Sonship is.

I have said often to you that you cannot truly make a wrong turn, and no one has ever made a wrong turn in his or her journey. How could this be possible in the field of pure Love that is God? Only Love is real.

You have allowed yourself—as God—to formulate shapes of experience merely to experience it. Every tear that you have cried, every loss that you have felt is yet only God choosing to have the experience. *You have remained eternally free in each moment to choose again.* And indeed, you *will* choose again without end. For there is not a "time" that God will cease to be. For if God *could* cease to be, then God is not God, for there would need to be a field of energy in which non-being could exist.

The mind that is awakened serves only the Holy Spirit, and the Holy Spirit is merely right-mindedness. And what is right-mindedness if not true knowledge?

The Way of Knowing, then, is a way of unobstructed feeling, unobstructed allowance, not only of what is around you, but what is arising from within you. The work that I do communicating this lesson is not done because someone else is requiring me to do it. It arises within the field of the Mind of God that *is* the essence of all that I am as Christ. It arises, is witnessed and allowed by me. And therefore, the work is done.

This is no different than what you experience in your moment-to-moment experience. When you watch a raindrop fall and touch the window through which you look, you have utilized and are the presence of the power of awareness that is no different than that which pervades me and through which this communication is manifested.

All that is taking place in all attempts to awaken the Sonship is that that One is speaking to itself. It speaks of awakening because another aspect of itself, another wave from the ocean, is yet pretending that it has truly caused itself to lose awareness.

Look around you, beloved friends. For once I asked you to consider that you do not know what a single thing is or is for. I did this because you *believed* that you were a separate self, and that your judgments and perceptions and definitions of things had a reality *outside* of your mind. Therefore, I asked of you, "Look around in perfect humility, for you do not know what a single thing is, or is for."

For if you look upon a brother or sister and see them as separate from yourself, someone from which something can be acquired for you to gain in your journey, you have truly not known what your brother or sister is for.

This is the only thing that your brother or sister *can* be for: to be that which God looks upon and sees only Himself. A brother or sister is in the field of awareness you have learned to call your own for one reason: to be loved, to be celebrated, and to be joined with to create and extend the good, the holy, and the beautiful.

Does this mean that if you look upon another that they *ought* to get it? Not at all, for that One that you are, manifesting through them may very well choose, in its infinite, perfect freedom, to remain wholly insane. And so what?

Nothing can prevent you from looking with Love and allowing the play and display of form to continue its dance of birth and death, joining and distancing, creating and dissolution. All things that can be experienced must finally be allowed to flow without obstruction within your mind. Birth gives rise to death, and death gives rise to birth in a ceaseless display—not of something struggling *for* life, but *as* Life itself.

The reality of all that you are remains utterly changeless and pure. You are as the sky through which all clouds dance and play. Your literal moment-to-moment experience, even in the moment when you think you are only a separate self that is going to go bankrupt tomorrow because of decisions made yesterday, even *that* can be allowed, can be trusted, can be appreciated, can be witnessed from the spaciousness of the sky that can embrace each cloud from a place of perfect knowing.

There can be no greater joy than to arrive in each moment with nothing to be acquired, nothing to be accomplished, and nothing to be resisted. When resistance has been released, through the simple choice to release it, you will discover and know that all along, in reality, there has only been God.

LIVING IN UNOBSTRUCTED LIFE

How, then, does one live as they abide in true knowledge? One could simply answer, "Any way they want to." For in unobstructed Life, that One is allowed to *in*form your choices.

There is no longer anything you believe you need, nothing you believe will add something to you. For who by taking thought, who by taking action, who by belief in theology has ever added even one inch to their stature? For though the body arises and passes away, as a brief cloud of illusion in the field of creation, you remain unobstructed and vast. How can eternity be added unto? You are pure awareness. And nothing you have ever done has increased you, just as nothing you have ever done has taken anything away.

Each moment, then, is perfectly pristine and honest and innocent. Each moment embraced and allowed without obstruction *is* the literal and present state of Heaven. This is why I once said:

> Heaven is spread across the face of the Earth, yet mankind sees it not.

Yet, it requires Heaven to choose to see something else. This is the slippery point upon which The Way of Knowing rests. It is slippery only because *it requires no effort*. You cannot help but be the One showing up as the dance of a temporary play of energy that *appears* to be separate from all other plays of energy.

Yet, the Sonship is one. Every tree, every drop of rain, every molecule, every thought, every non-thought—these things are the Sonship. Is it not time to awaken beyond a particular language that speaks only to humanity?

Remember that your suffering has come only from the illusion that you are a separate body-mind subject to the ravages of time, the insecurities of the world, surely to become a victim of death. The whole time, in reality, you are the *power* by which you chose that belief!

Does this mean that you can merely say, "I am awake now and I don't need to feel that feeling that's coming up"? Not at all!

For Love does not resist anything. Love embraces all things. Love desires all things. Love awakens to the Truth that only God is. And God would embrace the totality of His creation *through* you, *as* you, *in* you, *for* you and for Himself! For there is no difference between God and you. *You are that One.*

How, then, does an awakened one live? I gave you the answer earlier: any way that that awakened one wants to! And here now, please understand, we come to the essence of what we will be doing in the lessons that follow. For no longer will we live in questions about what we *ought* to do. No longer will I ask you to live in questions of what went wrong, but rather, in the purity of the power of the one question that God dwells in constantly:

What do I want?

For here, in perfect surrender, is the mind returned to pure desire—not the desire to gain for a separate self, but that which expresses the totality of God. "What do I want?" is the question that God asks Himself *as you*.

Yes, it does mean you are perfectly free to enjoy the field of desire. Are you capable of knowing what you truly want? Absolutely, once you decide that you are not what you once believed you were. This requires only the decision to recognize that nothing can exist save God, and that, therefore, you are that One. You are whole and free—*now!*

I have often hinted to you that the totality of my life was *my journey* back to God. I chose it freely, not because I was separate from God, but because I had already awakened to the truth that:

What could possibly exist except the Love of God?

I chose to look upon the body-mind and live only in the question, "What do I want?" One thing I chose was to demonstrate the *unreality* of death.

What will you choose to demonstrate? For see not in my demonstration something grand and beyond you, but rather see that everything you demonstrate is *equal to* that same power. For it flows from *that* power, it abides in that power, it manifests that power. It is the living breath and reality of God!

Therefore, as we continue through these lessons, we will begin to focus attention in the perfect freedom of exploring what is wanted. For the awakened mind sees that in truly living in divine selfishness, you cannot help but dance perfectly with your brother or sister, regardless of how *they* are choosing to respond to you.

It is impossible to be separate one from another. It is impossible to cause another suffering. It is impossible not to be *one* with the one before you. There is only the dance and the play of creation. There is only the celebration of God's eternal reality. There is only the recognition that God is joy and not depression. All depression stems from resistance, the obstruction of the flow of awareness, the attempt to limit the unlimited.

The mind that allows all things, trusts all things, and embraces all things *is* all things. Yet though you will seem to live, yet you will not live. That One alone lives as you. You are free. You are vast. You are without birth and without death. You are as I am. You are the awakened one, the anointed, the messiah. You are the gentle touch of Love in a temporary illusion, attempting to be other than Love. And why not? It is all a simple game—an innocent illusion.

Therefore, we will end this lesson with one question that we ask you to live within:

> Beloved friend, oh holy One, what do you want?

And is that wanting generated by the freedom of Love or by the ridiculous creation of a useless fear? Want only from freedom and you will have your desire.

And with that, beloved friends, peace be with you. We are most certainly going to enjoy being with you. Go then, in peace. Amen.

LESSON 26
ALLOWING PURIFICATION

Beloved and holy friends, it is with great joy that we come forth to abide with you in this manner. The forms of communication are virtually unlimited. Communication requires only the willingness of any two minds to join in communion. Communion requires the willingness to rescind one's investment in being right. Rescinding one's investment in being right requires recognition that either mind does not know what a single thing *is* or is *for.*

For in the journey that began in The Way of the Heart, continued with The Way of Transformation, and begins to culminate in The Way of Knowing, you have heard me say to you countless times and in countless ways that to awaken in remembrance absolutely requires that you choose to want—above all things—to think with the Mind of God.

To think with the Mind of God requires that you be taught anew. To be taught implies a willingness to learn. And a willingness to learn implies that one is willing to create a space of emptiness within that can be filled with a new substance, a new elixir, a new alchemical substance.

CULTIVATING THE KEYS TO THE KINGDOM

Therefore, that pathway that brings the soul into perfect remembrance requires the cultivation of the keys to the Kingdom: desire, intention, allowance, surrender. The most essential of those keys, again, is allowance.

There is no one reading these words who has not already cultivated at least a sufficient desire. It may not be one hundred percent perfected, but the desire has been there. For no one would come into my presence, no one would come into communication with this group of beings—masters, teachers, friends, who choose as a group to be known as simply "the lineage," for which I remain the primary spokesman—who has not *already desired* healing, awakening, and remembrance.

Intention is the only place that you can begin to correctly use the will that was originally your Creator's gift to you. For the correct use of will or clear intention is to bring forth the good, the holy, and the beautiful. Any mind that reflects upon its experience and has come to see that often fear has been in the driver's seat more than love will rightfully use intention to ask for help in gaining correction of the mind, that that mind itself, that soul, might again come into alignment with the will of God.

Coming into alignment with the will of God is not an act of subservience, although it feels as such to the insane ego. But to the pure of heart, to the meek who shall inherit the Earth, to those who recognize their insanity and want a transformation to perfect sanity, aligning with the will of God through clear intention is to seek for that which is one's greatest good. It is not a loss at all. It is perfect remembrance.

Coming into that alignment, then, is like one who gives up one of your golden coins to receive ten million golden coins. It is as though one would give up a rag doll in order to step into a true love relationship of flesh and bone and emotion and passion. It is as one who would give up the hope or wish for a drink of water and go to the faucet and fill the cup with living elixir.

Understand that intention, when it is focused wholly on wanting only God, can never take anything from you that you truly want. Rather, it will bring to you that which you have always wanted, have known in the ancient past, and are calling back to you now.

Beloved friends, there are many of you that have come to taste the truth of what I am to say. Allowance is the greatest of keys to the Kingdom. For allowance requires a rescinding—slowly, patiently at times, painfully at times—of every perception you have ever held of everyone and everything. It is the descent into complete recognition of your ignorance, a complete recognition of your joy-filled dependence on the corrective power of the Holy Spirit.

Allowance requires cultivation *in time*. When there has been the desire for healing and awakening, rest assured, that already your Father, through the Holy Spirit, is working to reshape every moment of your experience—*every single moment*. So that the correct teachers, the correct lessons, the correct books, even the correct weather can come to force you to look at your edges of unhappiness, your edges of judgment, your edges of insecurity, your edges of fear-based definitions of what Love is, what it should look like, and what its effects should be.

In other words, the entire world that you have made in error must be brought to the surface of the mind for correction.

Allowance is sweet above the taste of honey. For allowance is that realm in which miracles can finally begin to occur. What is a miracle? It is not really a change at all. It is merely the recognition of what has always been—that there is a Love, a *power*, that would live through you, that would guide you in all things, that you need not be the captain of the ship, you need only be willing to take the cruise.

These three keys, which are *active* in a sense—that is, they are experienced in time, they bring up questionings, they require some resolve and commitment and faith—culminate in surrender. But this culmination is not something that you do for yourself.

Rather when the seed has been well planted, when the ground has been tilled and cultivated, when the wise farmer has made sure that the weather conditions, the watering conditions, and everything is just right so that the seed can be well nurtured, surrender is much like the petals which emerge in their own time. Here the farmer can do nothing, but wait for grace to descend.

He may not see that the petals are emerging as the result of all things that have gone forth before: in the selection of the seeds, in the waiting for the perfect time to plant, in each day's cultivation and weeding of the garden. In other words, *choosing* to enter times of prayer. *Choosing* to see where fear has made a home in the mind and surrendering it to the Holy Spirit. *Cultivating* turning over each decision, day by day, moment by moment. He may not see the causal connection. He will only see and witness the emerging of the petals.

That emerging has been called in some cultures "extraordinary gifts," such as clairvoyance, clairaudience, the ability to leave the body, the experience of communicating with beings like myself, or the ability to see and read the soul of another.

But more important than all of these is peace. Peace is the culmination of the spiritual journey. It becomes the *field* in which one has entered the Kingdom and now journeys within it in perfect freedom—a freedom that cannot be understood by the minds of humankind that still live in fear, doubt, separation, and even the most subtle traces of egoism. Peace is the goal. But peace is not passivity. It is really the seat of creative power. For you were created to create the good, the holy, and the beautiful.

For a while, you learned to create something else. Yet, that creation has occurred nowhere, save within the mind. It is merely a chimera or an illusion. But as you cultivated the power to create illusion, the journey to God requires purification, that process whereby you surrender your will, the egoic mind, over to correction by the Holy Spirit.

This journey will take you into the essence of what you do not know that you do not know. That is what makes it unconscious. For you have used the power of the mind to push down out of yourself your fears—where they actually gain power, but you do not need to confront them directly. Denial or suppression, as they speak of it in your psychological language, is the very root of the creation of the ego. That which has been hidden must be made known. And in its being made known, purification can occur.

As I have shared with you many times: Give thanks to the saviors that are sent unto you. They come in many guises and forms. Some of you would look upon me as your savior. In the sense that I am sent unto you as a teacher, I am. But it is only the *teaching* that saves you, not me.

Your saviors will more often show up unto you as those who evoke within you your deepest reactions, your vehement judgment, and your *certainty* that *you* are right! When these things occur and your peace is disturbed, your greatest reactivity has been triggered, your greatest emotionality is triggered, *there* is the *edge* that calls for your attention!

For remember always, that nothing can come to you unless you have called it from within yourself in order to grow more deeply in forgiveness, in wisdom, in love, and in the power of Christ.

As purification begins to touch the most fundamental or most radical levels, the *sweetness* of peace begins to be remembered—faintly at first, and then more and more. One has a realization. Remember the whole journey is merely one with no distance to it at all to a goal that has never changed. It is just a change of mind, a remembrance. Realization, then, may be the recognition that, "Oh, I used to think this way, but now I see the emptiness of such silly things."

That quickly, that fast—it is over; it is gone. Where did the illusion go? It got erased by the cosmic eraser on the end of the pencil held by the Holy Spirit because of your desire, your intention, your allowance, and your cultivation of all of those tools that support you to choose again, to want only Love.

Grace purifies the mind. Grace is a direct gift of your Father. It is that energy or power of Love that descends into a mind and heart that prepares a place for it. You could say that your greatest preparation is to admit that you do not know what anything is for.

If you are feeling emotions, if you are feeling like you want to run, if you feel like you want to avoid taking responsibility for something that has been dropped in your lap, rest assured, right there is your edge. There is the place you need to turn back and embrace.

Once the journey has begun, the end is perfectly certain. Peace is the perfect goal. But there are few, still, who truly understand what peace is. It is not the avoidance of pain. It is not the avoidance of responsibility.

It is the doorway to the greatest of responsibilities in which the mind, the heart, the soul, and even the body, while it lasts, have been so purified of dissonance and become so aligned with the will of God, that one looks upon all things with the compassion of Christ. Such a one walks in this world of yours *unknown* by those around him or her. That one serves only the voice of the Holy Spirit. It is not the least bit concerned with others' reactivity.

For the only goal of the awakened Christ—*and peace and Christ consciousness are one and the same*—is to be an agent through which the power of grace works to transform illusion. That Mind serves the atonement. That Mind may not be understood by others, but how can the insane understand the sane?

Surrender is like the petals of the flower. They emerge in their own time. One cannot necessarily see the causal connection of all that has gone before with the sweet nectar of perfect remembrance: the flowering of the soul that is no longer fearful and abides in the world—awake, in peace, open—through which the flow of grace descends to touch the world. Surrender flowers from the only three things you can do: desire, intend and allow.

ALLOWING PURIFICATION TO OCCUR

Allow purification to occur. Be willing to visit every dark corner of the mind. For, in truth, it is not necessary to seek for Love, for Love already embraces you. But it *is* necessary to seek for what is false:

> Where am I fooling myself?
> Where am I committed to my image in the world?
>
> Where am I committed to thinking for myself because underneath I do not truly trust that God loves me?
>
> Where am I lying to myself or to others?
> Where am I in denial?
> Where do I need to understand what projection is?
>
> Where do I need to understand more deeply how the viciousness of the ego works within my own mind?
>
> Where am I pointing a finger outside of myself?
> Where am I denying my fear?
>
> Where am I demanding that the world show up as I would have it, instead of surrendering to the structuring of the world in the hands of the Holy Spirit that serves entirely my healing, my growth, my maturing into true responsibility?

Indeed, beloved friends, in The Way of Knowing, it is absolutely required that you pause often and look around you and say:

> I abide in the perfection of a loving universe. Nothing can occur by accident.
> Where I am in this moment must be the perfect place for me to be.
> How can I find the doorway to stillness within now?
> Where within me can I rest in peace, and ask the Holy Spirit's guidance?
> Where, in this moment, am I clinging to another or to a thing?
> Where am I looking upon another person or another thing in this universe
> and claiming it is my possession?

For what you do not give to be shared that you say you have loved, rest assured, beloved friend, in that moment, you are in the viciousness of specialness. The egoic mind believes that if it shares what it has, it loses. Therefore, in your world, when you perceive that someone or something has brought you a great source of comfort and love, and even security, to see that being shared elsewhere activates the fear of loss within the ego.

Much like, many of you might remember that when you were teenagers, and you began "going" with a certain boy or certain girl in the seventh grade, and then two weeks later, they decided to "go" with someone else. Oh, how crushing it was, for the source of your love had been stripped from you! Never will you enjoy the smell of a flower again. Never will food taste good again. There could surely be no one else in this universe that could provide you this great source of love and attention! Such is the immaturity of the child. Such is the immaturity of many "children" who live in fifty-year-old bodies!

For, beloved friends, there is *no one* and *no created thing*—and the body-mind is just a created thing—that can be your *source* for love. Relationship was never meant to be a device for finding sources for love. Relationships were designed to be *holy*. In holy relationship, two have come together—not to *get*, but to *create* out of loving devotion to the grace that has awakened and purified their mind and hearts to the realization that only Love is real. There is no such thing as loss, and only Love is worthy to be celebrated.

In perfect Love, there is no possessiveness. In perfect Love, there is perfect allowing. In perfect Love—guess what? There is not even you! There is only God loving through you!

Therefore, indeed, beloved friends, look around your very home. Is there an object that you could not see yourself giving up? If you truly want to hasten your awakening, go and give it away. For in the end, all that you *believe* you possess must be given away. And what you believe you possess is the right to possessiveness, the right to be right. When all things created as a substitute for the reality of God have been rescinded or surrendered, then indeed, the flower has emerged, and the sweet fragrance blesses everyone.

The awakened mind, the mind that rests in perfect knowledge, looks upon all things that it has previously loved and sees that their *form* is not what is essential. It is the *essence* or the *content* that they express that matters.

A beautiful painting, in and of itself, means nothing. Hit it with a hammer, light a match to it, throw dirt and mud on it, and it is not the same. It is not the structure that matters. It is that in a timeless moment, you looked upon it, entered into relationship, and experienced the essence of beauty flowing through it.

That essence or content is timeless. That essence or content is all around you! It sustains you! It breathes you! It is the heart of your heart, the soul of your soul, and the mind of your mind!

Whenever you see any object, whether it be a body, a person, a mind, a thing, a flower, a pencil—it does not matter—when you feel what you call "being in love" evoked within you, it is because in that moment you have slipped between the cracks of the world of the egoic mind, and you are experiencing the essential content of reality: Love. You are experiencing your own living true reality, for only Love is real.

When you come to see that that Love can be experienced at *any* moment, in *any* situation, with *anyone*, with *any* flower, you are experiencing true reality. When you say, "Well, I like roses, but I don't like gardenias," that is nonsense!

Love is what you should love! *Love* is what you should assume responsibility for detecting as it flows through each living thing. And a rock, in this sense, is a living thing. If it exists, within it, you will find the good, the holy, and the beautiful. For only that which contains these things, which is the presence of God, can ever take form in the first place. Nothing can be without the essence of what you are seeking!

When you understand that it is the *content* that matters and not the *form*, suffering begins to finally be alleviated. You can begin to embrace the comings and goings of this transitory realm of the dream as a dream. People enter your life and you embrace them and see the good, the holy, and the beautiful. They flow through their ever-changing changes, and then they die.

Now, death can occur not just at the death of the body. Death occurs at any moment in relationship when another changes their mind. They may decide to leave you. They may decide to awaken, which means that the being that you were relating to is dead. A death has occurred, whether they leave you physically or not. That is really rather irrelevant.

But when you come to attune yourself to the essential thread of Love that flows through all things, you are abiding in a deeper sense of knowing. Whether an object, person, place, or thing enters your life and stays, or whether it flows through in a moment, or whether it flows through over the course of a lifetime, begins to be less and less relevant to you. Less and less do you grasp at it.

Indeed, the mind that is truly awakened and rests in the eternality of Love that is all things can lay the head of a loved one down, watch them take their last breath, feel a little wave of emotion pass through—that is the disengagement of the auric fields at a physical level, that is all it is—and let the little shudder of tears come through. You smile and say, "Oh, how sweet it was. How sweet it is, for Love is eternal. And wherever two minds have joined in Love, separation is absolutely impossible! So what's the big deal?"

And you allow something your world calls "death" to occur. Yet, death is unreal to the mind that rests in the perfect peace of knowing.

Beloved friends, you who have journeyed with me for longer than you would care to remember, it is always a journey of remembering and forgetting. That is what makes it your journey. You get a little glimpse or a taste of God, you tell the world that is what you want, but then, right away, you decide to forget it again so that you can experience the sweetness of *seeking*. You have become addicted to being a seeker. And to seek, you must first cleverly *push away* what is always yours anyway, in order to embark on yet another journey of seeking.

GIVING UP THE GAME OF SEEKING

Finding is the same as resting in knowledge, the same as Christ consciousness, and the same as perfect peace. *Finding* requires giving up the game of seeking. Such a one cannot be known by the minds of the world. Such a one walks in the world, but inwardly is empty. Such a one is merely a conduit through which there are no longer any obstructions to the offering of God's grace.

Indeed, beloved friends, many of you have journeyed with me for so long that you have taught yourself the only way to be in relationship with me is to be dependent upon me. You have journeyed with me so long that you cannot imagine, or would not let yourself imagine, being my equal. You would not let yourself imagine letting go of me. Yet, I say unto you, stepping into the fullness of Love requires letting go of *everything* you have possessed, even if that possession is me. For Love requires, finally, that you step through the door into the Kingdom and declare:

> I am that One sent of the Father, created before all things.
> I am only Love.

> I am not my mind. I am not my body. I am not my personality. I am not my history. I do not belong to the world.

> I am that vibration, that note of Love. I am the Christ, and as such do I abide.

I love equally. I love without reservation. I love without possessiveness. I love only to extend the presence of God that another might touch that place within them and be set free.

Love cannot possess. Wherever there is a trace of conditionality, rest assured, the viciousness of fear is in the ascendancy. Therefore, if you cannot surrender your pet, if you cannot surrender the object that sits upon your counter in your kitchen, if you cannot surrender a beloved into death, if you cannot surrender a beloved who changes their mind and decides to move to Antarctica with celebration, rest assured, there is yet a place within you that requires correction.

Correction requires willingness, intention. And intention requires your desire that you dissolve even more deeply into the Love which *is* God.

BE THE PRESENCE OF THE LOVE THAT GOD IS

Listen very carefully. Indeed, listen *very*, very carefully! If you would know the Love of God, you must *be* that Love. You cannot know *about* it. You must literally *be* the presence of that Love. Only then do you know God. This, then, is the essence of The Way of Knowing: knowing by *being* that which you have knowledge or direct experience of, and by choosing to be only that.

This is why knowledge is a mystical experience. This is why true knowing has an immediacy. It is not mediated through a theology, a religion, a philosophy or any words. Words are just symbols of symbols. They are symbols of ideas, and ideas are a step still away from reality. One who knows Love knows it because every cell of their being is the *presence* of Love. The Way of Knowing culminates with your perfect resolve to *be* the presence of the Love that God is.

Now, if you would truly know Love, look upon the things that you fear. Discover them. Dig them up and out of yourself. Rest assured, any time you must look at another and analyze them, there is something you fear. Anything that pushes your buttons is a sign that something is still requiring your love.

The Way of Knowing, beloved friends, can culminate *only* in the transformation of your mind to such a level of completion that you sit in your rocking chair and say:

There is only God. There has never been a separate me. There never could have been.

There is only this moment in which Love can dance, can be celebrated, and can be extended.

Father, what can we create this day that offers to the world the grace of the good, the holy, and the beautiful?

I once described the highest state of consciousness, highest state of purification, as one in which the child has awakened, and looks around him or her and sees to infinity. They see not where they begin and the Father ends. For such is their union, such is their marriage, such is their dance—the unformed and the formed, the Source and the created, the Creator and the creating—such is this alchemical marriage that one cannot look and see where the soul ends and the Creator begins. Yet, the awakened mind knows that it is still the created and it surrenders in perfect joy each moment:

Father, what would you have me do? What is your will for me?

The awakened mind surrenders not in subservience, but because sanity has returned. It recognizes that it has never been the tiny gnat, whining and complaining and trying to make life work the way it thinks it ought to work. It surrenders each moment. It dissolves in each moment. It abides in each moment. It knows that only the Love of God is real and says, "Father, what would you have me do?"

And it opens itself and it receives the pebbles being dropped into its pond, now not by its own hand, but by the hand of *grace*, the perfect hand of mystery I have called Abba, that Love, that creative Source, that power, that joy, that sublime, sweet, sweet mystery that is constantly creating. For Love must extend itself!

No longer is there concern or worry over the body. No longer is there concern or worry over the state of the world. No longer is there concern or worry over anything. There is only the eternal dance of creation. The awakened mind knows that it is a participant in perfect mystery. There are no longer any blocks or fears whatsoever.

And wherever you find yourself, if you are asked to be crucified, dead and buried so you shock the world into realizing that there is something else besides "surviving," you do it! If it is given unto you to write books, you write them. So what?

You are not attached. The flow of creativity is moving through you. If you are asked to take a simple picture that I placed in the mind of a certain artist and distribute it to fifteen million people, you simply do it because you are no longer attached to your ego. If Love asks you through me or through another to move to the far ends of the Earth to build a hut and to chant, you go and do it. What is the problem? There is not any!

You are free as the wind. Only those born of the Spirit *know* the Spirit. The Spirit comes and goes where it does. You do not know where it came from. You do not know where it is going. You totally confuse the minds of humankind. You are free! For you listen to no other voice but the voice for Love! What would you hold onto in a world of illusion?

Learn to discover the content that pervades all form, and you will taste the perfect freedom, the alleviation of pain that comes with attachment to the form—even your own. Even your very thoughts that yesterday you thought were true.

Today you have been taken even more deeply into Love, and what is in the past is allowed to pass away:

> Yesterday I thought I knew God. Today I know God even more deeply because I have rescinded my need to be right about what I once thought I knew to be true. Father, give me even more of you! I want more! I desire more! You are infinite! You are my beloved! I want only to die in you— ever more, ever deeper! Give me more of you—to taste you, to devour you, to die in you, more and more!

"More and more" becomes an eternal journey without end to a goal that has never changed. A journey with no distance—only the sublime experience of tasting God and then surrendering that taste in order to taste even more. Love comes to supplant fear. And learning to jump in order to receive the parachute becomes a delightful game to play.

When I decided to allow the crucifixion, I jumped, "Can I find my Father even more deeply *here*?" For me, it was the culmination of a life in which I developed trust that my Father would always catch me. That journey, by the way, has never ended. And those of you that would come to where I am, rest assured, you best not waste a single moment. For I am continually dying more and more into God.

Beloved friends, we will end this lesson with this suggestion. Ask yourself:

> Where is fear still abiding in my mind? Is there anything that I still fear? Is it the death of a husband or a wife? Is it the growing up of a child? Is it the loss of a job? Is it being without shelter?

> Where is the edge of your fear?
> Can I imagine abiding without a man in my life? Can I abide without a woman in my life?

This is nothing more than unhealed mother and father issues. It is an *authority* problem.

The awakened abide only with God. They cannot any longer comprehend possessing or being possessed. They allow all things, and trust all things. They love without reservation the one who stands before them as the embodiment of their very beloved—the content or essence which is the presence of God. For when you look upon your brother or sister and see only Christ, you have seen with the eyes of Christ. And Christ simply loves.

Therefore, indeed, beloved friends, be at peace. Amen.

LESSON 27
THE PURPOSE OF YOUR LIFE IS TO LOVE

Beloved and holy friends, we come to abide with you in order to instruct you yet again in The Way of Knowing. Remember always that knowledge is perfectly certain. Knowledge is that which is unchanging, unchangeable and unchanged forever. Knowledge is reality and reality is Love. Knowledge is the essence of your being, the essence of your soul.

If anyone says unto you, "I do not know," they are a liar and a hypocrite, though I would not suggest that you use those terms in your communication with them. But rather, whether in your own life or in relationship with a friend, wherever *doubt* seems to arise in the mind, remember only this: This mind is not currently choosing reality. It must, therefore, be choosing something else.

The something else can only be that experience, that world of the ego. For we use the term ego to differentiate that state of awareness that is characterized by *confusion* wearing the mask of *certainty*. When anyone says unto you, "I don't know" or whenever the thought arises in your own mind, "I don't know," rest assured that in that moment, that mind— your mind—is choosing to be *other* than what it is.

What is it, then, that you know?

I and my Father are one.
I am intimately connected with that very Source
from which all things have sprung forth.

Because this is the truth, because it is the Truth of your being, this means that for any situation that requires a decision, you have within yourself access to perfect knowledge. And perfect knowledge seeks to extend itself. Extension requires the realm of manifestation, the realm of form, the realm of individuation.

Therefore, you—as a body and as a mind—abiding in space and time on a tiny planet, *you are* reality's decision to manifest itself in form, for no other reason than to extend its own nature. The happiness of the soul depends on its decision to extend only that which is loving.

Because *you* are the manifestation of Reality itself, of Knowledge itself, of Love itself, it must mean that in any given moment, there is within you a part of the mind that yet remains free from the ego's authority. That part of the mind in which there already abides perfect peace; that part of the mind in which there already abides perfect certainty; that part of the mind in which there already abides the willingness to extend Love without attachment.

There is already within you that part of the mind that can deliver up to you the answer for each decision. The answer that helps to extend Love, first into your own beingness, and then through it. For you can only *give* what you first *receive*. And in your giving, your receiving is completed.

Therefore, indeed, beloved friends, if you would look to see what the purpose of your life is, it is quite simple. Being only Love, you can have no other purpose than to extend the treasure of your very Self.

Christ is God's only creation. Christ is that medium through which the unfathomable, mysterious, beyond comprehension Source that I have called Abba (and goes by many names) extends itself into the creation of temporary forms to reflect throughout the universe. It reflects that which the universe itself is made of, where it comes from, what it is enveloped within, and that to which it eternally returns.

Because *you*, like a wave unto the ocean, have been birthed from that reality, emerging from that reality, you are one with it. Therefore, you are Christ eternal. And that is unchanging and unchangeable forever.

Within you, then, even in this very moment, there abides a part of the mind that already knows the Truth that sets all things free. That part of the mind can be accessed at any time by anyone under any condition. It does not require years of cultivation. Although in the field of time, it can appear that you are getting better and better at it. Simply because you are enjoying it more and more and giving value to the fear-based egoic ways of arriving at decisions less and less.

That part of the mind is like an empty and open channel. Nothing can obscure its purity—*nothing*. Nothing you have ever done, nothing you have ever thought, nothing you have ever miscreated obscures the perfect silence, the utter purity, of your connection with the Source of your being. For Love is always connected to itself.

What does this mean? First, anyone who truly enjoins The Way of Knowing must make a decision to accept the atonement for himself or herself:

I am one with my Creator—now.
I choose to fulfill my purpose
by extending only the reflection of my Self,
and I am but Love.

Second, anyone who would enjoin The Way of Knowing must also look and embrace the very fact that their attention is involved in the world of space and time, the world of the body itself.

But in The Way of Knowing, the world of space and time is *seen* differently. The world is seen as something that exists *external* to the mind itself, not as something which has a power over the mind, or something to be feared, or that one must be conformed to.

Rather, the things of space and time are seen and embraced as that which is given of the Creator to the son, to the daughter, in order to be utilized as devices for assisting Christ to extend Love. It does not matter whether it is a pencil or a computer or a trip to your grocery store or a party in which you invite your friends to come and play. All things finally come to be seen as having only one purpose: *the extension of Love.*

PUTTING YOUR PURPOSE
INTO PRACTICE

Imagine a businessperson sitting down to negotiate the closing of a deal, who goes to that part of the mind that is sane and says, "What price should I place upon this land that I am about to sell to this other corporation?" While his accountants and realtors have been telling him that the property is worth one million dollars, he goes within. And the answer comes, "Ask only $250,000 and ask that another $300,000 be donated to such-and-such a charity." In *your* world, which is the world of insanity, the businessman would say, "Oh no, I can't do that. I cannot listen to that voice."

But in The Way of Knowing, in the way of enlightenment, the businessman smiles and says exactly what was received. When the shock on the other person's face settles down, they will be quite happy to know that they have saved a lot of money, for in *their* world, they think that the only way to *have* is to *possess.* But in The Way of Knowing, and in the way of reality, the only way to *have* is to *give.*

Now, you are like that businessman. You abide in the world in which the business of your reality is to extend only Love. Be you, therefore, not afraid of the world. For when seen through the eyes of the enlightened soul that accepts its oneness with God, the world of space and time is perfectly benign and has no purpose whatsoever except to serve Christ in the extension of Love.

This is why anyone who comes to answer only the voice for Love miraculously finds that the universe comes to support that one in ways that the egoic mind can never understand. Miracles do occur as creation flows from a mind unencumbered with the pressures of trying to make life go the way it thinks it needs it to go.

And here we begin to touch upon the essence of my teaching:

> I need do nothing.

This is not a passive state, of just accepting the fact that, "I need to do nothing so I'll just show up, and follow my impulses and not think too deeply or wonder what I'm doing. I really don't need to do anything, since none of it matters." That is not it at all.

It means quite *actively* to learn and master the art of "you *need* to do nothing" to find that spaciousness within you in which you are willing to allow that voice within you that is eternally connected to your Source to be the vehicle through which you receive your guidance. In the pure recognition that you have no purpose—save the extension of Love.

It is not your purpose to survive as a body-mind. It is not your purpose to keep the same house you have had for the last twenty years. It is not your purpose to be in relationship with this person or that person for the entirety of the life of the body-mind. It is not your purpose to accomplish great things. It is not your purpose to be wealthy. It is not your purpose to do *anything* except be that conduit through which Love extends itself.

As you come, truly, to allow Love to be your greatest beloved, as you set aside all other idols—the need to hold onto the house, the need to have certain dollars in the bank, the need to have certain people in your life—as you come to see that all of that is part of the world of illusion, as you come to love *Love*, you will have come to *love yourself.*

For you are love, and only this. As you come to love *Love* as your beloved, more and more, you will discover that you are guided on a path of miracles in which more power seems to be getting extended through you. You will begin to witness that the universe seems to support you, more and more, in ways that you could have never imagined.

Out of that you might, indeed, see the life of the body-mind changing—the car you drive, the home you live in, and the quality of the beings that come into your life. Yet, you will be unattached to these things for you will not see them as ends in themselves. But merely as the proof that the great wisdom of Love that underlies all things is connecting you to new forms and new contexts because it knows that now it can flow through you more powerfully, more certainly, more maturely and more wisely.

Therefore, seek not to improve your life by adding even one cubit unto your stature. But rather, seek to improve your life by realizing your nature as Love. How do you do that? By recognizing that in each moment you are in the right place at the right time. *This* is the moment in which Love can be remembered, can be restored, and can be extended. *This* is the moment in which you can decide to listen only to the voice within you that *knows* how to extend Love.

Beloved friends, in The Way of Knowing, the illusion that there is something to seek vanishes. The mind is liberated from the misperception that there is something wrong going on in the world.

The mind is so liberated that it knows as long as it chooses Love, as long as it follows the mysterious, quiet voice within its own heart, that the choices it makes, the decisions it embraces, the actions it takes, and the thoughts that it thinks cannot help but serve in the further awakening of every one and every thing, so perfect is the Love that embraces the whole of creation—God!

You have heard me say to you many times, that wherever you know a fearful thought, it can only mean that you are not thinking "rightly," that is, you are not thinking with the Mind of God. For God is but Love.

If a million dollars were to come to you, as Christ, you would say, "This must be the perfect experience for me now. How can I extend Love in this moment?" And if in the next day, your wallet is perfectly empty, the enlightened Mind of Christ says, "This must be the perfect event for me to be experiencing now. How can I extend Love in this moment?"

The changing can never be the source of peace. The world of form—whether dollars in a bank, houses, cars, people, friends, lovers, pets, plants, and all the rest—can never be the source of perfect freedom. These things arise and pass away and are like ephemeral shadows, wisps of foam dancing in an ocean. When the mind becomes identified with the form, that mind suffers. When the mind is liberated from attachment to form, it is free. For it is identified only with content or simply the reality of Love.

In any given moment, you have the power within you to experience the reality of Love, unobstructed, unmediated—now—without need of magical means, without need for the universe to arrange itself in any certain way whatsoever.

In any given condition, you have within yourself the power to decide to literally feel and experience Love. Love or the experience of it is a decision. It is not something earned, and it is not something created. It is that which is eternally present *now* as the very identity of your being, the very Life and existence of your being.

Once, I said to a beloved brother:

> Merely stand, with arms outstretched and palms up.
> Open the heart deeply, and ask whatsoever you will.
> And it shall be given you.
> But ask as the awakened Christ,
> asking from that place that knows only Love is real.

Therefore, take just a moment, right now! Stand wherever you are, with your arms outstretched and palms turned heavenward. Think about your own heart for just a moment, and simply ask to *feel* and *know* the reality of Love's presence. Breathe it into your heart. Open the cells of the body. Open the mind and simply *receive* what is available.

Good! Now you can allow yourself to sit down again if you wish. If you think you "did not get it," you are simply fooling yourself. It requires only this.

DAILY MEDITATIONS AND EXERCISES

We then give you this as a meditation to do in The Way of Knowing. At least once a day, arise from your chairs and stand with your arms outstretched and the palms up and say simply:

> I open and receive the reality of Love for myself—now!

You see, Self-love is the pathway to perfect peace. Self-love opens all the doors. Self-love dissolves every illusion. I am not speaking of love for the illusions of the egoic mind with which you have become identified. I am not saying that you should say, "I love my self because I now have "x" amount of dollars in the bank. I love my self because I have a wonderful husband or wife. I love my self because I have a great dog." No.

> I love my Self.

The Self that is beyond time is that Self from which even the body has emerged.

Whenever you are in doubt, whenever your energy seems to have dropped, try a dose of celebrating—a simple dose of celebrating that you are in a perfect universe, and you abide as Love. The very fact that you have a body that has emerged out of consciousness in order to be used to extend only Love is pretty miraculous. And you are free to celebrate that simple, essential truth in any moment. Then ask:

Who can I extend Love to now? How can I experience Love now?

It is all much simpler than you think.

In The Way of Knowing, there is *knowing*. If that statement seems puzzling to you, contemplate it as a meditation:

In The Way of Knowing, there is knowing.

There is no more powerful state of consciousness to act from than the state of knowing.

For indeed, beloved friends, if you truly accepted yourself as Christ, you would *know* that you could not fail. And if you could not fail, what would you do with your time? If you knew you could not possibly fail, that the universe will support you completely at all times, as you choose *only* to act, to do, to think in a way that extends Love, would you be living where you are currently living? Would you be doing with your time what you are currently doing? Many of you have answered "no" because you think you must survive *first*, in order to find a way to teach only Love.

In The Way of Knowing, the Christ Mind recognizes it has no purpose whatsoever, except to extend Love. The body-mind need not survive more than the next moment, if in that next moment you have extended Love and your guidance is, "Time to be beamed up."

Those that know that only Love is real are not concerned with what they eat and what they drink. For these things come into the body and leave through the body. They are concerned only with whether or not that which they consume for the sake of the body was consumed in Love.

For love is what allows the transmutation of anything that comes into the physical system and allows it to be turned to that which supports the energetic wholeness of the physical system itself. It is far greater to have a bottle of Scotch for breakfast in a state of total Christed Love, than it is to have nine thousand vitamins with one tiny little fearful thought. So that is something for you to think about.

For you see, it is fear that causes you to be unable to digest what you place in the body— the body of the emotions or the body of the mind. It is what causes stress in the subtle system of the body and the subtle nonphysical bodies—the emotional body, the mental body, and the causal body.

What causes the greatest problem is your refusal to *digest* what you have taken in. Just as food is a physical substance taken into the body, an *experience* of any kind is a "food" that has been called to the soul. Anything that arises that cannot pass through you, through your unwillingness to embrace it with Love, to feel it completely, will cause "indigestion" of the physical, emotional, mental, and causal beings or bodies.

Therefore, beloved friends, learn to digest all things in Love. Learn to digest the traffic jam in Love. Learn to digest the dying of a pet in Love. Learn to digest an apple in Love. Learn to digest a hurtful thought in Love. Learn to digest a misperception that there is something wrong with the world around you with Love. Transform all things by the power of your only reality.

Now, I want to ask of you: What is it that you have refused to digest in this one incarnation? Was it an "unfairness" bestowed upon you by your mother or father? Was it the "bad break" at the office in which you got passed up for a promotion? What is it in your life that remains undigested?

There! Something has come into the mind. Trust it. Stay with that one thought, that one picture, that one memory. For it has arisen in the conscious mind to be healed and transformed *now*. Bring your attention to it in this very moment. Look upon it, breathe with the body, and say simply within the mind:

> I choose now to fully digest this by bringing love to it, by actually loving the event just as it was—loving the picture, the memory, the thought, just as it is.

If you wish, you can stand with your arms out wide and your palms turned heavenward and receive the Love that transmutes all things. *Breathe* that Love! *Feel* that Love in and through that picture, that memory, that feeling—whatever it is that is occurring for you, until it literally dissolves. If you do not feel that happening, even in your body, there is a part of you that is resisting letting go of what has been undigested. If that is the case, you need to ask yourself:

> Why do I need to uphold my illusory perception about this event?
> What in me is committed to withholding my love?

We would highly suggest that you spend some time each day asking the same question:

> What is it that I have not been willing to digest about this life
> and about this world?
> Where am I refusing to bring my love?

Is it to your government? Is it to your Internal Revenue Service? Is it to the mate? Is it to the children? Is it to the pet? Is it to the school system? What is it that you have refused to bring your love to?

For the greatest joy in life is to be the lover of Life. For as you love, you experience Love. Therefore, do unto others what you would have done unto yourself. And is that not to be loved?

When you choose to love in any given moment, you are the one who gets to receive the benefits of Love first. It is an immediate experience, and it cannot be taken from you. You are free to "juice yourself" any time you want by choosing only to love.

In any given condition, you are the presence of that One to whom all power under Heaven and Earth has been given. Not just to extend love as a duty—for it is not a duty—it is a pleasure. It is the supreme pleasure that can be experienced in the depth of any mind, whether you happen to be in the world of space and time, or like me, out of it.

You are the one that can experience Love and let your cup overflow. You are the one who can enjoy each and every moment, regardless of the conditions. For the conditions are only the interpretations of the egoic mind. All events are neutral. They are there for you to love that you might experience Love!

That is really how simple it is. It has always been that way, and it will never change. You are the lover. The world can be the reflection of your beloved.

Let each moment, then, find you in the simple, quiet, inner enjoyment that comes from the decision to love. Love the taking out of the garbage. Love the rain that hits the windows. Love the crying of the child. Love, Love, *Love*! Love embraces all things, allows all things, trusts all things, and therefore, transcends all things. That is the power that abides within you when you finally choose to be that One who *knows*.

Look well, then, this day and seize this day. Where can you simply change your mind and bring love to something that you have been withdrawing love from? For example, "Well, I've got to go to the office." No, you do not! You are *choosing* to go to the office. You might as well *love* it!

Where, beloved friends, are you being presented with opportunities to experience Love coursing through every cell of your being this day? What can prevent you from experiencing Love if it is not but your own decision? For in The Way of Knowing, the liberated Mind of Christ knows:

There is nothing outside me.

And with that, peace be unto you always, oh holy Child of God. Amen.

LESSON 28

YOU AND YOU ALONE
CREATE YOUR TOMORROWS

Beloved and holy friends, feel and understand my delight as I seek to look upon the world in which you abide and allow myself to receive the guidance of my Father in how I can best create communication devices that can touch as many hearts and minds as possible.

There is a great advantage to living outside of the realm of the body. I need not spend "time" on the body. I can see that that strikes some chords among you. The body is not right, and the body is not wrong. The body simply *is*.

In reality, as you have fallen under the spell of the world that you have created for no other reason than you wanted to, you have come to perceive the body in a certain way. First of all, you think it is quite solid when, in fact, it is not. You think that the body separates you from others, since as your scientists well know, no two solid objects can occupy the same point of space and time. They are quite right about that.

As you look out, then, through the eyes of the body, you would actually believe that you dwell within it, and therefore, have a private domain that is all yours. This leads you to the great delusion that you can have private thoughts. Like one who comes home after a day of work and closes the front door behind them and then rants and raves about their boss or their coworkers, thinking that the walls of the house are around them and that, therefore, they have something called "privacy." Rest assured that this is quite a delusion!

In reality, the body does not contain you. Rather, you contain the body. Mind is vast, eternal and unlimited. Mind is what every being that you know participates in, like waves participating in the ocean. This means that any time you think a thought about anyone, that thought is communicated to him or her.

Now, it is quite true that unless they have done enough work to become sensitive to the subtle levels of creation, they will not necessarily be aware *consciously* that you are thinking a certain thought about them. They may only be aware that suddenly *they* have had a thought of *you*, and a rather funny feeling is going through their body. They will pass it off and give it not a second thought.

Likewise, if you think a loving thought, ten thousand miles away someone may suddenly think of you and feel good in their body and not even know why and just let it go by. Why? Because the belief system says that they must be doing that inside themselves, and it has no connection to you.

In reality, thought is the substance of all things. Thought is an impulse of pure energy. It is more subtle than anything in the physical domain. Thought travels far faster than the speed of light. In fact, light is actually a physical occurrence that emerges long after the birthing of the dream of separation. So while a light year can seem to be quite a vast thing in your world of physics, rest assured that thought travels instantaneously. In fact, thought is immediately present everywhere.

As you are a conscious mind, a body-mind, abiding in the ocean of pure Christ Mind, you literally receive the impressions of all thought being thought anywhere. It comes into your auric field. And your auric field is really nothing more than the trough that seems to separate one wave from another. But in fact, the trough of those waves *joins* them one to another.

YOU DECIDE WHICH THOUGHTS WILL INFLUENCE YOUR LIFE

All fields of thought, then, in a sense wash up to the shoreline of your being. *You* elect what influences will enter into your sphere. Some of those will pass through, and some you will begin to become identified with. You will take them on as *your* thought. You will form an agreement with the nature of that thought. You will value that thought, and therefore, create experiences that flow *from* your agreement, your valuation.

For virtually all beings born within the human sphere, one such agreement is, "I am just the body, and therefore, I am separate from all others." That is merely an agreement, a decision to create experience. You are equally free to say within yourself:

> I am more than a body. My mind is vast and unlimited.
> And that is the deeper essence of my identity and my existence.
>
> I am in perfect communication with all forms of life at all times.
> I need only withdraw my attention from my perception of my body
> to access communication with anyone at any time.

I once said in *A Course in Miracles*, "You have never forgotten the body, even for a moment. And yet, a moment is all it takes to realize that you are not the body." I did not mean by this that you should *deny* the body, but rather that you be willing to surrender your perception of what the body is, that it is not a device that separates you at all.

Why is this so? You once decided to dream the impossible dream: the dream of separation. The body is the result of that thought—the *attempt* to create something that succeeds in separating you from the Mind of God. But you have never succeeded. For in the moment that that began to emerge, the Holy Spirit already translated it into something that is not a *separation* device, but a *communication* device. You failed. The Holy Spirit did not!

This means that the body itself is *constantly* receiving input in the form of subtle energy vibration from everything and everyone around it. You are like a giant radio station that is picking up and transmitting signals constantly.

If you would like proof of this, and especially if you would like proof of how powerful thought is as it expresses vibration through the body, simply create what you call in your world dowsing rods. Take two pieces of metal. It could be two parts of a coat hanger. Bend them so that you can gently hold one end, and hold them in your hands about six inches from your body.

Then have a friend stand about twenty feet away and have them think thoughts of negativity, such as, "I am unworthy. I am not worthy of being loved. I have no energy. I'm not worth anything." As they are doing that, walk toward them and see how close you get before your dowsing rods of metal begin to move around. Then, back up and find just the *edge* where their energy field is influencing the rods.

Then back up about twenty or thirty feet, and have them change their mind. Have them begin to think loving thoughts, such as, "I am one with God. Love flows through me perfectly. I am so glad to be alive!" They need not say it out loud. They need not move a muscle. They need only think differently. Then again walk toward them, and see when you find the point where the rods in your hands begin to move about. You will find that their energy field is much larger with the positive thought than with the negative thought.

Now, your body is like a divining rod. And so is everyone else's. Therefore, those with confidence, those who love themselves, those who are not concerned with the good opinions of the world, who just go forward in the direction of what they love, are the ones that seem to gain the greatest support in the universe.

Why? Because when such a one walks into a bank to get a business loan, already knowing that this is a great idea and they are going to bring the fullness of their being to it, and that they could not possibly fail, by just walking in the door they are bringing an energy field that influences and touches the loan officer.

Those that walk in thinking, "God, I wish I could get this business loan, but I just don't know; I don't have any experience in this; and they're going to look at me like I'm a jerk," walk in with a much reduced energy field. It is very weak. The quality of vibration of the thought is emanating out and touching the energy field of the loan officer. If you were the loan officer, whom would you rather do business with?

Therefore, when Love leads the way, when Love is the field of energy that you are abiding within, everywhere you go, you are touching the universe in a way that is much more subtle than the conscious mind. And the universe will respond to you, because Love responds to itself like a flower that opens to sunlight.

Now, I am not telling you anything you do not already know. But you have not stopped to consider how profoundly important it is in the nature of your own life. You know that *you* respond to a happy person, to a kind person, to a loving person more than you would to a person who is being wicked. It is simple common sense.

You know that you love to be around beings that talk about unlimitedness, that talk about great vision. Why? Because they are reminding you that you too are a great visionary, that unlimitedness is the natural state of the Kingdom of Heaven.

The problem is that you have unwittingly taught yourself to live from fear, to think negative thoughts, to believe that the opinions of the world mean something. You have literally created a world in which people are negatively minded, do not want to support you, and do not think you are worth anything. Yet, *you* are the one that is projecting that belief about *yourself*. And you, therefore, will attract a like vibration. For like attracts like.

If you, therefore, want to attract beings who will support you and love you, decide to be a being who supports and loves *yourself*. Decide to open your arms wide, as we spoke of in the last lesson, to receive the Love, the presence and the pleasure of God's presence.

Think only loving thoughts. Learn to master forgiveness. Dare to follow your heart! Celebrate life! Do what brings you joy! Walk as one confident in the Light of Christ! Dare to look out upon the world and say:

> My Father has set the table before me, and every being and
> blade of grass is here to support my enjoyment of God!

As you cultivate that kind of discipline, your life will change, as it must. For the universe responds to the vibrational quality that you are emitting from the radio station of your own mind.

Beloved friends, you are, indeed, Love. But when you decide as you get up in your day, that you must fear the attitude of the boss, that you must safeguard the feelings of the spouse, that you must sacrifice in order to be conformed to the opinions of the world, you shrink your energy field.

And the only thing that leaks out is something like the statement, "I choose to live in fear. I'm not willing to be bold and big and happy. I don't want to laugh too much today because somebody might be offended. I won't tell you my truth because it might disrupt your energy field."

All of that is delusion. You are free. You are here to celebrate. You are here to be outrageous. You are here to extend Love, and Love cannot be extended through a contracted energy field.

Therefore, teach yourself to notice each fearful thought. Teach yourself to notice when your energy field is contracted, and do the opposite: Choose to receive Love! If you start to go through a single day, and you notice that by five o'clock your energy field is not feeling very good, ask yourself:

> Where have I been waiting for love to show up
> as a gift of something or someone else to me?

Stop what you are doing and be the one who gives Love to *yourself*—simply so that you can enjoy it.

NOTHING CAN OCCUR THAT YOU HAVE NOT CALLED TO YOURSELF

The essence of this lesson is this: You, and you alone, are completely responsible for the quality of your experience of each moment. No one is doing anything to you. The world is not an unsafe place. And what you experience in life is the direct result of what flows from the inside *out*. For there can be no flow from the outside *in*, except that which you *receive* and make your own. Is there any point, then, to be fearful of something? Of course not!

If you *are* fearful, at least accept that you have *decreed* it to be so, by saying, "I choose to be fearful of being a millionaire, and therefore, I will not take this opportunity and run with it. I am fearful of the opinions of others; therefore, I will not give speeches in public." At least say, "I choose to have the experience of being a contracted and fearful human being." At least take ownership and recognize the simple truth that as the world shows up to reflect that fear to you, it is doing so only out of *loving service to you*.

The universe is only Love. And beings will respond to you according to what you want to call into your being; that is all. Nothing else is even possible. It is quite true that you may be calling a calamity to yourself because you, as a soul, are ready to discover a greater depth of Love and forgiveness in yourself. Life might bring you challenges, but only because you have asked it to bring you challenges so that you can grow your capacity to maturely direct Love in this world. *Nothing can occur that you have not called to yourself.*

I could not begin to tell you how many times I have conspired to create opportunities for many, many beings to step into the fullness of their Christed consciousness with full power and glory in the shortest possible time, only to have them say, "No, no. I can't do that. That's just not who I am. I have to go do something else." And the something else is always something based on fear. Something the egoic part of the mind thinks that they can be comfortable with. And something that will take them many more lifetimes to reach the same result.

The Holy Spirit always knows the shortest route to God. It *will*, when presented to you, bring up for you your deepest *fears*, since it is *fear* that obstructs the light of Truth.

HOW TO DISSOLVE THE POWER OF FEAR

How, then, do you dissolve the power of fear? By recognizing it, by feeling it, and by owning the simple fact that fear is not your master and continuing to walk on. The "ring of fear" of which I speak quite deeply in *A Course in Miracles* is simply that. The ring of fear is something constructed from the inside out.

In reality, all power under Heaven and Earth is given unto the holy Child of God. When you are presented with an opportunity, you are not presented something in which you are asked to walk alone. If you accept the Holy Spirit's function as your own, *every obstacle is removed before you reach it.*

Therefore, beloved friends, where in your life are *you* resisting the opportunities that have been presented to you? Where have you resisted and said, "Well, that's just not me, I'm not that way, I really can't do that"? When, in fact, you are merely afraid of the world. Fear has defeated you. In The Way of Knowing, fear has no power. One simply abides and does, gives it back to God, and goes on.

On the day when your body-mind returns to the dust of the ground—which is an old way of saying that the energy that is holding the subtle forms of matter, your molecules and atoms together to create an appearance of something solid—when that energy of intention and will is gone, the mind is shifted somewhere else and the body dissolves. Yet you will remain as you have always been: pure intelligence, pure potentiality, pure perception. You will still be creating, and you will merely generate energy fields that will create experiences in worlds around you.

You abide—now—in the perfect opportunity to walk through your rings of fear. Therefore, look well. Where do you feel a contraction, a fear, and a hesitancy? Is it in something that needs to be said to a friend?

The more transparent you become, the more you merely speak when you feel moved to speak, do when you feel moved to do, go where you feel moved to go, laugh as you feel moved to laugh, and cry as you feel moved to cry. The less resistance you have to the flow and movement of life emanating from your own heart and soul, the more you recognize your perfect innocence and the perfection of all things.

The more you do that, the more you will create for yourself a mindset, a state of being, so that when the body dissolves and you are in your infinite magnificence, fear will not contract you. You will simply say, "Oh! Well! What can I create now? I seem not to have a physical body any more. Hmm, how interesting!"

Where you choose to resist moving through your rings of fear, *as you know they exist in your current life,* you are building a prison for God's child—pure and simple. The world will tell you, "Do not trust the impulse of the heart." Not the impulse of the ego or the mind, but the impulse of the heart. Yet, it is in the heart that the guidance of the Holy Spirit speaks.

THE DOORWAY TO GREATER GOD CONSCIOUSNESS

Indeed, beloved friends, In The Way of Knowing, there is a certainty of knowing that it is the places in which fear seems to be cropping up that is the actual *doorway* to greater God consciousness. If there is something that you feel fearful of sharing with another, *there* is your doorway.

Go and share your truth, for no other reason—not to persuade, not to be right—but just to do the sharing so that you get through the ring of fear. That is all. If you feel your heart constantly calling you to live penniless on the streets of London, and it has been calling to you for thirty years, go and sell all that you have and follow your heart.

Now, I know that the world has not taught you to live in such a way. But the world is the opposite of the truth of the Kingdom. Love all. Become the one that serves all, by loving first yourself. Learn to quiet the roar and the din of the world, which is nothing more than your decision to place *value* on how the rest of the world is thinking.

Serve only that voice of Truth within yourself. That voice of Truth within you is the voice that says, "Go start a garden today!" First, you think, "Oh, yes!" Then you realize, "I don't know how to garden. How am I going to figure this out? But I really want to start a garden." Go start a garden!

Some would say this is living from your authenticity. I do not speak of what is authentic as being what the *mind* thinks, that is, its social image. That is not authentic at all. That is a mask, a persona.

What is authentic is what you feel in the core and the depth of your being—in innocence. What do I mean by that? The innocent heart is not needy. It does not require selected individuals to agree with it. It does not wait until the universe nods its head in approval. It merely *knows* it is innocent and acts from it, and is not attached to the opinions of the world.

Authenticity is the core through which Christ Mind grows. Any time you look and see that you have not been living authentically, and decide to take a deep breath and let your illusions be shattered by becoming transparent, telling the truth, and allowing whatever changes that need to occur to occur, then indeed, you are growing your Christ Mind.

In The Way of Knowing you ask yourself constantly:

Where am I being inauthentic?
Where am I just showing up the way that I think
Harry down the street needs me to show up?
Where am I being a vegetarian so that I can feel superior
to those that are not?

Where am I controlling my diet because I am afraid
that this substance will make me less spiritual?

Where am I denying my humanity in order to present an image to another?

Where am I getting up and going to the same job every day, when I know
in the depth of my being that I just do not want to be there anymore?

To live authentically, in some sense, is to live alone. To live alone simply means that you no longer are run by needing to look a certain way, succeed in a certain way, so that the judgment of the world will nod its head and give you a "10" instead of a "1."

In The Way of Knowing, the mind comes to grasp the simple metaphysical truth that:

I and I alone am creating my tomorrows.

If I create inauthenticity now,
I can rest assured that I will experience it tomorrow.

If I create imprisonment for my soul now, I will experience it tomorrow.

Because creation is eternal, it is impossible not to have a tomorrow—whether in this world or another.

Beloved friends, you were created to create. You were created out of an overflow of joy and Love. Therefore, live joyously, live lovingly of *yourself.* Dare to consider that your Self is *so important* that you have an obligation never to settle for less than your own authenticity.

Sometimes that requires beginning the process of discovering what is authentically yours and not merely the influence of others.

Where are you still being inauthentic? Where are you responding with a smile when you are actually feeling anger? Where are you responding with an "okay," when inwardly the answer is "no"? Where are you responding in fear to the substance you would put in your body? For example, "I can't eat that because that's a very bad substance, and I want to be healthy." It is the very fear that is creating a tomorrow of unhealthiness.

Love heals all things. Love transmutes all things. Love embraces all things, and thereby, transcends all things. Where are you not allowing Love to be your reality?

Beloved friends, consider well the theme of this lesson. Do not be in a hurry to merely put this lesson aside. Read it a few times. And wherever you see a question instead of a statement, pause and spend some time considering it—quietly, as though you were allowing the answer to emerge from your innocence. Then ask yourself:

What changes can I make
so that I am truly showing up in a more authentic way?

For those of you that truly choose to, you will find that if you abide with the message of this lesson, engage the simple quiet questions that are asked, and contemplate certain key thoughts that were repeated, much movement can occur, much liberation can occur.

You are Christ. And you are free in the world of space and time to know it as deeply as possible. And with that, peace be unto you always. Amen.

LESSON 29

FREEDOM IS LOVE UNDER ALL CONDITIONS

Once again, beloved friends, we join together with you because we remain as committed as you are to discovering ever greater depths of God's presence, ever greater depths of our own presence, ever greater depths of what alone is true always, of what alone is unchanged, unchanging and unchangeable forever.

We would speak unto you in this lesson of that which deepens the understanding of abiding in perfect knowing, in perfect knowledge. We want to address a theme that you have heard before, though from a slightly different perspective. The theme goes by a term that most of you are familiar with. That term is karma. Karma as popularly considered means that for every action, there is an equal and opposite reaction. For everything you put out, a similar energy returns.

Now, I have said before that karma can exist only where unconditional loving does not. This means that to the degree that your mind has not been purified of fear, that the mind has not been purified of need, that the mind has not been purified of its tendency toward idolatry—that is, creating something which is a substitute for Love, mistaking form for content—wherever this is occurring, you are, indeed, experiencing the creation of karma.

What do we mean by that? Each time you hold an unloving thought you are going to experience the effect or the fruit of that thought. In reality, there are two levels at which this occurs, or two ways in which it occurs. The first is immediate. The second is mediated through the forms of time.

UNLOVING THOUGHTS ALTER THE CHEMICAL BALANCE OF YOUR BODY

In the first, in that which is immediate, the very moment you think an unloving thought as a physically embodied being, you immediately alter the electrical flow of energy throughout the physical system. You immediately alter the chemical balance of the body and, thereby, experience tightness in the body, sadness perhaps, depression, an overall illat-ease feeling. For every negative thought, not just the big ones that you really get your attention wrapped around, but even the small ones, this is still true. Depression can only occur in a mind that has been denying its pathway to joy.

Depression, then, is the result of a resistance to the true flow of Life throughout the body-mind. This resistance occurs in many ways. It can be the result of not feeling a feeling to its completion, withholding a simple truth, and more often than not, from denying the impulse of the heart.

As you begin to walk a spiritual path, you realize you need to be open to the guidance of the Holy Spirit, and that, in fact, you cannot awaken yourself because if you could, you would have already done so. Then the opportunities are presented that contain within them all that you need to awaken from your illusions, but you resist it because it does not conform to your image of yourself.

There are many ways in which you can resist and create a blockage in the flow of energy through the system. It is all around some form of a negative thought. All negativity is an expression of fear. All attempts to control another are really fear. Anger is merely a form of fear. So the very moment in which the mind is used to think a negative thought, there is a very immediate karmic effect. Given that effect over a period of time, an illness is created in the body. Depression is created in the emotional field.

THE WORLD WILL MIRROR YOUR
THOUGHTS AND BELIEFS

Second, there is a *mediated* form of karmic response. Namely, that the world around you will over a period of time coagulate, create itself in a context that will *mirror* to you that which seems to prove the negative thought that by now you have forgotten you even created. Then you will have the negative thought again and you will mistakenly believe that the negative thought is there *because of* the conditions outside of you.

An example would be for someone to see an event occur in life, such as the government raising taxes, and then say, "Yes, I've always known that that's the way it is. You cannot trust a single politician." Yet, that one is not seeing that fifteen years ago, he decided that politicians could not be trusted because he heard it from his father and "knows" in his mind that the politicians will always do something to take more money out of his pocket.

Then fifteen years later, when taxes are raised, the mind says, "I knew it. I think I must have been right all along. See what they did? This means that politicians can't be trusted." When in fact, the politicians are merely the manifestation that fulfills the prophecy.

In this way, I want to invite you to look at your life. How are the events that are occurring and the quality of life you are living possibly reflecting a self-fulfilling prophecy? In other words, how could it be merely the fulfillment of the karma of how you are using the mind? Usually in this secondary form of the way karma shows up, the beliefs or thoughts are very, very old, deep in your unconscious. As you go back in time and look at your life, ask:

What must I have believed previously for this effect to be showing up?

For instance, if you have no money, look well at what you have believed about money in the past. Especially look to see: What were the beliefs about money that my parents held?

For indeed, as we have touched on before, each soul drops into this world through the context of the parents. There is a context of perception, belief, and attitude that you begin to be colored by because you are accepting that coloration into the field of your own energy, as a means of making contact with this world and emerging into it.

If, for instance, the parents believe that spirituality and material wealth cannot go together and, therefore, to be spiritual means to do without materially, then look at how your life has evolved. Do you find a block at receiving money for being of service to others, but no block in receiving money for doing something you dislike?

Live in that question, beloved friends, and begin to apply it to the whole of your life. As you look at your life, look at the effects you experience as your surroundings and your context. Are you alone, with no lover or friends? What have you believed about the world previously?

For somewhere it is the nature of your thought—the agreements you have made unconsciously or consciously about what things mean, the agreements you have made with the family and the culture in which you have been birthed—that has actually generated the energy that is showing up as the effects you experience as your life. What thoughts or beliefs were you holding within the mind?

One common thought might be "Oh, I just can't really make it on my own. I need to be taken care of. I don't believe I have what it takes." Then twenty-five years later, you wonder why you feel resentment toward the mate. The resentment is merely the recognition that you thought a negative thought about *yourself,* acted upon it, and have created the effects of someone who is controlling and provides you with all your money.

You think there is a fault in *them* because you have forgotten to see the pebble that you dropped into the pond of omnipotent creativity, which *is* the domain of the mind. Karma, then, is an effect of how the mind is used.

Now, I have, indeed, said that karma can only exist where unconditional loving does not. What does this mean? When the mind unconditionally loves, it loves first *itself* and places no conditions upon what it receives as ideas from the universe.

There are many in your world that look up to those who take the greatest chances in life. For example, the actor or the actress who waits on tables at some cheap hamburger stand, sleeps on a park bench, keeps taking acting classes and finally gets the part and becomes rich and famous.

Yet, that one who became rich and famous is one who received the impulse of a desire to act, and followed up on it, and was willing to do whatever it took to be in the contexts in which something may or may not occur. They had the willingness to take the risk. Such a one is living actually in a state of unconditional Love of the self. Whether they think about it or not, they are carrying the subtle belief that the universe will somehow arrange itself and will support them to follow their heart.

KARMA DOES NOT EXIST
IN UNCONDITIONAL LOVE

In unconditional loving, karma does not exist. The example I have given you is just a rudimentary phase of unconditional loving. In its mature state, in its spiritual state, unconditional loving means that the mind has awakened and seen that nothing that occurs in life can *cause* it to contain or withdraw its love. In the perfection of unconditional love, the mind simply Loves.

Karma, then, cannot be said to exist because that mind is no longer experiencing effects coming back at it. It has transcended the world of cause and effect and regardless of what arises, it merely loves. And who can be imprisoned who simply loves?

So there is a transcendence of karma through unconditional Love. And unconditional Love is always the fruit of the decision to love oneself. Not because it is a duty to do so, not because it will make your husband love you more. You love yourself because you finally recognize that you might as well. That is all. You love the Self because your Creator loved you enough to create the Self.

There truly are no effects that are occurring as the result of a source of power outside of you. In other words, nothing is being done to you. Nothing. You are free, in each and every moment, through the power of Love to free yourself of what looks like the effects of the world. In truth, you are never at the effect of anything, but the illusions of thought and belief that you have learned to project onto the world.

Many of you feel somewhat fearful of telling your friends and neighbors that you are reading *The Way of Mastery* that contains the guidance of Jesus, or Jeshua. That very fear that you feel, that constriction, is karmic. Somewhere a long time ago, you decided that following your own pathway must stay concealed and is not worth very much—that nobody will agree, and that their opinions decide your worth.

I would ask you this question: Could there be fear in sharing with your friends that you study lessons on achieving mastery from Jesus of Nazareth? Could there be fear of sharing this, if there was no prior belief that the opinions of others have the power to decide whether you are good or bad, worthy or unworthy? If that was not in place, there could not be the fear.

So somewhere you have believed that there is a world outside of you whose opinions matter. Where, then, in your life do you limit your expression of your joy and your fun of simply being alive because you are concerned about the approval of others?

Karma is a most interesting concept and it shows up in many, many ways. Ask yourself:

> Where are the effects I experience in my life that are the result of karmically induced thought, as opposed to thoughts of unconditional self-acceptance?

Beloved friends, the fact that you are experiencing yourself as a body-mind is, in many ways, karmic. That is, it is the result of the vast expanse of mind to dare to think a tiny, mad idea and take it seriously that, "I could separate myself from the Love of God and create an experience that *convinces* me that I have succeeded at achieving separation."

Yet, unconditional love transforms the experience of the body into something quite different. Unconditional love of Self translates the life of the body-mind—the life of paying taxes, the life of keeping your car well oiled. All of it is translated so that the world becomes not something that proves your unworthiness, your separation, but rather as a medium of communication in which magic, in a sense, is always at play. Miracle-mindedness is always at play.

You go to take your car to fill up your gas tank. Because your heart is open, your mind is open; you are not in resistance to it, and your eyes are open. You look around you and you feel the energy of somebody at the pump on the other side of the island. Because your heart is open, you go up to them and say, "I'm just here pumping my gas. I looked up and saw you. You've got a great smile. You've made my whole day. Thank you!"

Then, a conversation is struck and it is discovered that they are looking for someone in their corporation who happens to have your skills. And you are looking for a new job.

The things of the world become translated into that which supports your ever-increasing joy, success, fun, pleasure, material improvement and new friends. It supports all of it when you see through the eyes of Love. Then you literally look at the world around you and finally get that it was never what you thought it was because you failed to separate yourself from God.

Everything you see is there to support your happy experience. You are free to live in your highest joy, to ask for what you want, and to open the heart and love. And the universe will respond *according* to the beliefs you hold about yourself, within yourself.

KARMA CAN BE TRANSCENDED

Look at your life, then, with respect to your karma or the action that is occurring in response to a former action. One of the most powerful things you could ever do is to ask the question:

> What must I have believed is true about the world
> to be living the life I am living now?

This is not to say that karma is bad or wrong. It is not. It is merely effect—cause and effect. Then ask yourself:

> Where in the effects I am experiencing now can I bring a greater degree
> of unconditional, loving acceptance?

> Where am I looking through the eyes of boredom instead of appreciation?

> Where can I bring a greater depth of unconditional love?
> Where can I let go of resistance?

> Where can I give up trying to direct my own life and allow the Love of God
> to direct my life?

Karma can be transcended by translating it into something else. Karma can become the fulfillment of your purpose, your very way to extend and teach only Love. For when you see that the effects, called your life, are the result of limited, fearful negative thoughts or beliefs you have held about yourself and about the world, you can embrace the effects you have created and see them in a new light:

> I choose to allow these very conditions to be those conditions
> under which I now learn to choose Love.
> What can I appreciate in this moment?
> What can I give forgiveness unto?
>
> Where can I overcome fear of speaking out and share a truth with a friend?
> What have I been avoiding that I can now embrace?

In that very means, any set of conditions created as the effect of fear-based thinking *now* becomes the very *pathway* that will lead you to transcend the negative thinking and enter a domain of the use of the mind that will create effects far more enjoyable, far more expansive than you have ever imagined.

Do not, then, lament your life as it is, for it is *absolutely perfect.* Each set of conditions contains within it everything you need to translate your life into that which expresses your Love of God. Never lament what you create. Never lament what you experience. Never judge yourself and say, "Oh, why did I do that? I should have done this other thing." No.

Appreciate what you have created. Find what can be appreciated within it. Wrap the arms of your love around it. Bring unconditional love to it. Thereby, you will find a window, a doorway to the creation of a new use of the mind that must necessarily *require* the universe to *rearrange* itself to accommodate the new vibration. Appreciation and Love and unlimitedness *require* the universe to show up in a different way.

In other words, karma is not your prison. Bringing your attention to the effects you create is a pathway to great freedom. What you did in the past to create the effects that you no longer want was not a sin or a mistake. It was merely a free choice in order to create experience. Fine, you have been there; you have done that. Now, bring love and appreciation to the very effects that you may be judging.

For example, "Why did I buy that stock? It was so silly. I didn't get enough information and now the company has gone bankrupt and I just lost ten thousand dollars.

"Ah, let me be in appreciation of this very effect. Yes. Well, this is fantastic! I created experience for myself. I can do more of this. This is great! Oh, I just love myself so much! I can decide to do it differently. Oh, this is great! I just learned a valuable lesson. Next time I'll get more information. I'd like another opportunity for a great stock opportunity to make money. Ah, yes! Oh, I'm going to be an expert at this—I can see it coming—through my unconditional love. Yes, yes!"

In fact, every time you think you have failed, celebrate! Celebrate your so-called failure as though it were a success. For remember, it is up to *you* to decide what you will perceive.

Events are just neutral. Therefore, you are free to celebrate what you *call* your failures. When you celebrate them, they are your successes. Any successful person knows that they never fail. They merely learn and become wiser.

Become one who is no longer at the effect of karma. Become one who uses karma *wisely* by looking honestly at their life, learning what needs to be learned—without judgment, but rather in celebration. Become one who translates their karma into the doorway to an ever-increasing awareness of God's presence and perfect Love spread across the face of the Earth, permeating everything you see, translating the world into the very means that can uplift you, awaken you, care for you, and heal you.

Beloved friends, again we ask that you study well the theme of this lesson, and that you spend time with the questions that have been given unto you. For in The Way of Knowing, the mind that abides in a perfectly liberated state *knows* that the world of effects that the mind is experiencing contains within it the very secrets to an ever-increasing delight in the presence of God's Love.

There is no such thing as failure. There is only ongoing success—as life evolves from good, to better, to best as the mind learns to be the presence of Love.

Freedom is Love under all conditions.

And with that, peace be unto you always. Amen.

Lesson 30
You Were Born to Create

Beloved and holy friends, I come forth to abide with you as merely your brother and your friend. Remember always that a brother or a sister is not someone who is above you, but who is your equal. Remember always that a friend is one who has chosen deliberately to see in you the perfection of Christ and all greatness that can be birthed through you until you are willing to see yourself in such a light. Then, that friend joins with you in holy relationship to create, to play, and to extend the Truth of Reality.

The Difference Between Creating and Making

For you were born and created to *create*, not to *make*. What is the difference between *making* and *creating*? Making requires the special efforts of the egoic mind. Making involves planning what one wants based on what one already knows. And then setting about to find the way to bring it into being according to one's own ideas. Making always has an element of fear, since the ego itself *is* the fundamental contraction of fear.

Creating, in the way that I am using these terms, is quite different. When I say that you were born to create, that you were created to create, I mean that being made in the Creator's image, your only function is to serve as a conduit through which the unfathomable mystery and beauty of Love can be expressed in ways that can be seen in this world. An artist can do that with a brush, a singer with a song, a writer with a word, a friend with a smile, a gardener with a garden.

You are in the act of extending creation whenever you surrender your own ideas of what a thing is or is for. And choose *only* to do what you do in order to enjoy the presence of Love and the offering of that Love to whomever or whatever will receive it.

Creation, then, is the process in which the creator extends herself or himself from the world of the formless into the world of form. When you choose to invite friends to dinner and have no ulterior agenda except to be with them and to create a good salad and some soup for them just because you love them and because you are in a joyful state of being, you are extending the reality and presence of God. Surely, this is much different than what your politicians do when they invite friends for dinner.

Indeed, they are involved in making, while your dinner is the flow of creation. In the flow of creation, the form itself is always recognized to be secondary. It is a mere instrumentation for the content.

In making, the form becomes very important. Why? Because in making, the egoic mind already believes it knows what things are and what they are for, since all things are for the ego's safety and continuance. Therefore, the form of how things are done becomes very important, for form is image and not content.

In creation, the form is as you most desire it to be because it gives you joy, not because you believe that it will coerce someone else into voting for your party.

Imagine, then, if those of your actors and actresses were more interested in wearing clothing for their Oscar nominations that brought them joy, as opposed to seeing how good they could look, what will be acceptable, what will be breathtaking, or what will grab the attention of others. Rest assured, many of them would show up in their pajamas.

The difference between making and creating is the difference between illusion and reality. Reality *is* the Love that is God. It is the Creator's will to extend Love. You were created out of the will of the Creator, and therefore, *your will* to express Love is the *will of God*. They are one and the same.

The egoic mind is interested in making love. It has very set ideas of what Love should look like, what form it should take, how other beings ought to respond, what actions are all right and what are not all right.

But in creation, Love merely extends itself with innocence. When your will is one with your Creator, you are not in the least bit interested in making love. You are only interested in celebrating the reality that you are already *in* Love, and you are already *as* the expression of Love. You are innocent and you are perfect, just as you are. The form of that expression becomes quite secondary, since it is merely a temporary instrumentation for the fulfillment of the heart's desire to celebrate the reality of being in Love.

Let me, then, ask you this question: In your own life, do you exert energy in trying to *make* love happen, or do you celebrate that you are *already* in the presence of Love?

For in the former, you must coerce other beings to join your making, and then try to persuade them of how they ought to be behaving, performing, accepting, and receiving. So that you feel you have succeeded in manifesting what you have already determined in the mind. *Making* love requires others. *Creating* Love, that is, extending love requires nothing but your will, your willingness. This means that you are perfectly free and do not require— do not *need*—the world to show up in any certain form before you decide to be *in* Love.

When you are *in* Love, Love will guide the expression of form.

That is truly how simple it is. You will know right away if a smile is enough, whether to another human being or to a leaf on a tree. You will know if you are with another, exactly how to express it. There will not be a question; there will not be a doubt. There will be no interference of the egoic mind. There will be no fear.

For when the mind is truly in the will of God, there is no time. Since there is no time, there is no reference to the past and no reference to the future. For these things abide in the duality of time. They are not part of what alone is eternal. The past has passed away. The future is, at best, a fantasy in the mind. The present is where God abides.

ABIDING AS LOVE IN EACH PRESENT MOMENT

The peace of Christ, then, depends on your willingness to abide in the present for no other reason than to extend creation. To be one who receives Love, acknowledges the presence of Love, breathes Love, and then allows it to flow through the body-mind, through the voice, through the handwritten word, through the wink of an eye—whatever it is. Then you are done with it and you are on to the next moment.

The peace of Christ comes only to that mind that withdraws valuation from the past and the future, and surrenders into the present. For only in the present can Love be felt, known and extended. Such a mind is a creator. And through that mind, the perfection of Love's extension flows—without impediment, without obstacle, and without mistake.

The mind then, that is free—free from the egoic need to make, to control, to shape—is free from identification with the past and anxiety over the future, abides in the perfectly eternal *now.* For no other reason than to receive the awareness that it abides in Love's perfect presence, and then allows that mysterious reality through that mind—right where it is—*as* it is. It does not need to make a show. This is not about having a prescribed set of activities to do. You are merely present in the moment, and *Love lives you.*

Holy relationship, then, is where any two beings choose to come together and each of them, individually, chooses to be *in* the presence of Love. Then, whatever happens, happens.

Perhaps one will sit in a chair and read a book while another one watches a movie. Perhaps they will come together and create a beautiful dinner. It really becomes quite irrelevant because they will be moved by the mysterious energy of Love itself, which is the will of God creating experience through His creations. And when that moment is gone, it is gone. The mind of each of them simply finds itself in a new present moment.

ARE YOU MAKING OR CREATING?

The difference between making and creating is essential in The Way of Knowing. Therefore, I want to invite you in this lesson's message to begin to look at your own life. Where are you resting in knowing and allowing creation to flow through you in each present moment, and where does your mind become absorbed in what you think you must *make* occur? Come to discern the difference between the two, and notice the quality of feeling that is within you when you are in each of those states.

If you are diligent, you will come to see that whenever you are in the mode of *making* love, *making* life conform to what you *think* it ought to be, you are in suffering. When you are *creating*, you are enjoying the miracle of creation itself. For you are in a very unique position. You both are that One through whom creation flows, and you are also the witness of, or the observer of, the act of creation, flowing from the Mind and Heart of that creative center I have called Abba, who is but Love.

Celebrate, then, and embrace the uniqueness of yourself as the Son of God. You are one who gets to experience Love, create Love, and also observe and witness the flow of Love. If you do not understand that that is *miraculous*, then spend as much time as you need to alone, without moving a muscle, until you get it.

For that is the Truth of your reality. It is timeless and eternal, and far transcends the boundaries of the physical body and the boundaries of your ideas about your physical self—your personality, your personal history, your children, your mates, and your bank accounts. It far transcends everything that is temporarily arising in the field of form.

As the holy Son of God, as that created Spirit birthed to create, your ability to be aware of the flow of Love is unborn and undying—you will never lose it. As the holy Son of God, the power of your ability, the power of your beingness to allow Love to flow through you is unlimited forever. And it will never be taken away. As the holy Son of God, your capacity to enjoy the very act of being the one through whom Love is extended is without equal in all of creation. And it too is never taken from you.

Those three aspects are really one thing. They are the Truth of who you are. Any time your mind has fallen under the power of the egoic mind, which is just to choose wrongly and insanely for a moment, the reality of your being never goes away. It is never changed or altered in any way. All that has occurred is that you have used time to lose awareness of the Truth. And in the next moment, you are free to choose again. The healed mind is one that accepts its true knowingness:

> I and my Father are one. Only Love is real. I cannot possibly be a victim
> of what I see, since what I see is what I choose to see. And if I choose to see

with the eyes of Love, all I see is perfect innocence and the will of my Father clearly at work.

The healed mind is simply one that rests in that simple reality. It has merely trained itself to always choose the voice for Love. It does not matter what arises and passes away. The healed mind is not a mind that can *make* whatever it wants to happen, happen. That is the egoic attempt to become absolutely powerful. The meek of heart, the pure of heart, realize that *making* is the illusion. *Being* is the reality.

The choice is yours: making (*doing* frantically) or creating (*being* the presence of Love), out of which creative contexts emerge because it is the will of the Creator to extend Himself through a myriad of forms that arise and pass away. The forms change, but the content or the essence does not.

The awakened mind is awakened to the ever-present flow of content, pervading all form at all time. This is why for the awakened mind, loss is not possible and death is seen as unreal. For death can pertain only to the form. Forms begin in time and end in time, such as the body. That is a form you are very clearly aware of. Ideas have a beginning and an end. Love is the only thing that knows neither beginning nor end, being the fundamental energy of God Itself.

The healed mind does not plan. What does that mean? It does not mean that it does not structure a day—that is, make decisions whether it is going to make this phone call now and that one later. But it does not plan what the day shall be for. It merely surrenders into Love and allows Love to birth the day. Do you see the difference?

The egoic mind arises in the morning already believing it knows what this day is for. And this day can have no purpose, but the sustaining of the authority of the ego and trying again to make the world conform to what the egoic mind believes must be so.

The awakened mind knows that this day has no purpose, save that which the Creator would give to it—through the Christ Mind, through the Self. So it seeks first the Kingdom and then all things are added unto it. The day flows *out of* its surrender to Love.

The healed mind—the truly healed mind—is one who is like the wind. When you look upon the wind, you cannot tell from where it is coming, and you do not know where it is going. It is not a logical thing; you cannot control it. You can see its effects. You can try to measure it. You might even try to predict it. But it will always leave you guessing.

A healed mind is not interested in making. Its only interest is the delight and joy of creating. It merely shows up where it is asked to be. It no more laments or complains if it is asked to work twenty-three hours a day at bringing forth some creation that extends the presence and Love of God. It merely does what is asked. The healed mind is no longer attached to the world's definitions of success or failure. For those pertain to the realm of making. It is no longer attached to what others think of its creation. For it trusts the mystery that has birthed it and that operates through it in each moment.

Indeed beloved friends, consider well: Are you devoted to making or creating?

EXERCISES TO OBSERVE YOUR CHOICES AND CHOOSE AGAIN

By way of a simple exercise, in this very moment, how are you approaching the reading of this lesson? Did you remember to begin it, as we have suggested many times, as one who knows that they are already Christ and they are merely sitting down to abide with a brother and a friend who is their equal and sees the Truth of them? Did you remember to open the heart and trust that what emerges in the form of your experience as you read these words is exactly what is perfect for you in this moment?

Or did you sit down determined to *make* yourself like Jeshua by memorizing the words, by getting the concept? The *relaxed* mind absorbs all knowledge. The *making* mind misses all knowledge. The relaxed and healed mind is like a sponge that is constantly learning and being shaped by what it learns.

The making mind has no room in it to receive anything new because it has already decided what the truth is, what it should look like, and what it should sound like. It misses the moment in which it can observe and be the conduit for, as well as the one who is creating, an experience of Love.

In this moment, then, you are quite free to truly open the heart and relax the mind and to realize you are present with a brother, and together we are *in* the field of Love. All that arises, arises in mystery and returns to its Source. If you can enter into such a field of Mind—in this very moment—you are free. And you are, indeed, one who knows.

If you can join with me in such a Mind—in this very moment—then you can prove to yourself how infinitely powerful you are. What you can apply to this moment can be applied to all moments.

Likewise, if your mind is currently insisting that you cannot be that One in this moment, you are doing the very same thing. You are using the infinite power of the mind to choose to remain a *maker*, and therefore, to reside in suffering. Either way, you remain quite right. Either way, you are expressing your infinite and perfect freedom—to *create* or to *make*, to be in Love or to be in fear, to abide in peace or to abide in anxiety.

Now, ask within yourself:

Would I choose to experience what is unending—myself—as a creator or a maker?

If you choose the path of the creator, then the first thing you need to do is to remember that creating is not the same as making. Creating involves seeking first the Kingdom of Heaven.

What does that mean? Well, it means that you have to sell all that you own, get a backpack, buy a ticket to Katmandu, and spend seventeen years hiking through the Himalayan Mountains until you find just the right cave. And then another seventeen years of astute meditation and prayer before you begin to get your first glimpse of God. That is what seeking the Kingdom involves.

Or you can simply turn the mind to the peace of God—right where you are—and accept it. And in that very moment, you will have gained what all the yogis in their caves have ever gained, what all of the Buddhas and Christs have achieved in their austerities. The Kingdom is but a choice away:

I choose now for the perfect peace of God.

And just like that, you have achieved all that needs to be achieved—*if* you will receive it.

To create means that you are committed to seeking first the Kingdom of Heaven. Then allowing yourself to celebrate that, regardless of what your physical eyes show you. Regardless of how the brain-mind is interpreting or creating perception of what the physical eyes reveal to it. Regardless of all of that, *you are free*. For whatever is arising is perfectly harmless. Forms come and go, Love remains. Where else can you possibly find freedom, except as one who is merely abiding as the decision for Love?

If you would be a creator, you will need to give up striving, for striving is part of the world of making. And you will need to give yourself permission to cultivate a mastery of allowing. Allowing is not passivity. Allowing is not sitting on your pillow waiting for the universe to manifest good things in your life. Allowing is an act of turning within, appreciating your oneness with God, and simply asking:

Father, what would you like to create in this moment?

Suddenly, a thought comes. The thought reveals you driving your car thirty-five miles to see a friend and inviting them to dinner. Well, then, get on with it! Driving your car for thirty-five miles is an act that takes energy. It is not a passive act at all.

Allowing is a very powerful state of being, for allowing does not resist anything in the field of action—anything! And if you are asked to create a retreat center in northern New Mexico, well, you simply get on with it, even though you have no idea how it is going to come to pass. You merely make yourself available and you show up.

On the outside a creator—a true creator—may look very ordinary. A creator may look to be one who is not getting the applause of the world. Their picture may not be on the front of *People Magazine.* They may not be the centerfold in *Playboy* or *Playgirl.*

A creator is one who is delighting in allowing the flow of Life to find ways to touch hearts and minds with Love. The creator is not about storing up golden coins for a winter's day. The creator is merely about watching, being a conduit for, and being involved in the creative extension of Love. That creation might require the storing up of golden coins, for the creator resists nothing of the world. Nothing is seen as good or bad. It is just an instrumentation for carrying out the will of God, which is the extension of Love. When you are involved in *that*, your will is one with the Father.

The difference between making and creating is essential in The Way of Knowing. It would behoove you, then, to spend some time in merely abiding in the innocence of observing your life and beginning to notice when your energy gets caught up with making instead of creating. Where have you, perhaps, given your life over to making, wishing you could create?

Begin to observe the moments in your day when you can choose to create. Remember that to choose to create means:

> I give this moment over for the Will of my Father. I wonder how I could simply surrender into being the presence of one who has accepted the Kingdom for him or herself? And then I will see where it carries me in the next second.

So that you begin to see that regardless of what is arising in the conditions around you, or what other minds are doing in this world, the world has no effect on you. I have said that this world is a big clash of dreams, and the vast majority of minds are still far more committed to illusion than reality. There are just events arising and passing away. And in any context, your mind remains free to give up making for creating, and to surrender that moment to the will of God.

Accepting the atonement for yourself is another way of saying accepting Love's presence, breathing it in and celebrating it. "Ah, yes! This is all that is really real anyway. I wonder what would want to be created in this moment?" And then observing the delightful expression of that *will* in that moment.

When I said, "The meek shall inherit the Earth," I meant that eventually there will be established as the pervasive quality of human consciousness just this state of being. The world will be populated by creators who arise in the morning and say:

> The day really belongs to the Creator. I am just created to extend the Creator's will. Father, what would be a groovy way to hang out this day?

Some of those minds might hear, "Oh, just hang out in the forest and listen to the birds." So those beings will give their day to delighting as deeply as possible in the experience of the singing of the birds. Others will hear a different message. And they will set about and do whatever they are asked. Why? Because the mind of the creator is no longer in resistance. Sanity has been re-established and there is nothing to fret about.

The mind involved in *making* listens for the impulse of God, and then has a million reasons why that cannot be. And those reasons are always linked to learning that has occurred in the past or anxiety about an imagined future. In other words, the mind of a maker is never present. It is caught up in the illusion of duality, not the reality of perfect oneness.

One who knows is a creator. And a creator is empty of himself; that is, empty of the self that was made in error. The knower of Reality is the presence of Love, the spaciousness through which the Creator extends Its perfect will. It has no attachments and no illusions. It is not run by what other people think of it. It is not run by what it has accomplished in the past, or what it perceives it must have in the future.

The mind of one who knows and rests in true creativity is merely present, witnessing the extraordinary, mysterious ways of Love. For Love allows all things, embraces all things, trusts all things, and therefore, transcends all things. Perfect peace can only exist where the mind has transcended all conflicted states of duality. Transcendence is not denial. It can come only through embracing, through allowing, through being present.

Your mind is a mind that *has* been healed. You do not need to heal it. You only need to accept that healing has been accomplished by the grace of that Love that birthed you to create. That is what I meant when I have said a teacher of God need only accept the atonement for himself or herself:

> I am already healed. Time to get on with it.

All forms of healing, then, are merely contexts created by Love through a mind that has accepted healing—a context created that would give the mind that perceives itself as unhealed an opportunity to choose differently.

Therefore, I want to create a context for you in this very moment. This is a way of demonstrating to you exactly what I have been sharing with you in this lesson. For in this moment, as a brother and friend who loves you and loves my Father, I am merely allowing myself to create words that are being formed into a lesson that help to create a context that I am literally observing emerge. I have not planned it. I am not trying to make anything happen. I am abiding in Love.

And out of that Love I am now receiving the thought from the will of my Father. I am observing it flow through my mind and being translated through electrical impulses into that which creates words that are being formed into a lesson that are then read by your eyes that send vibrations to your brain-mind, giving you permission to access it with the deeper Self that knows the Truth. I am witnessing all these things even as it flows through my mind toward yours.

I invite you, now, into the context of healing. Say this within your holy mind:

> My mind has already been healed by the grace that birthed me in its image.
>
> I need only use the power of the Christ Mind to choose the perfect peace of God. I do so now and forevermore.
>
> I am one who knows.
> Father, what would you create in this moment that is an extension of Love?

Do nothing but observe what comes into your mind—what feeling suddenly flows through the body.

There! A short exercise. A context to demonstrate how it all works. No magic, no pilgrimages, no special pills, no special diet, no special love affairs—nothing special at all. Simply the presence of Christ Mind.

And rest assured, in that moment, if you were truly joining with it, you had no thought whatsoever that you are a separate ego who does not know God. You were that Christ Mind engulfed in the creative process itself. You were in your right-mindedness. And in that moment, you are the knower. And as a knower, you are free to have as many moments of that knowing as you want to experience.

So, beloved friends, merely observe the mind for a while, until you learn to detect the difference between making and creating. You will come to discover that creating is much more fun, takes a lot less energy or effort, and creates a whole lot more joy within your own experience, your own energy field.

Delight in that simple practice, and remember: you do not have to go to a temple in Tibet to perfect it. For wherever you are, you are in the temple created for you by the Creator who loves you and knows exactly how to enlighten forevermore the mind of the creator that He has created. Enjoy creating!

And with that, indeed beloved friends, peace be unto you always, you who are eternally perfect co-creators with our Father. Peace be unto you always. Amen.

LESSON 31
PLACING YOUR TRUST
AND LOYALTY IN LOVE

Beloved and holy friends, As always, and though I have repeated this to you often, I say it to you again, and yet again: It is with joy that I come forth to abide with you. For relationship is the holiest of all places—relationship between any two who choose to look upon each other, having looked within and found no lack. For those two can then look out upon one another and see only perfect innocence, only perfect peace, only perfect Love.

Therefore, it is with joy that I join with you, for I look upon you with perfect peace, and perfect Love, and perfect trust. My *loyalty* to you is unshakable. No event that occurs in the realm of your space and time can taint the loyalty which I know to the depth of Truth that is your very Self—that which is unshakable, unchanging, unchangeable and unchanged forever. For my loyalty is perfectly pure. My trust of you is unfathomable and immeasurable.

How can this be so? For perhaps, even now, your mind says, "Well, yes, but last week I got a little angry with my spouse, and three weeks ago I forgot to pay for that candy bar I picked up in the store. Since I'm such a horrible person, your loyalty, Jeshua, is misplaced."

My trust in you emerges *from* my trust in my Father. My trust in you emerges from the perfect knowledge that you belong *only* to that One that I have called Abba.

My trust, then, is the expression of what I have come to know as I have looked into the depth of my own being, both within my physical incarnation that became rather famous, and also since then, where I discovered the perfection of Love that pervades all things, and can be seen beneath the surfaces, and through the appearances that the body's eyes and the ego's thought system would show to you.

What do I mean by that? As you abide in your physical world, the greatest challenge that you have, moment to moment and moment to moment, is to be vigilant against identifying with the perceptions which are born and birthed as a result of the physical apparatus of the body itself. That is, you look out through a body—that is where your attention seems to be. Your apparatus called your eyes immediately shows you a world of objects separated by space.

If you identify with that level of perception, you can only conclude that you are separate, one from another. When you see events happening, it is absolutely impossible to see the subtle interconnection of all events. You fall into the trap of forgetting that you live in the universe. And universe means simply one turning, or one song—one event occurring, like an ocean is but one event, expressing as many waves. So too, do all events in the field of space and time, in the field of physical matter merely emerge from that *one* universe.

From the body's level of perception, the thinking mind in association with the body creates interpretations of what it believes it is seeing. And now, your attention, your awareness is already twice removed from reality. First, you have become hoodwinked, thinking that what the body's eyes show you is what is truly real and significant.

For instance, you love someone. They are here today and tomorrow they leave. You see them pack their things and their body leaves. And your eyes show you that they are "gone." Then the mind says, "Woe is me. I have lost my love." Neither of these is true.

The soul, the level at which reality is far deeper than the level of the body, can never "go" anywhere. No one you have ever met or known can ever be outside of your heart through his or her *own action*. The body-mind, yes, can leave, but that is not what takes someone out of your heart. It can only be *your* decision to withdraw Love. It is only the withdrawing of Love that creates separation in the experience of your awareness.

So you are now sitting two levels removed from reality. First, you have become hoodwinked, thinking that the physical eyes show you what is true. Then you draw conclusions and create interpretations of the events the body's eyes show you. This creates the emotional effect that is like a soup that runs through you and around you, and will remain so—until it is healed.

The third level of being removed from reality is the trick of the mind in which it *insists* that its interpretations are fact. It is to this level of the mind that I asked within *A Course in Miracles:*

Would you rather be right or happy?

For happiness can only be the result of perfect trust. And perfect trust emerges from perfect loyalty. And perfect loyalty emerges spontaneously in the mind that has rested in surrender.

We have spoken often of the keys to the Kingdom: desire, intention, allowance, surrender. In allowance, you go through a period of deep undoing, in which you disconnect the wiring that has led you to *insist* on the rightness of the interpretations that you have created and then linked to events that the physical body-mind has perceived.

So as allowance is perfected, one has come to see that their whole world, everything they have constructed, has been undone. That is, your perception of belief, your perception of feeling nature, your perception of what is, has been undone. The mind is unraveled.

Now, the perception of the body-mind, of course, goes on. The physical eyes seem to show you that there is someone in another body over there, and they are doing what they are doing, and you are doing what you are doing, so there cannot be any connection. That level goes on as long as there is a body. However, the mind that is healing does not identify that as the primary level of reality.

So as allowance surrenders the construct that has been made up in the mind—and exists nowhere but in the mind—one rests in an unobstructed allowance of how the body-mind goes through its days until it returns to dust. But there is no longer a "being hoodwinked," no longer being attached, no longer being swept up with that level of identification because there is no longer a need to identify with the interpretations. And there is no longer—quite happily—any need to be right.

As allowance comes to completion, something quite magical occurs. It is beyond all comprehension of the thinking mind. The ego could never comprehend this! It is as though something that was existing because it was contracted in fear dies and dissolves like the mist before a rising sun. And all that is left is a quiet spaciousness in which awareness has been purified.

Events still arise and pass away. One continues to talk with their friends, perhaps as they always have. One notices the tendency in the body-mind to create interpretations, and some of them are quite necessary, "That light just turned red. My interpretation is that it might be wise to stop." But there is now something that is wrapped around all of that. So that what is arising is seen as, ultimately, quite inconsequential, quite innocent and devoid of any deep value.

For you will place your loyalty on what you have *decided* to value. And in that spaciousness, in that perfect stillness, in that deep peace, mind—or *self*hood—dissolves in surrender.

Anyone who has awakened knows exactly what that feels like. Anyone who has begun to awaken has touched on moments of perfect surrender. For in surrender, the mind beholds that all things that are arising and passing away are perfectly harmless. They can hold no value because they abide in time. And the things of time are like the waves that arise from the ocean—because they have a beginning, they *will* have an end. In their beginning, their end is certain.

Only a fool would create loyalty to that which is temporary, temporal and ultimately, unfulfilling. But the wise of heart have decided to place their value on that which is eternal.

And what can be eternal save God? And God is but Love.

Therefore, in The Way of the Heart and in The Way of Transformation, and now in The Way of Knowing, all that we have sought to share with you has been by design, to lead you to see that love is the only thing worth valuing. Love is unconditional. Love merely loves in order to abide in its own nature.

And because God is but Love, as the mind disentangles itself from the perceptual level of the body-mind, from the interpretations selected and created in the mind and overlaid upon those events, and especially as it disentangles itself from the egoic need to be right about its *makings,* that which you are—pure intelligence, pure infinite creative possibility—shifts itself into being identified only with valuing Love. This is the same thing as saying:

I value only God.

Then, the soul begins to reawaken, the soul—this drop of pure light, which is pure intelligence—begins to realize that to know God it must *be* God. And since God is only Love, the soul desires to be only Love. For in loving as God loves, God is known. As God is known, Self is realized and remembered. And the dream of the dreamer is transcended.

Therefore, indeed, beloved friends, my trust in you is perfect, for I have come to value only God. My loyalty to *you* as the offspring of my Father stems from having received that enlightenment for myself, having awakened from the maze—the complex web of perceptions in the body-mind, the interpretations that the body-mind places on events, and the ego's construct of what it feels it is right about. Because I have dissolved all of that, I abide in pure devotion only to what is truly real and perfectly unconditional: the presence of my Father, which is the same as the presence of Love.

WHERE HAVE YOU PLACED YOUR LOYALTY?

Indeed then, look well then to see what you have chosen to be loyal *to*. And if you have chosen to be loyal to something of the world, you have actually been using loyalty as a way to overcome fear. Think about it. I have often said that what is not Love is only fear.

In a state of Love, there is no clinging; there is no denial. There is nothing obstructed in the nature of the body's experience. One renders unto Caesar that which is Caesar's. One sweats in the hot summer sun. One simply is where one is, but the mind—the essence of your identity—is as Love. All of the rest of it is superfluous.

And so, you find yourself in a maze of events called space and time. By this, I mean you find yourself going to a job. You find yourself in a certain third-dimensional relationship. But you are not hoodwinked into thinking that this place, this context, is the all.

It is only an opportunity for you to be the one who loves in the midst of that context, simply for the sake of knowing Love. The career, or the mate, or the car, or the garden, or the boat can come and go, for whatever is begun in time ends in time. But your delight is in loving and embracing and being the field in which these events rise and fall.

If you are loyal to a person, place, or thing, look well to see: Is there, underneath, a fear that you have not yet been honest about? Are you being loyal in order to have this person, place, or thing approve of you and stay with you so that you get something that you want?

And there is nothing wrong with that. Do not think that because you look and see, "You know, the bottom line is, I really like this job and the hundred and twenty thousand dollars a year that it pays me; I really like the sense of security that gives me," that there is anything wrong. It doesn't mean you have to give it up and go live penniless on the street.

What matters is that you become perfectly honest with what you are doing, and withdraw the tendency of the mind to say, "Well, I'm really doing this career because I believe that the product that we create is making a huge impact on the planet. I believe we can really make things different. And besides, we give jobs and we give money to charities. That's why I'm here." Oh, nonsense!

In the world, you will do what you do because of where you place your value. This is why I have often said:

> If you want to know truly what you idolize, what you are committed to, what you most deeply believe, merely look at where you are, who you are with, and what you are doing with your time, and how you feel about it—truthfully.

Those that insist on saving up money for a rainy day are merely stating, "I believe there can be a rainy day unless I do something to prevent it." Their trust has been placed in their power to manipulate and use the world to create what they perceive they must have.

And it is very, very different than the trust of the one awakened in God who knows that whatever arises and passes away in the field of space and time is inconsequential. Because *that* mind is so identified with being the presence of Love that the body-mind could contract cancer tomorrow and say, "Who cares!"

The mind that rests in freedom has learned to transfer trust and loyalty to Love. That mind has come to enjoy the peace that comes with only loving. For what harm can come to the mind that simply loves, who looks upon all things and sees its perfect innocence and plays in the Kingdom provided by that one's Father—the kingdom of the body-mind, the kingdom of space and time, the kingdom of the power to choose Love over fear?

This is why I suggest this simple thought:

> Suffering comes from being identified with form, whether it be the body, a belief, a career, or a context of experience of any kind. For all experience comes and goes. Liberation and deep peace come from being identified with content.

By content, we simply mean the matrix or the source out of which all possibilities are possible. It is like a musician who comes to appreciate the field of silence out of which notes can arise in a certain sequential order, in order to create a beautiful melody. If it were not for the silence between the notes, no song could have ever touched your heart.

The matrix of Love, which is the presence of the Father, the pure intelligence, the field in which all things arise and pass away and never change, that field is like a canvas upon which the grand artist paints. But the master artist knows that without the canvas, there is nothing. And therefore, honors the blank canvas first.

LIMITING BELIEFS NATURALLY CRUMBLE AS THE SOUL AWAKENS

Loyalty and trust are significant things to ponder. There is a process of growth, of course, for each time you begin to see that what you have placed your trust in cannot really, truly fulfill the soul, it is as though a structure crumbles.

Now, what is actually occurring? You, as infinite being, have merely realized that you have been hoodwinked. And you are withdrawing value from what you placed your trust in. That feels like a crumbling. And it literally is a crumbling at the subtle level of energy that constructs a perceptual belief system about the nature of experience.

For instance, to give you a simple example: If one believes that they must have coffee every morning in order to get going, and then later in life for whatever reason, they come to see that they never needed it at all. They may go ahead and enjoy their coffee, but it will never be for the same reason. That structure of belief will crumble and they will, literally, see life differently.

Each and every one of you can pause in this lesson right now and merely ponder what structures of belief have crumbled in your life. Has it not always led to a sense of greater expansion, deeper wisdom, a more certain knowing?

In other words, life proceeds from illusion to reality. As the soul awakens, it literally feels a sense of expansion and growth. But the growth has nothing at all to do with the body getting bigger, or the bank account growing, or having more children. You all know that as wisdom is reawakened in the mind, there is a sense of growth. And that kind of growth becomes all attractive to you.

PLACE YOUR TRUST IN
THE LOVE THAT BIRTHED YOU

When you become so much a lover of the wisdom of perfect union with God, so that that is all that matters to you, you are already ninety percent free of illusion. And the world will never have the power to truly bind you again.

Place, then, your trust in the Love that birthed you. When I say, "birthed you," I am not talking about the body. I am not talking about your personal history, your ego. The "you" that I refer to exists within and prior to all of that.

It is as though your Father has created you as the powerful ocean in which *you* have been—knowingly or unknowingly—emanating all of the waves that have become your particular experience as the soul. *That* is what God has created. Trust the One that created *you,* as an infinite source of awareness that is perfectly free in every moment to decide what experience it will have.

Why is this important? Your world would teach you, and the level of perception of the body-mind would say, "Well, I want to have an experience. Oh, I just had a thought of having an ice cream cone. Well, I've experienced driving my body to the ice cream store and eating ice cream." That event does occur.

But if you look closely, you will discover that your experience is the value you place upon the event. I know that seems subtle to you, but it is very, very important. *Experience actually occurs nowhere but in the field of the mind.*

You could just as easily go to the store and eat ice cream and have your mind on a book that you are writing, or the remembrance of a great love affair or a great movie from the night before, and never even notice the taste of the ice cream. You get home, and your wife or husband says, "Well, dear, did you have a good trip to the ice cream store?" And you reply, "Oh! Oh, that's right. I did stop at the store. You know, to tell you the truth, I don't even remember what I had!"

So where does experience occur? It does not occur at the level of the body-mind itself. It occurs at the level of mind. And mind shapes experience according to what it chooses to value.

Now, does that mean that you just drop doing anything in the world? No. An awakened being in the world simply delights and has fun—from a state of clarity of knowing that whatever they choose to do with the body-mind is merely a free choice based on what they are choosing to value in the moment. And if they own that valuation, they can totally enjoy the experience they are having.

Then, they have come full circle. If they want to design a Website, if they want to be a banker, if they want to be a dancer, a prostitute, or a farmer—it no longer matters! For the mind that is awake, while the body lasts, merely sees experience arise and pass away. It takes total ownership and realizes that it has the power to create its experience as being delightful, fulfilling, and a blessing—regardless of what the body-mind is actually doing.

There can be no difference. It does not matter if you are a teacher standing at a boat on the shores of a great lake in what you now call Israel talking to a hoard of hundreds, or perhaps seeing if you can actually make a few fish and loaves of bread feed five thousand. And then saying, "Oh! How about that! That was fun!"

There is no difference between that and driving a truck in New York City and delivering frozen fish, if the mind within the soul is taking complete ownership and delighting in the mystery of creating experience, and choosing to bring enjoyment and freedom to that moment.

This is why events of the world can never bind you. All suffering comes because of the *interpretation* you are *overlaying* over events. And in that very moment, you have used God's gift to you, which is the power of awareness, to create its experience.

Once again, my crucifixion was my final learning lesson in the realization that I had broken the spell. I was no longer under the spell of the egoic mind, or the body-mind. I merely looked upon my experience and decided to freely be in a state of Love in the midst of that context.

You are free to be in a state of love in the midst of any context, as you watch and observe the waves of temporality come and go.

As you see that happen, and as you develop that capacity within yourself—through the choices for Love, through the choices for forgiveness, and through the choices to be happy instead of right, to live in innocence and wonder instead of certainty and dread, and to rest in true knowledge, true knowing, rather than the relative knowledge of the world—you come to see that all that is arising and passing away can never leave you. That loss is impossible.

For where the mind chooses to rest in Love, all things that arise and pass away are remembered and restored and sanctified. There is perfect peace.

Though a beloved friend passes away in what you call "death," because you do not identify the friend with the body-mind and because you do not, then, perceive that you can no longer love your friend, you just enjoy loving your friend. As you abide in Love, you begin to experience the reality that nothing dies. Nothing dies!

For pure intelligence can go nowhere. One of your scientists once said, "I think I have figured it out. Energy is what makes up everything, and it can never go anywhere. It can only change form. But the essence, or the energy, remains."

This is not unlike a mystic, or a sage, or a great savior or messiah, or a very ordinary everyday person waking up and saying:

> You know, only Love is real! And in Love, all things exist forever.
> I am not separate. I am not lost. I am free!

The great journey in the field of space and time is to allow that awareness to settle into your beingness so that that quality of awareness permeates and pervades the level of the egoic mind, the level of interpretation, and the level of perception of the body-mind—the apparatus of the brain and nervous system.

All of that is still going on, but you begin to pervade it with the growing awareness that only Love is real, that:

> I have the power to extend forgiveness.

Every time the mind trusts in the One that created it and rests in that peace, a miracle occurs. Every time that you have extended forgiveness, a miracle has occurred, for you have withdrawn valuation of an old perceptual system and chosen for reality.

The enlightened sage is merely one who has cultivated the practice of training the mind to choose the reality of Love under all circumstances. Through that one's many successes, they have come to know that what they have chosen is true. God has been revealed. Loyalty is no longer a question.

WHAT WILL YOU CHOOSE TO VALUE?

Trust and loyalty, then, must flow from the mind and its power to choose what it will value. Be you, therefore, *loyal* to Love. Be you, therefore, *loyal* to your perfect union with God. Trust that One who birthed you and who has been guiding your journey home all along. For remember, I have said often that from the very moment the dream of separation began to be dreamed, already the answer was provided—called the Holy Spirit—the right-mindedness in the depth of your being that cannot be touched.

Rest in the right-mindedness of choosing only Love. Extend complete freedom to the waves that come and go. In this sense, the weather is a wave, Caesar is a wave, your spouse is a wave; that is, as you would look at them as a body-mind. They are a wave. They will come and they will go. But if you abide in the field of Love, you abide in timelessness and eternity. You abide as the spaciousness that embraces all things, trusts all things, and thereby, transcends all things.

Here, then, beloved friends, is the pure essence of loyalty and trust: If your loyalty is in anything that can crumble, you have merely not yet fully chosen to place your loyalty in that which cannot crumble. If your trust is in a requirement that individuals act and behave in a certain way, you have not yet come to trust the perfection of Love that is already at work in everyone's lives, calling them to deeper levels of remembrance.

See, then, the perfection of all events. For the waves that arise in the temporality called the world have no power, in and of themselves. They are already held in the arms of a perfectly loving God, and each event truly serves no purpose save to nudge that soul, that spark of pure awareness or intelligence, to look deeper beyond its illusions.

When anyone attacks you or projects upon you, they are merely crying out in their own fear and insanity. The awakened one looks upon them with love and merely says, "Oh, is that so? Well, very well. Yes, thank you for sharing. Have a nice day." And goes on trusting and lets their life be an expression of the loyalty that they give *only* to the voice of the holy One within them.

Look and see where you are with trust and loyalty in your own life. Simply ask yourself, "Where are my idols? What am I attached to, and why?" Remember that those with thoughts of "I" and "mine" know not the true nature of things. When you say, "my car," or "my wife," you are not dealing with reality, for all things belong to God. There is nothing that you can possess *except* the reality of what you *are* as the thought of Love in form.

WHEN YOU CHOOSE LOVE, YOU BECOME FREE

Come to see, then, that when you choose love, you become free. Who can harm you? What gain or loss can affect your peace? In each moment as you remember love, *you give Love*. Everywhere you go and everyone you see is touched in a quiet and secret place. They may not know why they feel attracted to being in your presence, but *you* will know. You are simply choosing to *be*—and mark my words well here—you are merely choosing to finally *awaken* and *be* God incarnate. For God is but Love, and when you love, there is only God.

Remember then always, beloved friends, that that which crumbles can only be form and not content. Love can never crumble, because it is the content that is the presence of God's reality. Because Love is content, it is unchangeable, unchanged, and unchanging forever.

Perfect freedom comes to any mind that shifts its identity from the level of the body, from the level of the interpretive mind, from the level of the egoic mind that insists its constructs are real, correct and valuable, and becomes *identified* with Love.

Identity with what is conditional and temporal can never produce what is unconditional and eternal. The power of mind can leap from the conditioned to the unconditional through the decision to place value only on *that.*

Well do I understand that what arises within the body-mind is a fear of survival. Yet, it is a useless fear, since the body-mind from the moment of its conception has been marching inexorably toward its demise.

And if the body-mind itself is completely powerless, which it is, to exist as eternity, everything dependent on the body-mind must crumble with it. Everything, then, built as a house upon the foundation of your having become identified with the perceptual level of the body-mind, the interpretations of the thinking mind, and the insistence of the egoic mind on being right are all like floors in a house built on a foundation of error and illusion. You might as well own it now—they are going to crumble.

Illusions have no life. That is what makes them illusions. Only in reality is Life finally found. Yes, you do feel that crumbling going on, for what crumbles in the mind sends a shock wave, like a ripple, down through the body-mind, through the brain, through the nervous system. And the body shakes and groans, and maybe it complains and cries, but it is nothing more than the crumbling of illusion.

Eventually, the body itself must crumble as an illusion. For the mind that grows in the radiance of its awakening must finally put away the entire physical dimension as a toy outgrown. The body-mind, the nervous system, can no longer contain you, for what you value is the radiance of merely *being* the presence of God's Love. You begin to realize that you do not need a body-mind at all in order to extend Love. While the body-mind lasts, love it, embrace it, allow it. Do not expect great things from it. Just use it as a temporary communication device.

Since what you want is Love, practice teaching *only* love. Teaching love is not talking *about* love, not about the philosophy of love, and not about the metaphysics of love. You teach love by *being loving* in each moment. And you can only be loving by allowing yourself to *feel* the presence of Love in, and as, your moment-to-moment experience.

Because Love is unconditional, you are free *now*. No set of circumstances must change *before* you have the power to be in Love. This is the same thing as saying that God is given to you by grace in each moment, and you are asked *only to open and receive*.

Only Love is real. Only Love allows you to transcend the great fear, the great suffering, that comes only from a temporary, mistaken identity problem—an authority problem. You think your construct of the world is your authority. You think the body-mind is who you really are. This is merely an identity problem, an authority problem. When you come to know that you are merely the expression of that One—pure Spirit, Love—you are free from the world.

Now, will the world "get it"? Will the world say, "Oh, I'm really glad that you are free"? Of course not, since the world is the attempt to be *other* than the Truth of the Kingdom. Therefore, when anyone projects upon you at any time, when anyone is in any way anything but loving, it can only be because they are still choosing to insist on the rightness of their construct of the sensory data that has come through their nervous system, which they have been identified with. In other words, they are living in illusion.

Only Love is real. If you want to be with one who is sane and awake, be only with one who chooses to teach only Love. Let *those* be your friends. Let *those* be your playmates. Let *those* be your lovers and your spouses, for only they are capable of honoring the Truth that is true always, and seeing it as the very essence of your soul.

That is why there is a great attraction to anyone who is awake, for they "see" you. They see you to your essence because they see *from* their own. These two are but one and the same, for the holy Son of God is one. Therefore, choose Love. And transcend the suffering that is the world.

REVIEW WHERE YOU HAVE PLACED YOUR LOYALTY

Look well, then, beloved friends, over the next thirty days. Enjoy merely looking at where you have placed your loyalty in the past, and where you are placing it now. Look at the grand journey that you have made. What on earth has changed your loyalty from your teddy bear to God, if not God Herself?

Think not, then, that you have been apart from that One. For in each moment of your experience, even as you believed in the illusions that the body's eyes would show you, already that One who is but Love was working to dissolve your illusions, one by one, in the way unique to the dynamics of your own soul.

When the ship sails into the harbor, it is home. The long journey is forgotten. Perhaps there will be a few stories told in the pub as everyone has a beer. But in a day or two, a week or a month, the journey fades from awareness. And friends merely abide together, growing flowers, dancing in the evenings, observing the sunset, and giving hugs and kisses.

When the ship sails into the harbor, the journey is over. And there is only calm water, though around it the storm may rage. Let it! *Let the storm of life rage.*

Merely identify with the peace beyond all understanding, the peace that comes as a mind comes to choose only identity with Love. Peace, beloved friends, is the result of the *shift of identity* which emerges by placing your trust and loyalty only in that One who is only Love.

Allow, then, everything else to crumble. Does that mean you must give up your golden coins? Of course not! For that would be to say that the golden coins have a power to bind you. They do not! Neither the having of them or the lack thereof can bind you. Only your decision not to love can bind you and make you suffer.

Give, then, perfect freedom to all created things, for they belong not to you, nor were they given to you to give you security or to boost your ego or to make you happy. They are given for your enjoyment and for you to bless.

For the Christ who walks this Earth knows that his or her primary purpose is to bless the Father's creations, to set all things free in the sanctity of their own deep and perfect union with God.

Seek to possess nothing or no one. Seek to change nothing and no one. Seek only to love. And in Love, you are set free.

So then, as you conclude this lesson, simply make the decision to spend five minutes doing nothing but loving all that you see through the body's eyes, all that you notice arising in the mind as a memory or an image of a friend, or what-have-you, or an event— any event that has occurred. Simply decide to love it. That is all. Then, try to tell yourself that peace is a long way off. It is present in every decision for Love.

Therefore, indeed, with perfect trust and perfect loyalty, I look upon you and already know that you are borne on the wings of that Love that carries you away to itself. In perfect trust and loyalty I look upon the holy and only begotten Child of God, and *know* that the dream of separation has already been corrected, and you abide in perfect safety *now*!

For the events of space and time can never touch or alter the Spirit, the pure intelligence, the infinite awareness, that is the Truth of who *you* are. It is up to you to decide to enjoy that power of awareness by selecting only loving thoughts.

Peace, beloved friends, be with you always. Amen.

LESSON 32
THE LONGING OF THE SOUL
IS TO KNOW LOVE

Beloved and holy friends, we come forth to speak yet again of the essence of all that you seek and all that you are. With great devotion and with unceasing praise, we share with you that which alone can set God's child free, that which alone enlightens the mind, purifies the heart, and brings about the serenity of the soul.

What, then, could such a subject be? What theme could all of these words point to? Indeed, what does the morning sunrise point to? What does the sound of a child's laughter point to? Beloved friends, what does the very breath you breathe point to? What do all things of creation point to? For I have said unto you before, there is nothing you can create that does not express your longing to awaken.

Therefore, all "doing" of the body-mind is but the attempt of the soul to break free of all limitation and to once again rest or recline in that perfect peace which is the certain knowledge that only Love is real.

The yogi in his cave but expresses the longing of that one's soul to recline in God. The lovers entwined express only the longing of the soul to taste, to touch the reality of Love. And Love is but God, for God *is* but Love. All things, then, reflect to you through the sensory apparatus of the body-mind the longing of all creation to *know*, with perfect certainty, the living presence of that One whom I have called Abba.

In The Way of Knowing, it must come to pass that the mind is converted from fear to Love, from doubt to perfect faith. Perfect faith is not that beginning and intermediate stage in which one is *choosing* to have faith in things unseen in the hope that they might materialize, for perfect faith casts out all fear. Faith—when purified, when matured, when totally realized—is the same as complete forgiveness, the return to peace, and the *knowledge* that only Love is real.

Love, beloved friends, is the essence of all that you are. Love is the essence of *all* that dances as a temporary reflection before the eyes of your very body-mind. There is no one—nothing—you can look upon whose essence is *not* Love. There is *nothing* you can experience whose essence is not Love.

THE ONLY QUESTION

The only question, then, is:

> Are you willing to make the journey from fear to Love
> as you look upon any thing,
> as you experience any emotion?

For there can be nothing that obstructs from you the light and presence of your Creator. To perceive the real world of Love is to know with perfect certainty that you and your Father are one.

When you remember only your loving thoughts, Love is all that you will see. To "remember your loving thoughts" does not mean that as you look upon the past, you decide to ignore those thoughts that were less than loving. It means that, in truth, you never do look at the "past."

Rest assured, if you are having a memory *now*, you are having a very present experience. It is absolutely impossible to think about the past for thinking occurs *now*. You will look upon the past as you *choose to be* in the present.

If you are still carrying the effects of less than loving reactions and the perceptions you have made from them, you will continue to see the "past" as you always have.

Yet, as you look upon the past, if you will choose to be the presence of Love first—wanting only to see with the eyes of Christ—there will not be one event you have ever experienced as a soul that is not immediately translated into perfect harmlessness, into the perfect realization that only a dream has occurred.

For Love looks upon all things and sees that there is no substance to them, except the Love out of which those involved in that situation were longing to find a way to know the reality of themselves.

Listen carefully here: There is nothing you can experience that is anything but the soul's longing to be the perfection of what it is—Love. Everything—your tall skyscrapers, your busy freeways, your armies—is an expression of the longing of the soul, that spark of divinity that rests in all created things to know Love.

Has it become distorted? Oh, yes! To think that one can awaken to Love, to know Love, and to have Love by building weapons of destruction must be wholly insane. But the *longing* from which it arises is absolutely no different than the pacifist who would place a flower in the barrel of a rifle. It is no different than the mother who picks up and suckles her newborn son. The *longing* is one and the same!

This is why I have said often to you that what is not Love is fear and nothing else. Fear is merely the contraction that has occurred in the soul that has lost, temporarily, the sanity of knowing that it need not *seek* for Love, it need only *open* and *be* Love. For the attempt to seek Love only reveals that sanity is not ruling the domain and the dominion of your heart and soul and mind.

Any attempt to *get* is insane. Likewise, any attempt to *refrain* from receiving or giving is also insane. Getting and receiving are not the same. Giving to get is not true giving. Giving and receiving are one. For in either case, the heart must open, the defenses must be laid aside, and the soul becomes wholly vulnerable.

Yet, in the perfect paradox of the spiritual journey, when vulnerability is fully allowed through mastery of the keys to the Kingdom (desire, intention, allowance, and surrender), when this, indeed, is accomplished, Love is known. For in perfect vulnerability, the soul remembers its perfect invulnerability. The world can do nothing to the one who only loves.

Oh, indeed beloved friends, the beauty of every flower, the song of every bird that sings— these things are given to you, the holy Child of God. The sparkling waters, the vast expanse of the desert—these things are given to *you*. There is no creation that has within it the capacity that you, as a human being, possess.

Not even your whales and dolphins can truly experience and *realize* the presence and the mystery of the Creator. They flow in perfect innocence in creativity, in the Creator's Love, but their capacity to reflect, to know, and to embody *consciously* that which Love is, is not the same.

And those that would perceive that seeking out a whale, or a dolphin, or a wolf, or a bear, or a crow, or what have you, will add something to their own nature, are yet caught up in *projecting* onto another form of creation that which must be embraced in and for *oneself.*

For the body is the temple of the living Spirit, when it is seen through eyes that have awakened. Where you are is where Heaven is fully available. That which you are is the Love of God made manifest. And when you remember only your loving thoughts, that means that in the very present moment, you are re-membering, you are bringing the facets of yourself back into the wholeness of the realization that only Love is real.

For example, "Yes, my dog just died. Yes, my husband just left me." These are just the external forms bouncing about in the field of change. "But the essence has not left me, for I am free to love. I am free to make the energetic transition from one set of circumstances into the present moment. I am free in each moment not to abide in fear, not to abide in that great fear that I can't possibly survive because my teddy bear has been stolen."

And what are husbands, mates, careers, cars, and money in the bank if not the attempt of the little child within you to have and hold onto the "teddy bear" that you think can comfort you? Yet, the *Christ* within you can *love*!

In each moment that you seem to be confronted with the challenge that brings up within you your deepest fears of security, your deepest fears of "managing the estate"—the domain that you call your "life"—these things come not by accident. And they must come without ceasing in a world of unceasing change. For all that you look upon and say that you love that you perceive as a temporary form of creation, is already dying and dead to you.

There can be no peace in the world. But *you* can be the *embodiment* of peace when you look beyond all form and perceive the essence of all things as the *longing* for Love, the *longing* to remember.

When your spouse leaves you—no matter what they say—they are leaving you because they *long* for Love. Does this mean that you have failed them? Absolutely not! For that would mean that they are a victim of you. But you have heard me say to you many times: There is no cause, save that which arises within the field of the sovereignty of each soul. Love is always present, and there is no reason for staying or going. There is only reason to awaken to the voice for Love and to allow *it* to move *you*.

So in the world, peace cannot be found. For in the world, there is only the deep belief that Love is absent and must be sought, pursued and gotten—extracted—from the forms of creation, whether it be career, flower, ocean, desert, lover, mate or money.

The forms of the world contain no reality. By that, I mean that when you look at someone or something, and the energy of wanting to possess or extract runs you, you are already in insanity. Insanity is wholly illusory, which means any attempt to live from that energy can only fail.

Yet at the very same moment, the world awaits you in perfect transparency. Nothing can obstruct you. In the busiest of your malls, in the most horrendous traffic jam, there is nothing that is preventing you from choosing to remember only your loving thoughts.

There is nothing preventing you from choosing to look upon a brother or a sister and to see their perfect innocence, to see their unchanging essence, while allowing them *complete freedom* to journey as they must, until they elect to remember that essence within themselves, until they have chosen to learn to be the stillness of God's presence.

Stillness is not opposed to activity or movement. Rather, it pervades the very body-mind. There is a quality of stillness in the awakened that is ever attractive. Yet, the awakened are ceaselessly involved.

Why? Because they no longer resist the flow of this dream world, including the body-mind. They have reversed the thought structure of the world within themselves. The body-mind is no longer compelled by fear. Unobstructed, it serves but one purpose—the extension of Love.

Can you extend Love by restraining the energy of the body? No. Can you extend Love by holding on to rigid thoughts and beliefs about how relationship should be? No.

The only way then to remember Love, the only way to rest in the certainty of The Way of Knowing, is to come to the realization that what is not Love is fear, and only fear. In any moment—any moment of experience—regardless of what is occurring, where Love is not present within you as a known commodity, you are in fear.

We do not speak here of the emotion, or the wave of energy, that might be passing through the body when you walk around the corner on a hiking trail to behold a very angry mother grizzly bear who will protect her cubs by having you for breakfast. Those are just emotions passing through the body-mind part of the system that would help you to flee or to stay. Do not make the mistake of perceiving that as fear. It is just a biochemical, electrical impulse, programmed into the body-mind. For even the wise and enlightened will pay attention to that!

Yet, the wise and enlightened will look quickly and possibly say, "Perhaps this is my time. Go ahead, bear, eat me. Go ahead, crucify me." Or perhaps, that very same enlightened one will say, "Take me from the city. The crowds are too great. We must flee across the lake, for they would press upon me and eat me up if they can. It is not time. This is not the place."

Peace, then, is not passivity. Peace, the very state of Love, is a state in which *no experience* is obstructed within you. Do not make the mistake, as so many do, of thinking that experience has something to do with what is outside of the very body-mind. For remember, nothing is caused by a single event occurring beyond the boundary of the body-mind.

If two human beings come together—they may not know why, but for some reason their heart is open—they are walking around with a neon sign that says, "I just want to love and be loved. That is the only reality. I am a little tired of putting up a wall of resistance." They walk around the corner and oh, my goodness, the sparks fly! They say, "Oh! Love! This is it! It's the real thing! Oh, my God! Oh! How could this be? Oh, this *must* be a gift from God."

Nonsense! It is a gift from yourself. *You* are the one who chose in the depth of your being to finally become sane enough to allow the context for the experience of Love's sharing to be called to you. And guess what, it is occurring in your lover for the very same reason. Two souls have sent out the call and have come together in a field of space-time within the body-mind for a moment, in which each has said, "Yes!" to the possibility of remembering the purity of Love.

Love does not condemn, and Love does not judge. What is not Love is fear, and nothing else. Therefore, remember always that *no* act of love should ever be judged. For *each* act of love is to be cherished. Each *moment* of Love's presence and reality is to be cherished. Each *moment* in which a soul, two souls, three souls, ten souls, a country of souls, a universe of souls—it does not matter—makes the choice to drop the defenses, to open and gesture as the presence of Love—that act is to be *cherished*! For it is rare in the world.

Those that would seek to possess a mate, to create an exclusivity, are truly only expressing some subtle level of fear. Love denies not to anyone the perfect freedom that is the sovereignty and right of every soul. For you cannot know Love until you have set all beings free. You cannot know your Creator until you love as your Creator loves. And there is no one who is reading these words that does not long to know Love completely, to come home again.

COMING HOME TO LOVE

To "come home" means to know Love. And to know Love means that you can no longer tell where you end and the Creator begins. Such a one merely loves. Such a one rests in the perfect certainty of Love so deeply that the thought of restricting another's freedom cannot arise. Why would it? If your cup is truly overflowing, would you require another to place their half-filled glass before you, demanding that you need to possess their glass? Love allows all things. Love embraces all things. Love trusts all things, and thereby, immediately transcends all things.

If you would know Love, spend the next thirty days, in which each day without fail—remember it is wise to use time constructively—you spend some time with yourself and a piece of paper and a pencil, and truly look back over your past honestly. Where did you refuse to give total freedom to the ever-changing expressions of creation?

Have you ever judged a politician? In that very moment, you were refusing to extend perfect freedom, for judgment flows from fear and not from Love.

Were you ever in a relationship in which some part of you felt at least a little urge to try to convince the other that they do not really love that person they met in the supermarket, they really love just you? Have you ever, even politely for a moment, insinuated to another that their passion for anyone but you might be some sort of "biological abnormality," or certainly, they are being insane and need to sit down and do some serious thinking? All of that is fear, and nothing else.

For Love is satiated in its own being. Love overflows. The thought of possessing, controlling, or limiting can come only from one who feels emptiness. Love sets all things free. Love sets the world free to be as the world is. Love sees perfect harmlessness. Love sees that because things are as they are, they are as they are. Think well about that statement. Because things are as they are, the mind in perfect freedom lets them *be* as they are, and sees them as utterly harmless.

Love sees that the world that is shown to you through the body-mind—this world of buildings, automobiles, pollution, pristine beaches, desert expanses, towering trees, lakes, ponds, this world of torment in the mother whose child has just died, this world of torment in the heart of a child who has just buried their parent, this world of peace, this world that contains all possible expressions of consciousne*ss—this world is perfectly harmless.* This world that you experience *in this now moment* cannot add anything to you, and it can take nothing away.

In this *now* moment, where are you? Are you in Love in this moment? Did you just lose your job? And you think the problem that is disturbing your peace is that you have no job? That is not it.

What is disturbing your peace is that the loss of job has flushed up for you your deep identity with and as the body. You think the body must survive and continue, and perhaps you say, "Darn it, it has to do it in the same level of material comfort that I knew yesterday!"

Can you understand that when your love is so complete, it no longer matters if the body-mind exists tomorrow? For where would you go? You are but the field of Love itself. Your essence is unchanging forever. You are pure Spirit.

If you just lost your job, sit down and breathe and open the heart and decide to love your employer unto the death of your illusion. Then, open and receive all that is around you—the singing of the bird, the first rays of a new day's dawn, the grasses beneath your feet. Receive the field of infinite possibilities that has been thrown wide open for *you*. For that which passes away in your experience cannot do so by accident. It can only be occurring through the complicity or the agreement of the world around you with the soul within you. *Nothing arises by accident.*

And if you come home to discover that your child has died sleeping in her crib, feel indeed your feelings with great curiosity. Such as, "Oh, this is how a human being feels when they perceive that loss has occurred. I will bring Love to this moment and feel this as deeply as I can because I want to embrace it with reality."

Then look with gentleness upon that tiny form of lifelessness, and know that the soul who animated it for a brief moment has gone nowhere, except into the furtherance of their destiny and yours—always by *perfect agreement*. Not the kind of an agreement in which a child says, "Yes, Mom, yes, Dad, whatever you say," but the agreement of the perfect sovereignty of two unlimited souls.

You have heard me say before that the spiritual path cannot begin until a mind accepts complete responsibility for the entire field of its experience. This must include the comings and goings of all beings.

You will realize: "I called them in, I called to them and asked them to leave me. I wonder why I did that? Oh, God, here's this feeling again. I'm all alone. I've been abandoned. That's why they've had to leave me. For I *must* heal this ridiculous belief that I have been abandoned. I must overcome all separation. I must awaken beyond the dream of the dreamer."

Nothing you create can arise by accident. And everything you experience calls you to the field of unchanging and perfect Love that transcends, supersedes, and underlies all that arises and passes away.

THE DECISION TO TEACH ONLY LOVE

Love is the most critical of themes, beloved friends. The Way of Knowing must be the completion of the decision to teach only love. And the only way to teach love is to *be* Love under all circumstances.

This does not mean that you paint a plastic smile on your face and never feel any emotion. That is not enlightenment. That is the height of the ego's attempt to usurp power from God. The spiritual ego, the spiritual personality is the last "egg" to be cracked.

One is only awakened when one allows all things, trusts all things and embraces all things, which is the same as feels all things. For in that very moment, the very thing arising is transcended because it is not obstructed or resisted. And what is not obstructed or resisted is embraced and *consumed* in the spaciousness of Love.

You have within yourself, then, all power under Heaven and Earth to translate the body itself from a contraction of fear to a spaciousness that reflects the reality of God's Love. For the very body-mind that emerged first from fear can be reopened so that the energy of truth flows through it. So that nothing arising in your experience in the emotional field obstructs the remembrance of Love.

Quite frankly, the emotional field is the *only* place you can experience anything. All the rest are merely thoughts *about* things. The gap between a thought *about* things and the feeling nature of *experiencing* things is exactly the same gap that exists between illusion and Heaven.

It is for this reason that no *idea* of God is the same as God. No concept *about* love is the same as Love. No *philosophy* about enlightenment is the same as enlightenment. Unobstructed feeling embraces all that arises and passes away. Unobstructed means without judgment. Even that which arises as fear or anger should never be judged or obstructed. That which arises as sadness or joy, that which arises as the passion of the body, all things must be opened to and embraced. Or the beingness of your soul has not yet transcended the world.

Love is the ability to be wholly present with what is, devouring it like a child devours candy: "Umm! Give me another bite. For this dream cannot contain me. Therefore, bring it on!"

EXERCISES TO AWAKEN IN LOVE

Beloved friends, if you would truly use this teaching of The Way of Knowing as the time in which you awaken into the decision to be the presence of Love and nothing else, so that you can move into the rest of your experience *as* the enlightened Christ that you already are, look well in each of the next thirty days:

> Where in my life have I refrained from love?

> Where have I chosen behavioral patterns and decisions and choices with a smile on my face, while all the time attempting to control and manipulate the world in order to keep me safe from feeling and facing my own insecurities?

> Where have I demanded that the world show up in a certain way so that I can pretend to have peace, and pretend to be happy and loving?

Anyone can be happy and loving in a candy store. Anyone can be happy standing in front of a crowd when everyone is applauding you. Anyone can be happy being held by twenty friends who say they love you. But only the enlightened can be happy when those twenty friends have chosen to crucify you.

Therefore, indeed, it is in your darkest moments, it is in the crumbling of the structures you have made, where you are best given the opportunity to realize the great power within you to teach only Love.

Yet, the ego would convince you that to know love, you must set up your world so that you never experience the challenges and the insecurities of abandonment, aloneness, and not-knowingness—the kind of insecurity one might feel when they know not where their next meal comes from. The attempt to create material security flows only from the egoic mind. *For the enlightened mind is in complete abundance, always.*

When I walked this world as a man and was taught by the Essenes, I and my brothers and sisters learned to practice a way of life that was also known in other cultures in ancient India. A conscious decision was made to give up all materiality and to walk, literally, naked in the world—owning nothing, possessing nothing—facing the stark reality of the body's perfect vulnerability, relying on the expressions of grace and love through others. We would walk around with a begging bowl and simply say, "The body-mind is hungry. Would you be so kind as to fill my bowl?" And receive the "yes" or "no" with the *very same* appreciation.

Many of you have no idea what it means to be hungry. You think hunger is that temporary gnawing that occurs because you have not gone to your refrigerator in the last few hours. Go and abide in the forest with nothing to eat. Take nothing with you but perhaps some water, and abide alone, open to the elements for three days and three nights. Then, you will know something of what it means to be an Essene, to be one who goes without any attempt to protect the body-mind from the deepest fears of its own demise.

Once a rich man came unto me, and asked me to teach him. And I simply replied, "Go and sell all that you have and follow me." He did not want God *that* much.

Of course, as I have said unto you many times, it does not mean you must go and give away your material wealth that you have in your world. It does mean you must give away your *attachment to it*. You must see that it is merely an illusion, which cannot provide you the safety that you truly seek. For safety can come only in reclining in the Heart of God:

> The body-mind is not even mine.
> The mate is not mine.
> The career is not mine.
> The bank accounts are not mine.
>
> These things of the world cannot keep my soul safe.
> They cannot awaken me.
>
> Only my decision to surrender the world,
> to transcend the world, to abide as empty in the world,
> only my decision to teach only Love can awaken me to
> the invulnerability beyond the vulnerability of all created things—
> even this very body-mind that I once mistakenly identified with as my self.

The truly awakened come and go as the wind. You know not from whence they have come, and you know not where they are going. For they do not even know these things. How can you? But they listen to the voice of Spirit. And Spirit is like the whisper of the wind, that says, "Come. Go. Touch. Speak. Refrain. Leave. Abstain. Embrace. Eat. Fast. Pray. Dance."

The one who abides in unobstructed feeling nature flows with that which comes from the depth of a perfectly still heart and mind, and dances while knowing stillness. For the body-mind that others see is no longer inhabited by the contraction of the ego. The enlightened cannot be understood. They can only be appreciated by the enlightened.

Who, then, will you choose to be this day, beloved friends—one who walks in the ordinary world, or one who walks in Heaven, side by side with their Creator? Will you walk this day in the world as one who has everything figured out, or will you walk as one who in perfect innocence merely loves and laughs and chuckles within at the great illusion of the drama of this world?

For this world arises and passes away in the twinkling of an eye. It is merely like dots on a screen that have created a temporary movie. Once the movie plays out, the screen remains as it has always been, until the next movie comes to town.

Your consciousness is like that screen. It witnesses that which arises and passes away, even within the body-mind itself. Identify with that pure screen, the pure witness, the spaciousness that is wider than all universes. Notice that part of you that is simply aware of what is arising—a feeling, a thought, a word, a song heard, a car crash witnessed. It does not matter.

Anything arising in the field of your experience arises in the field of this spaciousness of awareness that is God's gift to you as your very *existence*. For pure Spirit is awareness itself. And that awareness can be fueled by the decision for Love or the belief in fear.

Beloved friends, if you have truly chosen to enact The Way of Knowing, do not waste time. Look well over the next thirty days; look deeply at the truth of what has been running you.

What are the patterns that created the choices, the reactions, the responses, the rationalizations, the great words, the great seeking, the great striving—all of it! Look well and perceive and know that which was birthed from fear, no matter what it looked like. For indeed, the wolf can come in sheep's clothing.

Where have you been a ravenous wolf coming in sheep's clothing with false smiles in order to get another to give you what you believe you lack? Where have you refrained from love? Where have you refused to become perfectly vulnerable? For it is only on the other side of that decision that your perfect *in*vulnerability arises.

You are Love and nothing else. In any moment that you behave, speak, or perceive yourself to be other than Love, *you* have used the power of your awareness to decide for what would attempt to stand against the Kingdom of God. And *you* are the one that has suffered for it.

Love, beloved friends. So many of you that have read my words look upon me with *such* great love. You look upon me and say, "Oh, Jeshua. He just loves so perfectly!" Well, of course I do! Because I have come to see that there is not anything else *worth doing*! I know that sounds almost simplified, but the Truth *is* simple.

You must come in your own Christed nature to see that in perfect innocence there is not anything else to do but love. To love without limits, to love without fear, to love by extending perfect freedom to all of creation to be and do what it wants to be and do.

Then, and only then, can you know that nothing can betray you, nothing can hurt you, and nothing can bring anything to you or take anything away. *You* have the infinite and perfect freedom to love! And in *that decision*, you know your Creator and can say quite simply with me:

> Behold! I and my Father are one and the same!
> Now, let me give you a hug. Now let me set you free to have your experience. Now let me watch this great movie. Now let me enjoy my salad.

It is all so very simple!

Never identify yourself with your *doing*, but let your *doing* be infused by your *being*. For while you are in the world, the body-mind will *do*. Its very nature is action and activity itself, just like it is the nature of a leaf in autumn to fall from a tree to the ground. Would you say, "Oh! Well, that shouldn't have happened! The leaf shouldn't have had to die. It shouldn't have had to change colors. Oh, what's wrong with this universe?"

You are like a leaf on the tree. And you are already falling to the moment of your death. How much more time will you waste before you decide to break through the chains of fear held in the very tissues of the body-mind? How much longer will you wait to enjoy the dance of the fall from the branch of birth to the ground of death of the body-mind in order to experience the total freedom of the fall?

For the great fall from grace, the great dream of the dream of separation must finally be embraced and lived with perfect Love, obstructing nothing, knowing that the very momentary experience of the body-mind in a perfectly insane world is all right because it is illusion. To resist illusion is to insist that the illusion is real. It is only in the full *embrace* of an illusion that the illusion *dissolves* before your eyes. *Love sets all things free again.*

Over the next thirty days, do only this: Dedicate and commit each moment of each day to teaching only Love. Take upon yourself the commitment to discipline the mind and the heart, *while* opening the body without obstruction. In each moment, set all beings free by being only committed to Love. See how much joy you can experience by being the lover of all Life.

Want nothing from no one. Need nothing from any one. Express your passion. Express your longing. Look upon the falling leaves, if they are happening in your neighborhood. Wherever you are, look upon all things and decide to love the hell out of it. For the hell in it is only what you have projected upon it. Take back your projection and embrace it with love.

For thirty days, you can do it! For thirty days—such a small time frame in one human life! Would you not give yourself permission for thirty days? This is not a difficult assignment! Anyone with any degree of intelligence and maturity can *surely* decide each morning, for one day, to teach only Love and string thirty of them together!

If it is, in truth, the transformation of your soul that you seek, so that only Christ is present where you are, complete this one assignment. And when it is done, simply do it again, and again, and again—worlds without end.

Heaven awaits you. Love waits on your welcome. Yet, that welcome is but the decision to finally *embrace yourself* and to live the Truth that has already set you free. Love and give all things complete freedom to be and to do as they will. For there is no other doorway to the perfect freedom that you have sought for oh, such a long, long time! Let time end, that eternity might be remembered. Only Love can set you free.

And indeed, with that, beloved friends, peace be unto you always. For indeed, it is dripping through the ethers of your very atmosphere, waiting for you to drink it in. Peace be with you always. Amen.

LESSON 33
THERE IS ONLY GOD AND YOU ARE THAT

Beloved and holy friends, as always, I come forth to abide with you because you have asked. As always, I come forth to abide with you because in truth, there is nowhere else that I could be. For where you are, I am. And where I am, you are. We abide, then, as the one Mind, birthed from the very Heart of Abba, or God. There is nothing outside of us. And from within, there is nothing hidden. Though the dimensions of creation are infinite, they abide within the Mind, or the field of consciousness, that we share as one.

THE SIMPLE TRUTH

Because this is true, and I assure you that it is, there is only one task that must be accomplished, one realization that must be realized, one reality to be expressed and lived. That simple truth is that there is only One, that there is only Heaven, that there is only Love, and that there is only the perfect peace that passes all understanding that keeps your hearts *in Mind*.

For your heart or your soul—that which is all that you have experienced throughout the multitude of your lifetimes upon this tiny planet, all of the experiences that you have garnered since before the beginning of time throughout all of the multitude of dimensions—resides within the Mind of God, within the Mind of Christ. For these are one and the same.

Therefore, beloved friends, know always that the only truth that must be lived, as you enter into the firm commitment of *choice* to abide in The Way of Knowing, is simply that there is only one thing. You are that One. Your brother and your sister are that One. And though bodies come and go, though time seems to arise and pass away, though the dance of relationship, of career, of weather patterns, seems to come and go, it is only the unenlightened mind that looks for great signs in these things.

In truth, within the field of your soul, within the entire field of experiences that you call to yourself, the same gift is being offered. The gift is offered to you that by grace you might decide to see that the world of ever-changing form means nothing—*the world means nothing.* It does not, nor has it ever existed, except in the perceptions conjured up within the field of mind that seems to be particularly related to your soul. Now even that is a bit of an illusion.

But the point is simply this: In The Way of Knowing, there is a quiet decision to accept the Truth that is true always, to surrender, to open the palms of the hands and to release the tight grip upon the value, the meaning, and the rightness of the perceptions you have made to veil Reality. You are that Reality. All things are that Reality.

The forms that the physical eyes show you arise and pass away. Yet, in each moment, Mind remains perfectly clear, perfectly One. Only the *spell of the mind*, that believes itself to be the body creates suffering, creates doubt, creates illusion.

Wherever you are, then, in this very moment, *you* can only be where, in truth, *I* am. Wherever I seem to be in this moment, *I* can only be where *you* are. For indeed, in The Way of Knowing, what must come to be released is the mistaken perception that there is, or has ever been, a *separate I* that is localized where the body-mind is.

To release this illusion is to see that all things are simply one thing. They appear in different forms—automobiles, plants, trees, clouds, thoughts arising and passing away—but they are but one thing.

Because an enlightened mind no longer sees the veil of the *false I* standing between itself as a filter and its recognition of its union with—its identity with—all things arising and passing away, such a mind looks out upon a transfigured world, a world in which the veil has been lifted. And that mind sees only itself. It sees that the very things it had been judging as imperfect, as it looked out upon the world—that it had been judging through fear, that it had been judging through self-doubt—that those very things of themselves are perfect and that they are, indeed, the Kingdom of Heaven.

This is why the distance between where you are and where I am, indeed, is a distance that cannot be measured. For in Reality, there is no gap. In Reality, separation does not exist. In Reality, your fall from grace and your movement into unenlightenment itself has been but an illusion.

The very life you have been living is *absolutely perfect.* The life you are living now is *absolutely perfect.* And it has not anything at all to do with where the body-mind goes. It has nothing to do with whether you watch a movie or read a book, whether you make money or do not, whether the body-mind lives or dies. The life you have been living is the life of awareness, of consciousness, of perfect freedom to create whatever perception you choose to hold.

You are free, then, in all moments, to see that what has been arising as the Life of your very Self *is* the Life and Mind of God.

A mind so awakened looks out and sees that there are no problems. Such a mind looks out upon the world and sees no reason to change it, for it is now looking at a world that has already been healed, already been transfigured, already—through alchemical fires—been purified and made whole again. For in reality, it sees that that wholeness was never once lost. The dream of separation occurs within a space of mind that is nowhere, which holds no value and no purpose.

Fear, then, has no power over you. Death has no power over you. You abide in the only place ever created for you. You are not localized to the body or the particular personality that you have associated with as your "I." That in itself is part of the spell, or the drama or the dream of separation.

In The Way of Knowing, there is a simple and quiet decision to behold that as the body-mind plays itself out—as the coming and going of all forms *around* you and *within* you, as your own unique perceptual field changes and dances and ebbs and flows, as all of these things that seem to be within you in your private world (and that is a bit of a misnomer) and in your external world (that you think is yours and not someone else's)—all of these things are innocent, harmless. They hold no power. There is no Reality in them.

Yet, they are Reality itself, when seen through eyes that are not identified with the *false I*, with the localized sense of identity. Even the body-mind, that you once called your "self," is merely seen to arise and pass away in the vast expanse of your true Self, the Self that is shared by all beings in all dimensions—always.

It was this understanding that allowed me to simply choose to give myself over to what was called the crucifixion. An enlightened consciousness knows that loss is impossible. An enlightened consciousness knows that gain is also impossible. Yet, an enlightened consciousness resting in the certainty of perfect knowing, merely abides in Reality.

That means there is no resistance to the coming and going of the body, no resistance to the grand display of energies that make up what you call your world. Governments rise and fall or a new model automobile is unveiled to the flash of a thousand camera bulbs. Some minds take it as being a very serious thing, some do not even notice. And *all* of it is *you*! All of it is arising in the vast expanse of the perfectly free Mind that belongs to no one, and yet, in which, all ones arise.

An enlightened mind, then, whether it is experiencing sadness, joy, anger, guilt, hurt, ecstasy, lovemaking, a piece of fruit, or cold wind on the skin temporarily in the body-mind, merely allows all of these things without resistance to be exactly what they are, while that mind perceives and knows them to be harmless, vast, eternal, radiating the Light that God is.

As we near the end of the study of The Way of Knowing, the truth must be told ever more simply and ever more simply. There is only Reality. That Reality I have called God. That One is one with me. And I am that One. That One is one with you. And you are that One.

In the end, then, what seems to be radical to a world caught in the spell of the small self, seemingly playing its drama out through the field of many, many body-minds, the truth does, indeed, become radical. The truth is that all that arises and passes away is, indeed, God. There is only God. There can only be God. And you are that One. For in the end, even the creative teaching device of God and child, Creator and created begins to slip away, as duality becomes the One, as illusion—the last traces of illusion—finally give way to Truth.

All things that arise and pass away are perfectly okay. All opportunities to experience the awareness of Love's presence are okay. Every opportunity to experience the contraction of fear is okay. For these things arise only in the field of the perfectly free Mind of God that you are.

So in the end, it is not so much about cutting out certain experiences and having only certain ones that you have decided hold value. It is, rather, to see that *all* such experiences are transitory. A moment of ecstasy or a moment of sadness is *one and the same* for the enlightened mind. There is only that vast expanse that allows all things.

And when *nothing* is any longer unacceptable to you, in the field of what seems to be your own unique, particular experience, you will know that you are home. Things arise and pass away, and you remain.

Beloved friends, I am indeed that One that birthed Christ. I am indeed that One that walked this Earth as a man and manifested the fullness of my Self, to reveal my Self to my Self. You are that One that birthed Jeshua ben Joseph. You are that One that set in motion the great drama of the dream of separation and its correction. You are indeed that One, which alone exists unchanging, unchangeable, and unchanged forever.

And yet, when the mind has been under the spell of thoroughly believing it is a separate body-mind, and that the body is the source of the "spell" that creates the illusion of a localized, separate self, a soul that has no connection to anyone else or anything else, it has forgotten the Truth.

In the field of the body-mind, if I were to have come to you three, four, five, ten, or two thousand years ago and said, "You are, alone, that One. You are God and only God exists," your fear, already present, would have been heightened. And so I came to you in the guise of a man known as Jeshua ben Joseph. I played out a perfectly clear drama, like so many body-minds. I allowed myself to be perceived as a unique individual, since *you* believed that unique individuals exist.

You saw me as separate from you. So I appeared in the way that you could see me and understand me. And I have gone on, without ceasing, to appear in ways that you can see me and understand me, to speak in languages and words, metaphors and parables, teaching tools that you could receive without increasing your illusion of fear. Even the appearance of myself as Jeshua ben Joseph was but a teaching device, a temporary teaching tool.

All teaching and communication devices have one, simple goal: to reduce fear so that that particular mind can release its grip on itself and surrender the illusion of separation. And thereby, be bathed in the Light of Reality yet again, seeing that God is *what* I am. I am God. You are God. Only that One exists. Only the "I" that we share as the One exists.

I appear as every blade of grass. I appear as every thought. I appear as every desire. I appear as every cloud in the sky. I appear as you. You *are* That One that I am. I am speaking to you, and yet, you are speaking to you. You hear me, but you hear only your Self.

Understand well, then, that I, as Jeshua ben Joseph, am but the appearance of God in a particular form, so that you could come closer to the truth of your nature without recoiling in fear. It is, indeed, said in the Bible that, "No man looks upon the face of God and lives." That statement means simply that the mind that is not yet enlightened, therefore, living in fear, living in the perception of itself being separate from God, cannot look upon the face of God, the reality of God, and *live.*

It was not a fearful statement at all. It was simply the truth. For when the mind looks and beholds, "There is only God and I am That One," the false self has, indeed, died. Where did it go? Nowhere. Because it *never existed* in the first place.

THE DECISION THAT CLOSES THE GAP

That which closes the gap, though it may be said to you in many forms, is the *decision* to give up seeking and acknowledge that you have found.

All teaching devices, all forms of language that I have brought forth have been by design to woo you, to seduce you, to calm you into knowing that you are God. The final gap then—indeed, the final step—is taken by me. And that final step taken by me is the final step taken by you. For that final step into the fullness of enlightenment can only be God recognizing that only God is. And you are That One.

Where else could we come to in a series of lessons entitled, The Way of Knowing? It was never intended to be a set of lessons that will *someday* get you there, but rather the very *way* of knowing to walk the journey of creation, *knowing* that it is God doing the walking. And to walk in the knowingness that all things that arise here are in God, and you are that One. And to finally be willing to look at a tree and know that the eye of God is seeing God, and the tree of God is being eyed by God.

You are, indeed, that One, infinite, eternal, unbounded, so intimately linked with every one of your brothers and sisters that there is no such separation, nor anything to fear. And there is yet this infinitely magical process in which the Mind is realized within a body-mind.

That is, you can be perfectly enlightened now, by simply seeing the truth that the thought you have held of yourself has never been true. It was only a temporary spell—God forgetting, God playing to be other than God. And yet, that play is the very fullness of God. For in the end, the "fall from grace," the separation from union, that very thing itself, cannot be outside the Mind of God.

All that your eyes show you is innocent and free. All that the mind can conjure as thought is innocent and free. You are free to be that one who has the Mind of Christ—which is God—and shows up in the transfigured body-mind. Where once there was a false sense of "I," now there is only the free, unobstructed field of awareness of God observing creation *through* His creation—God observing His creation *through* His creation.

Imagine, then, that you are, indeed, that One, and *you* choose to pick up a particular body-mind that everyone *thought* was called Fred or Nancy or Harry or what have you. You put on the body-mind for the simple enjoyment of looking out through it to observe what creation is like from that perspective. Not unlike one who would go to a costume ball, puts on a certain costume just to play at being Louie the Fourteenth or Lady Godiva, or Mother Mary. Or if you want to be very radical, Jesus of Nazareth.

You have already put on all of those costumes. You are the creator of all of those costumes. You are God. There is *only* God. There can only *be* God. And as you read the words, which produce insights and pictures that are flowing through the field of the mind, the "you" who is reading and the "I" who is speaking are all *one thing*: God.

Fear not, beloved friends. Fear not the coming and going of the life of the body-mind. For that life in itself is already perfectly unobstructed and free. It cannot hinder the Truth of who you are when you choose to see from the truth of what you are. As we begin to conclude this study of The Way of Knowing, dare to live the "impossible dream." Dare to begin to see that you are God, perceiving, looking out upon God's creation. And God's creation is only God!

Yes, in the end, you can even say that God has created nothing. For nothing can be *outside* of what God is. I have given unto you many clues throughout these lessons. I have told you that if God forgot to think about you for one moment, you would cease to be. Think about what that must mean.

It *must* mean that you are inhering so much in God that a simple thought in the Mind of God either creates you or destroys you. In the flash of an eye, you are either in existence or you are not.

Yet, what could be in existence but the will of God? If you *exist*, you *must be* in the Mind of God—that perfect power by which all things arise and pass away.

God's creation occurs nowhere. That is, it has no location. The planet Earth, the bodies that inhabit it, the physical universe in which the planet Earth is spinning about—all of these things are not at all unlike what you experience when you close your eyes and imagine having ice cream. You create the image. You have the experience. You see yourself giving the cashier your money. You eat the ice cream. You see yourself smile. You can feel it move down into your belly. Where did all of that exist? Could anybody find it outside the power of consciousness to create? No.

You are like the ice cream in the Mind of God. God sees Itself, appearing as you, doing exactly what you are doing in each and every moment. If God, for one split second, dropped the thought of you, you would entirely disappear. And all of those beings around you, who you think are different people, would instantly have no recollection of you whatsoever.

REALIZING ALL POWER IN HEAVEN AND EARTH RESIDES WITHIN YOU

There can only be God. You are God's dream. You are God's creation. You are God's child, in the sense that you are God shaping Herself into a temporary expression of Herself. And for what purpose? To simply extend creation. You *are* that One! *All power in Heaven and Earth resides within you*! When you bend to pick up a glass, God is embracing God! And if God were not choosing that, in that moment, you would cease to be. Even the body would vanish from view.

As Jeshua ben Joseph, then, I have appeared to you to be your brother and friend, because *you* have believed that you needed some *one* to be a brother and friend, who will let you know that you are safe so that you can give yourself permission to nod your head "yes," and say, "I can accept that now. Thank you for being here, Jeshua." Yet, in truth, you are God merely playing out that field of relationship, the quality of experience that seems to require an elder brother who has gone through quite a change and now has the voice of authority.

But I have no voice unless you give it to me. And what can give such authority, if not the Mind of God? For it takes One to know One. You have heard me say that many, many times. It can only be the Christ Mind *in you* that could perceive the Christ Mind in Jeshua ben

Joseph. And the Christ Mind *is* the extension of God's perfect being into, and as, creation.

When you look lovingly upon anyone, *you are God*. For God is but Love. You have also heard me say many times, Love is the essence of what you are. If God is Love, and Love is the essence of what you are, this can only mean that the essence of *you is* God—right here, right now, with not one thing that must be done to earn it, to shape it, to get it.

This is why no form of technique brings the son to the Father. This is why I once said in *The Jeshua Letters* that no prayer or supplication brings the son to the Father, but only the release of illusion. And that illusion, when you have peeled it all down in the way you have insisted on peeling it down, is to come to see that the notion you have held of your self, as having a separate existence, being a separate "I," has been false. It is a smoke screen, a guise, a veil. Your perception or belief that that is what you were, as opposed to being everything else, is the illusion that must be released.

CHOOSING TO DECREE THAT ONLY GOD EXISTS

In The Way of Knowing, what I am offering to you as indeed your Creator, and the essence of all that you are, is the opportunity to choose this context to decree that only God exists. To choose that the very body-mind and the self you once thought you were is now embodied, inhabited by the Creator Itself. That when the hand moves to pick up the glass, it is no longer 'I,' but God, it is no longer "me," as a separate struggling being, but God who *moves* the hand. It is God who is *aging* the hand, and God who is *the aging of* the hand. All things can only be That which I Am. I am One and singular and whole.

The Creator says, "You should have no other gods before Me, no other thoughts or illusions before Me, not even a sense of an 'I' going to God." Then there is only God. And Reality has descended to make its home in the field of awareness where once you thought there was something else.

We created The Way of the Heart to begin to speak in such a way to you that would not elicit fear, to which you could nod your head and say, "Yes, yes. That sounds true to me. I'll accept this."

Then we spoke to you of The Way of Transformation, where you perceived yourself as one in *need* of transformation. Again, you nodded your heads and said, "We'll accept this. Yes, I am still in need of transformation. I'll buy into this as the context in which I receive more of the truth about myself."

And now in The Way of Knowing, we begin to bring you full force into that which you have chosen to bring yourself to—to stand at the doorway of the temple of Heaven, to begin to open it, to let the golden light stream out.

As you look into that sanctuary to see, it is *yourself* upon the throne. This is why I have also said that Self-love, the simplicity of Self-love, is that doorway that brings about the release of illusion. This does not mean that you just hang out in a state of consciousness that says, "Well, I'm really kind of a weak being, but I accept and love myself." That is a good beginning. But eventually you must say:

> I am God and I love myself.
>
> I am that One abiding as the leaf that falls from the tree.
> I am, indeed, that One that shudders against the cold of a winter storm.
> I am, indeed, that One that is the warmth of the sunlight that comes to
> caress the flower. I am the flower that receives the sunlight.
> I am this body-mind arising and passing away.
>
> I am the quality of awareness that I choose, now!

For there is only God. Only the Truth can be true. And the Truth sets *all things* free. For if Truth is given only to humankind, but not to a blade of grass, the blade of grass remains imprisoned. But the Truth that sets all things free does so because all things are the Truth.

This is why, when you encounter *anyone*, it is, indeed, a *holy* encounter. "Holy" means wholeness. In wholeness there is only One.

I hope you are beginning to see how simple it really is. Each moment of relationship is "holy," not because the mind decides to hold the thought, "Well, I heard this was holy. I guess I better be a nice person." No! That is egoic thinking, and the ego *is* the dream of separation. Who is dreaming the dream? You are. And *you are God*.

Each relationship or each moment is a "holy encounter" because there is only *wholeness* showing up as that One thing. Existence is not really two beings coming together and having an experience. There is only the One thing, which is the experience itself.

Do you know that all along you have never forgotten me for a moment? That is, in any moment of true perception—true, clear, immediate perception—you have been unaware of the thought of an "I" having the experience. There is just the experience itself. It arises innocently. It arises uncaused. There is no judgment about it. There is just experience.

Then in the next millisecond, the next slight moment, you create the thought, "Oh! I am having this experience and it's with that separate being over there." You have merely elected to use the power of God consciousness to identify that another body-mind is something separate from you. You are the creator of the game. You are the players in the game. You are the result and consequences of the game. You are the end of the game. And you are that in which all games disappear as though they had never been.

Beloved friends, look around you. This means the world is not outside of you at all. It *is* you. You are playing a game. That game is going to take this very planet into a transfiguration in light. And you will all be transformed in the twinkling of an eye.

Well, of course you will be. You are God making up the game. That is all that is going on. That is all that has ever been going on. There is only That which I Am. There is only That which I Am. I Am, indeed, that perfect impersonal I. I Am the creator of all things, the sustainer of all things, the destroyer of all things.

There has never been a separate "I" where you are. There has only been me, showing up as you. You are perfect and whole, and you are innocent. You have never failed and you have never sinned. How could these things be, that I have spoken to you time and time again as Jeshua ben Joseph, unless you are already whole? And wholeness is God. You are *it*. You are the destination of all you are seeking.

In the beginning, the Mind—which is me, which is God, pretending to be separate—plays itself out and tries to make itself be as separate as it thinks it can be. But separation *never* succeeds. The first step in the awakening process is to *hear the word*. You will hear the word when you decide, as God, to have the experience of being a being awakening to the Truth.

Everyone reading these words has, indeed, heard the word. And the word will be given unto you in a form that you choose. Everyone reading this *The Way of Mastery* chose to hear the word through me, as Jeshua ben Joseph.

That vibration received by you set you on your course toward perfect remembrance and enlightenment. You are the One that created the drama of the crucifixion. You are the One that set in motion the return of Jeshua ben Joseph as the primary teacher in this world. Why? Because you are that One that has decreed that it is this context in which you will give yourself permission to edge ever closer to the reality that the whole thing is God, and *you are That*.

What has been playing out, then, for these past thirty-three lessons, and even longer than that—indeed, been playing out for 2,000 years—is your creation. It is the game of God, remembering God, through the guise of God's creation.

As you come, then, to accept a savior or a teacher or a teaching, that is a stage in the awakening process. And when you decide to release your grip of fear a little deeper, you begin to have what are called mystical experiences. You begin to realize that you can be aware of someone else, not in the room with you physically. You begin to have unique and extraordinary experiences of communicating with beings that do not have bodies. And oh, my goodness, it all looks to be so incredible! Yet, even that is but a stage of the journey.

OPENING THE DOOR TO THE TEMPLE OF HEAVEN

As the mind becomes more and more transparent to itself, the more it is simply choosing to release illusion and abide in Reality. It *must come* to the door of the temple of Heaven. It must open that door, which is to release any final sense of being outside the sanctuary of Truth.

It must come to bask in the Light that flows from the Source and essence of *All That Is*. The separate seeker, the one who would know God, realizes that they already know God perfectly. And that they have indeed been God, seeking God, for the enjoyment of finding and knowing God again.

Yes, that is your challenge now. Would you be willing to simply be God? Do you know what that requires? Absolutely nothing. How then, do you show up as God? If you are thirsty, drink your water. If it is cold, put a sweater on. If you want to make love, make love. If you want to sleep, sleep. There is no difficulty in this. The only practice is to be that which you are, and you are the Light of the world.

How many times have you heard me say that to you? Be that which you are. And you are the Light of the world. You have heard the words and said, "Oh, now if I could only be who I am, then I'd be the light of the world. But I'm not being who I am, so I must be the darkness of the world." But the whole time, you are, indeed, being who you are.

You are the light that lights the world. For in being whatever you have chosen to be at any moment, *you* are that which generates awareness of experience. And that is all that we are as the Mind of God—that which generates experience—for experience is the extension of creation.

You have not failed in separating your self from your Self. You have not succeeded in shaking the hand off of your own arm. The joke has been on you, because you wanted to be "joked." *In each moment of your existence, you have been the perfect expression of God*. Even in the moments of your deepest so-called suffering, when you believed that everybody else had it and you did not, when you perceived yourself as being light-years from knowing God, you were the very power of God creating that perception.

You are also that One who has dared to be bold enough to allow Shanti Christo into your life—a rather radical organization. You created it as the context for your awakening. And you are free to use that context, that organization, to enlighten the entire planet if you want to. You are also free to let it crumble into an ancient echo of memory. There is only God, and you are That.

God extends creation without ceasing. You will, therefore, always continue to exist as the One who creates experience. This is why there is only one question worth asking:

What do I truly want?

For you will experience the answer to that question. And, in fact, your experience *is* the answer to the question. You can lay in bed with the flu and ask yourself the question, "What do I truly want? Well, this body-mind has the flu. I am experiencing exactly what I have wanted." And you can embrace it and love it, and see it as perfectly innocent because that is the truth of it. Having the flu is not a sign of failure. The death of the body is not a sign of failure. It is just what is arising as the extension of creation.

So, the final and greatest truth that can be told sounds like complete nonsense! It is unacceptable to the egoic mind that wants the power of making the false, separate self all-powerful and invincible, standing against the world—in other words, the gnat shouting at the universe. For the mind that is awakened to the Reality of God allows all things, trusts all things, embraces all things, transcends all things, and sees the shimmering perfection literally showing up as all things.

You are perfectly free in every moment. Nothing can imprison God. If you choose to leave a relationship, you are merely using the complete freedom of God to generate experience. If you choose to stay in a relationship, you are merely using the freedom of God to generate experience. Neither is right. Neither is wrong. Both options are totally free and uncaused. And each expresses God. It is, indeed, time to give up perceiving some things as being more perfect than others. There is only God. There has only been God. There will always be only God.

When a wave is cast up out of the ocean, it does not lose its wetness. And who would say that this wave is better than that wave? Yet, I say unto you, the mind that chooses one wave over the other *is* the Mind of God creating creation. For in the very moment when one wave is chosen as having a greater value, experience has been had. And experience is the extension of creation.

You, therefore, are a creator. And you create without ceasing. You remain, today, exactly as you were when you were created by your Self. You remain free to create whatever you want to perceive. And you do it from within the mind and you extend it out, you radiate it out, with every thought you think.

When an enlightened master shows up on the planet, it is simply that God has given up playing the game of the separate self through that body-mind. That is all. An enlightened mind realizes that there is only God. And that in that freedom, it is free to show up as the body-mind in whatever way it wants, while the body-mind lasts.

Whether it shows up with saffron robes or a beggar's worn-out clothing makes no difference. An enlightened mind is an enlightened mind. It might smoke a cigarette. It might drink carrot juice. It becomes irrelevant. And the one smoking the cigarette looks at the one drinking the carrot juice and smiles. The one drinking the carrot juice looks at the one smoking the cigarette and smiles. And in that smile, there is only the One, beholding the One.

You, then, are free to be at peace. You are free to release all judgment. You are, indeed, free to give yourself the exquisite experience of being the One who allows all things. You are the One who is free to embrace the innocence of each moment. You are the One who is free to require sunglasses against the morning sunrise. You are the One who is free to be *free*. And to be free is to be authentic. And to be authentic is to *demonstrate* the Reality that only God exists.

There is only God. Though it seems that you are receiving information outside yourself, yet I say unto you, you have received information only from your Self—God. Only the Mind of God exists. And you are God choosing to remember that you are God.

If you would go back and read *The Jeshua Letters,* not all of those communications were from the perspective of Jeshua ben Joseph. There was also direct communication from the Mind of God, given as a clear and obvious sign unto you. Things were said even in that book that revealed the Truth that there is only God. If you looked past it and did not see it, it is because you still thought it would be too fearful for you to know the Truth that sets you free. You needed to perceive there was an individual who had an experience opening to Jeshua ben Joseph and you were receiving information through the medium of a channel. And yet, I say unto you, you have received information only from your Self—God.

This is why all giving is receiving. This is why loss is not possible, and why death does not exist. God can only dissolve into God. And in that realization, the final step, beyond even The Way of Knowing, is to release resistance to creation itself, and learn to show up as God in individuated form to have a good time, to love, to create, to extend.

Therefore, indeed, beloved friends, our Love will be without ceasing. Our creativity will be without ceasing. For we are that One showing up *as* creation for the *joy of the dance.* There is nothing but this. There is nothing above or below, nothing behind or ahead. You are indeed that One *now.* And if you rest upon your couch with eyes closed, who is doing the resting? Whose eyes are closed?

In this lesson, I have given unto you the very rock bottom, most fundamental core that you can now sit with—or dance with—if you wish. You can take it to bed with you. You can have a cup of coffee with it. You can strive to understand it. You can analyze it, saying, "Well, there must be some message here. This must be metaphor, somehow." Or you can simply give up being identified as a separate self still struggling to know the truth.

In *A Course in Miracles*, I said unto you:

> "Holy relationship is when any two have looked within and found no lack, and therefore choose to join to create, to make happy."

If any two have looked within and found no lack, they have seen that there is only God. Who cares whether this body-mind goes there or this one goes over there? It is all the same. Where do you feel like playing? That is all.

And when you see your brother or sister say, "I am moving from this location to that location," the awakened mind says, "Oh, this is a part of my Self wanting to go live in Cleveland now—perfectly fine." For the enlightened mind gives perfect freedom to all beings because it sees that the expression of all beings is the freedom of its own Self, of the One Mind which is God, showing up as that being who would rather take the body-mind to Cleveland instead of living in Florida.

When the lover awakens at three in the morning and says, "I now need to move to a monastery and live in perfect silence in a solitary cell, I will never see you again," the totally enlightened mind receives that and smiles. For that enlightened mind knows that the lover can never truly leave because separation is unreal. Therefore, the enlightened mind allows all things, trusts all things, embraces all things and transcends all things. There is only God. And you are That. You are as I Am.

The only question, left, then is: *Who do you want to play with?* Who do you want to play with—*knowers* of God or knowers of fear? They are all God. And yet in that play and display of creation, you are free to decide who you will play with, who you will dance with, who you will create with, and what you will create.

As any mind awakens to itself as God, it becomes more and more interested only in being with others who are like-minded. It can no longer tolerate unenlightenment. Why? Because it is not as much fun. It is not as loving. And God is but Love.

Therefore, beloved friends, review well what has been shared with you in this lesson. If you have been noticing, quite a shift has just occurred. The "cat is out of the bag." For Jeshua ben Joseph has been but a guise, a disguise, chosen of me, to present myself to you because you have required it.

Indeed, beloved friends, be at peace always. Let us play together as that one Mind, extending creation without end, inviting aspects of our Self back to our Self. Only Love is real. Only Love exists. Only Love is worthy of Love. And God wants only that which extends the good, the holy, and the beautiful.

Therefore, indeed, peace be with you always. For in truth, where could it go? Know I am with you always. Amen.

LESSON 34

YOU ARE HERE TO EXTEND THE LOVE
OF GOD INTO CREATION

Beloved and holy friends, I, we, come forth to abide with you because again, you have asked. You have asked that that One that we have called Abba appear through His created forms as I, Jeshua ben Joseph, and as we, which we will call "the lineage," who serve as the conduits of that wisdom, of that energy that in truth the Father is.

The Father *is* what *you are*. Therefore, *you* have asked to be guided into the recognition that only God exists, by sending forth a prayer unto me, and unto this lineage, and unto your Creator to appear unto you in a graded way. That is, in a slowly emerging way that does not elicit an increase of fear.

Yet in truth, your prayer has been to desire the awakening from the dream of the small self into the reality that there has been nothing *but* God and *you are* That. Therefore, indeed, beloved friends, as that One created and birthed from the Mind of Abba, even as you are created and extend the Love of God in the realm of form, I come forth as your brother and your friend. Yet, only God exists.

I will be with you always, even unto the end of all *worlds*. That is, unto the end of all *illusions*. From that moment, creation will extend itself with perfect clarity, with perfect transparency, as God merely extends God in a joyous, ecstatic act of becoming the forms of creation, merely to celebrate and praise God. For the very purpose of all created forms of consciousness is to express praise of the Creator.

It is impossible to extend praise of the Creator without *fully* loving oneself. Without embracing and loving the particular manifestation *of God as you*, you cannot *fully* step into the complete expression of the praise of the Creator. Therefore, you have heard me say unto you many times, that the veil that keeps you from the Kingdom is the lack of Self-love. Self-love is essential to return to the Kingdom. For Self-love is the love of the Creator. You cannot love the Creator while rejecting the Creator's creation.

Indeed, then, beloved friends, know well that we who would come unto you, we that *have* been coming unto you since the day and hour and moment that this work began, have always been a "we" and not just an "I" as Jeshua ben Joseph.

For there are, indeed, many of us who are linked together, in what we call "the lineage," that extends far back in your history of time, creating what you might call in your scientific terms a resonance of energy that links the Mind of the Creator through the epochs of time, through many individual minds, even unto this moment.

It is, indeed, that lineage that brought forth the strand of salvation that culminated in my incarnation as Jeshua ben Joseph. The script was written thousands of years before. The linkages of energy were created generation unto generation unto generation unto generation, culminating in the birth of me as a man, who opened to the Reality of Abba as the *only* Reality through which the Creator could extend the perfect Love of Himself, and make it visible to His children abiding in the spell, or under the spell, of illusion.

That work has never ceased. And, indeed, let it be known that this work that is done through Shanti Christo is an extension of and a collaboration with the entirety of that lineage, that strand of light, extending from the Mind of God into the forms of time with one purpose—to *awaken* every aspect of the Sonship. And what can the Sonship be but the extension of God into form, into that which appears as an individual—that which can create, that which can enter into holy relationship, that which can remember the fullness of Abba, *while* being the particular individual in the field of space and time.

The purpose, then, of the lineage has never changed. And it has, indeed, gained in power through practice and through adding to its numbers. Imagine then a *field of energy* that attracts minds floating by it. As those minds begin to resonate with the message or the word of God, as it is being expressed through this energy field, this lineage, they become like unto the field of energy itself. As one of us once said and is still recorded in your Bible:

> Let that Mind be in you which was also in the one we have chosen to call
> our Lord, the one known as Jeshua ben Joseph or the Christ.

When Paul wrote those words, he was referring to just this process in which you, under the spell of separation, release the spell and begin to resonate with the Mind of the Christ. And you begin to take up your seat within this expanding lineage of light—a direct descendant, a direct disciple of God.

YOU ARE PART OF SOMETHING EXTRAORDINARY—ULTIMATE TRANSFIGURATION

Therefore, indeed, beloved friends, understand well the role that you play wherever you are upon this plane. You may be living in a farmhouse with very few neighbors. You might be living in a condominium in New York City. And yet, wherever you are, you are about something *extraordinary*. You are about that process whereby from the moment the tiny mad, serious thought of separation was dreamed, you are about the very process through which the Creator is correcting the illusion of separation.

There is nothing occurring upon your planet that is not about that. It either expresses separation, or it extends the correction of separation. There is only Heaven or the *illusion* of hell. Therefore, understand that you are an extraordinary being. You, right where you are, are given opportunities moment to moment, to be the truth of who you are, and therefore, be the Light that lights the world. You are part of an ancient lineage that stretches back to before creation began. That strand of light has never been broken or lost.

I, as Jeshua ben Joseph, am merely the culmination of the expression of That in the field of space and time. From that moment it has begun to spread out and to seep into more and more minds as the Sonship is awakened to the resonance with the field of energy that is the Christ Mind.

You are in the process of ultimate transfiguration. *You* are part of an ancient lineage with but one purpose: the complete transfiguration of human consciousness into being the literal field of Christ Mind, extending creation throughout the physical dimension.

There are many extraordinary things ahead for humanity. There are many extraordinary things ahead for you. No matter how deeply you have stepped into this journey, no matter how many transfigurative experiences you have had, as the false self melts away, and the reality of Abba is birthed in the mind made by God, there is always more. There is *always* more.

For the Father never ceases in extending Himself into the forms of His creation—*never*. That which the soul *is*, even beyond the life span of the body, can never die. Nor will it ever be completed. For creation is an infinite process of extending the good, the holy, and the beautiful.

Understand well, then, that you are not an ordinary person. You no longer walk this planet asleep. You may have thoughts saying, "I'm still not there. I still don't quite get this Way of Knowing. It takes my breath away to hear 'there is only God, and I am That'!" Let it take your breath away! Enjoy the experience, knowing that *that is* precisely the most perfect thing that can be occurring in the process of transfiguration that *you* are undergoing.

YOU ARE PART OF A VERY ANCIENT FAMILY

You are already *in* the hands of Abba. You are already embraced and supported by many, many beings abiding in a nonphysical dimension, that are part of this expanding circle of energy that we call "the lineage." Our numbers are numerous. Many of our name*s* are known to you. Who are we, then? Well, you know me. You know that of St. Germain. You know that of Mary. You know that of Abraham and Moses. There are many, many others. You know the names of the prophets of the Torah.

The entire lineage expressed itself down through the birthing of what was called the Jewish Nation, which carries the great strand of the messiahship, culminating in the birth of me, Jeshua ben Joseph. You are part of a *very* ancient family. You are becoming one and the same as that field of shimmering, radiant light that is the purity of the Love of God shining through consciousness into the realm of matter, into the physical dimension.

This makes you not ordinary, but extraordinary. For without fanfare and without external ritual, which often casts only a spell over the heart and mind—the ego loves ritual—you have, indeed, gone through many initiations. The day and the hour in which you first opened to me through this pathway, you underwent an initiation. You gave your consent to your Creator to transfigure your beingness so that it becomes the conduit through which the Creator extends Himself.

And God is but Love. God is the wisdom of the Christ Mind. God is the Sonship. I want to invite you in this hour to *know*, to accept wholly, that you are in *extraordinary company.*

You are not sleepwalking on the planet any longer. You have already begun to see beyond illusions, to penetrate what your eyes used to tell you were just the form and dance of matter and molecules, personas and egos and bodies. You have begun to see the invisible strand, the invisible dance that is truly going on. You have begun to have visions and dreams. You have begun to feel inspired. You have begun to learn forgiveness, healing and even Self-love.

THE PERFECTION OF ALL SPIRITUAL PRACTICE

Self-love is the *perfection* of all spiritual practice. Self-love is the final, shining ray of light that illuminates the heart of the individuated ray of light that you are. Self-love transfigures the mind, the emotional body, and even the physical body to the degree that it strongly shines into the cells of the body.

Therefore, indeed, beloved friends, as we enter into this last part of The Way of Knowing, we have come in this lesson to share with you that we do not so much come to a culmination or an end, but to a *springboard* for what shall be.

In this *The Way of Mastery*, we have sought to help you dismantle your illusions, to soften your heart and your mind, and to be more and more willing to be less fearful. By becoming less fearful, you have, indeed, opened more and more to the guidance of the Holy Spirit.

Every choice for Love has been the result of a transfiguration that has been going on in the alchemy of your soul. You are an extraordinary being. You have been initiated into the strand of light of the lineage, the sacred family, dedicated to the manifestation and the fulfillment of the atonement, *the awakening of the Sonship as the Mind of Christ.*

All that you do, in each moment, when you dedicate yourself to Love—whether you be living in a farmhouse or in a condominium in New York—adds to the field of energy being created that will one day tip the balance and dissolve *all* illusions from *all* minds. Your life, then, is a life in service to the Sonship, regardless of the forms in which you find yourself living.

YOUR ONLY TASK

Your only task, then, is to decide each day to surrender anew, desire the atonement, intend the atonement, allow transfiguration to occur, and surrender into the truth:

> Abba, you are the only thing that exists.
>
> Therefore, it makes no sense even to say,
> "Not my will, but thine," for yours, alone, is.
>
> How shall we spend this one day?

Each experience that you go through is the reshuffling of the cards as your life changes, and ebbs and flows, and miracles begin to come. Old friends go, new friends come. All of it is the process whereby *your particular expression of Abba* is being transfigured into the power and purity of Christ.

THE POWER OF THE LINEAGE IS AVAILABLE TO YOU

The second thing that I wish to share with you this day is that *the power of the lineage is available to you.* For in the first moment you chose to read these lessons, you entered through the portal of an initiation. And transfiguration has continued from that moment, to the degree you have been willing to *allow* it. In that moment, you plugged into the circuitry of the lineage. We are with you wherever you go.

I want, then, to invite you in this lesson to recognize that it is not just Jeshua ben Joseph who has manifested the fullness of the Christ Mind, but there are a host, a heavenly host. That is where all that language came from within the Jewish Torah and even the New Testament, taken over by something called "Christianity," which is not something I know much about since as a man I was a Jew. But beyond that, I am of that strand of Light, expressing itself through the tradition of the Jewish family. And all of this has been by perfect design of God. It is not the only strand. There are others—universal strands that encompass the entirety of human experience. All souls have their lineage. There are strands expressed through India. There are strands expressed through Tibet. There are strands or lineages that extend themselves through the South Americas. There are strands or lineages that have extended themselves through the North American Indian.

All of these strands are like spokes emanating from the hub of one wheel, reaching out to the farthest reaches of the dream of separation, attracting and calling the Sonship back together. So that whether one is Incan or Mayan or Anasazi or Tibetan or Indian or Jewish, or even if you are from New York, you are beginning to become part and parcel of One Mind that recognizes the reality of the *invisible* permeating the realm of the *visible*.

You are, indeed, taking up your place at the *right hand* of God. The phrase in your language, "the right-hand man" or "the right-hand woman" means one who is in alignment, and acts only to fulfill the will of the one in charge. It is a beautiful phrase, and it expresses right-mindedness.

Therefore, understand well, beloved friends, even if you are eighty-five years old sitting in your comfortable rocking chair believing that your life is just about to end, it can never end. The body-mind will be put into the dust of the ground, but you have already entered into a *fast track*.

You are, indeed, a *mystic*. You are, indeed, going through the process of transfiguration, and you are adding to the power of this lineage, to bring about the restoration of Heaven on Earth, and the re-establishment of the Christ Mind throughout the Sonship. And even when the body drops, you will be "assigned to a new office," that is all.

You—*you* reading these words—are of *infinite importance* in the expression of this work that is called Shanti Christo. More than an organization, and much more than a sacred piece of land to which many, some day, will come and will be healed—that is, will enter into the Christ Mind just by the power of stepping into the vortex of purity that has been established there.

You are already in that process. As that purity is established in you, you are literally effecting the creation and extension and expansion of the vortex on that land that has existed for a very long time. It is a portal, a doorway—there are many names that can be used—that takes the mind and transports it into other realms. It is transfiguring to simply abide on that land.

Therefore, understand well your great importance. Many of you will perceive that you are merely a *receiver* through this organization. Yet, as you receive, you are giving, and as you give, you receive. You are a part of the lineage—the field of energy creating a vortex that has the power to overcome illusions. Many of you are seeing this in your personal lives.

What Is to Come

You are, literally, witnessing the forerunning effects of what is to come, when the day will arise when no one will need to say a word. And yet, through the gathering of the lineage, individuals who are attracted will heal—spontaneously—and immediately drop into enlightenment.

All of you are part of this. This is how extraordinary you are! And this is the invitation that we constantly extend to you. Think not that that which is called Shanti Christo is simply another worldly organization. The *deepest levels of transfiguration* are already occurring through this lineage, through this strand or ray of light.

Therefore indeed, embrace that which you are, honor that which you are, extend that which you are. *Go and teach all nations.* Let them know that I *have* come again and that this expression, called Shanti Christo, shall become, increasingly, a primary vehicle through which the lineage is creating the vortex, the portal, the initiation, the energy of transfiguration that will quicken in its enlightenment, or atonement, of the Sonship.

Therefore, understand well, that what will be coming in the future is a growing body of those maturing in the way of the Christ Mind, maturing in the level of commitment, because they will come to see the extraordinary role that they are playing in a much bigger picture than their own personal lives.

The family will indeed, grow. And much is being put into place for this to occur.

The lineage never ceases working in establishing the network of light that allows the expression of this light—visibly through this vehicle called Shanti Christo. We recognize well that as you live your personal lives, seemingly many, many miles from one another, often with little third-dimensional contact, it is easy for the mind to cast a spell upon you that not much is occurring. And yet I say unto you: *It will occur with or without you.*

The invitation then, is to take up your rightful place by stepping into full commitment for this *extraordinary expression* that shall indeed, eventually touch all corners of your planet. That has been its purpose since long, long, long ago. The birthing of Shanti Christo is perfectly an expression of that which was just as important—called my birth, and my crucifixion and resurrection. It's all part of the same script.

Something in you has attracted you to me. Something in you has attracted you to the lineage. Something in you resonated with Shanti Christo. For those words carry the vibration of the call, that I have told you from a time quite ancient, you would one day "hear" as you become "quickened from the dead," to use a Christian phrase. The awakening of the soul, the call back home to the family, to the lineage, to the purpose of the atonement.

You Have Come with a Mission

Indeed, then, beloved friends, you cannot have an ordinary day any longer. You might as well accept the fact that you have come with a mission. You are a bringer of light, a bringer of a new day or a new dawn. You are that which extends the Love of God into creation by your willingness to let the light transfigure your humanity. Your humanity is transfigured as you embrace your humanity and see it all as sacred.

For the spell of illusion is to believe that life as a body-mind is a mistake. That it is a fearful world. That one is limited and small, that the only thing you can do is put all your energy into trying to survive. That all you can do is block your feelings and pretend they are not there in an attempt to deny the power of the Christ that you are. The power to bring the miracle of Love and remembrance and atonement to each moment.

You are, indeed, unlimited in all ways *forever*. The mind that serves the Holy Spirit *is* the Christ Mind, the Mind of Abba, the Self of your very soul—they are all the same. And the mind that serves the Holy Spirit is, indeed, *unlimited forever*. And this Self is part of an extraordinary family, the lineage that can, indeed, be traced through the Jewish nation, the Jewish families, and can be traced even back before that lineage, that family, that nation, was birthed. It shapes itself back through Egypt, back through Persia. It has some roots in ancient India. And it, indeed, has roots beyond this physical Earth.

You Are Incarnating Christ Into the World

You, therefore, are not alone. And your role should never be minimized by you. Please understand that the culmination of The Way of Knowing has been the desire and attempt to invite you more and more and more deeply into knowing the Truth of who you are and what you are here to do, into awakening as Christ.

And yes, we know that the mind hits its points of fear and must plateau out for a week or a year or ten lifetimes before it is willing to step further. Yet you are free, even in the midst of your deepest fears, to say, "Yes!" to transfiguration.

For darkness holds no power over light. It is *always* when you are at the point of your greatest sense of darkness, or your greatest feeling that the light just cannot quite get into you, that you could not possibly ever be enlightened—it is at that moment that you need only *invite* the light. And the light begins to transform the darkness. It is when you are at your edge of darkness that the dawn is but a breath away.

As you transfigure *your* humanity, you are transfiguring the energy field of *humankind*, pure and simple. You are incarnating Christ into the world. You are resurrecting and awakening the dead into Life eternal.

Take up, then, your *rightful* place and begin to give up hiding your light under a bushel. It is, indeed, time to start standing up to be counted as one who is committed to the transfiguration of human consciousness, through the lineage of the Christ Mind, pure and simple.

Step Forward

You are extraordinarily important. You must begin to discipline the mind to not perceive yourself as a small part, not to perceive yourself as separate from one another, to begin to take action to create the lines of communication, even in the third-dimensional realm. It is time for you as individuals to step forward in the birthing of Shanti Christo, instead of waiting upon the handful that seems to have gone a little further ahead. You are that One—you, the reader of these words. If you will but step forward, the whole *power* of the lineage will support you.

So, the invitation is indeed bold. And the "stakes" have always been high. It is the great dream to transform the dream of separation into the dream of perfect remembrance. You are not small. And you are not alone.

Many of you are beginning to be more deeply aware that you too, hear me. Let that process continue and deepen. Become an equal conduit which extends the atonement through the Mind of Christ, through that which is called Shanti Christo, through you.

For this work to reach its fulfillment in the quickest possible time requires the invitation of this lineage to you—a part of this lineage:

Where can you step forward with greater boldness?

Where can you find your edge of fear and call in the
support of light and move through it?

> Where can you drop the pebble into the pond that radiates
> the vibration of this lineage through you out into the world?

For the world holds no power over you.

I hope in this simple sharing that your mind has been a little shaken and you have been brought to a deeper stillness, that your mind has been brought back to the reality of what attracted you to this vibration in the first place. For in that moment, your heart was thrown open, through the *portal of initiation*. Your soul is what has attracted you back to me, for your soul has always known the Truth, and it has simply answered the call.

Yet it takes vigilance and discipline to always remember each day not to fall asleep again. For the temptation of the world is just that: to begin to think that all of those walking asleep in the world have greater knowledge than you, and since so many of them are asleep, maybe being asleep is the way to be. *It is not*!

For all those sleeping will be transfigured in the twinkling of an eye. The sleeping call out in their slumber for someone to stir them from their sleep by modeling and expressing and communicating the quickening vibration of light which is the presence of God.

Indeed, you have chosen to come into this dimension as part of a very grand work that is going on *multidimensionally*. You are, indeed, part of a rather large family.

Many of you will continue to deepen your ability to communicate with me. Honor and love one another. Recognize that you have come, not to live ordinary lives, but to play out the greatest drama ever enacted upon the human plane. That is your role, your function, your purpose, and your life.

It has, indeed, been a great honor to be the one selected of my Father to undergo the laser beam purification, called the crucifixion and resurrection, as part of a much larger picture. It has been a great honor to be the One through whom you have opened your heart to the Love of God. It has been an honor to serve as a savior and messiah. But in truth, that is not the end.

For the end can come only when perfect equality as Christ is established in all hearts and minds. Join with me, then, in this great work. Join with me—do not shy away from that which your heart would call you unto. Rather, dive deeper!

I will never leave you, and will never take my hand from this work until all is, indeed, completed. I love you always. And I participate with all minds called to awaken. I am but your brother and your friend, ever dedicated to revealing that which my Father would reveal to you through me—in just the right way, at just the right time.

You are as I am. And together we transfigure humanity. I was a prototype for what is to come, an expression in space and time of what all of you are destined to be. Yet, that destiny is but the *remembrance* of what you have always been beyond the veil of illusions.

Peace is with you always. Hear the call. Accept the invitation. And let us continue in the greatest story ever told! Amen.

LESSON 35
LIVING AS A SOVEREIGN MASTER

Beloved and holy friends, I come forth to abide with you because I love you. Always and forever we are joined in the place of Love. Always and forever we are joined in the place of Reality. Always and forever I am but your brother and your friend.

You have many brothers and many sisters in what you call the disembodied state, who know you and who love you and who do not come closer to you than you are willing to allow. And that allowance is always the result of your decision to claim your *worthiness* to have communication that can enlighten you.

You are, indeed, entirely sovereign at all times. You and you alone create the thoughts, the beliefs, and the perceptions, that you wish to experience. These then crystallize into the forms of your experience, even into the physical dimension.

Remember, then, in this conclusion of The Way of Knowing, that there is never a time that you see anything that exists outside of you. Everything you see originates within you, since the only thing you *can* see is the way in which *you* choose to cloak or drape the mysterious energy of creation.

Every neutral event, every moment of arising, is merely energy given to you on a silver platter, given to you freely that you, as consciousness, might choose to have the opportunity to create experience by cloaking that energy that has been presented to you with the perceptions and beliefs that you have chosen for yourself.

You have heard me say unto you many times that only Love is real. You have heard me say unto you many times that it is not necessary to seek for Love. But it *is* necessary to seek for what is false.

CREATING AS A MASTER

In all the previous lessons, you have been given many, many tools and much deep and profound understanding to assist you into the simple decision of complete responsibility for every moment of your experience. For in the end, I can give you only this. I cannot relieve you of what you may perceive yet to be the burden of the fact that you are constantly creating—that you are, indeed, a creator.

Likewise, I would not wish to unburden you from the incredible, shimmering awareness and responsibility—the freedom, the fun of knowing that as a sovereign master of your domain, you are free to create whatever your heart most truly desires.

The secret then, as I have shared with you many times, is to practice seeking first the Kingdom. Never let a day go by in which you fail to ponder the great mystery of God's presence. Never let a morning go by that you fail to begin your day, except in this way:

> Surrender all thought of what you know and have believed.
> Rest in gratitude to the One who has birthed you.
> Ask only to be revealed for you greater truth, greater wisdom,
> greater capacity to know and extend perfect Love, perfect trust and perfect
> peace.

In The Way of Knowing we come to the great culmination—that you are, indeed, as I am. That in each moment of your soul's journey, you have literally created the worlds of your experience, just as I did when I walked upon your plane, just as I continue to do now.

How, then, has it occurred that this form of communication could take place? It is not so much that I cleverly set up a labyrinth of doorways to draw you to this teaching, so that I could connect with you. But rather, I rested in my desire to extend the atonement.

By creating that desire, I began to create a vibrational field emanating from my Mind out through creation. That vibration, alone, is not enough. But where it resonated with the deepest desire of my brother to know the Christ Mind, to find a way to serve, to indeed heal and awaken from any last traces of illusion, a connection was formed. It is like two wires dancing about—their dance caused by the movement of energy through them, until their energy touches, joining the tips of the wires together.

This process has occurred between my Mind and yours, or you would not be reading this book. You would not have heard of Shanti Christo. And you would not have heard of me. Recognize, then, *your own power.* For you have attracted me unto yourself, as I have attracted you to me. In each moment of all of your relationships, whether they be with people, places or things, learn to pause long enough—which only takes a few seconds— and say within yourself:

> I am in the moment of this relationship
> because I have called this to myself.

> There is, then, something within me
> that vibrates or resonates perfectly with the "other."

Again, this is true whether that be a person, place, or thing.

True change, then, can occur, not when you recognize that you do not like the relationship you are in, of person, place or thing, and therefore, take steps to get yourself out of it, but rather when you recognize that the relationship and what is occurring within it must be the result of something within your own consciousness. Therefore, what is unlikable in that moment of relationship is merely the flowering of a seed potential or vibration that you have been holding in the depth of your own being.

It is, then, a simple thing to seek first the Kingdom, to rest in that simple knowingness, and to gently inquire of the Holy Spirit to teach you, to reveal to you what you have held as a true belief that is, indeed, false. As you then see why you have been holding that belief, and how it has manifested the world of your experience, you then are quite free to choose anew.

It is just at this point where so often the mind becomes fearful and says, "But at least I know *this*. I do not know what is unknown." But I say unto you, there is nothing unknown. There is *nothing* unknown to you. For there *is* nothing until *you* decide to choose for it. This is why desire is the first key to the Kingdom.

Freedom can only come to the mind that truly assumes complete responsibility for the creation of its experience. So that in any moment, it recognizes that the thoughts, the perceptions, and the feelings coursing through the emotional body are arising within the sovereign domain of that soul's being. They are *uncaused* save, again, for the seed thoughts or perceptions that that mind, or that soul, has chosen to value for itself.

Life, then, offers you your way out. When things don't seem to be working and your peace is missing, this is actually a sign to you that there must be some belief or perception that you are clinging to which does not work. You are free, then, to seek it out, to inquire, and then to change it.

I have often recommended to you that you cannot transcend what you first fail to embrace. Therefore, look well upon your creations, and bless them. If it is the fact that your car has just broken down along the freeway, and the wheels have fallen off, and the motor's stopped, and the doors have crumbled to dust, bless it. For that context of experience will take you into your tomorrows.

There is no moment, then, *there is no moment*, in which you have failed. As a sovereign master, indeed, the literal embodiment of the Mind of God, you have used your freedom to create experience. Embrace it. Rest in gratitude for it. Own it as completely yours.

Then simply ask:

> Do I wish to continue it, or would I like to start a new adventure?

You will be creating new adventures eternally. For there is no moment that creation ends. *Mind* or *soul* is the *vortex*, the *vehicle* through which creation extends itself from the field of infinite possibility into the realization of manifold particularities.

Beloved friends, you are, indeed, as I am. I am rather enjoying my domain. I am unlimited by space and time, and have no longer any need whatsoever for the unique forms of experience that can come through the crystallization of what you call the body— what some of you still mistakenly call *yourself*.

You, then, are very much at play in the Kingdom, like a child in a sandbox. And each event that arises for you need not be judged. I have shared with you many times that it is the egoic mind that compares and contrasts. Therefore, *never* compare or contrast your experience with another person's. Yours is unique.

And though the world would say, perhaps, that your experience is not as valuable because you are only worth twenty thousand dollars and somebody else is worth four hundred million, therefore, they have manifested more powerfully, that is simply not true. For manifestation is simply the expression that reveals where the mind has been focusing.

The *real* power is the very mystery that anything can be manifested at all. And you are free to constantly choose anew.

Cultivate, then, a very childlike attitude toward all of your experience. Learn to ponder it, to wonder about it, to look upon it like a father does to a child, like your Father does to you:

> Behold, I have created all things and it is good!

In your Bible in the creation story that is told there, it is said that God said something like that. For God looked upon all that She had created and said, "Behold, it is very good!"

You are the father of your creations. You are the father of your thoughts, your attitudes, and your choices. Look upon all of these things and say, "Behold, it is very good." For goodness begets goodness. Judgment begets judgment. For nothing can produce except that which is like itself. An acorn cannot produce a fish. A man and a woman cannot produce an acorn. The thoughts you hold about yourself will reproduce themselves. When you look upon all things as good, goodness will be begotten from that decision.

Each time, then, that you have chosen to hold a negative thought about yourself, or about anyone, you have only insured the kind of inconsistency in your mind that interrupts the power of your ability to create, more and more, as a living embodied master. This can only be because you have held deep within the mind some belief that says, "No matter what I do, it won't work out." There is some *conflicted* belief. A belief in goodness and a belief in evil create a conflict that must entrap the soul.

PERCEIVING AS A MASTER

Therefore, indeed, beloved friends, if you are to complete this study of The Way of Knowing, then know this—*as you think, so shall you be*. How you think, how you choose to perceive and believe will determine what you see in the world. And what you believe you see will determine how you act. It will determine the friends you keep, the kind of career you create, where you live, and how you feel.

In other words, if you hold the thought that you cannot trust the universe to support you, you will look out and see a world that seems, self-evidently, to reveal to you that such a thought is true. You will then create behaviors to insulate yourself and never let the world know what you want. And then, of course, you will wonder why life seems to go on as it always has.

Learn always to inquire, not out into the world, but into yourself:

If I am having this experience,
what must I have believed to be true about myself and about the world?

The truth will come through prayer and through honesty. When you discover it, you will know it. Then use the sovereign power of free choice given unto you, which is the Truth of the Kingdom to choose otherwise.

A master cannot *blame*. And a master can never perceive himself or herself as having been victimized. Yet, this mastery does not come through special spiritual power. It comes only through a simple and free choice. Remember, I said earlier that you are constantly creating your experience. You are free in this moment and in every moment to simply say:

I think I will adopt the perspective of a master—
no sense in blame, no sense in feeling like a victim.
What I am experiencing is wholly mine.
I must, therefore, have wanted it.

Always be very careful that you do not judge what is occurring. For that is the fault that people fall into, saying, "Why did I call this to myself? This is a horrible experience. Why, oh why did I want this?" All of that is judgment and not gratitude.

I learned at the crucifixion that I could feel and experience gratitude for my persecutors. I could feel gratitude for the whole context of experience that *I had chosen to call to myself* in order to discover that there are *no* circumstances powerful enough to prevent me from choosing for Love.

In the end, can there be a more powerful experience to call to yourself than that? Not the crucifixion, with nails in your wrists but rather, the power to see that in every moment of birth and of death, of comings and goings that nothing prevents you from the deep peace and joy of choosing to Love. For Love is not conditioned by the conditions of the world. How can it be, when the world does not exist? Only you exist, as a field of awareness that chooses to create perception and belief.

Beloved friends, the world *is* unreal. In the end, the body is unreal, at least as you perceive it to be. For the body cannot limit you in any way. You already extend so far beyond it that it seems unimaginable and completely unbelievable.

You are, indeed, the thought of Love in form. But that form is not the body. It is merely the thought or the reality that is Christ. Christ is the essence of your higher Self. Christ is the truth of who you are. The role of the body, then, can only be to bless, to comfort, and to extend Love.

Two lovers find the fulfillment of their lovemaking in your physical plane when each delights only in blessing, comforting, and extending Love. Each learns to receive that desire from the other, as an act of love toward that one. One says, "Oh, let me massage your shoulders." And the other responds, "Okay!" For relationship *is* the means of your salvation. And holy relationship is always a simple, joyful dance of two who recognize, truly, that only Love is real and they want nothing else.

You are, indeed, a sovereign master of your domain. You cannot fail at any moment. Any form of experience that is unfolding for you is merely the fruit of the seeds of thought that you have planted within your mind. Look at the outcome in order to discover the thought. First say, "What a good girl am I (or good boy am I). That was a rich experience." Then merely ask, "I wonder what I might most want to experience now?" For rest assured, you *will* experience it.

You can either claim dominion over your life and become the conscious director of your life experience, or you can abdicate it to someone else, such as your government, your employer, or what have you. You are totally free to do that if you remember to claim it as a sovereign act, such as, "I am commuting two hours on this freeway, to a job that I don't like, and commuting home for two hours every day. Because of the sovereignty of my total mastery, I choose to do so." For that is the only reason you can find yourself in any place at any time.

As a sovereign master, you are free to follow me. You are free to choose only your loving thoughts. You are free to remember only your loving thoughts. You are free to embrace whatever comes up that may be unlike love and simply accept that it must be an old seed getting cooked, and that you are free to embrace *it* with love.

This is why there can be no feeling that must be judged or avoided. Feelings of despair or feelings of sadness are merely something left over from a past thought. In the act of embracing them, you have already decided with Love. And Love, alone, heals all things.

Just think of this. As a sovereign master, you chose, without lifting a finger, to call into the domain of your experience a form of communication with an ancient friend, Jeshua ben Joseph. Out of the field of your sovereign domain as a living master, you have chosen to bring *The Way of Mastery* into your domain, you have chosen to bring that called Shanti Christo into your domain. There must be a reason for it. There must be a desire for it. Is that not the desire to discover, ever more deeply, if there is anything possibly obstructing you from experiencing greater joy, greater peace, greater wisdom, and greater Christed consciousness?

Indeed, beloved friends, a master never ceases in growing himself or herself. A master is never finished. Do not think that you can come to the end of some form of experience, perhaps even the death of the body-mind, and suddenly be at the finish line. For there is no such thing as a finish line. There are only realms that you can grow into in which creation is indeed far more blissful than it is in the physical domain. But creation continues. Your responsibility and your sovereignty and your dominion continue.

For the further you go into God, the greater the responsibility, for you are dealing with greater power. Thus the need for vigilance and discipline does not go away. It *increases*, but a master welcomes it. For through it, even greater creations can flow through their holy mind. Did you know that it is possible to birth an entire solar system with a single thought?

Now, if you have ever baked a very good chocolate cake, you know something of what it means to create. If you have ever written a poem, if you have ever birthed a child, if you have ever planted a seed and watched it grow, then you know and understand the great satisfaction of creating. Imagine merely holding a thought in the mind and then experiencing the actual birthing of an entire solar system. It is, indeed, a great delight.

Imagine birthing that which is called *A Course in Miracles* merely by holding the thought of it in its completed form, and then letting that wave emanate and join with another mind, who happens to be in the physical domain and does all the work. That is the power that is available to you.

BLESSING ALL YOUR CREATIONS

As you choose to embrace yourself as a master, as you choose to look upon each and every moment of your experience as wholly self-created that is waiting for *your* blessing, you come to see that there is power and freedom in choosing to bless with gratitude *all* of your creation.

And then to say, "This has been so fantastic. It might be fun to have something even greater happen now! It was great being with that lover, but what the heck, they have just recently died, so I think I'll open up to something even greater."

It is that kind of an attitude that expands the Kingdom, the domain of your consciousness, until the day arises when the physical universe can no longer contain you. And you will simply outshine the body itself.

This has occurred. Some minds have outshined the body before the body was ready to die. They merely dissolved in light and that was the end of it. It is not necessary, however, to do so.

For the experience of what is called "death" in your world is *just another experience*. If you bring your awareness to it, you will discover in the day of what you call death that it is actually rather delightful. As your attention withdraws from the body, you become the witness of the gasping of the lungs, the building up of the fluid, and you watch it with disinterest. For you are already vibrating in the energy of bliss, which *is* the essence of your soul. Death, then, is quite simply, nothing.

CLAIMING SOVEREIGN MASTERY

Beloved friends, in the culmination, then, of The Way of Knowing, I ask you as your equal, and as your brother and as your friend eternally, to claim in this hour *complete sovereign mastery* over your domain.

Discover what has not yet been embraced and owned. For those things that are "dissociated" in your psychological language, that which has not been *embraced* by you *imprisons* you.

There is the doorway to perfect freedom. There is the doorway into what looks like the unknown, except that there is no such thing as the unknown. For nothing exists until you call it to yourself.

In this study, then, of The Way of Knowing, let its culmination be that as this lesson ends and you close the book, let it be the *last act* you ever do with a mind that says, "I'm still trying to get there. I'm still a victim of the world I see." When you finish this lesson, let those attitudes be finished entirely. It requires only the willingness to say in each moment:

> This must be what I have called to myself.
> Do I wish to continue it, or would I choose something else?

The world you have made is only an illusion. Nothing that has been constructed must remain *unless you desire it*. If you continue the structures of your life—career, relationship, whatever it is—recognize that you are doing so out of the sheer delight of wanting the experience.

If you prefer, you can let it crumble and start anew. You are free to clear out your bank accounts, give away all of your material possessions, sign over your house to somebody else, give your car keys to somebody and simply start walking down the road with nothing but the clothing on your back. You are totally free to do that. And out of the power of your desire, you will attract situations that provide a place to sleep, food to eat, new experiences and new friends.

At no time can *anyone* be a victim. Yet at any time, consciousness is free to perceive itself as having been victimized. That is merely the choice to create a form of experience. We might share with you that victimization is one of the "booby prizes" chosen pervasively by humanity—the victim game. Many are quite committed to seeing how well they can play it out. One could say that the victimization game has affected virtually every mind in the human domain.

You are not a victim. If, indeed, tomorrow, your doctor tells you, "You have cancer and you have fifteen days left to live. I wish you would have come in earlier. I could have given you, possibly, forty-five days." Simply say to yourself, "Oh, what a rich experience this might be. I have fifteen days to go into the death of the body with total consciousness, complete forgiveness, and perfect peace. Wow, what an amazing opportunity I have called to myself!" For cancer is not a failure.

Indeed, we would behold, in much of your so-called new age movement, that there is much judgment, *much judgment*, much abhorrence of anything that does not look like manifesting wealth, having perfectly curved hips, and a multitude of loving friends. That is a naive attitude.

But the soul's sovereignty is rich beyond measure. Wherever you are as you read these words, you are living sovereign mastery *now*. You are free to create anew any time you wish. But understand that the experience you are having, when embraced and loved and accepted totally as being uncaused by anything but your own awareness, when you can delight in that, you are free. You are free! And you have already risen above and gone far beyond the most successful beings that humanity would say are successful.

Do not, then, be succumbed to the shimmering lights of the world, the great tinsel on the tree. For all that matters is this:

> Am I at peace? Do I bring love to each moment?
> Do I accept with great humor, that all that I have experienced
> has been by my own design, an interesting game,
> and perhaps a joke, played upon myself?

Look upon the world and say:

> There is nothing I need here.
> But I choose to be here to see who I can love,
> how I can love, and what enjoyment I might create.

Peace, then, is always the goal of a spiritual journey—that peace that passes all understanding. For if you have listened well to what I have shared with you in this lesson, ninety-five percent of it seems like mere gibberish to the world, that would say, "It cannot be that way!" It turns the world upside down, rips it inside out and makes it valueless. But it makes *you* valuable. It places you at the right hand of God. This is what you were birthed for. This is where you remain. For Love waits on your welcome.

So I greet you, indeed, beloved friends, as my equal. I greet you as sovereign masters, co-creators, perfect divine expressions of creativity, ceaselessly creating all that you would choose to experience. I never lament the pain that you experience. I never feel sorry for your suffering. I merely wait, in Love, for the truth of your being, and offer assistance to you, when you are willing to grow, to heal, to forgive, to expand, and to enlighten your being.

Great freedom can come when in the midst of something that you feel to be great suffering, you choose to laugh and say, "Look at this one! What an amazing script I have written here. I ought to win the Oscar. Who could have done this one better than this?" And rest assured, you are speaking to one who had some experience at writing rather interesting scripts of suffering.

Beloved friends, look *lovingly* upon the world you have created. Look with perfect forgiveness *now* upon the simplicity of your physical domain. For the life of the body-mind arises and passes away in a few cosmic seconds.

You can delight in sensory experience in the cruel beauty of time, without ever believing that it should be different than it is. It is merely shadow. It is merely a disguise that you have laid upon a mysterious energy. For you, indeed, have birthed the physical domain itself. You might as well relax and enjoy it.

BEHAVING AS A MASTER

In each and every one of your days, live and behave as a master lives and behaves. When first you realize that you are awake in the physical domain in the morning, choose Love. Choose to relax the body-mind into a state of deep prayer and give thanks to your Creator. Hold in the mind's eye all of your domain—your relationships, your careers, your physical objects—and say, "Behold, it's been a lot of fun!" Then simply ask:

> I wonder if there is anything I might like to move toward changing
> in order to experience greater joy, deeper peace, more certain wisdom,
> and more loving relationship?

If something comes into your mind, do not blame it; do not judge it. But simply begin to *wonder* about how you might like to see it changed. Hold that as a desire in the depth of your consciousness. If its energy builds during the course of the day, simply begin to say it, write it out, get a picture of it, hold the desire in your heart. And you will, indeed, bring it to pass. For you see, manifestation occurs *instantaneously* in the field of a mind that is no longer conflicted with opposite kinds of thoughts.

So if anything seems to be manifesting slowly for you, first of all it simply may be that that is part of your script. That is the journey you are taking. A walk from one village to the next allows a much richer experience than taking a taxi.

It may also be because you have some conflicted belief in your mind, and therefore, in the cells of your body, that is not in alignment with what you would wish to desire. For instance, often the human mind will say, "I desire a perfect loving relationship." But deep in the quiet of the mind is the thought, "Except I don't deserve it. I'm unlovable."

When that has been repressed or dissociated, it will run you and will conflict or take away from you the power to create or to attract the desire. Therefore, when you desire, look well and watch with subtle vigilance, what *contrary thoughts* seem to also come up in the mind.

Then follow those contrary thoughts so that they become crystal clear. You may even discover where they began. Feel whatever feelings may be associated with them, and then return to what you desire until you feel that all of your being is in perfect alignment with it.

For then you begin to create yourself as a resonating station to which those things will be called that help align your external world in the physical domain to express the desire you have created.

One who, for instance, creates a lifestyle of financial independence after twenty or thirty years from one perspective has accomplished a great deal, but from another, has taken a very long, slow way to get there.

Everyone is free to create what he or she desires. Everyone is free to do so because they are doing it, now. Look well, then, to the feeling and the thought coursing through you. Look well to the physical environment in which you find yourself. Look well to the objects that you have surrounded yourself with and simply say:

> All of these things demonstrate to me what I have chosen to desire.
> And it is very good!

That statement of love and acceptance is the doorway to expansion of your mastery. For in truth, as the master awakens to what they have been doing all along, the most natural thing in the world is to create greater joy.

SERVICE IS THE GREATEST SOURCE OF JOY

And the highest level of joy is to manifest service to the atonement. That is why, perhaps one gives up a job in a corporation to go and start to make videos that can help get a good message out to the world. That is why someone ceases to work in a doctor's office and becomes a messenger for Jeshua. That is why someone drops what they are doing in a corporate career and becomes a minister. Because within them the soul has said:

> All right, enough of that experience. I want greater joy.
> And the pathway to greater joy is to join with like minds that are creating
> and extending contexts in which other minds can awaken.

That is why many of you have been attracted to Shanti Christo, to join together, to use your golden coins, to use your voice, to use your lips, to use your hands, to use your feet, to help participate in the creation of contexts in which the atonement can occur.

Service, then, is the natural outflow of a heart filled with the gratitude of grace. Masters are never found struggling to survive in something they do not like. They would frankly rather sit on a street corner, asking passersby for a nickel or two to get a cup of coffee. Meanwhile they are too busy smiling and waving and blessing everyone that walks by because they would rather love than look good in the world. A master has no choice but to serve—but to serve not from duty, but from joy. For the greatest joy can be to extend the good, the holy, and the beautiful.

Therefore, when you choose active participation in serving the atonement, you will discover that you will, indeed, be well supported. And all of the events that occur are merely opportunities to deepen your capacity for wisdom, for peace, and for Love—to create within yourself a conduit for the extension of greater Love into the world—not because you *must*, but because you have *chosen* to serve. And you have chosen to serve because it is the greatest source of joy.

If, then, you resist service, it must mean that there is some seed thought within you that is in conflict with the desire to serve. For once you have achieved mastery, there is nothing else to do but serve.

So, indeed, beloved friends, we come, then, very gently, and by way of summation, to the culmination of The Way of Knowing. The truth is, you have been a master all along. You cannot help but be one, for you are constantly creating your experience. You are free now to create *differently*. How to do that? Do not get up out of your chair and rush about. But why not decide, right now, to experience happiness, to experience peace, and to experience the knowledge that you *are* a master.

How do you do that? By *choosing* to. Simply decide right now for the next thirty seconds to be happy. And then choose another thirty seconds to be at peace, and then another thirty seconds to simply and quietly look around you and say:

> Behold, I am, indeed, the master of my domain.
> And all of it has been very, very good.

Thank the chair that you are sitting in for coming into your domain. Thank the vase of flowers on your table. Thank the electricity bill that comes in the mail. Thank all things as blessings that come to you.

For to fail to do this contracts your power to continue to expand and to create what you enjoy. To *believe* that you are in lack at any time is to *create* lack in your tomorrows. Therefore, choose now to *feel* perfect abundance and joy. And then *behave* as one who *knows* they live in abundance.

I love you. You love me. This communication will never cease. Why? Because I have no intention of withdrawing myself from extending the Christ Mind to anyone who will receive it. We are, indeed, joined in the place of perfect Love.

Creation is merely a harmless game, done for the simple enjoyment of creating. Become, then again, as a little child, for every master *is* a little child, delighting in the great mystery and the seeming surprises of discovering the power that can move through them. *Always move toward what you enjoy. Always follow your heart.*

Do not follow the reactive ego that says, "Oh, no. I don't want to go there because that feels uncomfortable." Nothing is uncomfortable. It is just another opportunity to have an experience to broaden your capacity to love. How can I say that? Try the crucifixion. It was not uncomfortable, once I embraced it.

This is why, by the way—and some of you have done this—why human beings can walk on fire and not burn their feet. Why? Because they choose to do so and have a good experience. And everything in them is unconflicted for at least the minute or so it takes to do the firewalk. That gives them a taste of what is possible always.

Use then, your time to cultivate the garden of a healed mind. Never believe that you do not hold the power to change the energy you feel in your emotional body, to change the thoughts held within the mind. *You are free to birth whatever you so desire.* And nothing can serve as a limit to you.

You are free. You are home. You are, as I am.

Peace then be unto you always, precious, precious friends. Amen.

Shanti Christo Foundation

In 1994, Shanti Christo Foundation was founded as a 501(c)3 non-profit organization dedicated to holding a vision inspired by Jeshua ben Joseph (Jesus). That vision is incorporated into our mission, which is to awaken the Divine Self within by offering the teachings of Jeshua ben Joseph. These transformational teachings include hundreds of hours of recorded conversations, available in CD and MP3 format. His more formal lessons—*The Way of the Heart, The Way of Transformation,* and *The Way of Knowing*—are now offered in this volume, *The Way of Mastery.*

The vision then, inherent in our mission, is the bringing of Heaven to Earth. Shanti Christo means the "Peace of the Anointed One," an awakened state which empowers you to be all you are created to be, so that our world can be blessed by the divine gifts of each and every unique, worthy, and precious individual. Shanti Christo is that pure and ever-present, perfectly innocent, and completely awakened vibration, which is peace.

If this book has touched your heart, you will enjoy listening to the original recordings of *The Way of Mastery* along with the other Jeshua material.

For a complete listing of recordings by Jeshua, and other related products, and to learn more about the Shanti Christo Foundation, please visit our Website at:
www.shantichristo.com

Shanti Christo
FOUNDATION

A Partial Listing of CDs Available From The Shanti Christo Website

The Way of the Heart—Set One

Twelve consecutive recordings, each designed by Jeshua to build on the previous lessons, which help anchor, inspire, and teach us to awaken in Christ Mind. 12-CD set

The Way of Transformation—Set Two

The continuation of the formal lessons from Jeshua. 12-CD set

The Way of Knowing—Set Three

The third set of formal lessons from Jeshua. 11-CD set

The Heart of Freedom

Described as one of the most powerfully rich recordings of Jeshua's message. CD

The Holy Instant

Originally recorded as a Christmas message in the year 2000, this is regarded as a favorite. CD

Heaven on Earth

A four-CD recording set of Jeshua's early talks on bringing Heaven to Earth. 4-CD set

Healing Through Self-Love

An uplifting offering on the importance of loving oneself. CD

Love Heals All Things

A two-recording set with a "live" audience of *A Course in Miracles* students. 2-CD set

Mastering Communication

A remarkable message on how to have genuine communication. CD

Death and Earth Changes

Jeshua addresses the "end of an ancient dream," the transition of the Earth and humanity during these times. He also answers the question, "what happens when we die?" CD

Grace as Reality

A two recording set describing Grace as that which brings perfect Peace to those who allow it. 2-CD set

Visit us at:
www.shantichristo.com